ON SECOND THOUGHT

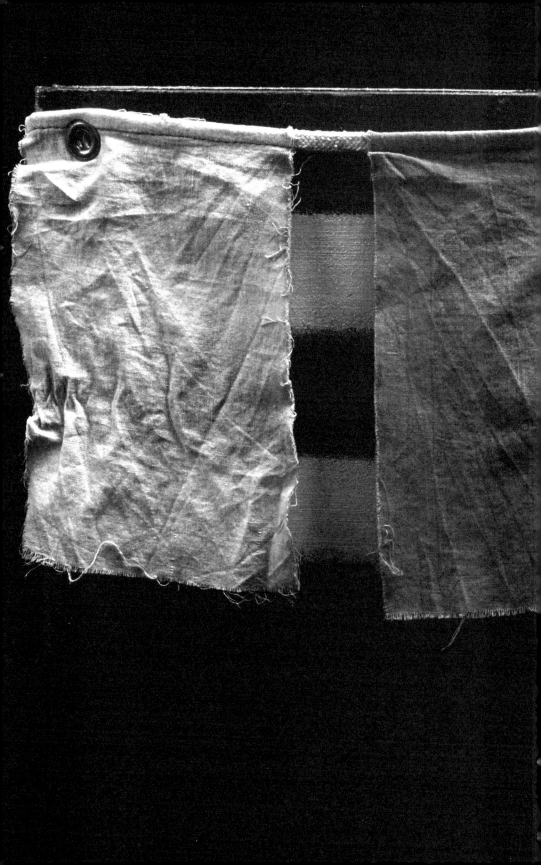

ON SECOND THOUGHT

Scholarly Women Reflect on Profession, Community, and Purpose

Edited by Luisa Del Giudice

The University of Utah Press | Salt Lake City

The Defiance House Man colophon is a registered trademark of The University of Utah Press. It is based on a four-foot-tall Ancient Puebloan pictograph (late PIII) near Glen Canyon, Utah.

21 20 19 18 17   1 2 3 4 5

Library of Congress Cataloging-in-Publication Data

Names: Del Giudice, Luisa, editor.
Title: On second thought : scholarly women reflect on profession, community, and purpose/edited by Luisa Del Giudice.
Other titles: Scholarly women reflect on profession, community, and purpose
Description: Salt Lake City : The University of Utah Press, [2017] | Includes bibliographical references.
Identifiers: LCCN 2016040294| ISBN 9781607815358 (pbk : alk. paper) | ISBN 9781607815365 (ebk)
Subjects: LCSH: Women scholars. | Women scholars—Religious life. | Work-life balance.
Classification: LCC HQ1397 .O5 2017 | DDC 001.2082—dc23
LC record available at https://lccn.loc.gov/2016040294

Printed and bound in the United States of America.

CONTENTS

ACKNOWLEDGMENTS

If we are lucky in life, we encounter helpers and mentors to assist us on our journeys. Some of mine have been enlightened teachers, musicians, dancers, spiritual leaders, colleagues, activists, friends, and family—as well as many, many books: the learned ones packed with information and those that explore existential questions of life's meaning. Yet other sorts of helpers have been those who have made intellectual work possible by helping us care for children and households, thereby freeing us to sit quietly and alone in our studies. Little of my intellectual work would have been possible without the extraordinary care of Maribel Gonzalez (sometimes known as "Saint Maribel" in our household). I thank my distant and near ancestors and my families of origin. Even those of us who seemingly live solitary lives locked away in our offices, tap, tap, tapping away at our computers, trying to connect with them, know that we are not ultimately alone and that an entire host of those we have met along the way, and those we have never actually met but of whom we have heard speak, are nonetheless with us, filling our thoughts, guiding and advising us. This is the larger backdrop of presences among those I acknowledge here—not all of whom I can name, but all of whom I indirectly address in the pages of my own contribution to this volume, "Making Dead Bones Sing."

I thank first and foremost the first circle of women in my life: my mother, Liliana, and my own honest-to-goodness sisterhood—Claudia, Franca, and Irene, with whom I have shared family life as a child and young adult and who remain my surest points of reference throughout all the peregrinations of life. Who has known me longer? I also thank my daughters, Elena and Giulia, who are becoming my next most intimate group of family women and with whom I look forward to a tight and never broken circle. I also acknowledge my stepdaughter, Thérèse, and my stepdaughter-in-law, Leslie, my family women's circle. And I thank the next generation of younger women and women-to-be, especially all the nieces (Marlene, Marzia, Luisa,

Vania, Christine), and grandnieces in our Toronto-based Mermaid's Club: Annik, Aiyana, Zoe, Maia, Victoria—thank you for your love. I look forward to witnessing your flourishing as women, hoping that you too will learn to create circles of love and support to sustain yourselves and others through Wise Women's Circles of your own.

Of course, we know that those who sustain and support us are not all women but also loving fathers, husbands, brothers, nephews, and male colleagues. I express some of my largest measure of gratitude to my irrepressible father, *buon'anima* (rest his soul), who, despite his tyrannical ways, taught me much about how to survive and how to prevail, and especially how to celebrate life with others. And I am grateful to my sweet, dearest husband, Edward, who has generously given me the freedom to go where I would and as needed, gently sustaining and supporting all my dreams, while weathering the slings and arrows of life with me.

I thank all my current spiritual advisors for their keen ability to listen to stirrings of my soul along with me: Susan Klein, Joanne Leslie, Linda Schultz. I also thank those who, over the years, have helped hone my attention to the spiritual life of women as it intersects the hard facts of women in the world, through the St. Alban's Interfaith Beijing Circle's focus on the Millennium Development Goals: Joanne Leslie (co-convener with me), Bisbee Goldfarb, Deborah Kennel, Hugh Leonard, Karen MacDonald, Ava Stanton, Paula Tavrow.

And I thank those who helped me tinker with words and ideas, carefully reading and assisting with the editorial revisions of my own contributions to this volume: Edward Tuttle (always my first reader); Mary Allen Macneil (editor extraordinaire); as well as the reviewers of the original manuscript, Christina Bacchilega and Kerry Noonan, who suggested how we could improve the text. Of course, it is the University of Utah Press editors who completed this editorial process. An especially big thank you to John Alley for his faith in my work over the years and for this third vote of confidence—twice with the Utah State University Press and here as editor in chief of the University of Utah Press. It has been a great pleasure.

INTRODUCTION

A Convocation of Wise Women and Reflections on Lives of Learning

LUISA DEL GIUDICE

Wisdom is not the gathering of more facts and information, as if that process, in itself, might eventually coalesce into truth. Wisdom is a new, different way of seeing and knowing the "ten thousand things." . . . Presence is wisdom! People who are fully present know how to see fully, rightly, and truthfully.
—Richard Rohr, "Seven Themes of an Alternative Orthodoxy" (Meditation No. 10, November 18, 2013)

What would happen if one woman told the truth about her life? The world would split open.
—Muriel Rukeyser, "The Poem as Mask" (1991)

KNOWLEDGE AND WISDOM

The pursuit of knowledge and the pursuit of wisdom may appear dichotomous, divided between communities of scholars known as "the academy" and those searching for existential truths in myriad spiritual and faith traditions. Some may object to this division, however, arguing that the business of critical research to which we devote our energies, the gathering of knowledge, and the scholarly syntheses of natural and human phenomena that we devise are the very foundations upon which higher, universal truths or wisdom ought to rest. Indeed, as multifaceted and complex human beings, scholars themselves can make their most profound contributions when learning is informed by a fundamentally "new, different way of seeing and knowing the 'ten thousand things.'"[1] I contend that it is the integration of matters of the head (a pursuit of knowledge) with those of the heart (a pursuit of spiritual truth) that can teach us to see "fully, rightly, and truthfully" and that it is just such an integration, often achieved through profound spiritual transformation, that marks our greater thinkers and our best scholars. This volume focuses on how women of learning have addressed such issues across a multitude of disciplines, life experiences, and paths to spiritual knowing.[2]

As is true for any other group, scholars experience and are sustained by spiritual impulses and experiences, in and through our work, although relatively few are inclined to articulate this core of being—even when it impacts their work more than casually, even when their very disciplines explicitly treat matters of spiritual tradition and religious practice. Instead, within the academy, we are encouraged to remain silent, to keep our "private" lives to ourselves, at the risk of mild censure or severe ostracism. My response instead is that we must seek after our own motivating spiritual paradigms in order to gain a better understanding and more consciously fulfill our vocations as teachers, guides, mentors, and advocates (and sometimes the very topics that we are studying). Infusing our work with consciousness and a consciousness of purpose makes these roles integral to our life's work, not merely to our work life. An examination of the whys, wherefores, and ways that have led to the present is a task of life review that we most frequently engage during its second half (compare Bateson 2010). But we needn't wait for that later season of life. I invite you here to join this circle of women as they reflect on their own arduous tasks of integration and self-expression.

WISDOM AS A WOMAN

How many cultural traditions represent Wisdom as a woman? From the ancient and classical Mediterranean world we remember Sophia/Sapientia and Athena/Minerva; in Irish culture we find Cailleach; in the Tibetan Buddhist tradition we find Tara; and in many other vernacular settings we find an old woman, a wizened crone (such as Befana, Spider Grandmother, and Frau Holle), devoted to the domestic crafts and healing arts. Such iconic wise women are frequently presented as knowledge-bearers attuned to the life and nature cycles, the earth, and the hearth, and as spiritual guides. Their sisters instead actively focus on sustaining, defending, and civilizing the world as warriors and women of justice and peace in the public sphere, such as sword-wielding Athena.[3] Sometimes these split roles of women of learning (and contemplation) and women of action fuse together. Further, while Wisdom and Just Action may be personified as mythological figures, many sage and activist women also come down to us through historical time, including Teresa of Avila, Catherine of Siena, Hildegard of Bingen, Mechthild of Magdeburg, Julian of Norwich, and more recently Peace Pilgrim, Dorothy Day, and Jane Goodall as well as Sisters Helen Prejean and Joan Chittister. We may honor them all, whether women of learning, social warriors, or peacemakers, as enlightened women (compare Flinders 1993, 1999, 2006). We also know that wise women present themselves within our more intimate circles of sisters, mothers, grandmothers, and daughters, no less than among colleagues and friends.

The image of a woman carrying a lamp to illuminate and explore the darkness might best symbolically represent the woman of learning. One such example recently figured on a volume of Zen teachings, *The Hidden Lamp: Stories from Twenty-Five Centuries of Awakened Women* (Caplow and Moon 2013).[4] But we also know from our experiences as women in society that illuminating the darkness around the actual lives of women, seeking to shed light on the issues negatively affecting women, often meets with resistance. Moreover, to carry the metaphor of light one step further, faced with these societal attitudes, women often unwittingly dampen their own inner light, thanks to their "inner critic." In extreme cases, especially (but not exclusively) in the developing world, women's lights are intentionally and sometimes violently extinguished from without—by censoring cultures, exclusionary laws, repressive religions, and other patriarchal institutions. While male curiosity in the Western world has generally been hailed as a positive trait, expressing itself as adventurous exploration or noble seeking after Knowledge (the very essence of expansive progress through learning), female curiosity instead has repeatedly invited ridicule, punishment, revenge, and even death.[5] Pandora-like, female curiosity has been blamed for unleashing chaos on the world; just as biblical Eve, by tasting the forbidden fruit of the tree of knowledge, is blamed for ushering in all suffering for humankind.

WISE WOMAN ASPIRATIONS

As a woman of deep curiosity about the physical, social, and spiritual realms (learning, social action, and spirit), I confess that I have long harbored wise woman aspirations. When once asked, during a spiritual exercise, to ponder the question: What do you wish for your future? I had no hesitation in answering that I wanted to be a wise woman. I have gradually come to understand that a wise woman might seek knowledge both in the world (as a scholar) and apart from it (as a spiritual seeker), achieving wisdom through an active and thorough engagement with the ordinary and daily stuff of life, while also exploring its larger meanings in places of worship and retreat houses.

My search for meaning began by studying my own small corner of the world, through Italian ethnicity, migration, and orality. Through such studies I began to gain a better understanding of my own place within family, culture, and history. I went on to apply this learning across geographic, historic, and cultural boundaries, eventually learning how and why to engage with issues of social justice and peacemaking, through an evolving awareness of the "common good." From culturally specific knowledge, I have ventured toward more universal truths, grounded in a growing awareness of (my) life's spiritual core. I have concluded that this combined form of understanding can transform our sense of purpose, consciously drawing us toward a worldly pursuit of the good, the beautiful, and the just. What follows is my own "travel tale" of how such an evolution of my scholarly mission came to be articulated. (It should be read in conjunction with my own essay in this volume, "Making Dead Bones Sing: Practicing Ethnography in the Italian Diaspora"). It is offered merely as an introduction to the many other "travel tales" that are included in this volume.

Even after a decade of higher learning at universities in Canada, Italy, and the United States (first in Italian Medieval and Renaissance literature, then in folklore and oral history), I knew that being a collector of information (whether in the library or in the field) could never be enough. I concluded that knowledge had to be sifted and assembled into personally meaningful and collectively useful syntheses. (I needed learning that was useful, not just interesting.) And as I matured as a scholar, I became increasingly impatient with scholarship that seemed a mere assemblage of facts and footnotes on topics that I found ever more trivial and inconsequential. Ultimately, this sense of an underlying lacuna provoked recurrent deepening reflection about my own evolution and trajectory as a scholar. In fact, a professional crisis launched me headlong into deeper consideration of my life purpose, an enquiry that first led me to spiritual direction and then circled back toward framing a more engaged professional mission within my own disciplines of ethnography and oral history. Anguish at the closure of my Los Angeles–based nonprofit research institute, the Italian Oral History Institute, in 2007 became so acute that I suspended scholarly activities altogether. It would take years for me to emerge from this impasse—transformed, however, and with renewed and clearer resolve. How was this reaffirmation accomplished? Guided by a lifelong practice of research, I had already begun a new "research" task in 2004, gathering spiritual intelligence in disparate places—in Zen sanghas, Benedictine monasteries, Christian churches, Jewish synagogues, Pagan covens, nature quests, and sacred women's circles—gleaning here and there, reading, attending gatherings, programs, retreats, engaging mind, body, and soul—through various spiritual traditions. Each, I discovered, delivered glimpses of wisdom of one sort or another. I even trained as a spiritual director.

Spiritual direction is a mindful practice of listening to others' sacred stories and accompanying them along their personal journeys, helping them to discern responses to the "where to now?" questions. I especially applied this learning to groups organized for women and around women's issues. One such organization was New Directions, assisting homeless women veterans. I volunteered in their group home for two years of monthly meetings. Most of these women had indeed lost their way in the most extreme circumstances imaginable (addiction, violence, trauma) and were seeking physical and spiritual redirection "home." More broadly woman-focused was the St. Alban's Interfaith Beijing Circle, a spiritually oriented group that I co-convened with Joanne Leslie, which centered on how the UN Millennium Development Goals especially affected girls and women worldwide. Still other groups were expressly convened to function as a sounding board (or Discernment Committee) for those considering ordination to the Episcopal priesthood. I often pondered how such discernment practices might benefit many more of us attempting to navigate tough spots or impasses on other vocational, professional, and personal journeys. From extreme examples of women tragically losing a sense of direction to others merely negotiating a fork in the road, practices of mindfulness, stillness, and listening became critical, life-giving, and even life-saving to me.

These spiritual practices had redirected me homeward. I also learned how deep personal suffering could deepen my dedication to others, to a common purpose, and to the common good. I experienced a heightened sense of compassion for the suffering of others as well as a stronger desire to help them integrate *their* lives. Could my work inside and outside of the academy, as well as the personal knowledge that I had gleaned in all these diverse places, serve this better purpose? If so, how? My growing consciousness of the world's brokenness called me toward peace and justice causes that specifically addressed poverty, hunger, migrations, and women's issues. Sometimes I engaged these causes in Los Angeles (my own backyard), and sometimes they took me farther afield. Recession, war, and the widening socioeconomic divides that characterized the first decade of the new millennium made me more attuned to the deplorably regressive policies that increasingly polarized political discourse and mired us in stasis. I sought to address some of these issues through the prism of my own disciplines, attempting to raise awareness while addressing social and economic inequalities in concrete ways (for example, St. Joseph's Tables and Feeding the Poor, within the Watts Towers Common Ground Initiative).[6] I accepted a visiting professorship in the Department of Ethiopian Studies at Addis Ababa University to teach the praxis and theory of oral history, which I partly envisioned as a symbolic way to right historic wrongs visited upon that people by my own during the fascist colonial adventure. Most projects in which I engaged during those years needed to serve some larger purpose or I was not interested.

I have long been attuned to women's issues, especially to the status of girls and women in the world, learning about and participating in many initiatives that address education and women's health. While on the home front we witnessed so many setbacks in domestic and public policy (often referred to as the "War on Women"), globally girls and women were being physically oppressed, brutally maimed, and killed at a furious rate. It became all too evident to me that we needed to awaken a new generation both at home and abroad and that the battles would be fierce. As Hillary Clinton has asserted, the plight of women is the unfinished business of the twenty-first century. Certainly it remains one of our greatest challenges.

Although I have always considered myself a feminist (albeit not a book-learned one), I fear that I have not always known how to translate my beliefs into corrective action. Because it took me years of "catching up" on the feminist front, to see more clearly through the fog of my youth, one of my battle cries has become: Wake up girls! Don't be duped into reviling the f-word ("feminism"). Learn to respect and defend yourselves and your sisters! Too many girls and young women in the developed world were either naively uninformed about the struggles faced by the preceding generations of women or else willingly turning their backs on those struggles, buying either into the Right's social backlash or into the Left's postgender worldview. In the developing world, in contrast, the struggles seemed more basic: women's right to education, health care, economic and environmental stability, and personal safety—basic human rights denied in increasingly oppressive fundamentalist regimes (including homegrown fundamentalisms threatening our own). I sought to engage in various forms of activism, including "Facebook activism," sometimes joining others on the actual barricades (for example, Miss Revolutionary and StandingWomen),[7] while also helping to organize and lead groups devoted to women's initiatives (such as St. Alban's Interfaith Beijing Circle), supporting local and global networks of women (including the Global Fund for Women and Ms. Foundation), and serving on the advisory board of the Fregenet School (Fregenet Kidan Lehitsanat), an elementary school educating both girls and boys in Addis Ababa, Ethiopia (for which I organized a fundraiser in 2013). Today my feminist activism also includes encouraging women peers and colleagues to reflect upon their life purpose and to pursue it more fully, and to help lift up the disadvantaged (women among them) in whatever way possible. Our global liberation must include all of this.

As I worked through my crisis-driven search for meaning, I learned that it was indeed possible and critical to reconcile my warring selves: public versus private, academic versus spiritual. My own chapter in this volume describes the process, first explored while in the very midst of my existential storm, in a paper delivered at the 2004 Société Internationale d'Ethnologie et Folklore (SIEF) meeting in Derry, Ireland, entitled "Spiritual Direction and Ethnography: Varieties of Listening" (later published: Del Giudice 2009a), which ultimately led to the present volume. Back in 2004 I agonized over that intensely personal account, about whether it was wise to expose myself in so public a fashion before my colleagues. I pondered appropriate language: should I affect the aloof critical voice of an academic, or use the aggrieved voice of the excluded ethnic and feminist, or emulate the lyrical voice of a contemplative mystic? I concluded that I would write in as natural a "mother tongue" as possible. In any case, I resolved not to employ the bookish approach that I had been trained to use over years of academic writing—even if such deviation might prove academically compromising. I concluded that I had paid my academic dues by producing learned publications, scholarly conferences, and public programs and by serving on society boards; that I had earned the privilege of personal self-expression within the academy; and that such personal reflections might even benefit others. Nonetheless, I ended that essay wondering if what was left to do in my life would require a renunciation of the academy in general and ethnography in particular. Not quite yet, it turned out.

I began asking myself: was the accumulation of knowledge to which I had devoted my entire adult life enough? Did I wish merely to continue meeting an ongoing cycle of publication deadlines and conferences? Why keep slogging in the scholarly trenches? I felt constrained. My heart sought expansion beyond the forces driving the first half of life. I wanted off the treadmill of the relentless pursuit of gold stars (publications, conferences, grants and awards). My scholarly résumé was respectably long enough. The critical question became not: Had I accomplished enough? But rather: how well had I lived? Had I fulfilled my deepest purpose? What was I to do with the time left? How should I "make things whole" (compare Magliocco 2001)?

Perhaps this volume is timely, as my peers and I approach the so-called second half of life, naturally inclining toward the task of life review. The idea of inviting other women to join in this self-reflective process suggested itself soon after writing that 2009 essay exploring how my spiritual, feminist, and professional lives intersected and informed one another. Three years after publishing that essay, in the spring of 2012, a new project took shape. I began encouraging women whom I considered spiritually integrated human beings, as well as clear-thinking women of learning, to reflect similarly and write candidly about their own lives.

The volume that you have begun to read represents the reflections of women who accepted my personal invitation (not all did). It gathers together women engaged in a range of endeavors. They are women of learning who are spiritual as well as spiritual leaders who are scholarly. Some contributors emphasized the professional side of the equation, while others focused on the more personal, yet all points between these poles were treated. Such a diverse gathering of voices posed challenges regarding a unifying title for the volume. Was my title too wordy? Too mundane? Not clever enough?

More critically, did it gather in all contributions? A witty colleague, Paul Harris, to whom I described the project, suggested that I rename the volume *Second Thoughts from the Second Sex*, playing on Simone de Beauvoir's feminist work *Le deuxième sexe* (1949). I settled on the notion of "second thought" first, because it addresses the ruminative activity of thinking and rethinking (that is, the general task of academic work); and second, because it contains a subtext of hesitations ("second thoughts"), reservations, even regrets. In fact, this title did reflect the mental attitude of some of my contributors, whom I sometimes needed to persuade, encourage, cajole. I hope that no one turns out to have lasting regrets about participation in this project!

I ponder whether it has been my specific field experiences as a folklorist (collecting ballads from women singers in Brallo, studying the St. Joseph's Day tables of the women of San Pedro, California, or doing research on female faith healers in my family) or my woman-dominated nuclear families (from my sisterhood of four and the mothering of two daughters) that have repeatedly drawn me into circles of women. I feel most at home among mothers, grandmothers, aunts, sisters, daughters, women friends, and the sacred feminine. All these generations of women have nurtured and guided me within intimate networks of love. I am so confident of their worth that I lend my voice to many others who call for an increased role for women in a variety of local and global platforms. We should become more willing to ask, especially in times of crisis: "What would the grandmothers say?" Our world craves a council of grandmothers deeply rooted in their own communities and cultures to care for the human family, teaching us how to live responsibly and sustainably for our own good, for the good of generations to come, and for the good of Mother Earth herself. Who possesses a deeper knowledge of life? Women have given life, nurtured and swaddled it, healed the sick, accompanied the dying, and tended the dead. Women have an intimate knowledge of the entire life cycle through the intimate nurture of small children, as midwives, as caregivers for the old, and mourners of the dead; of the earth, as tillers of the soil and gatherers; of the ways of the spirit, as healers. They create and care for networks of family and community. As United Nations monitors of the progress on the Millennium Development Goals have repeatedly noted, women tend to be "multipliers of good" out into the larger community, valuing, enhancing, and sustaining the common good for the generations that follow. And as direct creators and sustainers of human life, they incline toward protecting it against violence, destruction, and war.

In women's circles of learning ("homeplaces"), grounded in listening, a "tradition that has no name" (Belenky, Bond, and Weinstock 1997), leaders arise from within the community as they are listened into being, ready to speak from the experience both of and for the collective. Jean Shinoda Bolen (1999), in *The Millionth Circle*, explores how small-circle interactive work creates real change in the world by prompting organic change from within. Small circles added to other small circles eventually create a tipping point, a paradigm shift, achieving change that previously seemed impossible.[8] I envision this volume as a circle of thirteen women (lucky thirteen) to be one of those innumerable circles, ever widening and reproducing, aiming for a paradigm shift, a transformed academy, wherein spiritually enlightened scholars become agents of positive change from within.

In many instances within these pages we acknowledge the guidance of wise women elders within our families. We remember our grandmothers fondly, having known them as sources of knowledge, love, inspiration, and leadership. My own grandmother and namesake, Luisa Palmacci Del Giudice, was a powerful matriarch, a faith healer and community leader in her Italian village, the medieval San Domenico parish of Terracina in the region of Lazio, central Italy. Sadly, I paid closer attention to her life activities only after she passed away, gleaning biographical fragments from her daughters (my aunts) and in the process discovering also that there were other women healers within the Del Giudice line (grandmother, great-aunt, and great-great-aunt: Del Giudice 2001 [2011]). I can no longer ask Nonna Lisetta directly the many questions that I am now so interested in exploring as I also begin to understand why she had been so concerned with the spiritual well-being of her family. (In her specific case, she was worried that the younger generation had lost its belief in the saints and had stopped praying.)

Others too remember their grandmothers. Literary scholar and teacher of memoir writing Edvige Giunta, in "Bridging the Spiritual and the Political: My Scholarly Becoming," pays homage to and integrates into her own life her grandmother's devotional practices of the sacred quotidian. Public health scholar and Episcopal archdeacon Joanne Leslie, in "Repining Restlessness," recounts how her grandmother's love of books and libraries influenced her own bibliophilia. Sabina Magliocco ("Walking between the

Worlds: Reflections on a Life of Scholarship") attributes her professional interests, in part, to her grandmother's mastery of storytelling and engagement with spiritualism as well as to her mother's passion for classical literature and myth. But no contributor dwells on the impact that a grandmother has had on her life more deeply than Jennifer Guglielmo ("Rising and Falling and Rising"), who credits her grandmother (her surrogate mother) for an all-encompassing approach to spirituality, infusing her sense of purpose and shaping her professional pursuits as a historian and nurturing teacher.

Ancestors, as Senegalese poet Birago Diop teaches us, are "never dead." After our own ancestors have departed, we learn about their lives, we attempt to live better within their memory, embodying them in ways fitting to our own. In my chapter I explore how I have sought to make my ancestors' dead bones sing through my own acts of remembering and embodiment, in my private and public scholarly life. Somehow we must transform their wisdom and ways of being in the world, into our own lives, striving both to honor the elders and to mentor the next generation. Thus we become conduits. Grace Schireson, in her work with female Zen ancestors ("Finding My Female Zen Ancestors: Is There Such a Thing as a Woman?"), shows how to take their hands and walk forward together, for the benefit of our own granddaughters. Jennifer Guglielmo envisions the energy and learning of her female ancestors as having seeped into her cells, deep into her mind and heart, continuing to ignite creative power. We must learn to breathe the ancestors in through our own lives and back out into the world. Eventually, we may—literally or metaphorically—become those grandmothers. For her part, after a lifetime of striving and achieving as a public health professional and as an ordained deacon, Joanne Leslie, for example, tells us that she proposes to embrace a newfound grandmotherly role: to sit on a stool and tell stories to her grandchildren.

MENTORSHIP AND WOMEN'S CIRCLES

Those who have not been blessed with the presence of women elders such as these in their personal, familial, or professional networks nonetheless have many opportunities to search elsewhere for surrogates. Conversely, sometimes they must strive to become the wise women that they seek and in turn mentor others, sharing what they have learned. In our transient modern

lives, frequently disconnected from family networks of origin, we must ourselves assemble support networks among women whom we may consult in
times of joy, calm, and success as well as in times of trial, loss, and turmoil.
In the absence of familial and community "traditions that have no name,"
we must convoke our wise women to help us accomplish the task. We hope
that this volume will be one such resource, a "consciousness-raising circle,"
a surrogate women's council.

Academic environments can be harsh, competitive, lonely, and emotionally arid places, where supportive colleagues are few and far between.
How can we create ad hoc networks of care and support, forging a coun-
tervailing culture within them? My own circle of wise women has come
to include a parish priest, a spiritual director, spiritual companions, and
colleagues, no less than family and friends. On rare occasions colleagues
and spiritual companions are bundled into a single person, such as Joanne
Leslie or Sabina Magliocco.[9] We all benefit from the support of an encouraging, concerned community, to listen with us and deeply reflect on life
direction and purpose—as well as on our day-to-day teaching and collegial
duties. They become cherished friends, colleagues, spiritual companions,
and mentors.[10]

As in many other areas of my life, among friends, family, and ethnic
and religious groups, I have tried to listen deeply, seeking always to identify,
articulate, and act on behalf of unspoken shared needs. I trust that I am
doing the same here. As I gather together this group of scholarly women
(both inside and outside academic circles) to reflect upon and narrate
lives fully lived and lessons learned, I realize how much, as a young first-
generation academic, I would surely have benefited from mentors such as
these. Artist and teacher Karen Guancione, also a first-generation college
student, viewed these uncharted waters as liberating, freeing her to "make
it up," "to orchestrate herself"—a positive outcome of her working-class
upbringing of benign neglect (wherein she became a young leader within
her family and community). I instead felt less confident and moved cautiously as I traveled this route for the first time with precious few guideposts
along the way. Charlene Villaseñor Black ("Chicana Art Historian at the
Crossroads"), who experienced educational and economic disadvantages in
her own life, turned her pioneering experience into a pledge to mentor similar minority college students at the University of California at Los Angeles
(UCLA). Many, like us, had scant knowledge about what would be required

in academia and learned to negotiate elite educational environments on our own. I surmise that I likely gravitated toward the Italian Department at the University of Toronto, from earlier academic interests in philosophy and history, precisely because the department was peopled with other first- and second-generation bicultural, working-class Italian diaspora students. For me, understanding and negotiating the "between and betwixt" of socioeconomic and academic systems may have been more personally urgent than pursuing philosophical abstraction.

In other words, and with hindsight, it does not seem to be a coincidence that I eventually came to make diaspora cultural identity, recoverable through oral history and folklore, the prime focus of my scholarly life. Increasingly, I sensed that my entire cohort had been cut off from any academically sanctioned access to our ethnographic histories (save for what we could glean from our own families). My academic mission became helping my generation remember our ancestors and their class history. I therefore rejected the more traditional study of Italian literature because it had little to do with my own Italian sociocultural experience. I scarcely could have foreseen that it would take eleven years of university learning in various departments of Italian studies on both sides of the Atlantic before a chance encounter with folklore, mythology, and ethnomusicology at UCLA would expose me to the idea that a legitimate course of study in tune with my own cultural and historical experience (Del Giudice 2009a) was even possible. I concluded that this precious knowledge—so hard-earned, given the establishment—needed its advocates within and outside the academy. This became my mission.

Advocacy for folklore and oral history went hand in hand with an increasing feminist consciousness, as I sought to "make the invisible visible" and "give voice to the silenced"—me included. Had I more fully participated in the Women's Movement during the 1970s and been encouraged to take a few Women's Studies courses, I might have known more (and known sooner) about consciousness-raising and advocacy of this sort. I reiterate that as a young scholar I was busier finding my bearings in the foreign world of higher learning and was not sufficiently empowered to deviate from the standard curriculum. I had known limited formal encounters with the Women's Movement, even though I counted myself part of that world. I had read every single issue of *Ms.* magazine from its inception, had been elected to the Student Council of the University of Toronto in the mid-1970s, had served on its Women's Commission (even though that experience was not especially enlightening, inasmuch as the commission was largely manipulated and "managed" by male council members), and had spearheaded the founding of a Sexual Education Center on campus. All of these activities heightened my own growing feminist sensibilities.

As a naturally contemplative child who spent hours in her inner world, I was always on a search for quiet places to think and frequently longed for a secluded women's community. The convent life (or other such intentional community) secretly appealed to me. It continues to be a leitmotif in my life. I have organized and participated in many women's retreats, as well as women's peace and justice groups, and continue to be inspired and supported by them. I learned that seclusion and community, contemplation and social action, go hand in hand for me. Organizations such as Sister Simone Campbell's "Nuns on the Bus" and the Center for Action and Contemplation earn my fullest admiration. On a cultural tour to the Grand Béguinage in Leuven, Belgium (during an International Ballad Commission meeting in 2002), Mary Ellen Brown (see her essay, "Predestination?") and I encountered this medieval institution for the first time. We were captivated by the idea that *béguines* (women) and some *beghards* (men) organized themselves around a semimonastic way of life that included contemplation and serving the poor but did not require that its members relinquish independence or personal property or take vows or pledge obedience to a motherhouse.[11]

Only half in jest, I have proposed that we revive the concept of *béguinages* in our own times to help sustain women in communities that favor contemplation, learning, and social action. Might similar communities be envisioned to sustain us as women of learning and compassion when the usual institutions will no longer do (or, frankly, do not yet exist)? Absent such structures, might other (adapted) paths serve just as well? For example, Leslie became a deacon in the Episcopal Church, the "eyes, ears, and hands" of the church in the world (she is now archdeacon of the Los Angeles Diocese), seamlessly extending and intertwining her life as a UCLA professor of public health with her spiritual calling (while conversely, bearing witness to the life of the spirit within the academy). Others seem to have felt similar needs as they undergo ordination processes, frequently training others to follow. While continuing to be women of learning, they may also become ordained Christians (Leslie), Pagan priestesses (Magliocco), Zen abbesses (Schireson), yoga teachers (Giunta), or spiritual directors (Del

Giudice).[12] For most of us, though, integration of the professional and the spiritual remains hidden from public view—even where it may form a significant part of who we are, how we view the world, and how we practice our professions.

LIFE CYCLES AND OTHER CHALLENGES

The cauldron of parenting two daughters and coming to terms with the biological realities of a woman's life cycle, while also attempting to forge a professional path, forced me personally to confront entrenched gendered inequalities in our social systems. This private sequence of revelations made me a more pronounced (and yes, enraged) woman's advocate. Motherhood at first made me feel thwarted, invisible, defeated. As this collection demonstrates, I was not alone, even though few express the rage that enveloped me over such life-cycle events. Others also negotiated nonlinear professional pathways as they assimilated to their traditionally assigned female roles as mothers, wives, and caregivers. I sometimes feel pangs of guilt. I trust that my daughters, Elena and Giulia, will forgive me for any rage that may have spilled over into their lives, while I assure them of my deepest love for them and my most cherished memories of baking cookies, reading bedtime stories, making art projects, taking field trips, and other shared mother-daughter experiences, which I genuinely loved. Indeed, one of the most memorable but also most challenging chapters in our shared life was during my Fulbright research stint at the University of Pavia in northern Italy in 1991. Alone as a parent and intensely together with my homesick four-year-old and a three-month-old nursing infant, we created a wonderful six-month adventure in parenting/scholarship. We were visited from time to time by my husband, a UCLA professor, who accepted as many Italian university lecturing invitations as possible in order to be near us.

I consider all my parenting experiences—the mundane, the extraordinary, the difficult, and the joyous—to have provided a life seminar in how to love deeply and care thoroughly for my most precious daughters. But, as they have also witnessed by watching me (and will likely learn through their own lives), the life of a woman trying to balance profession and family is a rather complex achievement. Their paternal grandmother, Helen Fowler Tuttle, one of the first women petroleum geologists to graduate from the

University of California at Berkeley, became a professional casualty of her times, forced out of her Shell Oil surveying job a few years after becoming a mother. And although she was a highly competent member of the workforce, the men returning from World War II service were granted ipso facto priority. Nonetheless, when I recorded her life history (a future gift from the ancestors to my daughters), I noted that she maintained a high degree of ladylike dignity while narrating those years, vigilant not to complain. Alas, I have never quite mastered such equanimity and detachment. Even after the many advances that women had made in the intervening decades, my own experiences of turmoil as a young mother and budding academic found more varied forms of expression, witnessed by daughters, husband, sisters, and parents—all of whom supported me through the toughest times as best they could. I can only hope that my daughters will be equally surrounded by love, intelligence, and support within their own families. But as a result of my own experience, I have also strongly encouraged them in the direction of professional and economic autonomy first—before integrating these into any loving family life and even motherhood of their own.

Mine proved a complex career path—and one rarely remunerated. Relegated to occasional contract work, small grants, and visiting professorships, I have nevertheless been a highly productive academic, all the while questioning whether such efforts might actually constitute an academic "career." Many of these endeavors became a means of staying deeply engaged through research and publication. They saved my life. Further, listening in community also became a vital part of the process, as I struggled to listen, think, and write my way into consciousness and into action. I continue to do so.

My nuclear family and home life has especially grounded and nurtured (and also distracted) me. A continuing connection with my family of origin (in Canada) has provided a marker by which to assess my own place in ancestral time. I listened to and through my families, the better to heed my own spiritual impulses, finding my way forward and adjusting for speed and distance. Time and again, I ventured farther out, overcoming fear, returning home to reflect, assimilate, and write, in order to venture forth again and again. And throughout this process, I have increasingly gathered around me kindred spirits, creating communities of "elective affinities" inside and outside the academy. Some are present in these pages.

PROCESS AND GOALS

The present volume did not begin with the usual open and anonymous call for papers but rather evolved by word-of-mouth. This process represented a first for me. Indeed, I had previously always insisted on general calls for papers for the publications and conferences that I organized. For this experimental project instead I applied a more organic, oral methodology, which seemed more in tune with the actual networks of women's friendships and community lives. I also wanted to be assured through the extension of direct personal contacts that this volume would indeed gather together women that we knew embodied integration of head and heart.

This project differed in yet another way. Although it would be geared toward academics, it was not to be academically onerous or employ academic jargon but instead would offer an exercise in self-reflection and self-expression, gratifying to the writer herself, and be accessible to all. This process required patience on all of our parts. I encouraged ever more personal (rather than expository) prose. We collectively dealt with fluid and periodically renegotiated deadlines, as contributors inevitably faced diverse personal crises, heavy teaching workloads, administrative responsibilities, and medical leaves. Given the reality of women's lives (as scholars and otherwise) doing double-duty as professionals and caregivers, I took what was for me an uncharacteristic laissez-faire attitude toward deadlines, because my goal was full participation. This editor has learned the rewards of patience. I encouraged, cajoled, and waited, as did others on the project's behalf (thank you, Edvige Giunta and Lauren Vitiello), because I had faith that each would keep her word and because I firmly believed that we would all benefit from each and every contribution. Had there been even more time, I might have extended the evaluation process to include reciprocal readings of all contributions and collective rewritings. I chose to push the project toward publication instead. Indeed, most contributors are also reading these essays for the first time.

This is one of the first publications I have edited that is not primarily a collection of Italian and Italian diaspora writing, notwithstanding its remote origins as *On Second Thought: Italian Women Scholars' Internal Dialogs.* In dialog with others, my own thinking evolved and our circle widened across many disciplines and interests, while remaining gender-centric.

"Women of learning" is here broadly defined to include women who may not consider themselves "scholars" in the strictest sense but who have spent their lives in scholarly pursuits of one sort or another, in a variety of work settings. Many do research, assemble facts, write grants, publish, lecture, organize conferences, mount exhibitions, and teach—all the varied activities that typically characterize a scholarly life. Professionally, some may be medical doctors, artists, yoga instructors, and federal agents, involved in teaching, training, and imparting knowledge in a formal setting. Many have taken their expertise into the wider world, to health clinics, congregations, women's circles, writing groups, dream circles, yoga studios, peace and justice forums—on local, national, even global fronts. They are thinkers and doers, at times even activists who turn individually acquired knowledge to benefit some greater common good. I hope that their strong voices will serve as touchstones, attesting to the many roles that we can fill as we bring together lives of learning with living in the world.

I asked these contributors to give "a second thought" to their lives of learning and share those internal dialogs with us. I wanted to know from them what I had been asking myself—the whys and wherefores of the intersections of their personal, professional, and communal lives. I was especially eager to plumb the processes of how and why they had chosen to devote their energies to the things they had. How had their deeper personal convictions (or encounters with "ultimate reality") determined their career paths and affected their work? What role had family, culture, religion, and gender played therein? What life lessons had they learned and which did they wish to impart?

What came forth from this process of self-reflection may indeed serve others, but the dialogic process has especially served the contributors themselves. Despite lives of learning, critical thinking, and reflection, many had never before turned such intense scrutiny on their own lives in quite this way. They expressed how difficult the process had proven to be but how surprised, illuminated, and satisfied they were with their results. Through contributors' reflections on this writing exercise, I have learned how valuable it has been for each, affording an opportunity for self-nurturing and compassion through the process of examining their lives and speaking their piece. This moment of rest, amid lives of endless professional activity, family duty, and life's assorted challenges, has helped us focus on what is of lasting value in the life of both the mind and the heart, helping us maintain our "true" direction. Some discovered patterns within their lives that they had not fully considered. Others experienced epiphanies. I was delighted but not surprised. What I had garnered through spiritual retreats could be achieved in virtual (writing) retreats such as this one. Part of my mission had been accomplished. The remaining part will involve our readers.

At least one such epiphany proved to be my own. Although I had participated in many contemplative writing retreats—virtual and otherwise—it was a more recent invitation by folklorist Pravina Shukla to participate in the 2013 American Folklore Society "Leaders in Folklore" forum that prompted another important self-discovery.[13] Shukla posed a series of questions prompting a closer consideration of my curriculum vitae. Had I encountered this handy set of diagnostics when inviting the contributors to this volume to submit essays, their process of (self-)examination might have been even more keenly honed. So fruitful have these questions proven that I might suggest that scholars use them at regular intervals, to monitor evolutions and shifts in perception, focus, and growth.[14]

I gained further insights into my own life. I recognized a persistent malaise about not having had a "real" career, despite a scholarly life marked by tenacity and high production. But I came to understand that career paths, albeit nonlinear and sometimes unremunerated, are nonetheless careers and perceived as such by colleagues. I also had to admit that my path had largely been self-forged and defiant. A critical exception to this narrative of the self-made was due to a highly motivated high school teacher of Canadian History, John Biernat, who set me on my way. It was he who intervened to convince my reluctant father that Luisa must go to college. To Mr. Biernat I will be forever grateful. Yet what had propelled me forward thereafter? It was my innate and increasingly assertive nature as a contrarian. My life journey had been propelled forward by resistance and headstrong opposition to the repeated "No"s that I had long battled (from beloved but authoritarian father to other road-blocking gatekeepers). While my father provided a strong model of survival, defiance, and strength (for example, as a prisoner of war in Germany and as a determined but impoverished post–World War II Italian emigrant to Canada), his patriarchal control taught me paradoxically to resist his authority in order to maintain my own sense of self. I was indeed "my father's daughter." Like him, I am a survivor with an uncommonly strong will—for which I am grateful.

But there were other, less pointed ways in which I resisted and refused to accept "No." For example, when denied a critical graduate scholarship, I left my Canadian university to study in Florence on an Italian government scholarship (for Italians residing abroad). Years later, when I encountered reluctance by a Ph.D. dissertation chair about folklore and diaspora as legitimate areas of Italian Studies, I rearranged my committee and replaced him. A dead-end in university teaching led ultimately to founding my own nonprofit institute for oral history and the immigrant experience. And finally, when this nonprofit was denied institutional affiliation (academic or museum), I closed it. Thus, *nolens volens*, I was finally released from any institutional affiliation. Untethered, I continue to pursue research and community programming as an independent scholar. Again and again I have had to re-create myself, using the strength, agility, and tenacity that are my birthright.

One of my guiding dictums has been that the difference between stumbling blocks and stepping stones is how you use them. I have converted obstacles into guideposts, while learning to meander, bypass, negotiate, and eventually (when needed) ignore obstacles altogether. At times I have chosen patience, waiting for the situation to resolve itself. On other occasions I have vociferously advocated for change and acceptance. And in a few instances I have simply battered down the door. In retrospect, from my place ever on the margins, I have become a keener observer of hierarchies and power struggles, mostly (but not all), male-dominated. It has made me more alert to the many and alternative ways of achieving ultimate goals. I call it the art, skill, and practice of "Finding a Way" (Italians call this *arrangiarsi*, "making do"). Ultimately, as I have written elsewhere, my status as an independent scholar has brought me collateral benefits, as I learned to embrace the margins as a place of freedom, autonomy, and even power. Here, on these pages, for example, I can speak freely and candidly as others, more institutionally bound, perhaps cannot. I repeat: not everyone accepted my invitation to do some truth-telling here.

I am especially grateful that my professional struggle prodded me to grow by extending my projects beyond the academy, into society at large. Some have called me a public intellectual—which at first baffled me. The truth is that I have been baffled by labels throughout my postgraduate years, given my peculiar situation vis-à-vis the academy. What should I call myself: an ongoing visiting professor, a public sector folklorist, an (in)dependent scholar? As my own understanding of what I do, and why, has evolved and expanded, I realize that "public intellectual" suits me fine and is particularly appropriate with respect to my recent work around the Watts Towers Common Ground Initiative (www.wattstowerscommonground.org), which integrates the scholarly, the personal, the public, and the spiritual.

A label that I would now willingly discard, however, is "contrarian," because it no longer serves. This mode of being seems restrictive, reactive, and externally driven; it is time to adopt a more self-and-other compassionate model as my modus operandi. It is also time for me to embrace the concept of "enough" and to abandon the perpetual motion machine of academic production. The fact is, the gaping maw of the professional résumé can never be appeased. While raw survivalism and innate perfectionism have been my driving forces for decades during which I sought to leave no stone unturned, attempted to catch all the balls in the air, and said yes to all new adventures while taking risks and overcoming fears, such an approach to life may deny more natural rhythms and stalls the season of reflection and renewal. It is also exhausting. Collaborative projects such as this collection of self-reflective essays instead now seem more poignant and seasonable.

PRESENTATIONS

I am delighted to present this collection of essays by some of the most extraordinary women it has been my fortune to know, to work and share life with, and to enjoy as friends and colleagues. We are women who have worked in the fields and borderlands of holy writ, law, medicine, public health, art, art history, literature, cultural anthropology, ethnography, oral history, gender studies, and psychology as well as American, Chicano, Italian, and Native American Studies. In our many life trajectories and paths of learning—in laboratory, studio, library, archive, and community—we have spanned disciplines as well as cultural and spiritual traditions. Among us are an Italian Pagan anthropologist (Sabina Magliocco), a Sicilian American literary scholar and yoga teacher (Edvige Giunta), a (Jewish) Zen Buddhist abbess and psychologist (Grace Schireson), a Scottish Canadian Californian Episcopal archdeacon and professor of public health (Joanne Leslie), an Episcopalian Anglo-Scottish ballad scholar (Mary Ellen Brown), an Italian American Catholic integrative medical doctor (AnnaLisa Pastore), a New-England Californian Jungian analyst (Willow Young), an activist Chicana Episcopalian art historian (Charlene Villaseñor Black), an Italian Jewish American historian (Jennifer Guglielmo), a scholar of Polish, Italian, and Native American oral traditions (Christine Zinni), an Italian American artist and professor (Karen Guancione), an Italian American refugee officer and poet (Lauren Vitiello), and an Italian Canadian Californian Episcopalian ethnographer and oral historian (Luisa Del Giudice). We are middle, upper-middle, and working class and include first-, second-, and third-generation immigrants as well as long-established "Americans."

Our lives and our work have spanned continents as scholars and spiritual practitioners but also as adventurous and curious world travelers. We have been at home in many places while in at least one case homeless in several others (Guancione). Some were born abroad, while others precociously discovered foreign lands, new languages, cultures, and class differences, already as girls (Leslie in Brazil), and still others displayed mastery, competence, and leadership in their own world at a tender age (Guancione). "Foreign" worlds come in other forms, as several first-generation scholars navigate the foreign milieux of higher learning, pioneers from their own families (Guancione, Villaseñor Black, Del Giudice). Some instead venture into new territory by expanding disciplinary boundaries, such as integrative medicine (Pastore) or journeying deeply inward through autoethnography (Del Giudice, Brown), memoir (Giunta, Guglielmo), spiritual lineage (Schireson), or depth psychology (Young). We represent established spiritual traditions and emergent ones (neo-Paganism). Many of us have held prominent leadership positions within public institutions, spiritual communities, and professional practices. Most have nurtured groups large and small, as mothers, grandmothers, godmothers, mothering teachers, and community mothers.

I have searched through these essays for threads that bind and found many. I encourage you to find others. Here are a few of the recurring themes that have caught my attention. For example, there is a general insistence that women's voices are critical and must be heard, even when doing so challenges the institution—often by exploding orthodoxies, seeking greater inclusivity (not exclusively relating to gender), and opening the gates. Another theme snaking its way throughout is that finding our voice requires hard work, an earnest and deliberate search, even suffering, but that having traveled that road and overcome its obstacles gives us the confidence and desire to support, advocate, and even create structures that recognize women's and other marginalized voices. Our authors do not shy away either from descriptions of pain and suffering or from spiritual awakening and joy but accept that the full range of emotions are both permissible and also worthy of articulation. We tend to share what we have and what we know with others within our own communities, with those we do not know, and even with future generations. We respect that each woman honors heritage according to her own lights, her own experiences, her own life. For example, with regard to this very publication, I respected the fact that each contributor offered her own life experience in her own voice. This meant that even where ideas and worldviews did not agree with my own, or expressed ideologies I did not share (or even opposed), such essays nonetheless were to be included with no disclaimers or editor's notes (nor will I allude to them here).

In the volume's narratives we encounter masters of bricolage and diverse resources who find meaning in lonely marginalized places, who struggle to weave together disparate aspects of life to make them meaningful, sometimes literally weaving threads together to make a coherent fabric (Guancione's artwork). Many strongly articulate a sense of being "between and betwixt," of "walking between the worlds." Notions of flux, multiplicity, and simultaneity abound. They are expressed in the figure of Persephone, a bridge between the underworld and earth, old and new worlds, or Italy and America (Giunta); in the spiritual "thin spaces" between realms in the Pagan worldview (Magliocco); in professional roles between the academic and public nonprofit worlds or in cultural peregrinations and suspension between continents (Del Giudice); or in occupying simultaneously a middle place that is both/and in the concept of "nepantla" (Villaseñor Black). These women feel that they span worlds, existential states, roles, and physical realities.

"Nepantleras/os" are "liminal" or "threshold people," bilingual, bicultural, biracial, and embrace this space between, as "productive space" (Anzaldúa 2009: 180). Like trickster coyotes, they move between worlds by stealth and intelligence and become agents of change. Folklorist and anthropologist Sabina Magliocco articulates the multifaceted theoretical and practical aspects of "walking between the worlds" as a scholar and a practitioner of ritual. It was modern Paganism that helped her, both as a scholar-observer and as a practitioner, to walk between worlds (the scholarly and the spiritual). She maintains that those who straddle worlds are healers who "carry gifts of the spirit back from the otherworld into the human realms—gifts that help make things whole" and that on some level "all scholarship is not only a seeking of knowledge but also a spiritual quest to achieve a better understanding of our own nature and how we fit into the larger patterns of the universe."

We search for mothers and other matrilineages (scholarly or spiritual) and honor female ancestors in our lives and our work. We recognize the Female Divine and even engage in female devotional practices. In several essays we are reminded of the foundational and symbolic role of grandmothers. These Ur-Mothers sometimes undergo mythic or symbolic transformations in our third-generation lives, pressed into archetypal service of one sort or another, guiding us and inspiring us along our paths. They may also teach us how to lead. A rapport with our grandmothers favors intimate reflection on ancestral time and legacies, as we consider our place within our own tribes, our evolutions within or away from our familial or religious worldviews. Cultural affiliations may inculcate in us the very love of (book) learning, shared as women of learning—as it has for two of our scholars of Scots ancestry (Leslie, Brown), both with a passion for poetry, both involved with religions of the Book. For example, as a professor of Scottish balladry, Brown recognizes the central place that her Scots family granted to religion and poetry and how the well-crafted word of poetry and song became for her an all-encompassing modus vivendi. Despite humble farming roots, Leslie's grandmother's marked love of learning motivated her to turn her home into a community library, a focus of learning for her entire rural Canadian village. Edvige Giunta returns to the devotional practices of her maternal grandmother, to whom she was fiercely attached as a child, gradually incorporating this spiritual mentor's rapport with the sacred quotidian into her own life. Guglielmo's grandmother, too, became her spiritual teacher. My paternal grandmother, a formidable matriarch and village faith healer, may have informed my own journeys in ethnography and community work. By contrast, in "The Arc of Becoming," Willow Young speculates that her affinity for the underdog and sympathy for the culturally different arose in opposition to a genteel grandmother who gave her earthier grandchild the sense that she belonged to a wilder part of the family. Magliocco likewise resisted her grandmother's sense of class entitlement.

One of the overarching themes, of course, and part of the volume's raison d'être, is the search for one's life purpose. Jungian psychologist Willow

Young has made a profession of delving deeply to identify and explore the subconscious mind and its archetypal guides on the journey toward greater consciousness: the "arc of becoming." That process takes account of the remembered, the inherited, the willed, and the occurrences fatefully visited upon us—as well as "symbolic language of soul, dreams, dream images, and intuitions." Dreams have literally been the stuff of Young's life, waking and sleeping. They have been an integral part of her professional and academic life (dream groups and teaching), while allowing her to navigate the alienating, logos-dominated world of the university. She reminds us that the work of becoming is never complete and that the struggle continues "to live the truth of my being, to stand on my own ground, consciously *choosing* a life in relationship with the psyche and not just live abducted by it." Even as an educator, her goal is tending to the "living image of the psyche as it makes its presence known."

As women, our lives are intimately intertwined and sometimes determined by life-cycle events such as motherhood—which we may alternately crave, accept, reject, or lament. Life-cycle choices and/or duties such as marriage, motherhood, childcare, and eldercare most frequently devolve upon us (trials of devotion, as Guancione calls them) but often represent distractions to careers. We are frequently taught to take care of others before taking care of ourselves. Few are taught to "put on their oxygen masks before assisting others," as we hear during air travel upon takeoff. Guglielmo, however, did receive such advice from the paternal grandmother who mothered her, from whom she learned the important lesson of reconciling family care and self-care and never to sacrifice the latter for the former. She learned many of life's lessons in the most sacred place of all—her grandmother's kitchen. In rare instances, however, our roles as nurturers do not distract but may actually enhance careers, as some find professional opportunities in and through these very experiences. Leslie's maternal experience of breastfeeding, for instance, and her reading about nutrition helped identify her doctoral research topic: the economic impact of malnutrition (which led to a career in public health). While my experiences as a mother and wife did not determine my career choice, reflection on these situations did contribute to publications on lullabies, erotic ballads, and the decidedly female phenomenon of (neo-)*tarantismo*, the therapeutic dance for the mythic "spider's bite." No amount of confinement, fatigue, mundane distractions, or anguish over professional marginalization, that is, can prevent an imaginative mind from working overtime—even as we nurse babies or change an elder's diapers (see Guancione). This ability to use what is at hand, grounded in our own lived experiences as women, as a resource for the life of the mind shows a thrifty way of "making do" and also a critical capacity to be fully present to all of life—doing the practical while pondering the existential. The nonlinear path, sometimes caused by family obligations on the early and later ends of the human life-cycle spectrum, can make us resilient and creative. Despite suffering from a sense of incompleteness regarding our not always well defined life purpose, or an abiding sense of "intrinsic restlessness" (Leslie), we muster energy and drive to do what we must, learning to keep dreams alive. And even when career choices have been well-defined, peregrinations may be imposed from without, as we pursue employment opportunities around the country (Magliocco).

Care for family, though, can frustrate or delay professional self-realization, as many attest. Guancione considers her role as designated caregiver for a failing, demented mother to be a form of "house arrest" (compare Zinni's "exile"). She describes the mind-numbing tedium of eldercare, the despair of being a highly effective and productive artist and teacher, caught up in the web of domesticity, sleep deprivation, lack of privacy, and loss of freedom. She also rails against the practice of "extolling the blessings of caregiving," juggling guilt and shame primarily through concealment, while hiding her travails from colleagues "as though this was my private shame." She contends with eroding self-esteem and "slow loss," with anxiety and dread, with humble patience and compassion, "learning how to stand still while believing I can fly."[15] She "flies" in her mind to the more carefree years of her youth, as she happily rambled across Europe and North Africa, always using art as the "magic key to entering all worlds" and also as a means of self-protection from the various dangers and risks of a woman traveling alone.

My wanderlust has never abated, perhaps a natural outcome of my own relentless "triangulation" between California, Canada, and Italy. More likely, however, it represents my own inner restlessness, a desire for learning and adventure. As for many others (compare Young), Mary Oliver's "The Journey" seems to represent a "women's anthem" of sorts, reminding us to pursue what we are meant to do in life relentlessly, despite family obligations, despite everything:

though the voices around you
kept shouting
their bad advice—
though the whole house began to tremble
and you felt the old tug
at your ankles.
"Mend my life!"
each voice cried.
But you didn't stop.
(Oliver 1992)

Our lives are often limited by the resistance of others (the voices telling us to stay), by bad advice, or by self-censure, but this poem seems to promise that the stars will burn through this obfuscating fog, lighting our way as we venture into the world.

On the positive side of the ledger, deep engagement with our roles as nurturers and caregivers also brings us face to face with the sacred dimensions of such work, at times compelling us toward nurturing larger communities (spiritual communities included). Several contributors have become publicly ordained wise women and mothers within their spiritual communities. For example, Schireson sees her role as a conduit between Zen female ancestors and their granddaughters, as she expands the list of ancestors to include women within the tradition. Leslie realizes the "something more I was meant to do," through ordination to the Episcopal diaconate, taking on faith-based health advocacy. Both Schireson and Leslie happen to be grandmothers who inhabit the role with deep spiritual conviction.

Others focus on their roles as mothering teachers. Giunta's cultural and political convictions as a feminist writer and teacher find expression in her birthing and mentoring of an Italian American Women Writers collective, Daughters of Persephone.[16] As mentor and editor, she understands how an anthology (this one too, I might add) "can serve as a spiritual circle," by nurturing new voices. She enhances her scholarly mentoring by teaching memoir writing and yoga. Villaseñor Black (a single parent or mother/father) concludes that "mothering was my most effective model for mentoring my students,"[17] even as she confronts the still vibrant institutional stereotype of the "nurturing female faculty member of color 'wasting' her career away, selflessly mentoring underprivileged students." Guglielmo credits her grandmother with helping her heal deep grief (the loss of her mother as a young child and abuse at the hands of her father in its aftermath). Her apprenticeship in compassion and spiritual practice led, in part, to her life's work as a scholar and professor of history, as she seeks to become a vehicle of healing for others, notably for the students at her all-women college. Like Villaseñor Black, Guglielmo concludes that teaching, like mothering, is about love. Guglielmo sees her twenty-year-long work, *Living the Revolution: Italian Women's Resistance and Radicalism in New York City (1880–1945)*, as "a series of altars in honor of my ancestors."

We find resonances that help define our purpose in our own traditions (mythic, historic, ethnic, and ancestral). Chicana art historian Villaseñor Black, for instance, asserts that her work in Spanish religious art is "an affirmation of my Catholic upbringing, Mexican heritage, and working-class roots." This identity guides her career and her activism. In her essay "Becoming Storied," Zinni considers how returning to old things, and listening to the lives of her own ancestors as an oral historian, completes the circle of her own professional and personal lives. Family narratives of tending lush vegetable patches and indigenous peoples' relationship to the land, their concept of "nature's rights," and their prayers of gratitude together teach her about service to family, community, and the earth itself—now the central tenets of her life. As her Native American and Italian diaspora studies converge, her own life becomes more complete and integrated.

The economic aspect of the academic life is another theme running through several essays. Villaseñor Black and Zinni both address issues of penury, the first as a student, the second as an academic who forewent a traditional career to care for her mother. Zinni invokes the images of "begging bowls," the "sacred hoop," and "the red road," connected concepts that point to "living small," enjoying freedom and flexibility, while enduring anxiety about the precariousness of living on the professional margins. Living on the academic margins, as a largely unremunerated "independent scholar," is a topic that I treat in my own essay. Several first-generation scholars of working-class backgrounds (Villaseñor Black, Guancione, Guglielmo, and Del Giudice) also describe how socioeconomic class and ethnicity have affected their academic identities.[18] For example, Villaseñor Black, who resolved never to work on any topic associated with privilege, such as elite patronage or portraiture, is dedicated to the mentoring of minority students of similar background, and also strongly advocates on behalf of public education. Intersecting expressions of inequality may also be identified in "hierarchies of knowledge" surrounding the written word, as Zinni has learned from the Ho-Chunk. I too have worked with similar issues along literate/illiterate divides as they relate to the oral culture and history of Italian peasants. Activist scholars such as John Mohawk taught Zinni how to combine praxis, local history, and social justice. Scholars of oral history and oral culture understand the value and power of the spoken word as a vehicle for giving sound to the unheard and for advancing social justice. I have advocated for oral culture through my multiple activities within the academy and in the public sector. Guancione uses her art in similar acts of consciousness-raising and activism. For instance, the materials, methods, and message of her art reflect both "the art of labor and the labor of art." Her art reaches deep into her family matrix, combining a quest for perfection and flawless craftsmanship with a natural sense of thrift, resourcefulness, use and reuse—learned from her mother. She engages provocatively with issues of equity, justice, and women's work, examined across class lines and through the prism of ethnic identity. Ironically, as a daughter under "house arrest," experiencing the drudgery of eldercare, she gets her firsthand experience of the life of a domestic servant ("yet another and uniquely female category of labor"), a role that she had shunned all her life.

The formal act of listening to the spoken word represents a core practice for professionals besides ethnographers and oral historians, such as Lauren Vitiello, a federal asylum agent who listens, and trains others to listen, to stories of incredible suffering. How do we prepare to meet such challenges, to discern levels of truth in such stories? How does a listener come to terms with the terrible responsibility and power of being a story-listening gatekeeper? She learned these skills from her moral formation in the Roman Catholic Church, within her southern Italian family, and from the stories that she was regularly taught to believe as a young child in parochial schools—especially the hellish and freakish ones. Years later she would be listening to "stories even more gruesome." That religious heritage—including fantastical tales of angelic flights toward heaven—contributed to the construction of her alter-ego: Astro Girl, come to save the world! (The world of childhood fantasy nurtured more than one of our contributors, shaping who they would become as adults: consider Guglielmo's practice of drawing and writing about witches, oracles, and other powerful women who could shatter curses and help new worlds emerge and Magliocco's enchanted worldview as a girl and adult.) As an evaluator of refugee stories, Vitiello realizes that she is "stepping into someone else's memoir" and must listen with openness from a respectful place of humility and deference. She has trained interrogating officers to question inconsistencies but also to conduct nonadversarial interviews. She commits to the core belief that "what matters is that we care and take care of ourselves and others," managing her responsibility as a gatekeeper with vigilance not to abuse this privilege.

Ancestors guide our personal, moral, and professional journeys. Guglielmo's grandparents told tales of their own southern Italian ancestors, both as cautionary tales and as stories of great suffering transcended, including a legacy of predatory madness. She credits the feminist movement with emboldening her to tell her own tale of abuse, helping other women address overlapping systems of oppression and develop their abilities in "bearing witness to one another." In my essay I consider the embodiment of ancestors through the practice of (auto-)ethnography and oral history, as a spiritual practice of deep listening. I envision my role as the active link in the chain of transmission, carrying forth vital lessons from our ancestors into the modern world. But it is also a dyadic relationship. I explore the question: "What do the ancestors want from me, and what do I ask of them?" Ballad scholar Mary Ellen Brown also considers how the inherited cultural and religious values of deep Scottishness (as a form of ethnic determinism) have strongly influenced her life and work, articulated as a focus on religion, on learning, and on the crafted written word. As a member of a family "of the Book," a long line of male ministers and church women (including Presbyterian missionaries), she too gives "language a heightened meaning." As a scholar of Scottish folksong editors, she recognizes a shared "habitus," infused with unstated beliefs and cultural practice that led her to literary and ethnographic things Scottish.

Sometimes, however, genetic (ancestral) determinism proves as much a force in our lives as family narratives and religious tradition. The theme of pain and suffering (physical and psychic) returns in the essay "Sacred Medicine: My Healing (R)Evolution," by AnnaLisa Pastore, a doctor of integrated medicine who articulates her professional calling as the care of bodies and souls. Thoroughly trained within the scientific academy, Pastore nonetheless chooses to practice outside its traditional parameters. She credits her

deep Christian faith for her commitment to "working with love" and seeing medicine as an expression of her "sacred contract" (Myss 2003) to the
"woven web of creation" and the "divine weaver of that web." Further, as a
child witness to so much suffering in her family, suffering that recurs within
her own nuclear family and in her own body, these experiences helped her
develop a "noncognitive, intuitive understanding" of the patients and illnesses that she was to later confront as a doctor. Through dealing with
her own ailing children, and the various tragic accidents befalling her, she
asserts that it was motherhood that "allowed me to deepen my understanding of healing," while prophetic dreams, miracles, premonitions, and faith
provided other messages from the spirit, leading to "beautiful transformations even through the most tragic of circumstances." Further, like yogis
"coming to the mat," medical practice is a "disciplined system for spiritual
growth," a sort of ministry whereby she engages patients in "leaps of faith
regarding their potential to heal."

Many in our circle of women occupy positions of leadership, some
within and others outside the academy, and still others are created by them
ex novo. For example, I founded and directed the Italian Oral History Institute, while Myōan Grace Schireson now occupies a prominent position
within established, male-dominated Zen Buddhism in America. She provides an exemplary model of how to challenge and expand such traditional
structures. "How do you speak to the Buddhist invocation of oneness when
it silences you and your personal experience?" Her effective strategy for
change was to seek "stories of *actual* not mythical women and their historical spiritual practice from the beginning of Buddhism," immersing herself
in their words, their images, and their art. She discovers and holds hands
with her "Zen mothers, aunties, and Dharma sisters tossed aside in one
historical account after another." Why was this urgent to her own practice?
As she took her teaching seat in 1998, she needed to decide: who would be
her role model? How could she formulate her own personal expression of
Zen, as a priest with a husband, children, and grandchildren? She found
many examples of how to balance love of family and the wider community with love of spirit—a model contrary to that of male monks, who were
routinely taught to cut all family ties. She also learned from female Zen
ancestors that, in fact, "there is nowhere to hide if women want to find and
maintain a respected place in Zen Buddhist practice." She understood the
need "to be strong, strategic, bold, unashamed, and visible."

Schireson never minces words, derived in part from the Zen tradition of grappling with kōans, but also attributable to her own temperament and experience as a feminist activist. Persistence does effect real change. Indeed Schireson has helped create a more balanced and less patriarchal Zen, helping it transition from Japanese, Korean, Vietnamese, and Chinese teachers to American practitioners and teachers, partly by co-founding the Shogaku Priests Ongoing Training Institute. And she has successfully introduced a chanted list of female ancestors, now accepted by Soto Zen teachers across America.

CONCLUSIONS

This introduction has only briefly touched upon the essays of our accomplished women of learning and heart, thinkers and doers in a wide range of settings. I consider the women here gathered to be a Wise Women's Circle. They tell of varied, full lives of learning, struggle, and spiritual transformation, while entertaining, informing, challenging, and surprising us. They generously share their personal experiences and lessons learned—some individual, many universal—offering guidance to us all.

I invite you to add our own voices to this chorus, to sing out your own song and narrate your own story, and by sharing them in communities of your own to mentor others—and even become wise elders in turn. May this volume of "travel tales" on the road of knowing and self-knowing be a resource for you. And may this project of ours also be seen as an example of modeling care for communities of women colleagues and friends, reminding us that such communities can be created solely by convoking individual women together—as I have done here. Put our stories to your own uses in community-building. Casting circles and listening in circles is a time-proven way of raising each other's consciousness and voice—bringing forth leaders inside the circle to effect positive change outside the circle. Our "consciousness-raising" Women's Liberationist foremothers knew this. As we face political and social backlash on all fronts today, we understand that there is still much to do, new strategies to employ, and that we must expand our circles to include feminist brothers, sisters, parents, and children. But we begin with ourselves.

I trust that these essays will especially inspire you to examine your own life, identify its purpose, and pursue it no matter what "bad advice" prevents you from doing so. Woe unto those who ignore these inner callings. A cautionary tale that I have shared in woman's retreats follows. This Indian folktale, entitled "A Story and a Song" (Ramanujan 1997), powerfully and eloquently articulates the dangers of a woman's loss of her own inner core or meaning (her "story" or "song").

After a long-suffering, dutiful wife stifles her story and her song, they take the form of a man's hat and coat and sit outside her door. Her baffled and jealous husband finds them, leaves her, and spends the night at the temple where he learns from the chattering monkeys about the goings on in their own households. When this suspicious husband hears about his own wife's innocence, he understands that he has not been betrayed. He returns to her and asks why she had never before spoken to him of her most intimate story and her song? The woman responds: What story? What song? She had suppressed them for so long that she had actually forgotten them. In the process however, her forgotten inner core seemed to have become distorted or disguised and taken revenge. Our repressed dreams, this tale seems to say, can create havoc and can ruin our lives.

Although our stories span a variety of disciplines in the humanities, social sciences, and sciences, we identify therein commonalities of experience, questions posed, and life lessons imparted. Among these is the realization that family cannot fully define, contain, or express all we are called to do with our lives. It is curious, nonetheless, that with few and fleeting exceptions (notably Pastore and to a lesser degree Leslie, Magliocco, and me), most stay clear of engaging the more intimate subtexts of their lives with partners and children. This lacuna seems important, although I am not certain why. Does the challenge of not being defined by our family roles of parent, spouse, or partner prompt us to minimize the actual impact that these roles have on our lives? Are these roles too enmeshed with other family members to foster a clear perspective on what constitutes "us" and what "me"? Or are they simply not a central component of our professional becoming? Indeed, despite the progressive goal of integrating work and home, are they for the most part actual distractions in our professional lives? Or should we recognize that such questions may still verge on taboo for many of us, because they question our fundamental and culturally designated family roles, seeming to point to the reality that they are not as central to us as our families, our religions, and our cultures might wish? More personal stories on the impact of children, dependents, and spouses on female lives of learning might make a fine topic for a volume on its own. Notable examples of women speaking out about the challenges that they face—from within, from family, from work environments—in becoming fully realized professionals are beginning to appear in other sectors, such as technology (for example, Sandberg and Scovell 2013; and something of a response to it: Shevinsky 2015). An exciting new current of publications by women speaking their truth, especially as it regards their place in the working world, is unfolding all around us. I am gratified that this volume may be counted among them.

This has been a deeply satisfying editorial task, but now, upon its completion, I assess my way forward once again—just beyond a few remaining writing deadlines. As I review years of service to various communities, intentionally drawing some to a close, I see a shift in my foreseeable future. After a life marked by restless pursuit, I concur with Leslie that the time may have come for "less *doing* and more *being*." Just as she experiences a "certain disenchantment with striving," I consider engaging with a "theology of enough" (McLaren 2004). We all need rest, stillness, and contemplative retreat as much as we need the active pursuit of life's purpose. How else can we clearly see our way forward?

"Where to now?" I calmly ask myself, knowing well my own heart's natural rhythms of expansion and contraction, the flowing in and out of life blood and life energies, ever replenishing themselves. For me, this ebb and flow seem to have alternated between private scholarship and public education; between periods of contemplation and others of intense social action; between retreat inward to myself and my home and venturing out into the world in never predictable ways. At times these apparent oppositions reach rare moments of equilibrium and integration (for example, in the Watts Towers Common Ground Initiative: Del Giudice 2014). I honor both the quiet places of contemplation and the open and unexplored roads. I am strongly inclined toward journeying—both inward and outward. I tend toward a cloister with an open door, so that my wandering heart and curious mind might remain free to explore new paths and new adventures.

I intend to wander off the "professional grid" for a while—in part to my new "hermitage," a two-room cottage in a Sierran woods to walk in nature, swim, meditate, and write memoirs, as the spirit moves me. Or I may simply keep still and silent, doing little more than coloring mandalas. Conversely, I may turn more to a physically active life of the body. Time will tell. I prepare for this retreat by declining professional invitations to assemble and edit more volumes, write reviews, articles, and attend conferences. Among women colleagues in the second half of life, I note echoes of this shift toward rest and contemplation, toward different sorts of work.

Those who know me best will no doubt remember previous such declarations and chuckle, knowing that, as in the case of Mr. Toad and his love of new vehicles, my eyes will surely alight upon yet another shiny new project or adventure to pursue . . . My backpack is literally always ready, at a moment's notice. In my experience, Ohmmm always seems to be followed by Ohhh!

NOTES

1. Richard Rohr, making reference to the words of Dogen Zenji: "To study the Way of Buddha is to study the self. To study the self is to forget the self. To forget the self is to be illumined by the ten thousand things."
2. We also add our voices to a growing self-reflective scholarship that embraces academic memoir and feminist writings: for example, Cynthia Franklin's *Academic Lives* (2009) and *Writing Women's Communities* (1997); Leanne Simpson's *Dancing on Our Turtle's Back* (2011), regarding contemporary Native feminism and spirituality in the academy; as well as scholarship from a wide range of disciplines, fusing academic and first-person writing, including my own field of folklore, such as Frank de Caro's *The Folklore Muse* (2008).
3. Having received a knighthood from the Italian Republic in 2008, I am of late especially wedded to this image of the woman warrior, a "lady knight," if you will.
4. The woman searching by lantern light in the hidden fairy world (the world of wonder and enchantment) is another intriguing image. See, for example, "Fairy Lantern" (1930s) by Grace Jones (http://saveflowers1.tumblr.com/post/47395383272/art -by-grace-jones-1930s-the-fairy-lantern); or consider the Victorian fascination with fairy imagery, especially "Midsummer Eve" by Edward Robert Hughes and Arthur Rackham's illustrations for *Grimm's Fairytales* as well as William Shakespeare's *A Midsummer Night's Dream* and others.
5. On rare occasions, male punishment has also elicited female revenge, as in the tale of Bluebeard.
6. See Del Giudice 2009b and www.WattsTowersCommonGround.org for further consideration of these initiatives.
7. I thank Nanette Barrutia-Harrison for inviting me to participate in the Miss Revolutionary rally and Facebook page. Standing Women all around the world have

gathered in small and large groups annually since 2007, reading this statement: "We are standing for the world's children and grandchildren, and for the seven generations to come. We dream of a world where all of our children have safe drinking water, clean air to breathe, and enough food to eat. A world where they have access to a basic education to develop their minds and healthcare to nurture their growing bodies. A world where they have a warm, safe and loving place to call home. A world where they don't live in fear of violence—in their homes, in their neighborhoods, in their schools, or in their world. This is the world of which we dream. This is the cause for which we stand" (https://www.facebook.com/standingwomen).

8. Within the Episcopal Church, for example, someone does not unilaterally become a priest by "responding" to a call. The call itself requires a response and affirmation from the community (a "lay discernment committee"), which helps ascertain what form the call might take. It represents a sort of "call and response" between individual and community.

9. Joanne Leslie and I have intersected on many fronts during the past decades, first in a small group of UCLA faculty/Episcopalians, at St Alban's Episcopal Church in Westwood (she as an adjunct professor of public health, I as a visiting professor of Italian folk culture). We continued to cross paths on diaconal committees, peace and justice projects, and retreats and together we coordinated the St. Alban's Interfaith Beijing Circle in Los Angeles, beginning in 2004. With psychologists, professors, Zen teachers, historians, former Jesuits, and others (male and female), we created a supportive circle of thought and compassion to consider these important issues in the world, in Los Angeles, and in ourselves. From that circle many projects arose. For me, this publication represents one such articulation. Sabina Magliocco and I have been colleagues within the American Folklore Society for decades, sharing research interests and more. She has contributed many lectures and essays to various publications and public programs that I have organized. In more recent years I have participated in several ritual gatherings of her Willow Lodge.

10. I have learned much from such friends. Indeed, upon turning fifty, I threw myself a women's garden birthday party and asked that my women friends bring only gifts of wisdom, in the form of a favorite poem, prayer, meditation, drawing, or image, and thereby share individual "lessons learned"—resulting in my own treasured wisdom scrapbook.

11. This movement of free spirits was widespread in the Netherlands during the thirteenth to fourteenth centuries.

12. Although formally trained at the Stillpoint Center for Christian Spirituality, and most familiar with Christian teaching and practice, I am comfortable with nonaffiliation with any one religious tradition (although my closest community is St. Alban's Episcopal Church). As a firm believer in lay movements within faith traditions, respectful of interspirituality and interfaith approaches to spiritual life, I myself have resisted ordination. I eschew "representing" or carrying on my shoulders any orthodoxy, generous or otherwise (compare McLaren 2004), and thus have been content to be a spiritual listener to all and any. I am currently involved with this practice only as a directee rather than as a director. On spiritual direction see Del Giudice (2009a).

13. This forum was loosely patterned on the American Council of Learned Societies "Life of Learning" series. Named for the first chair of the American Council

of Learned Societies, the Charles Homer Haskins Prize Lecture has as its theme "A Life of Learning" (see http://www.acls.org/pubs/haskins). The lecture is delivered at the annual meeting and published in the ACLS Occasional Paper series. The first decade of lectures (1983–1993) is collected in *The Life of Learning* (1994). The lecturer is asked "to reflect on a lifetime of work as a scholar and an institution builder, on the motives, the chance determinations, the satisfactions (and dissatisfactions) of the life of learning, to explore through one's own life the larger, institutional life of scholarship." Pravina Shukla had become acquainted with the series through her husband, noted folklorist Henry Glassie, the 2011 Haskins Prize lecturer. The panel that she chaired for the AFS Forum was videotaped and deposited in the Fife Folklore Archive in the Merrill-Cazier Library, Utah State University, Logan, Utah.

14. The following questions were posed: 1. What brought you to folklore? 2. What does folklore mean to you? 3. What were some great influences and inspirations for you? These could be teachers, scholarly works, and/or informants. 4. What are key organizing concepts that you have found consistently interesting in your progress and your career? 5. Were there chance events and accidental encounters that forwarded your career? By replacing "folklore" with any other discipline, this list can be more widely applied.

15. An editorial aside is in order: Guancione's tale of suffering was excruciating for me to witness. Only in reading her essay did I come to learn of her heavy burden and the extreme efforts required to complete her writing. I myself had to assuage a sense of guilt for having requested this essay, adding to her burdens, and so am doubly grateful that she was able to find the energies to contribute this important project of making the personal public. She has since personally assured me of the vital importance of this writing project to her own process of dealing with her pain.

16. Note that Sicily is said to be "Persephone's Island," so for a Sicilian American such as Edvige Giunta the myth of Persephone is especially poignant.

17. It startled me when my graduate students at Addis Ababa University, perhaps expressing cultural paradigms new to me, first called me "Mom," evidently considering me to be an academic "mother."

18. I was a four-year merit scholarship student at the University of Toronto and have often reflected how fortunate I was to have grown up in Toronto, which afforded me an excellent public education, without economic hardship, something I might not have enjoyed in the United States. Even without a scholarship, higher learning is generally more affordable in Canada.

WORKS CITED

Anzaldúa, Gloria. 2009. "Border arte: Nepantla, el lugar de la frontera." In *The Gloria Anzaldúa Reader*, ed. Ana Louise Keating, 176–86. Durham, NC: Duke University Press.

Bateson, Mary Catherine. 2010. *Composing a Further Life: The Age of Active Wisdom*. New York: Knopf.

Beauvoir, Simone de. 1949. *Le deuxième sexe*. Paris: Gallimard.

Belenky, Mary Field, Lynne A. Bond, and Jacqueline S. Weinstock. 1997. *A Tradition That Has No Name: Nurturing the Development of People, Families, and Communities*. New York: Basic Books.

Bolen, Jean Shinoda. 1999. *The Millionth Circle: How to Change Ourselves and The World: The Essential Guide to Women's Circles*. Newburyport, MA: Conari Press.

Caplow, Zenshin Florence, and Reigetsu Susan Moon, eds. 2013. *The Hidden Lamp: Stories from Twenty-Five Centuries of Awakened Women*. Somerville, MA: Wisdom Publications.

De Caro, Frank, ed. 2008. *The Folklore Muse: Poetry, Fiction, and Other Reflections by Folklorists*. Logan: Utah State University Press.

Del Giudice Luisa, ed. 2014. *Sabato Rodia's Towers in Watts: Art, Migrations, Development*. New York: Fordham University Press.

———. 2009a. "Ethnography and Spiritual Direction: Varieties of Listening." In *Rethinking the Sacred: Proceedings of the Ninth SIEF Conference, Derry 2008*, ed. Ulrika Wolf-Knuts, pp. 9–23. Religionsvetenskapliga Skrifter. Turku, Finland: Department of Comparative Religion, Åbo Akademi University.

———. 2009b. "Rituals of Charity and Abundance: Sicilian St. Joseph's Tables and Feeding the Poor in Los Angeles." In *California Italian Studies*, ed. Lucia Re, Claudio Fogu, and Regina Longo (http://escholarship.org/uc/item/56h4b2s2).

———. 2001 [2011]."Cursed Flesh: Faith Healers, Black Magic, and Death in a Central Italian Town." *Italian American Review* (John Calandra Institute, SUNY, New York) 8, no. 2 (2001): 45–56. Revised in *Italian Folk: Vernacular Culture in Italian-American Lives*, ed. Joseph Sciorra, 189–96. New York: Fordham University Press.

Diop, Birago. 1984. *Leurres et lueurs: Poèmes* (1960). Paris: Édition Présence Africaine, 1960 (http://www.biragodiop.com/index.php/extraits/79-leurres-et-lueurs/109-les -souffles). Translated in *Death: An Anthology of Ancient Texts, Songs, Prayers and Stories*, ed. David Meltzer. San Francisco: North Point Press.

Flinders, Carol Lee. 2006. *Enduring Lives: Portraits of Women of Faith in Action*. New York: Jeremy P. Tarcher/Penguin.

———. 1999. *At the Root of This Longing: Reconciling a Spiritual Hunger and a Feminist Thirst*. San Francisco: Harper.

———. 1993. *Enduring Grace: Living Portraits of Seven Women Mystics*. San Francisco: Harper.

Franklin, Cynthia. 2009. *Academic Lives: Memoir, Cultural Theory and the University Today*. Athens and London: University of Georgia Press.

———. 1997. *Writing Women's Communities: The Politics and Poetics of Contemporary Multi-Genre Anthologies*. Madison: University of Wisconsin Press.

Guglielmo, Jennifer. 2010. *Living the Revolution: Italian Women's Resistance and Radicalism in New York City, 1880–1945*. Chapel Hill: University of North Carolina Press.

Magliocco, Sabina Magliocco. 2001. *Neo-Pagan Sacred Art and Altars: Making Things Whole*. Jackson: University Press of Mississippi.

McLaren, Brian. 2004. *A Generous Orthodoxy*. Nashville: Zondervan (HarperCollins).

Merton, Robert K. *A Life of Learning*. 1994. New York: American Council of Learned Societies/Oxford University Press.

Myss, Carolyn. 2003. *Sacred Contracts: Awakening Your Divine Potential*. New York: Three Rivers Press.

Oliver, Mary. 1992. *New and Selected Poems*. Boston: Beacon.

Ramanujan, Attipate Krishnaswam. 1997. *A Flowering Tree and Other Oral Tales from India*. Berkeley and London: University of California Press (http://publishing.cdlib.org/ucpressebooks/view?docId=ft067n99wt;brand=ucpress).

Rohr, Richard. Daily Meditations (https://cac.org/category/daily-meditations/?gclid=CNSHgs_njM4CFZFufg0dv9YIfg).

Rukeyser, Muriel. 1991. "The Poem as Mask." In *Cries of the Spirit*, edited by Marilyn Sewell. Boston: Beacon.

Sandberg, Sheryl, with Nell Scovell. 2013. *Lean In: Women, Work, and the Will to Lead*. New York: Knopf.

Shevinsky, Elissa, ed. 2015. *Lean Out: The Struggle for Gender Equality in Tech and Start-Up Culture*. New York: OR Books.

Simpson, Leanne. 2011. *Dancing on Our Turtle's Back: Stories of Nishnaabeg Re-Creation, Resurgence, and a New Emergence*. Winnipeg: Arbeiter Ring, 2011.

Standing Women: https://www.facebook.com/standingwomen.

Viola, Bill. 2008. *Three Women*. Video. Transfiguration series.

Watts Towers Common Ground Initiative: www.WattsTowersCommonGround.org.

One

BRIDGING THE SPIRITUAL AND THE POLITICAL

My Scholarly Becoming

IN THE BEGINNING

Nunziatina Nuncibello Minasola communed with God daily. Nothing fancy. No church, no altars, no priest, no pomp. I rarely saw her holding a prayer book, though I remember a rosary dangling from her apron's pocket and the holy cards she would place in the hands of her grandchildren, with the promise that they would keep us safe. Nunziatina's ways were those of mystics like St. Francis of Assisi, whose "Cantico delle creature" I memorized as a middle school student in Gela, my Sicilian hometown. Or the ways of Teresa Carmela Santangelo, a modern-day Bronx Italian American incarnation of St. Thérèse of Lisieux (the saint of the little flowers) and protagonist of *Household Saints* (1993), a film directed by Nancy Savoca.

A Sicilian Argentinean American filmmaker, Nancy was one of the women who first inspired me to abandon my work as a budding James Joyce scholar and to reinvent myself as a scholar activist devoted to Italian American women authors. That shift would in time lead me to other creative and spiritual experiences that would, in turn, take me back to my grandmother and her teachings. And it is with Nunziatina that I must begin. To her, I offer this meditation, this writing in which I retrace my steps and map out my journey as a writer, a teacher, an editor, a spiritual seeker whose first lessons took place in a grandmother's kitchen on the island of Persephone, beloved girl lost and found, inhabitant of two worlds, forever traveler, connoisseur of life and death and of the knots that tie them.

Nunziatina communed with the divine in humble ways. Her faith was rooted in the ordinary, the domestic, the mundane. She would ask her saints, Jesus, and Madonnas (she rarely importuned God or the Holy Spirit) for small favors. "I would like some fruit today." And lo and behold, her doorbell would ring and there was a friend at her door delivering a platter of freshly picked figs or apricots. "Padre Pio, help me find my glasses." The room would fill with a smell of flowers, the supernatural perfume that the faithful associate with the holy father, and her glasses would peek out from behind a basket on the kitchen table. Sometimes her requests had higher stakes and involved the protection of family or friends—a job interview, an important trip, an illness, a pregnancy, a marriage in trouble. Then she would get serious and warn her saints, Jesus, and Madonnas that they had better listen, that she was counting on their intervention. "Questa grazia me la devi fare"—"You must grant me this grace"—she would announce to Jesus on the Cross or Baby Jesus or the Madonna of the Carmel or Saint Sebastian. And yet she knew when to surrender, as she had when, as a young mother (she was twenty-one at the time), she had dreamed of a dark-robed Madonna who told her she would come soon to take her daughter Carmelina away. "It's time," the Madonna had told her. In the dream, Nunziatina had wept and wept, begging the Mater Dolorosa to let her little girl live—from one mother to another, she had pleaded, but to no avail. She had to acquiesce to divine will. Her firstborn daughter, whose tiny body was crippled by a bone disease that remains a mystery to this day, died a few days after the dream. She was seventeen months old.

This story of love, grief, and remembrance, of holding on and letting go, is one of the first stories I remember. The other was of the time I almost died of a delirious fever caused, so the story goes, by missing my grandmother when I was nineteen months old. I had lived with my maternal grandparents since I was three months old. My mother was busy teaching and tending to my sister, who was only four, and my father, a traditional man who did not do any domestic chores and demanded his wife's attention and assistance in many facets of his daily life. While I still saw my mother every afternoon when she came to visit, and on Sundays (which I spent in my parents' apartment, a twenty-minute walk from where my grandparents lived), during my early childhood home was with my grandparents, especially my grandmother. Whenever she visited one of her daughters in Catania, a three-hour bus ride from Gela, my grandmother would take me with her. "La nonna è mia, la nonna è mia," the bus driver would taunt me, declaring that my grandmother belonged to him. His eyes twinkled with amusement, but I was too young to understand. I would look at him suspiciously, holding my grandmother tightly, claiming her as my own with intense, territorial love.

Once my grandmother decided to leave me with my parents. She thought it was wise to wean me from my attachment to her and get me used to spending more time with my parents. As attached as she was to me, she feared the repercussions of the separation from my mother. Soon after she left, I became gravely ill. Over and over again, I heard the story of my miraculous recovery, which occurred only after my grandmother rushed back to my bedside; over and over, the mirror story of the death of her baby girl. I loved both stories. They had a profound effect on me. I rejoiced and mourned as the words poured out of my grandmother. I felt relieved that I had been reunited with her, that I was with her in the present. And I also came to love the child Carmelina, with whom I felt an intense connection. Her spirit hovered in the kitchen, amorously manifested through her mother's words.

While my grandmother sewed, I sat on a small wooden stool or stood on it beside her; while she kneaded bread or made *pignuccata* (a Sicilian cake of kernels of fried dough covered in a golden coat of honey), I listened to her stories and they sank roots inside me. Her stories were interspersed with prayers: "Gesù mio," she would invoke, shaking her hands joined in prayer up and down. "Ah Maronna mia," she would utter with a sigh, looking up toward an invisible divine force. She offered her sorrows, her pain, her tears to God as *fioretti*, her little flowers. It was my grandmother who taught me to pray. She taught me simple, rhyming prayers—like "Angelo di Dio, buon amico mio, guardami stanotte mentre riposo io" (Angel of God, my good friend, guard me tonight while I rest). When I was a child, her incantations soothed me as I fell asleep. Decades later, these prayers sometimes surface in my memory, sudden and unexpected, emanating an otherworldly aura. My grandmother also taught me standard prayers, like *Pater Noster* and *Ave Maria*. After almost thirty years in the United States, I struggle to recite them in English. I typically pray and count in Italian, visceral language of my origins, still resisting English. Although it is the language in which I speak, write, and dream, English remains foreign on my accented tongue. English feels cerebral, masculine. Yet I claim it as mine, intimately mine, as I do with my Italian American identity, believing and doubting at once.

THE WAYS OF DEVOTION

She was a simple woman, my grandmother, with little formal education. Not so her mother, Concetta De Caro. Through a series of vicissitudes that belong to another story, she had been an *educanda* in a convent in Palermo, Sicily's capital. She lived there from age seven to seventeen. It was the late nineteenth century and Concetta, against the odds for a Sicilian girl of her time and social class, became a literate young woman who sang arias and read books in the courtyard of the convent where Cardinal Michelangelo Celesia affectionately called her "Decareddra," a Sicilianized diminutive of her last name.

A few months after Concetta returned to Gela, a man saw her sitting at a window and decided that he wanted to marry that young woman with a sad face and quick, intelligent eyes. And so it would be. But Concetta soon learned that the man she had married did not appreciate the delicate life of the spirit. Efficient and brusque, Gaetano preferred the solitude of his orchard rather than communion with his wife. He spent entire days there, often even staying the night. Long after both Concetta and Gaetano were gone, I heard stories of arguments, of Concetta's desire to leave her husband. Disappointed in her marriage, she ached for companionship and comfort and thanked God for her children and, later, her grandchildren, who at night huddled in her widow's bed, eager for her stories. On that bed, she told them, again and again, the stories of her youth at the convent.[1]

Gaetano Nuncibello was the son of a rich Maltese merchant and a wealthy man himself. He was a man fiercely attached to tradition. He feared that if he allowed his only daughter to continue to attend school after the elementary grades, he would expose her to the dangers that life outside the home posed to feminine virtue. His daughter, destined to marry, did not need school. He would provide for her and find her a suitable husband. And so the girl who would become my grandmother, Concetta's only surviving daughter (two had died as infants), had no opportunity to read books, sing arias, or become adept with numbers, unlike her mother. "Sono ignorante" (I am ignorant), I remember her saying apologetically, whenever she offered her opinion, quietly deferring to her husband, to her sons, to her daughters (two of whom became schoolteachers), to their spouses, and even to her grandchildren.

As an old woman—she must have been in her nineties—Nunziatina would bemoan her lack of education. I could detect shame and regret in her voice, her sighs, the hands folded in apparent resignation. Yet I could read restlessness, too, and a desire for something that had been denied to her. Nunziatina never realized what a teacher she had been to me through her stories, her love, her devotion. She didn't know how I treasured her scarce writings, especially those letters that my grandparents sent weekly during my first few years in the United States to soothe the ache of distance. I was in my mid-twenties and making a new life for myself while also learning a new lesson in loss and separation. In her clumsy, childlike handwriting, my grandmother scribbled on the back of photographs, identifying their subjects, the dates, the occasions. She wrote on the back of the letters that her husband had written in an ornate handwriting using erudite language. She wrote at the bottom and on the margins, on whatever space had been left. She wrote slowly, pressing the pen hard on the paper. *Baciuzzi*, she would write above her signature. Kisses. And I, the granddaughter she had raised who now lived three thousand miles away, yearned to read her writing, moved by those tentative consonants and those trembling vowels, by the old fashioned twirl of the initial "N" of her signature.

When she was fifteen, Nunziatina was promised in marriage to a young man she had never met, a man she would nevertheless grow to love and to whom she would stay married for sixty years, until the day he died. I heard the stories of that engagement from both my grandmother and my grandfather. Nonno Giacomo was a proud storyteller, careful in his choice of words, tone of voice, and accompanying gestures—a man who loved to entertain an audience. I loved his stories, especially of the four years that he had spent in Argentina in the 1920s, and of one of his brothers, who had settled there with his family in the 1950s. I fantasized about my grandfather's "America," about going there myself one day. But I preferred my grandmother's storytelling, and her voice, so quiet and tender, so intimate. I felt the pull of her stories, the visceral way in which they connected me to something larger than the world that its characters inhabited, something for which I had no words as a child.

My grandfather was not as deeply religious as my grandmother, for whom the divine marked every moment of her life, for whom both the trivial and the momentous were manifestations of God. Nonno Giacomo was a believer in a practical, masculine way. There were no subtleties in his relationship with God. One paid respect to and trusted in God. But I never saw him talk to the saints, to Jesus, to Mary, as his wife did. I never saw him pray to the Mater Dolorosa in sorrowful times. His relationship with the divine was discreet and measured—nothing like that of his brother Angelo, who, as a little boy, would run out of the house whenever the bells of the nearby church called to him. Angelo became *lo zio prete*, the priest uncle who every year called each of his nephews and nieces and their spouses and children on their name days. He was a holy man, a servant of the poor and the disenfranchised. The faith of his older brother, my grandfather, was instead pragmatic, never mystical. Nonno Giacomo went to church every Sunday and on all the designated holidays. He crossed himself before eating, after he tucked a large napkin under his chin. He would also cross himself when traveling, especially as a passenger in a car (he never learned to drive and traveled mostly by bus or bicycle). At any dangerous intersection, or if a car passed, his hands would move quickly, rushing through the sign of the cross, a simple gesture that I cannot help emulating decades later, whenever my daughter drives back to her new home in Boston, when the plane is about to take off, when I watch my husband's motorcycle disappear around the corner of our street. I cross myself coyly, privately, reconnecting with childhood rituals and with my grandparents, my guides in the ways of devotion.

My grandparents' oldest surviving daughter, my mother, cultivated her own variety of religion, dictated by necessity, custom, and decorum. The niece of Monsignor Minasola, she acknowledged that our culture's customs were embedded in the rituals of the Roman Catholic Church. Christenings, First Communions, weddings, funerals, anniversary masses for the dead: these were the events that brought my mother to church. I never saw her pray at home or invoke the help of the divine, or even cross herself outside of the church. When she was a child, my mother had often accompanied her devout grandmother, Concetta, to their parish, the church of Capuchin. Those memories became part of the stories she told me, though my mother was a reluctant storyteller. I had to coax stories out of her. Often her stories had the stark quality of a Verist tale, lacking the magic and mystery of my grandmother's, their gentle promise that the past was near, accessible, that you could commune with what was lost. The church of Capuchin overlooking the Mediterranean in Gela was a familiar setting for my mother's stories about her grandmother—but that was all. No descriptions of women on their knees immersed in prayer, no memories of the sweet smell of incense and flowers, no evocation of a priest who knew the family well. And no spiritual visions or yearnings—though I could recognize in her voice a longing for the grandmother who had raised her. My mother's sorrow over the loss of her beloved grandmother was still, after decades, hard, thick, firmly planted. We both felt connected to our grandmothers, to a female lineage of love, loss, and remembrance.

My mother was not interested in the intricacies of devotional practices and beliefs. Yet she was the child who, in her sick bed, had held in her feverish hands the holy image of St. Teresa, the saint after whom she was named. Her uncle, the priest, had ordered everyone to leave the child's room as he prayed by her bedside. He never left her, not even at night, not until she recovered. He prayed to the saint, asking her to save his niece, the little girl whose oldest sister and namesake had died a year before her birth, leaving his brother and young wife bereft. (There is a picture, one of the few from my mother's childhood, in which she is a chubby toddler dressed in the saint's habit, as was customary for those who received graces.) It was her uncle who chose each of her six names. First and foremost, Carmela Concetta—both names associated with the mother of Jesus—after her paternal grandmother; Gemma, after the mystical saint; Angelina, after himself; Natalina, because she was born on Christmas day; and of course, Teresa. My mother's collection of names is a religious and familial tale of the ways of love, tradition, grief, and devotion.

My maternal family embodies so many facets of devotion—mystical, ritualistic, conventional. Each of them still plays some role in my life as an Americanized woman who does not go to mass but has baptized both her children in the cathedral of Gela, a neoclassic style church built in the late eighteenth century on the ruins of an old church and framed by the columns of ancient Greek temples. I am the woman who avoids eating meat on Good Friday (without calling attention to it) and keeps a small collection of icons of Madonnas and female saints. I describe myself as a cultural

Catholic driven solely by intellectual and aesthetic interests. Yet deep inside I hear the voice of my grandmother, feel the pull of her faith.

FATHER

My father was a self-professed atheist, as was his father, Diego Giunta. Like his father, Vincenzo was a socialist, a man concerned with bettering the living conditions of his kind in the here-and-now, a man who mocked divine power and intervention and entertained the possibility of an afterlife only in the philosophical terms of Blaise Pascal's wager. A politician, a man of reason, a philosophy teacher trained in Immanuel Kant, G. W. F. Hegel, and Karl Marx, Vincenzo Giunta disdained religion, the "opium of the masses," and criticized the church for its dogmas and superstitious practices rooted in the Dark Ages.

I spent hours in my father's study, listening to him as he told me of Plato's cave, elucidated Kant's critique of pure reason, or explained the links between Auguste Comte's positivism and Marx's dialectical materialism. In his twenties, my father was already a political leader. I heard stories of the crowd of workers that had carried him on their shoulders during a labor protest. As a college student, he had been one of the closest collaborators of Ernesta Cok Tignino, a relative of his and founder of the Unione Donne Italiane (Italian Women's Union) in Catania, the second largest city in Sicily, where both he and my mother attended the university and where my siblings and I did too (Fiume 2006: 506). He supported divorce and the legalization of abortion. He was adamant that his daughters pursue ambitious professional careers. Still, my father's progressive outlook on public life and education did not apply to certain aspects of child-rearing. His was the lineage of Sicilian men, like my great-grandfather Gaetano Nuncibello, who experienced deep anxiety at the prospect of their women—wives, daughters, sisters—out in a man's world, risking their honor—which, after all, was the property of men.

If my grandmother's mysticism trickled into every particle of my childhood, my father's philosophical and secular outlook swept over my adolescence like a wave. The emerging feminist within me responded and understood there was something to be learned from this father who stuck to ancient Sicilian codes of honor and female virtue but also encouraged me to seek a life beyond the borders of our town, to envision a diplomatic career that would take me to distant lands. By the time I was sixteen, long gone were the prayers, weekly mass, the sign of the cross before a meal, and the kissing of bread when it fell on the floor. Many times I had seen my grandmother perform this tender ritual of our people. Decades later, I would encounter that ritual on the page, memorialized in a poem by Sandra Mortola Gilbert, one of the writers who inspired me to become an Italian American scholar (Gilbert 2000: 171–75).

Unbeknownst to my father, at seventeen I started recording feminist programs with titles like *Sfruttata con onore* (Honorably Exploited), *Spazio donna* (Woman Space), and *Dalla parte delle donne* (On the Side of Women) on the local station, Radio Gela. I was their ambitious and outspoken writer and host. After homework, I would stay up late, plotting the next program. I used the scholarly methods that I observed in my father, who was always reading and sprinkling his lectures and political speeches with compelling historical anecdotes. One of my programs included *Women's News*, which I gathered from television and newspapers, and a *Book Corner*. The program's main feature was a topic of the day pertaining to women's rights—whether abortion, violence, or gender discrimination in schools. My programs were broadcast at three in the afternoon, when my father napped, and without revealing my name. When, at eighteen, I left my hometown and moved to Catania to attend college, I was more than ready to march on the streets with my new sisters, *le femministe*.

In the end, I became my father's daughter. I followed in his footsteps by becoming a scholar, a writer, a cultural activist. As an adolescent, I defied him and felt silenced by him. And he felt defied and tried to silence me. But he also helped me to find my voice, rebellious and assertive, and to fight for my ideas—and my salvation. In time, I would find a way to intertwine politics and spirituality and to integrate my father's social idealism and passion for history with my grandmother's devotion and storytelling.

FEMMINISTA

I was eleven or twelve when Maria Rosa Cutrufelli came to live in Gela and scandalized the town. She was the woman with a mass of red curls that people stared at with suspicion. She was an out-of-towner, a rebel, a feminist. Born in Sicily to a Florentine mother and a Sicilian father, she had spent much of her life in Bologna. In 1971 she moved back to Sicily and lived in Gela while teaching literature in a school in nearby Riesi, the town where I too would teach nine years later. In Gela she organized the first feminist group in Sicily, Lotta Femminista (Feminist Struggle). Girls from the local high schools flocked to her and together they brought about a small revolution. Decades later she would write of her time in Gela:

> we formed the first group that attempted to analyze the situation of Sicilian women relying on strategies that, at the time, were new, original. Thus, in the customarily endless meetings, we questioned the concept of honor, the cult of virility, and the exclusion of women not only from politics but also from public life in general. At the same time, we managed to organize block meetings in the areas where the families of seasonal laborers lived, involving all the women, even those who had never opened the door to a stranger. We believed it was imperative not to separate the practice from the theory. Therefore, our mobilizing, our political initiatives, all of our "practice" had to be connected to a theory that always took into account our history—a history that was specific even if we discussed abortion and divorce, domestic work and violence in the family, that is, problems that all Italian women shared. (Cutrufelli 2005)

Three years after arriving in Gela, Maria Rosa left. The girls who had gathered around her graduated from high school and they too left. They moved to Catania, Palermo, Bologna, Milan. They joined other feminists, created collectives and consciousness-raising groups, and continued the political work they had started in the unlikely setting of our provincial hometown.

Too young to be involved in Lotta Femminista, I nevertheless knew of Maria Rosa. The aura of her work remained, and her lessons came to me a few years later. I received them and made them mine. At seventeen, I read her book *Disoccupata con onore* (1975), which inspired the title of my first radio program, *Sfruttata con onore* (Honorably Exploited). Then I read *L'invenzione della donna* (1974) and *Donna perchè piangi?* (1976). These books belonged to my older sister, but I claimed them as mine and put my stamp on each inside cover: "Biblioteca Edi Giunta."

Over two decades letter, from New Jersey, where I was by then living, I would write a letter to Maria Rosa, the woman who had mentored me without ever meeting me. She wrote back, and an epistolary friendship began. I asked if she would write an essay for a special issue of the journal *VIA: Voices in Italian Americana* devoted to Italian American women that I was guest-editing. I wanted to created bridges between Italian women on either side of the ocean. Maria Rosa wrote an essay aptly titled "In the Kingdom of Persephone": Persephone, archetypal traveler who shuttles back and forth between two worlds, claimed by both and belonging to neither. Later, I wrote an essay about Maria Rosa and my encounters with her, "Sicilian Lives at the Crossroads." In 2000 she visited me in the United States and was a keynote speaker at a symposium on Italian and Italian American women that I helped organize, the first one ever on the subject. I visited her in Rome a year later. Together we edited a collection of Italian translations of Italian American women's writings for the journal *Tuttestorie* (2001), which would be the first Italian publication of that kind.[2] Our essays would appear together, in conversation with each other, in an issue of *Women Writers* on feminist mentoring (2005). There was something serendipitous and powerful about our encounter and collaboration, so many years in the making. And so I began to connect my Italian American feminism with the Sicilian feminism of my youth.

The feminist days in Catania, where I lived from the late 1970s to the mid-1980s, are a blur of flowered skirts and knitted shawls and wooden clogs, of women holding hands and chanting. Consciousness-raising meetings with young women I had never met before; listening in awe to historian Emma Baeri at the Collettivo la Maddalena; marching to protest clandestine abortion: these are some of my memories of Sicilian feminism. There is a photo of me, with my beloved girlfriend Sonia, taken on March 8, 1979, at the International Women's Day march in Catania. Sonia was a couple of years younger than I was. She was the sister of Ninfa Schlegel, one of the girls in Maria Rosa's feminist group in Gela. Sonia and I barely knew each other in Gela, but in Catania we became the closest of friends, sharing meals and politics, sleep and travel.

In the photo, Sonia is holding a rolled up flyer in one hand, her arm wrapped around my shoulders. Our heads are close, almost touching.

There's such tenderness, such intimacy in this political image of two young Sicilian women, framed by a colorful crowd of fellow *femministe*. I remember the excitement of those marches, the strength I garnered from my *sorelle* (sisters). We rejected the appellation *compagna* (comrade), which we regarded as masculine. We were fearless in indicting the chauvinism pervasive even among leftist groups. We were sisters, all of us, but Sonia was also my spiritual sister. We knew and understood each other with the passion of youth and the depth of two who have known and loved each other for thousands of years. Laughter, sadness, enthusiasm, despair, anger, regret—we knew each other in the passion and confusion of youth. We knew each other when we walked hand in hand on Via Etnea, when we chopped carrots and tomatoes for a salad to be shared at her kitchen table, when we sat on the beach on warm winter days, when we wandered the Van Gogh Museum in Amsterdam, searching for that haunting painting, *Wheatfield with Crows*. We knew each other in moments of silence. We recognized each other's yearnings and sorrows, which we often expressed in letters. I treasure those faded, slim relics, and once in a while I read them again and again, handling them gingerly, folding them carefully along the old lines, sliding them back into envelopes with old addresses. The photo of us taken on that March day is one of my holy images. It sits on a small bureau, where I keep my journals. The same red scarf that I wear in the picture embraces the frame.

In the 1970s, at the height of the feminist movement in Italy, we believed that International Women's Day commemorated the victims of a factory fire that had occurred in the early twentieth century in the United States. It was a context that connected us with other women across time and space and conferred a special meaning to our demonstrations. We marched to make sure that the sacrifice of these women's lives would not be forgotten. With their memory in our hearts, we marched for ourselves and for all women. I felt the power of this historical memory so strongly that I carried it inside me for years and took it with me to America. And so, some twenty years later, back in Italy, where I was giving lectures on my then forthcoming book, *Writing with an Accent*, I told a new generation of Italian college women students what I had learned about the fire long after I had marched on the streets of Catania. My Italian American sisters—women like historian Jennifer Guglielmo, working-class studies scholar Janet Zandy, and writer and filmmaker Kym Ragusa—had taught me about the history of the

Triangle Shirtwaist Factory fire. I had learned, as I shared with the women in the Italian lecture halls, that March 8, the day chosen in 1975 by the United Nations as International Women's Day, did *not* commemorate the fire. The fire had occurred later that month, on March 25. Yet the historical memory of the fire had mysteriously migrated into the Italian feminist understanding of this celebration of women.

The connection we felt to that event, so strong that it had become part of Italian feminist consciousness, had its own uncanny significance. This chapter of American history was much closer to us than we knew during those marches in the 1970s, since many of the 146 victims were Italian immigrant girls and women, a fact that entered Italian American consciousness only in the latter part of the twentieth century. The women who had died in the fire were needleworkers with names like Ignazia Bellotta, Josie Castello, Mary Gallo, and Sophie Salemi. It was one of these names—Isabella Tortorelli, age seventeen—that I shouted on March 25, 2001, with my twelve-year-old daughter by my side, at a gathering that I organized with my Italian American sisters in front of the notorious Asch building, the site of the fire in Greenwich Village.

Every year, on the anniversary of the fire, I remember Isabella. She is my Triangle girl. In 2011 the one hundredth anniversary of the Triangle fire was spearheaded by a contingent of Italian American fellow women writers, artists, and activists, like Annie Lanzillotto, Lulu Lolo, and Mary Ann Trasciatti. We marched on the streets of New York City, carrying banners in the shape of shirtwaists, each with the name of someone who had perished in the fire. And then we walked, in groups or alone, to the houses of the Triangle women—and men—and chalked their names on the sidewalk. I left the crowd and walked in solitary pilgrimage to Isabella's address, 116 Thompson Street. There I knelt down and pressed the chalk hard on the sidewalk, feeling her spirit, feeling the power of remembrance (Giunta 2014a, 2014b).

Italian immigrant needleworkers like Isabella Tortorelli became the protagonists of an anthology on the Italian diaspora that I edited with Joseph Sciorra, folklorist and fellow Italian American cultural worker: *Embroidered Stories* (2014). In the beginning, though, there is still my grandmother, bent over her needlework, and I, a child sitting on that small stool at her feet, and the stories she spun, which taught me to listen, to remember the dead, and to make sure they would not be forgotten.

My feminist days in Catania were vibrant with political praxis and intimate reflection, the memory of which is renewed whenever I look at the photo of two young Sicilian women celebrating International Women's Day on the streets of Catania. Although my feminist beginnings were explicitly political, it was through the study of literature that my feminism found its most significant and lasting expression. Charlotte Brontë, Emily Brontë, Sylvia Plath, Dacia Maraini, Oriana Fallaci, and Elsa Morante were among the writers I loved the most in my youth. And yet, when choosing a subject for my undergraduate thesis at the University of Catania, it was Lewis Carroll I turned to, drawn to his work as a writer, photographer, and illustrator and intrigued by Carroll's place both within and at the margins of Victorian culture. I studied all his Alices: the adventurous protagonists of *Alice's Adventures in Wonderland* and *Through the Looking Glass*; the visual rendition of Alice by the Victorian illustrator John Tenniel, who worked under Carroll's directives; the real-life Alice Liddell; the haunting photographs in which Charles Lutwidge Dodgson (Carroll's real name) captured her; and his own illustrations to the original manuscript, "Alice's Adventures under Ground," which he had given as a gift to his beloved Alice. Studying Carroll taught me how to become a close reader of life and literature and to recognize the slippery borders between worlds—the real and the fantastic, the physical and the spiritual, memory and fact. Carroll also taught me to recognize the subversive power and multivalence of language. I would return to Carroll a few years later, while writing my doctoral dissertation on James Joyce, a fellow islander and immigrant/exile who had also been fascinated by this odd, unconventional Victorian figure and by his literary characters.

It was the mid-1980s and I was an Italian student in a Ph.D. program at an American university. To choose Joyce as my literary father made sense. I had grown up in the shadow of my father's intellectual power. I was "the Professor's daughter." To contend, as a young scholar, with a literary giant such as Joyce was both inevitable and necessary. Joyce's self-imposed exile, his relentless return to Ireland through his writing, his European wanderings that led him to live in Trieste with his family (to his grandchildren he was *nonno*), his literary daring, his fascination with Greek mythology, his affirmation of the glory of the quotidian and its capacity for spiritual manifestation—all spoke to me. As a newcomer to the English language,

I especially appreciated his radical questioning of and experimentation with that language. I also felt drawn to Joyce's intimate connection with Italy and Italian language. In time, I internalized Joyce's lesson that I could return home again and again through writing.

Both Joyce and Carroll were idiosyncratic, radical, provocative *male* writers. I did not write about gender in my undergraduate thesis or doctoral dissertation. Instead, I wrote about language and literary influence. It seemed to me at the time that I was moving away from feminism. But Carroll first, and Joyce later, gave me access to literary language and linguistic experimentalism, which provided me with a critical training that would prove essential to my understanding of Italian American literature and the roles of literary tradition and influence. They also helped me gain insights into my own life, a life between different languages and worlds.

Joyce and Carroll indirectly taught me how to read Italian American literature as a "literature with an accent," but it was my work on H.D. that brought me to the brink of becoming a scholar of Italian American women, although it would take a few years for me to recognize the need for that scholarly shift. As a twenty-six-year-old master's student at the University of Miami, for a year I immersed myself in the study of this modernist writer. My thesis explored H.D.'s rewriting of the myth of Medusa and *The Winter's Tale,* in her *roman à clef HERmione*, written in 1927 but published posthumously in 1981. H.D., whose palimpsestic writing was rooted in spirituality, re-created ancient Greece in her imagistic work and gave voice to women like Helen of Troy, Circe, Calypso, and many other mythological and literary women whose stories had been framed within patriarchal mythologies. Joyce, Carroll, and H.D. had all in their own way deconstructed patriarchal mythologies through their radical approach to language. They became my literary mentors as I developed my own voice in a language that was foreign to me.

Transplanted in the luxuriant yet foreign tropical setting of Miami, I felt at home in H.D.'s Greece. I had grown up in a town that was once a Greek polis and a center of the ancient cult of Demeter and Persephone. The cult was associated with the Eleusinian Mysteries, which originated in Eleusis, the birthplace of Aeschylus. The Greek playwright spent his last years and died in Gela. His memory is still alive in my town's cultural memory—in the name of a school, a theater, a cultural award; in the Greek plays performed near the ancient Greek walls; in the stories people recount of his death and his never-found grave. Not much is known about the Eleusinian Mysteries, since initiates were sworn to secrecy, but we do know that they revolved around Demeter's search for Persephone and thus were rooted in the connection between life and death. The cathedral of Gela's Madonna dell'Alemanna rises where the old temple of Demeter used to be. Its Ionic and Doric columns, taken from Greek temples, unabashedly announce that people once prayed to a Greek goddess on this very site of Christian worship. Through layers and layers of sacred stone, traces of these distant times are still powerfully felt among the people of Gela.

Persephone embodies my cultural past. She is the girl stolen by Death and mourned by her mother, who searches everywhere for her daughter and negotiates her ultimately partial return, always to be followed by another separation, in an endless cycle of life and death. This myth of departure and return, of loss and longing, is evoked by the experiences of all those Italian mothers who saw their daughters sail off to America, and all those daughters who would never return home, except through memory and imagination. My mother, too, saw me leave at the dawn of one summer day in 1984, and we each took our place in the ancestral history of maternal loss and (temporary) reunion. Although I have traveled back many times to my native island, every arrival remains entwined with a looming departure. I have spent the last three decades of my life shuttling back and forth, home always elusive, desired and abandoned at once.

In an essay I wrote in the late 1990s, I called Italian American women writers and artists "Persephone's daughters": transplanted and displaced women who exist between worlds; women in search of lost foremothers; women seeking bridges between two countries, two (and more) languages, between past and present, between the dead and the living (Giunta 2004). The myth of Persephone was my gateway. It guided me as I began to intuit that my work had to transcend the pragmatic activism I thought was at the core of my scholarship: the research, the books, reviews, translations, the reprints of little known books, conferences, book readings—all the work focused on the seeking out of obscure and forgotten writers and bringing them to light. There was more, much more, to becoming a scholar, and it had to do with bridging the scholarly and the spiritual. I had to return to Carmelina, my grandmother's lost child, remembered through the stories she passed on to me, and realize my own relationship to and responsibility toward those stories.

EDITOR AND TEACHER

Editing has been at the center of my work as an Italian American activist scholar. Placing Italian American women in anthologies (fifty-four in my first), the obscure and the famous side by side, was both prayer and dare. I asked the literary universe to notice, to acknowledge the presence of these writers, and to value a literary tradition manifested through their collective voices. In a writer's life, editing seems an oddity, a hybrid. While it is more cerebral than creative, it does require an almost devotional attitude, a surrendering of the ego. It is humble and honorable work. I have often wondered about my passion for editing and its place in my academic life. I have dedicated years to it during my thirties, forties, and early fifties—what might have been considered the height of my writing years. I did write a single-authored book, *Writing with an Accent*: *Contemporary Italian American Women Authors* (2002), as well as essays, introductions, afterwords, and prefaces to books. In the after-hours of my work days, I also wrote poetry and memoir, though at first I did not feel the same ethical urgency about this writing as I felt toward my work as a scholar and editor.

And yet it was this writing about and editing of Italian American women's writing that led me to memoir. In 1995 I read an excerpt from Louise DeSalvo's then forthcoming memoir *Vertigo* (1996), which I included in my first edited project, the special issue of the journal *VIA: Voices in Italian Americana* devoted to Italian American women (1996) (in which I also included Maria Rosa Cutrufelli's "In the Kingdom of Persephone"). One day in August of 1995 I received the galleys of *Vertigo*. I started reading and did not stop. For two days I shuffled in a daze from my bedroom to the kitchen or the bathroom, holding *Vertigo* in my hands, until I reached the last line and knew that I had met another mentor. *Vertigo* would transform the course of my life as a teacher and writer. This book, by an Italian American scholar *and* writer, was unlike any other book by an Italian American woman I had read—and I had read most of them. It was a radical book that illustrated how memoir writing can transform our understanding of the past and thus the past itself: writing, then, can truly change a writer's life. But we must learn, DeSalvo (1996: 101) warns us, to yield wisely "the scalpel of language" as we cut deftly through the delicate layers of personal and ancestral memory. This is a lesson that I would carry with me as I began to teach and write memoir.

I wanted my students to follow the example of *Vertigo*. Memoir soon took a central place in my teaching, and in ways that have transcended the classroom. I have witnessed the development of a writing community across generations of memoir students; it is a spiritual community that acknowledges the power of memory and storytelling to connect us across differences. Many of my students have become fellow writers and friends, like writer and magazine editor Krystal Sital and Margaux Fragoso, author of *Tiger, Tiger* (2011). Margaux contributed an essay to *Personal Effects: Essays on Memoir, Teaching, and Culture in the Work of Louise DeSalvo*, which I edited with Nancy Caronia, a writer I met with Louise DeSalvo in the early days of my involvement in Italian American studies.

An anthology, I have found, can serve as a spiritual circle. The women and men who appear in my anthologies are part of the academic and literary circles so vital to my life. Looking back over five anthologies that I have co-edited, as well as the journals, conference proceedings, and newsletters, I understand the significance and necessity of my work, its purpose and timing at a delicate moment in the history of a literary tradition that had still tenuous roots. I have come to realize the extent to which my work as an editor has reverberated in my teaching. Teaching memoir is not very different from editing—it, too, is about nurturing new voices, recognizing a literature in the making, becoming an advocate for emerging writers, creating a community of writers and readers.

I am not a mystic. And I am not a politician. And yet those family lessons learned in childhood and adolescence have shaped me and defined and redefined my work. Straddling spirituality and politics, I recognize that the illiterate ancestors of the writers I sought out, anthologized, introduced, and pushed toward recognition were the contemporaries of Nunziatina. I became their ambassador, thus strangely fulfilling my father's hopes for me.

YOGINI

For years I yearned for a spiritual practice, but that yearning remained hidden, lodged in the crevices of my consciousness. I was almost fifty when I turned to yoga. At first, it was the intuitive recognition that I needed a practice that would heal and nurture body and mind that led me to the

Stone Center, a yoga studio in my adoptive hometown of Teaneck, New Jersey. There I again became a student under the guidance of a new mentor, Charlotte Chandler Stone, a Swiss American woman who had lived in Switzerland, where her father was born. I silently acknowledged something familiar about my teacher's foreign origins. Sonia, the beloved girlfriend who had marched with me on the streets of Catania, was also born in Switzerland, of a Swiss father and a Sicilian mother.

Yoga moved me, and my body began to flow into poses that stirred me with their gracefulness, with their poetry—sun salutation, sun bird, half moon, warrior. The mat was a devotional space and doing yoga felt akin to prayer (Giunta 2012a). Less than three years into my practice, I enrolled in a yoga teacher training program. Soon I was bridging memoir and yoga as practices that required one to surrender to the moment, to be present, to stay. While memoir overtly focuses on the recovery of the past, it is ultimately a constellation of singular moments, each of which captures the past made present—in stillness and movement—through new, transformative understanding.

As I familiarized myself with *asanas* (poses) and *pranayama* (breathing)—the third and fourth limbs of yoga as outlined in Patanjali's *Yoga Sutras*—I realized that yoga could help one be present and self-aware in ways that could sustain the practice of writing and teaching memoir; yoga could guide writers mindfully and safely through the meanders of memory. Having taught countless students and witnessed their struggles to translate memories of traumatic experiences into language, I saw that practicing yoga and meditation could soothe the body (*the body remembers*) and allow the spirit to speak.[3]

Whenever I write poetry or memoir, I feel like a scribe. I must listen, quieting everything within enough to make out the words waiting to be written. Yoga taught me to stay, with the breath, with the spirit. It taught me to listen. As I linked movement and breath, I began to connect with one of the greatest losses of my life, the death of Sonia. She had died at twenty-seven of breast cancer. I was already in the United States when she was diagnosed. At first, we kept close through letters and my yearly summer visits to Italy. But toward the end, though I did not know it at the time, I became afraid. I distanced myself from her and went into hiding. And then one day—after she had been dead for three years—grief began to erupt out of me, with the heat and vehemence of the lava that we had both witnessed spew from our beloved Aetna in Catania: quick, intense, incandescent. I had to let it cool before touching it.

A year after starting my yoga practice, I began to write a memoir titled, at the time, "Following Sonia." It was my husband who suggested this title. He had witnessed the aftermath of that first eruption of grief over the death of Sonia and had tenderly supported me as I followed the traces of the girl I loved and made my way through the labyrinthine path of mourning and self-forgiveness. I had written shorter memoirs before and even drafted a book-length manuscript that delved into five generations of my maternal family. But now this story was calling to me, and I felt compelled to make room for its steady flow. I had to teach myself to stay with sorrow and regret. I had to teach the body and spirit to surrender all defenses, to receive grief—just as my grandmother had taught me.

One evening, while at the yoga studio, I thought I recognized Sonia in the slender shape of a young woman stretching her arms into warrior two. I watched, mesmerized by the delicate back of her head as we flowed from one pose to another. I felt trepidation, excitement, and then a great peace. I felt spiritually connected to Sonia, to that stranger, to the universe. That night I drove home holding something new inside: the slowly emerging but deeply felt awareness that death does not cut off the ties with our loved ones, that death is not the end of love, that we are traveling through one great, luminous spiral, without an ending or a beginning, and are always becoming.

Deep, devotional love is what writing is now asking of me. All these years of guiding and nurturing other writers—students, peers, strangers— required that I ask my more personal writing to wait patiently on the sidelines. My work as a literary advocate, necessary and important, has led me to this moment. As I put away the lingering traces of the last two anthologies (now finally published), the room expands, grows lighter. It is time for another change. This new writing, solitary, almost monastic, is searching for and making a new place in my psyche. It is taking me back to that mystical communion with the quotidian, which I first observed in my grandmother and experienced at her side. As I write of my past life with Sonia, dead for almost thirty years, I gather the minute, fleeting moments we shared, asking them to reveal her presence.

The attic studio of my New Jersey home is flooded with light. Here I practice yoga, meditate, write. I kneel in front of two small altars where I have placed little totemic objects, each with its history and meaning. A baby Jesus in the manger, the same one that sat on my grandmother's dresser and that I used to admire as a child. An alarm clock with golden filigree decorations, a gift from my grandfather. A Sicilian blue ceramic cat from my oldest niece. Lava rocks gathered by my son during an excursion on Mount Aetna. A Thai Buddha, a gift from my daughter. A meditation bowl, a gift from my husband. Candles. Seashells. Mala beads. My grandmother's rosary. In a corner, a framed picture of Nunziatina, in her nineties, smiling. "I will watch over you," she used to say.

STORYTELLER

"You remind me of grandpa," my oldest nephew, visiting from Italy, tells me. It has been seven or eight years since I last saw him, and even longer since we both sat at my parents' table in Sicily, listening to my father. I am in my mid-fifties and both my father and grandmother have been dead for a few years. We are sitting around my dinner table. I have just recounted the stories of our ancestors. I have been piecing them together over the years from the older generations, especially Nunziatina. But this young man, who was the first baby I took care of so many years ago, when I was a young feminist in Catania, says that my storytelling reminds him of my father—my father, the professor, the politician, the historian who animated his lectures and political speeches with vivid historical narratives. There are the Greeks and Carthaginians, battling in the bay of Gela, and he evokes them and their stories for us, children and grandchildren, as if it were all family lore.

I have inherited my father's passion for history and have infused it with the love and care with which I received my grandmother's legacy, crumbs of family history offered to me in the quiet of her kitchen.

I keep the *immaginette* (holy images) that Nunziatina gave me. They are scattered in different places: in a purse, a drawer, a jewelry box, a book. Once in a while I am surprised by a Saint Sebastian, a Saint Anna, a Virgin Mary, a sign of my grandmother's all-encompassing presence in my life. I believed through my grandmother—I believe in my grandmother. She is my path to faith, to the divine, which ultimately means allowing tiny moments to become life-sustaining, life-defining, knowing when to surrender, when to follow a call.

I write of the beloved girlfriend I lost. In the sacred space of my studio—the space of writing, yoga, meditation, prayer—Sonia often visits me, as do Nunziatina and her child, Carmelina. I hear their voices. I write. And I feel I am another kind of scholar now—a scholar of my own becoming.

NOTES

I would like to thank Louise DeSalvo, Joshua Fausty, and Jennifer Guglielmo for their invaluable insights and suggestions.

1. I have written about my maternal grandmother and great-grandmother in a memoir titled "The Summer Mussolini Came to Gela" (Giunta 2012b).
2. Italian scholar Caterina Romeo co-edited this special issue.
3. Since then I have taught memoir and yoga workshops and developed a workshop called "Memoirs in Motion" with Charlotte Chandler Stone.

WORKS CITED

Caronia, Nancy, and Edvige Giunta, eds. 2014. *Personal Effects: Essays on Memoir, Teaching, and Culture in the Work of Louise DeSalvo*. New York: Fordham University Press.

Cutrufelli, Maria Rosa. 2005. "Seeds and Roots." Trans. Edvige Giunta. *Women Writers* (special issue: Lit Candles: Feminist Mentoring and the Text) (Summer 2005) (http://www.womenwriters.net/summer05/scholarly/cutrufelliinenglish.htm).

———. 1996. "In the Kingdom of Persephone." Trans. Edvige Giunta. *VIA: Voices in Italian Americana* (special issue: Italian American Women) 7.2 (Fall 1996): 101–9.

———. 1994. *Canto al deserto: Storia di Tina, soldato di mafia*. Milan: Longanesi.

———. 1976. *Donna perché piangi?: Imperialismo e condizione femminile nell'Africa nera*, Milan: Mazzotta.

———. 1975: *Disoccupata con onore: Lavoro e condizione della donna*. Milan: Mazzotta.

———. 1974. *L'invenzione della donna: Miti e tecniche di uno sfruttamento*. Milan: Mazzotta. 2nd ed. 1976.

Cutrufelli, Maria Rosa, and Edvige Giunta and Caterina Romeo, eds. 2001. *Origini: Le scrittrici italo americane* (special issue of *Tuttestorie*) 8 (March–May 2001).

DeSalvo, Louise. 1996 [2002]. *Vertigo*. Introduction by Edvige Giunta, NY: Feminist Press at CUNY.

Fiume, Marinella. 2006. *Siciliane: Dizionario biografico*. Syracuse, Italy: Emanuele Romeo Editore.

Fragoso, Margaux. 2011. *Tiger, Tiger*. New York: Farrar, Straus and Giroux.

Gilbert, Sandra M. 2000. "Kissing the Bread." In *Kissing the Bread: New and Selected Poems, 1969–1999*, 171–75. New York: W. W. Norton.

Giunta, Edvige. 2014a. "Isabella, piccolo italiana morta nel rogo di una fabbrica a New York." May 23, 2014 (http://www.lauraboldrini.it/news/lavoro-ed-economia/isabella -piccola-italiana-morta-nel-rogo-di-una-fabbrica-a-new-york).

———. 2014b. "The Reality of a Bridge." May 24, 2014 (www.i-italy.org/38077/reality -bridge).

———. 2012a. "Palm Salutation" and "Half Moon." In *The Poetry of Yoga: A Contemporary Anthology*, ed. HawaH, 104–5. Vol. 2. N.p.

———. 2012b. "The Summer Mussolini Came to Gela." *Ocean State Review* 2.1 (2012): 34–57.

———. 2005. "Sicilian Lives at the Crossroads." *Women Writers* (special issue: Lit Candles: Feminist Mentoring and the Text) (Summer 2005) (http://www .womenwriters.net/summer05/scholarly/giunta.htm).

———. 2004. "Persephone's Daughters." *Women's Studies: An Interdisciplinary Journal* (special issue: Creative Nonfiction) 33, no. 6 (September 2004): 767–86.

———. 2002. *Writing with an Accent: Contemporary Italian American Women Authors.* New York: Palgrave.

———, ed. 1996. *VIA: Voices in Italian Americana* (special issue: Italian American Women) 7, no. 2 (Fall 1996).

———. 1991. "A Raven Like a Writing-Desk: Lewis Carroll through James Joyce's Looking Glass." Ph.D. dissertation. University of Miami.

———. 1986. "HERmione Out of Shakespeare: H.D.'s Re-vision of the Myth of Medusa, in *The Winter's Tale*." M.A. thesis. University of Miami.

Giunta, Edvige, and Joseph Sciorra, eds. 2014. *Embroidered Stories: Interpreting Women's Domestic Needlework from the Italian Diaspora.* Jackson: University Press of Mississippi.

Household Saints. 1993. DVD. Directed by Nancy Savoca. Columbia TriStar (124 minutes).

Two

BECOMING STORIED

CHRISTINE ZINNI

Walking. I am listening to a deeper way.
Suddenly all my ancestors are behind me.
Be still, they say. Watch and listen.
You are the result of the love of thousands.
—Linda Hogan, Chickasaw (Hogan 1995)

TENDING THE PLOT

This essay is a personal meditation on a road that evolved from and led to ancestors and storytelling, a path that beckons to itself and calls for remembering. It courses through thickets, clearings, and crossings yet remains in the process of becoming.

Roads invite pauses and stillness along with movement. Like stories, they present dilemmas and decisions: quick turns, meanderings, and crossroads, all of which entail choices. Sometimes the turns lead to new places; sometimes they return us to old as this story does.

It begins in a garden—the garden I look out on from a second-story window of the house that was inhabited by three generations of my family. I see maple, ash, and wild grape, where the backyard was once filled with neatly tended rows of vegetables and guarded by sentinels of apple, cherry, plum, and pear trees. Some deem it to be overgrown, but I take pride in its slow growth and quietude. A footpath meanders below its canopy of

FIGURE 2.1 The author with her paternal grandparents, Frank and Grazia Zinni, circa 1952.

hardwood trees, bushes, and twisted vines, providing a shady refuge for birds and animals. The path appeared just a few decades ago, or was it a lifetime?

The path wends through the garden plot that once produced a cornucopia of tomatoes, peppers, and beans and moves past unmarked graves of beloved pets and a bower of bushes and trees that served as the childhood clubhouse for me, my siblings, and childhood friends then trails off. It conjures up images of the community of Italian and Polish immigrant families living in the twenty-block radius of our south-side neighborhood and calls to my mind how the bounty of their gardens, like ours, was shared.

Once smudges of earth on my Italian grandmother's apron and the scent of wild spearmint on her fingertips spoke louder than any words about a way of being. A locus of activity, the garden was also the site for prayers, reflection, stories, and learning—about my grandparents' devotion to patron saints, their migrations from the Abruzzo region of Italy, and the intricate web of connections among the people that formed our community on the south side of Batavia, New York. From year to year, there were comings and goings to our house and into the backyard. While my brother Frank, sister Teresa, and I helped plant, cultivate, and harvest foodstuffs, Aunt Carrie would relate the latest news of her younger sisters Mary (who joined a convent in New Jersey) and Nicolette (who became a teacher and moved to Virginia). Although Carrie's physical activities were limited to the immediate vicinity because she was disabled at birth by a spinal injury and unable to further her schooling, her stories transported us to worlds beyond the neighborhood, steeped as they were in the oral tradition. She kept alive the accomplishments and service of family and community members as well as the perils they faced when they journeyed away from the fold. Varying the stories ever so slightly depending on the occasion and the message or moral, she would retell aspects of the family's history until the past became so imprinted in our memories that time collapsed, turned in on itself, and became present. Again and again, she would return to the story of how my father survived 170 missions as an Air Force pilot in World War II while flying missions in the Pacific and how he met my mother in Washington, D.C. while on medical leave having tests done at Walter Reed Hospital for a cancerous growth that had mysteriously developed. Carrie paid careful attention to detail, as if she were relating each episode for the first time. The timbre of her voice altered as she recalled the family's support and my father's courage and resolve to finish his studies, practice law, and take up flying again after the amputation of his arm and shoulder.

Quieter now, the backyard hums with birdsong, where once it was filled with the sound of my relatives' voices, fragments of Abruzzese dialect, or the Polish of visiting relatives. My plantings are now confined to clay pots. Nonetheless I feel I have been tending the garden in other ways: I am teaching courses in Indigenous Studies, food and culture, and oral history at the Anthropology Department at a local college and have been working as folk art consultant and videographer in the documentation of regional stories. The work puts me in contact with local peoples and is attuned to a polyphony of voices, an expanding mandala of colors, textures, and forms. The numbers of students, storytellers, collaborators, and public(s) that I have encountered along this path have grown from year to year. Looking back on my life's trajectory, I know that I have been guided by ancestors. It was my parents and relatives, especially my paternal grandmother Grazia, her hands pierced by work in a garment factory and healed by the soil of earth and the touch of plants, who, we all felt, embodied the spirit of generosity.

66 | *Christine Zinni*

FIGURE 2.2
The author's father,
Nicholas, and mother,
Regina Pultorak Zinni,
outside Walter Reed
Hospital in Washing-
ton, D.C., circa 1946.

It was she who planted the seeds of compassion in our family. Considering the number of paths that I have taken, departing from Berkeley, California, to Boston, Massachusetts, and Stockholm, Sweden, in the sixties, to Athens, Greece, in the seventies, and to Chicago, Illinois, in the eighties and nineties, it was something related to "amazing" grace that brought me back to the homeland of western New York state to tell these stories in later decades of my life.

In some small way, during the last fifteen years, I have been able to repay this debt of gratitude to my ancestors by conveying the spirit of the gardens that they so lovingly cultivated. Along with ongoing documentation of oral histories in the region and religious celebrations and sodalities

FIGURE 2.3 Storyteller Chiara (Carrie) Zinni in the garden, 1950.

that honored the patron saints, I have also produced six video documentaries that revolve around the testimonies and collective histories of musicians, stonecarvers, and needleworkers in the region. With the encouragement of family members, especially my aunt, Sister Mary Agnes Zinni, and the support of Italian American scholars such as Luisa Del Giudice, Vincent Parrillo, and Joseph Sciorra, segments of the oral histories have been included in edited volumes and therefore preserved in written form.[1]

FIGURE 2.4 Grazia Zinni (in center) with daughters Carrie, Nicolette, Marie, and daughter-in-law, Regina Pultorak Zinni, 1950.

The path has also increased my awareness of the longer history of the land and has led to friendships with, learning from, and continued work for the indigenous people of this region: the Haudenosaunee or Iroquois people. Most importantly, travel along this path has allowed me to return a small bit of the nurturance and support provided by my parents, as I cared for them during the last years of their lives.

As I say good-bye to students at the end of a semester and bring video projects or written works to completion, sending them off into the ether of a virtual commons, I think of *ex voto* offerings and candles in the Catholic tradition, the prayer flags of Tibetan Buddhists, and the smoke rings of sacred tobacco among Native Americans. Each pulsing flame, gust of wind, and curl of smoke carries a silent prayer and message of gratitude upward. Seen in this light, teaching, as well as the very process and production of ethnographic projects, begins with inner reflection and "second thought" but evolves outward into a dialogue and interactions with others and with spirit. Like the spiritual aspect of flying that I experienced as a

FIGURE 2.5 The author at eight years old in her father's Luscombe plane, 1956.

child, accompanying my father in his small airplane, I view these encounters as flights of spirit, as offerings, and as forms of prayer (Zinni 2009a).

I am passionate about these projects and grateful to the people along the path who have helped me engage in such creative communicative work. But this journey—round about and returning to my region of departure—has not been without its spiritual, physical, and economic challenges. Living from year to year and sometimes month to month on grants, contracts, and scant stipends (despite my Ph.D. credential), I suspect that my economic means may not much supersede the yearly income that my grandparents achieved after fifty years of hard work! I press on, not only because I am committed to the "mission" of preserving stories that honor the spirit of ancestors and local knowledge, but because I am also committed to directing attention toward "nature's rights."

I fight against the scant monies and tenuous positions of adjunct professors, folklorists, and media artists but console myself with the knowledge that functioning underneath bureaucratic radar also allows for a certain freedom and flexibility. Funding may be precarious, but the classes and projects provide venues for dialogue about stories, poetry, ethics, spiritual traditions, and democracy as well as social, economic, and environmental justice issues.[2] Even as I identify with those on the margins—locavores (people who eat food grown within a 100-mile radius of purchase or consumption through conscious choice), storytellers, community activists, "guerrilla" teachers, eco-feminists, itinerant workers, monks, media artists, scribes, and *cantastorie* (history-singers of old)—I realize that my work is little interested in labeling who I am but more interested in how it might benefit others and the earth itself. Seen from this perspective, rather than generating anger, the practice of "living small" and seeking meager funds anew—similar to Catholic monastic tradition or the training of monks in the Buddhism Mahayana tradition who are sent out into the community with begging bowls—can be the ground for reflection, cultivation of empathy, gratitude, and awareness of our interdependence.

Among Native American peoples, acknowledging the "sacred hoop"—the interconnection of all things, plant, animal, and human, through words, practices, stories, and song—is spoken of as being on a road—the "red road."[3] The road involves living small but thinking large. It is based on awareness of humans' dependence on the renewal and regeneration of earth's bounty and the concomitant belief that everything needed for humankind to survive will be provided, as long as we are not driven by greed and live in balance with nature.[4] I have learned from the Haudenosaunee, the ancestral people of this region, to say a prayer that expresses gratitude for the distinct ecology of this Eastern Woodland region by listening to their Gano:nyok (Thanksgiving Address and Greetings to the Natural World or Ohen:ton Karihwatehkwen) at the beginning of their ceremonial and governmental gatherings. It is also taught to children at an early age. It starts with the basic elements of Creation, like water and plants, and works its way up to the SkyWorld. It begins something like this:

> Today we have to be gathered and see that the circle of life continues. We have been given the duty to live in balance and harmony with each other and all living things. So now we bring our minds together as One as we give greetings and thanks to the waters that give us life . . . so Now Our Minds Are One (http://danceforallpeople.com/haudenosaunee-thanksgiving-address; see also Swamp 1995).

Known in different spiritual traditions by different names, the metaphor of a path or road is used to convey a message that is simple but profound in its complex enactments. The road begins with the practical aspect of cultivating gratitude toward Creation in whatever form and by whatever term the divine spirit, energy, or Creator is known. And it involves seeking balance in daily life and working toward the benefit of others. It is a spiritual outlook that reflects our relationship to community, to the earth, and understanding the economic, social, and political ramifications of our actions. It is my understanding that setting out along "the good red road," "the Middle Way," or "the Way" does not mean that one is perfect or never strays from the "path" but that through awareness and meditative practices of mantra and prayer we continuously return to awareness of our relationship to all beings as aspects of Creation.[5]

RETREAT FROM THE CITY

Remind yourself every morning,
every morning, every morning:
I'm going to do something, I've made a "commitment."
Not for yourself, but beyond yourself.
You belong to the collective.
Don't go wandering off, or you will perish.
—Rosalie Little Thunder, Lakota, 2013 ("The Holy Road" 2014)

In contrast to other decades of my life, when I lived and worked in the cosmopolitan cities of Boston, Stockholm, Athens, and Chicago, the tempo and tenor of my days are now quite different. Residing in my grandparents' house in Batavia, a small town midway between Buffalo and Rochester, allows me to make relatively short visits to neighboring towns and cities to teach and to visit with colleagues, friends, and companions.

The turn in my life, the change from fast-paced city life to one more closely attuned to contemplative study and the rhythms of nature, happened because of a spiritual crisis. The death of my thirty-three-year-old sister and the diagnosis of my mother's breast cancer, twenty years ago, led to some deep soul searching at the age of forty. Within the span of two years of my sister's passing and my mother's remission, I had left the security of a job and connections in Chicago and was dividing my time between what is affectionately (and geologically) known as the Driftless Area of rural Wisconsin and Minnesota and my family's home in Batavia, New

FIGURE 2.6 The author at Arts in Education, Scandinavian storytelling session, Root River, Minnesota, 1994.

York.[6] Southeastern Minnesota was originally settled by Scandinavians. But the creation of a thirty-mile bike trail in the 1990s near towns along the Root River began attracting a diverse array of newcomers from a tri-state region, to create an oasis in the woods. I joined an informal group of exiles-from-the-cities and woodland mystics drawn to the ways in which the trail afforded access to the river and limestone bluffs. Freed from high city rents and living close to the bone, we formed an artist's cooperative called Cornucopia Art Center where we were able to sell our work. The experience of "communing" with nature and with one another—sharing meals and conversing about our work—led me to conceptualize a series of creative writing workshops focused on Norse myth and legend. I was drawn to the subject

FIGURE 2.7 The author with her brother, Frank Zinni, near the confluence of branches of the Root River, Minnesota, 1994.

of Scandinavian mysticism from my study of Icelandic sagas and comparative literature years ago in Uppsala, Sweden. I was eager to share some of the stories. At the time I was probably the only Italian American within a fifty-mile radius, but my workshops in Norwegian and Swedish legends were accepted with characteristic good humor as well as interest.

Warmed by the community of loving Scandinavian, Irish, and German spirits living along "the Root," and nourished by the company of artists and writers, I found inspiration and peace.[7] The austere beauty of the river and bluffs provided the backdrop for reading about poet Kathleen Norris's experience in a Benedictine monastery in *Dakota: A Spiritual Geography* and delving more deeply into the *Lectio Divina* practice passed on to me by my Aunt Mary, now prioress of a Benedictine monastery and spiritual retreat center in Texas.[8] I also continued to study works focused on Eastern spiritual traditions that dealt with the meaning of *bodhicitta* (compassion), and the works of *bodhisattvas*, such as Shantideva's *The Way of the Bodhisattva*—a Buddhist text that I had first come across in a Shambhala Center started by H. H. Chö-gyam Trungpa Rinpoche in Chicago.[9] Traveling most places by foot or bike, I found that the proximity to nature and silence of the woods provided the space to think about my life's direction and purpose.

If my sister's death and the move to rural Minnesota had put me on a road that led to nature and a group of like-minded artists, what occurred at the confluence of two branches of the Root River seemed to me a sign that events were being guided by spirit. I would go to a section of land adjacent to the confluence to meditate every day. The prospect of sched-uled development near the place where, legend had it, there were Indian burial mounds led me to seek out members of the Ho-Chunk (Winnebago) nation who were actively engaged in cultural preservation. I was introduced to a Ho-Chunk elder, Merlin Red Cloud Sr., and his family, who recalled the story passed down through oral tradition about a battle occurring right there along the confluence, hundreds of years ago, where many warriors were killed. Merlin and his friend Dennis Funmaker organized a delegation of Ho-Chunk people who met at the confluence. Based on their feedback, we scheduled a series of public hearings and conferences aimed at bringing the stories to light and preventing development of the area.[10]

Friendship with Merlin and Dennis and visits to the Ho-Chunk com-munity of Black River Falls, Wisconsin, were personally transformative. They not only opened doors of perception on the history of the land but deepened my appreciation of the oral tradition and local knowledge. In the efforts of the Ho-Chunks to communicate and legitimize the story passed down to them through oral tradition, I began to realize the extent to which Western culture had formed hierarchies of knowledge around the "written word." Moreover, if nothing was done to document and preserve oral nar-ratives, a good part of local history would be lost.

I began thinking of how to apply these lessons to my own community back in western New York State. During one of my extended visits with my parents, I was introduced to a Haudenosaunee elder and storyteller, Marian Miller. We collaborated on a creative writing workshop centered on Native American stories. With the encouragement of Merlin Red Cloud and Mar-ian that I should "do something for my own tribe," I began videotaping the stories of elders in the Italian American community where I had grown up. Dividing my time between Minnesota and New York state, I was in the process of simultaneously doing research commissioned by the Ho-Chunks

FIGURE 2.8 The author with Merlin Redcloud Sr. (Ho-Chunk) and Dennis Funmaker (Ho-Chunk) at the White Front Café, Lanesboro, Minnesota, 1995.

into the written record of the confluence to corroborate their oral history about a battle taking place there and working on a documentary that featured the oral history of community members in New York state. Then I received news that my mother's cancer had returned.

A HEALING BALM

> *We shall not cease from exploration*
> *And the end of all our exploring*
> *Will be to arrive where we started*
> *And know the place for the first time*
> —T. S. Eliot (1968)

Anyone who has accompanied a loved one on the sacred journey into the spirit world knows it is a privilege that changes you forever. Through the emotional roller coaster of prognoses about her illness, weekly blood counts, and the decision not to undergo more chemotherapy, we sought to maintain some balance and a sense of normality. In between doctor's visits and responsibilities as a caregiver, I would go out for an hour or two at a time and document celebrations dedicated to the patron saints and oral histories of community members then return home to review the day's footage with my mother. I was working toward a documentary about Saint Michael's Society with Italian American elders when it became clear that my mother's illness was terminal. We were able to honor her wish to die at home. The process of sharing images of the saint on murals and gardens in and around the parish church, along with conveying the stories and well wishes of longtime friends in the neighborhood, provided a measure of joy during her last days—and continuity derived from a sense of belonging and place.[11]

I realized through this experience how oral history work might be a healing balm and how I could contribute to the community with my skills of documenting and preserving the voices and history of the local people— stories of spirit with little or no written accounts or representation in history books. The process of researching and documenting the stories and testimonies of community members, shaping the material into narrative documentary form, and screening the productions in the region had all reconnected me to members of the diverse societies dedicated to patron saints in the parish. Parishioners such as Ester Rossi, a retired voice teacher, and Tom Rosica, a media specialist at the local community college, devoted their energies to helping me create a documentary record and community history of immigration to the region that featured stories and interconnections among our Italian ancestors and their *paesi* (villages). The work also introduced me to a new group of like-minded friends, folklorists Karen Park Canning and Daniel Ward, who had been working in the field for over a decade. In retrospect, I can see how this work gave me a renewed sense of purpose that helped me overcome feelings of loss and that deepened my own sense of place. In a very personal way, I was working through spiritual questions about impermanence, realizing that I could honor the stories of spirit in my family and community by remembering and communicating the oral narratives to others and in the meantime leave a record of their lives on earth. While our physical lives might end, the stories would live on.

Another decisive turn came less than a year after my mother's death, through visits and a growing friendship with the Seneca elder and storyteller Marian Miller. She encouraged me to hear one of the great Haudenosaunee

FIGURE 2.9
The author's sister,
Theresa Zinni, in 1985.

scholars and "storytellers" of American history, John Mohawk.[12] So, on a
cold and wintery night in November, I undertook an eighty-mile drive,
through what turned out to be near blizzard conditions, to hear John's mes-
merizing talk in Canandaigua, New York. The journey served as the catalyst
that prompted me to seek out and apply to the American Studies program
at the University of Buffalo where he was teaching. I was attracted to the
constellation of activist-scholars whose work, like John's, was grounded in
praxis and local history. My acceptance into a master's program was followed with an offer of a teaching assistantship and scholarship for a doctorate. My aunt, Sister Mary Agnes Zinni, counseled me on the benefits
of completing the "unfinished" academic studies that I had left behind in
Europe some decades before and encouraged me to move ahead with the

program. I felt the presence of a mandala of compassionate spirits in four directions urging me on: my father, my brother Frank, my sister-in-law Barbara, fellow folklorist Karen Park Canning, wonderful neighbors (the Barretts), community members like Rose Caccamise, Carol Mruczek, Kay Ognibene and Mary Ellen Wilber, and Marian Miller in the homelands of western New York state; Agostino Cerasuola in Chicago and friends Mark Brewster, Martha Greenwald, Diane Knight, Phyllis McCarthy, Yvonne and Glenn Nyenhuis, Luther Thompson, Dennis Funmaker, and the Red Cloud family in Minnesota and Wisconsin to the north; my long-standing friend Patricia Donnelly in Washington State and Mark Lancaster and Nadine Lau at the San Francisco Zen Center to the west; my Aunt Mary, cousin Rose Steele, and friend Don Carolan to the south; and Carol Donnelly and Rosemary Donnelly and friends Julie Kontoladis and Brigitte Perbandt in Greece to the east, I set out to get a doctorate in American Studies during the fifth decade of my life.

Fortuitously guided by spirit to a community of artists in Minnesota, I was also exceedingly fortunate to have arrived in the Department of American Studies at Buffalo at a liminal time when a unique group of scholar-activists were bringing issues of social justice front and center in the public sphere. Able to pursue an interdisciplinary program of studies in history media and culture, I was mentored by leading scholars in the field of oral history, ethnography, and cultural studies: Professors Dennis Tedlock, Michael Frisch, and Charlie Keil and community activist June Licence; Ruth Meyerowitz, Alexis Deveaux, and Elayne Rapping in Women's Studies; and Sarah Elder, Bruce Jackson, and Maria Zmarc Koczanowicz in media.[13] Moreover, as I came to understand, the very heart of the program in American Studies issued from the Indigenous Studies component and the work of Haudenosanunee scholars: John Mohawk, Oren Lyons, and Barry White. The commitment and work of all of these mentors struck a deep chord, stirring seeds of compassion that had been planted by my grandparents and aunts with regard to community service.[14] Moreover, the thrust of their scholarship on social justice issues resonated with what I had witnessed of my own father, mother, and brother's work in the field of law, advocating for the disadvantaged. More than anything else, I continued learning about local history through talks and small excursions with my father, who knew numerous people in the city of Batavia and outlying areas. Visits with Marian Miller in the town of Avon, New York, served to pique my interest in the ancient history of the region, making me feel that I had indeed, as the venerable poet noted, "come to know the place for the first time" (Eliot 1968). Documentation of local traditions kept me actively involved in community-based issues and oral history work, informing the very basis of my dissertation on the artistic traditions of music, needle-work, and stonecarving in the region. Shortly after receiving my doctorate, I was offered a position teaching cultural anthropology and Native Studies courses at a local university, the State College of New York at Brockport.[15]

SPRING, SUMMER, FALL, WINTER, . . . AND SPRING

I learned from life experiences, from those earliest times in the garden with my family, as well as from storytellers and mentors, about the ways in which a landscape becomes storied and infused with meaning.[16] I have tried to bring this perspective to my classroom by focusing on the local histories and narratives that convey a sense of place and respect for Mother Earth. In the food and culture classes I teach, I share firsthand experiences of music, dance, and celebratory feasts derived from my work as a local folklorist. Based on the lore gleaned from my voyages abroad and experiences with a Food and Culture Study Abroad program that I organized in Greece and Turkey in collaboration with Dr. Ralph Trecartin, assistant provost of inter-national education at the State College at Brockport, the Athens Centre, the Donnelly sisters, and Gregorio Altamirano,[17] students learn about the Greek gods and goddesses: for example, Athena and Demeter and their respective association with the olive tree and with wheat, grain, and the vine.

Purposefully, the touchstone of our days is derived from the stories of the Seneca people and their relationship to land. Students are introduced to the Haudenosaunee or Iroquois Creation Story, first related to me by Mar-ian Miller and later explored in independent studies with John Mohawk (2005b).[18] They learn how Skywoman came to earth and carried life-giving seeds with her to Turtle Island. Her story is connected to that of medi-cine plants like wild strawberries and tobacco and the Three Sisters (Corn, Beans, and Squash), also known as Sustainers or *Deohako* because of the way they support one another in traditional Native American agriculture (where they are grown together in mounds) and also support all the origi-nal inhabitants during the harvest.

Throughout the ancestral homeland of the Seneca, from the foothills of the Allegheny Mountains to the south, the boundary waters of Lake Erie in the west, Lake Ontario to the North, and the Genesee River to the east, fields of corn, bean stalks, and squash plants ripen in the sun. My father has passed on now, but as I drive down the back roads to get to class I am reminded of how well he knew the topography of the region from flying over its fields, hills, and waterways in his small plane. In the spring, summer, fall, winter, and . . . spring, guest lecturers from the surrounding community and from the reservations in a 100-mile radius of the college arrive to tell stories about Skywoman, the Three Sisters, and Corn Maiden. I accompany students on fieldtrips to local organic farms and to Ganondagan, a Haude-nosaunee history site situated on a hill dedicated to Jigonsaseh, the Peace Mother. The area was once the site of a large Seneca village of more than a hundred longhouses. Along with seeing a Three Sisters garden and walking trails with medicine plants, they hear about the Haudenosaunee Confed-eracy's influence on the forefathers of the Constitution, such as Benjamin Franklin, as well as early feminists, such as Elizabeth Cady Stanton and Lucretia Mott.[19] Sitting in a re-created longhouse atop Boughton Hill, they learn about the ways in which song and dance of the Seneca express grati-tude for the bounty of the world outside the door and the significance of the White Corn Project started by John Mohawk.

It has been seven years since John Mohawk has passed on. Over the course of the time since I first heard him speak in Canandaigua, the proj-ects he envisioned have flourished and grown. His White Corn Project has found a home at Ganondagan, which is in the process of building a new cultural center and performance space. They are spreading the word about their heirloom seeds nationally. On September 13, 2007, less than six months after he passed, the UN Declaration on the Rights of Indigenous Peoples was adopted by the General Assembly. The decision comes as a result of more than thirty years of work by John and his friend and col-league Chief Oren Lyons and indigenous peoples across the planet. As John predicted, it has become a place where indigenous people can advocate for their sovereign rights and nature's rights.

I think about how pleased John would be to know that recently, this past summer in fact, Oren and other members of the Onondaga nation and the American Indian Law Alliance of the Haudenosaunee Confeder-acy were involved in organizing a Two Row Campaign, which involved a

FIGURE 2.10 Photo of John Sotsisiowah Mohawk taken in 1993 for *Exit 16—Onondaga Nation Territory* (2014), a documentary film by Claus Biegert, during a winter walk in the Pine Woods of the Cattaraugus Reservation, western New York. The photo was used as the cover for *Thinking in Indian: A John Mohawk Reader*, edited by José Barreiro, © 2010, Fulcrum, Inc., Golden, Colorado, photo © Claus Biegert.

historic canoe trip from Onondaga Nation lands on Onondaga Creek to New York City. The international as well as national press have picked up the story of how Native American peoples and non-Indian paddlers formed two parallel rows of canoes, kayaks, and watercraft, acting out a symbolic representation of the historic Two Row Wampum Belt.[20] The event both commemorates and renews the promise of the 400-year-old treaty between the Dutch and the Haudenosaunee and the importance of environmental cleanup and preservation. On the shores of the Hudson River, on an overcast Sunday morning, Oren helped sound the call to the hundreds of people gathered: "Now is the time for people to come together and act to protect and heal our environment. If we do not act now no matter what we do it will be too late."[21]

As Onondaga spokesman, Jake Edwards holds up the Two Row Wampum Belt. He notes on the occasion:

> The belt refers to the *Ohen:ton Karihwatehkwen,* or "what we spoke about before all else," that described with thanks everything in nature and lastly the Creator. We (the Haudenosaunee) consider the *Ohenton Karihwatehkwen* as bringing ourselves as people together to honor and respect all in nature. I honor the Haudenosaunee and their allies in renewing their commitment to the land and water we share and to live respectfully side-by-side in two lines.[22]

Edwards goes on to explain: "These words, meant to brighten the mind, with their strong environmental message, would have been an integral part of any treaty with the people." Over the years, I have come to understand how the phrase Ohen:ton Karihwatehkwen, "the words that come before all else," refers to a deeply spiritual belief encapsulated in the Thanksgiving Address, the Gano:yok. I have heard the Gano:nyok spoken in the Haudenosaunee language countless times now, at every gathering involving Haudenosaunee people since I returned to the region. Native American guest speakers discuss its importance with students in the Native American and food and culture courses I teach. With each passing year of hearing, speaking, and teaching it, the text has deepened my appreciation of its spiritual weight. Like Haudenosaunee stories about Skywoman, the Three Sisters, and Peacemaker, the Gano:nyok acknowledges humankind's relationship to the natural world—reminding us about our dependence on and responsibility to the earth. It is based on the worldview, held by indigenous peoples everywhere, that for the beneficence of creation to continue it *must*, in turn, be recognized—that is, brought to awareness through memory and expressed in ceremonies, music, dance, words, and action. In short,

FIGURE 2.11 The author near a large old sycamore tree on a memorable excursion to Adamson House Museum and Garden with colleagues from the mandala: Luisa Del Giudice, Joan Saverino, and Joseph Sciorra. Pacific Coast Highway, Malibu, California, October 2014. Photo courtesy of Joseph Sciorra.

it articulates the belief that humans must cultivate gratitude with their whole being. This worldview points to our responsibilities to the earth and to each other—both as a spiritual covenant and as a civic duty. In effect, this worldview bears in mind how our actions impact the future of the earth and its people. Native American people call this "thinking about and acting for the benefit of seven generations" (Lyons 2008).

SEVEN GENERATIONS

Removed from the physical connection to the land, for the most part, students have not given much thought to where their food comes from, how it is produced, or who is harvesting it. The majority claim that they have not been engaged in any type of "communal" festivities, other than celebrating

Thanksgiving and holidays around the New Year with extended family and friends. Many of those born in the region are somewhat familiar with the ancient history of the Haudenosaunee through books or visits to the local museum. But only a handful, mostly those with some Native American blood, view it as a living culture and have been to Ganondagan (only a few miles away). Fewer still have heard stories about Skywoman and/or have thought about the sustaining qualities of the Three Sisters. It is gratifying to see how their perception of these matters changes over the course of a semester with our combined classroom and fieldtrip experiences. I also notice that each year brings a growing number of students involved in the locavore and Slow Food movement who are quick to see the connections between economic and political issues, food security, hunger, and civic responsibility.

I reflect on these issues from semester to semester and wonder what has happened in the decades since my grandmother and immigrant neighbors tended the gardens in our community, even as they came together to celebrate religious feasts and express gratitude for the gifts of Creation. Over the years I have come to understand how oral narratives and stories from the oral tradition are not without relevance to contemporary issues. On the contrary, in raising awareness about our relationship to the earth, these stories stand as spiritual antidotes to dominant narratives of our market economy and our exploitation of the earth in the name of progress, what Matthew Frye Jacobson rightly terms the "financialization of everything" in his recent address to the American Studies Association (Jacobson 2013).[23] To my mind Jacobson's words shed additional light on the long-standing work of indigenous activist-scholars like John Mohawk, Oren Lyons, Winona LaDuke, and noted Indian physicist and environmentalist Vandana Shiva on how greed has overcome any consideration of ethics. In our shared world, the issue of food democracy and the renewal and regeneration of heirloom seeds, which hold within themselves the preservation of cultural and biological knowledge, is related not only to the sovereignty and heritage of Native American people but to food security, civic responsibility, and the democratic longings of non-Indian peoples everywhere.[24]

I am grateful for the spiritual leaders, friends, and mentors who have been working on these issues for decades and who guided me along a specific trajectory. Most recently, that has led to work on a documentary in collaboration with Agnes Williams, Cynthia Pérez, and members of the

Indigenous Women's Network that focuses on the efforts of Native American women to preserve heirloom seeds. The work recalls a prophecy that I first heard in seminar sessions with John Mohawk and then read about in *Basic Call to Consciousness* (*Akwesasne Notes* 2005).[25] The story, based on historical fact, had to do with how a Hopi spiritual leader, Thomas Banyacya, helped form a Unity Caravan of indigenous peoples in the 1950s that traveled the United States. Alarmed by the use of the first two nuclear weapons on Japan, Banyacya attempted to call attention to a Hopi prophecy about the environmental consequences of continuing on a path where Earth is despoiled. Until his death in the 1990s, the Hopi elder worked with Oren Lyons, the Faithkeeper of the Onondaga Nation and a Chief of the Onondaga Council of Chiefs of the Six Nations of the Iroquois Confederacy, to bring this message to the United Nations. Janet McCloud (Tulalip) joined Banyacya on his travels to sound the call. He predicted that women would organize and be leaders in the struggle around these issues.[26]

The Two Row Wampum and the Hopi Prophecy occurred in different parts of the American continent and at different times in history, but their underlying message seems clear. The Two Row Wampum Belt of the Haudenosaunee people of the northeastern woodlands depicts parallel rows of Native American and non-Indian people, with the understanding that their paths converge in thanksgiving and understanding of our debt of gratitude for the beneficence of the natural world. A petroglyph carved by ancestors of the Hopi people in the Southwest depicts two paths that start out as parallel lines. One is straight, signifying balance with nature, and the other becomes jagged, warning of excess and a "life out balance"—what the Hopi call *koyaanisqatsi*.[27]

Thinking about these paths has given me pause and "second thought." My sense of purpose issues from the belief that we must convey the relevance and urgency of the choices involved. If I can communicate even a small part of this, I will have accomplished my goal. I am emboldened by the words of Oren Lyons (1992):

> So then, what is the message I bring to you today? Is it our common future? It seems that we are living in a time of prophecy, a time of definitions and decisions. We are the generation with the responsibilities and the option to choose the path of life for the future for our children or the life and path which defies the laws of regeneration.

The urgency of Chief Lyons's call about the environment resonates with that of leaders from other spiritual traditions. Daring to cross the red line between science and moral issues, Pope Francis's encyclical *Laudato Si'* centers on "integral ecology." He notes that the path of apathy and greed has inured us to the degradation of ecosystems and its effect on poorer nations. Underscoring the undue influence of consumerism and technology on society, he advocates for a change in course.[28] Similarly, for decades, Tenzin Gyatso, the fourteenth Dalai Lama, who has been living in exile from Tibet, has sounded the call that "peace and survival on earth as we know it is threatened by human activities."[29] He urges us to develop awareness of how our thoughts and actions affect sentient beings and a sentient universe. With ties to the land and seasonal rounds of planting, our own ancestors understood these connections in a deep, spiritual way, offering thanks for the continued fecundity of nature in ritual celebrations. With the loss of their stories and stewardship comes loss of knowledge and awareness of the natural world.

This story began with a path that issued from a small house to a garden onto the streets of the neighborhood and beyond; then it circled back, with twists and turns; it was the garden and the stories it contained that set it all going; it is the garden in each of our lives, (re)generated through love and compassion for those who came before and those who inhabit our present, that inspires purpose, as we recall their words and lives and grow in stories for future generations.

NOTES

1. I have been deeply inspired by the ethnographic approach and scholarship of Luisa Del Giudice (2009, 1993) as well as folklorist Joseph Sciorra's work documenting history and expressive culture (2011, 1993). Works by Fred Gardaphe (1996) and Edvige Giunta (2002) served as the impetus to enter the "discourse" on Italian American studies. The writings of Donna Gabaccia (2000, 1995) and Vincent Parrillo (2010) provided context by illuminating transnational elements of the Italian immigrant experience. I am especially indebted to musician and ethnomusicologist Charles Keil, my master's thesis advisor, and poet and ethnographer Dennis Tedlock, my Ph.D. dissertation advisor, along with committee members John C. Mohawk, Michael Frisch, Ruth Meyerowitz, and Barbara Wejnert at the State University of New York at Buffalo. Their critical eyes and patience guided me through the thickets. In regard to the home front, discussions and long-standing friendships with the

brilliant historians Agostino Cerasuola and Don Carolan, filmmakers Andy Golebiowski and Ryan Tebo, my sister-in-law Barbara Zinni, my sisters-in-spirit of the
Donnelly clan (Patricia, Carol, and Rosemary), and John Saverino and Luisa Del
Giudice urged me on. Most of all, it was my brother's support, the memory of my
mother and sister, and the example of my father, his love of nature and simultaneous involvement as labor counsel for immigrant Italians in the region, that set the
example for work on environmental and social justice issues.

2. For more on the subject of the "proletariatization" of academic labor see Goldstene
2012. The current focus on creativity and beneficial aspects of "mentoring-from-
the-middle" is the subject of recent discussions on pedagogy. See Charlie Sweet, Hal
Blythe, and Rusty Carpenter (2013).

3. Ideas about the sacred hoop and red road are expressed in the Gano:nyok (Thanksgiving Address) of the Haudenosaunee, spoken before all gatherings and ceremonies in the region. See Swamp 1995 and the published work of Haudenosaunee mentors like Mohawk (2005a) and Lyons (2005) in *Basic Call to Consciousness*; *Thinking
in Indian* (Barreiro 2010); and *Voice of Indigenous Peoples* (Lyons 1994). See also
LaDuke (2005, 1999).

4. This worldview was embodied in the practices of indigenous peoples who mentored
me: Merlin Red Cloud (Ho-Chunk), Haudenosaunee (Iroquois) elder and storyteller Marian Miller (Seneca), and Haudenosaunee scholar-activists I met in Buffalo: John C. Mohawk (Seneca), Barry White (Seneca), Oren Lyons (Onondaga),
Donald Grinde (Yamasee), Alan Jamieson (Cayuga), Agnes Williams (Seneca), and
Edward Valandra (Lakota).

5. Attunement to the sacredness of the natural world and balance is also evident in the
spiritual tradition with which I have grown up, in the many desert mystics of the
fourth century AD whose teachings influenced Saint Francis of Assisi's *Canticle of
Brother Sun and Sister Moon*, Hildegard of Bingen's *Liber Divinorum Operum*, and
Saint Benedictine's call to a monastic communal life in the *Lectio Divina*. Moreover,
Buddhist spirituality is based on awareness of the interconnectedness of all things,
as underscored in the teachings of Mahatma Gandhi and in the Dalai Lama's teachings on the environment. On a more secular note, this outlook is manifest in the
work of poets and writers like Henry David Thoreau and Ralph Waldo Emerson
on nature.

6. Southwestern Wisconsin, southeastern Minnesota, northeastern Iowa, and north-
western Illinois are called the "Driftless Area" because they escaped glaciation
approximately 500,000 years ago. "Drift" (silty sand deposits, boulders, and melt-
water streams) was left behind by the retreating glaciers, creating a mysteriously
lyrical terrain characterized by deeply carved river valleys and limestone bluffs
reaching elevations of approximately 1,500 feet.

7. My time in southeastern Minnesota was graced by a community of artists, writers,
and storytellers like Martha Greenwald, Diane Knight, Yvonne Nyenhuis, Phyllis
McCarthy, Luther Thompson, and Sid Sheehy who were attracted to the mystical
landscape. Discussions with long-standing friends who visited (like historians Agostino Cerasuola, Don Carolan, and Robert Wolf, a writer and publisher of oral histories) piqued my interest in local history and documenting stories. Along with frequent excursions to visit newfound Ho-Chunk friends in Black River Falls, I would
stop in at an alternative eco-village community of artists in the southwestern part of

the "driftless" region of Wisconsin—thus coming to know the physical characteristics as well as the ancient history of the terrain.

8. I have been exceedingly fortunate to have an aunt, Sister Mary Agnes Zinni, former prioress and spiritual director of a Benedictine Monastery in Texas, whose kindness and compassion has been a steady compass. She has been actively involved in contemplative outreach and the Centering Prayer movement. Monsignor Victor M. Goertz (2009: 23) notes how prayer is both an appreciation for and an acknowledgment of the deeper mystery of life: "For the most part, the journey of daily life is not experienced as a boundless exploration of mystery. In the ordinary, day-to-day living, the reality of mystery is shielded from view by the usual, the familiar and the routine." A personal friend of the family who was with my grandmother during her last days, Monsignor Goertz often remarked on her quiet mysticism. For more on contemporary Benedictine spirituality and the role of Centering Prayer and contemplative mediation, see the work of Jerome Kodell (2009), abbot of Subiaco Monastery, and Thomas Keating (2007), spiritual leader in the Centering Prayer movement.

9. See Norris (2001) and also Shantideva (2006: verse 101: 75): "directly or indirectly then, do nothing that is not for another's sake, and solely for their welfare dedicate, your every action towards the gaining of enlightenment."

10. See LaDuke (2005: 1) for a discussion of the desecration of burial sites. She begins by asking: "What qualifies something as sacred? That is a question asked in courtrooms and city council meetings across the country."

11. I continued to work on the video production about life in our community and Saint Michael's Society in *Backyard Angels* (Zinni 1997) after my mother's death, dedicating the work to her. Along with local screenings in the region, the film was also shown at the international documentary Festival dei Popoli in Florence, Italy. I am indebted to a number of community members, especially Ester Rossi and Tom Rosica, and media artists from Rochester, New York, who taught me how to edit on then state-of-the-art three-quarter-inch analog tape decks, thus helping me produce my first video: *La vita nuova* (Zinni 1995).

12. See Mohawk's "Epilogue" (1986).

13. My approach to oral history and ethnography is based on dialogical theory and inspired by discussions with my thesis advisor Dennis Tedlock on oral narrative and ethnopoetics; see Tedlock (1983). I gained immense knowledge about the theory and "craft" from working with the noted public historian Michael Frisch (1990). On pioneering efforts to digitize oral histories, see www.randforce.com. During this time, I was able to put some of this knowledge to work on a new media project with feminist scholar Ruth Meyerowitz (see Meyerowitz and Zinni 2008–9) that documented the work of local women labor activists. Time spent with a community of scholars and artists at SUNY Buffalo was fortuitous in other regards. I also met Maria Zmarz-Koczanowicz, one of Poland's most prolific documentary filmmakers, who was a visiting professor in Media Studies. I was honored to collaborate with her and community scholar and filmmaker Andrew Golebiowski on the organization of a six-week series of Polish documentary films in Buffalo. It featured many of the early films of renowned directors like Krzysztof Kieslowski and Andrzej Wadja and incorporated oral histories and interviews.

14. Among other important breakthroughs in the fight for social justice, SUNY Buffalo professors Sotsisowah (John C. Mohawk) and Oren Lyons wrote position papers delivered at the United Nations by the Haudenosaunee for the 1977 conference on "Discrimination against the Indigenous Populations of the Americas" hosted by the Non-Governmental Organizations of the United Nations in Geneva, Switzerland. The papers are included in the book *Basic Call to Consciousness* (*Akwesasne Notes* 2005). Underscoring the links between indigenous peoples' rights and nature's rights, the papers constitute the first written analysis and critique of Western culture by an official group of Native peoples. Mohawk was editor of *Akwesasne Notes* from 1967 to 1983, the largest American Indian publication. Oren Lyons has been a leading figure in the struggles for indigenous rights and environmental justice for more than thirty-five years.

15. See also my dissertation (Zinni 2007). I am grateful to Dennis and Barbara Tedlock for feedback and trenchant insights into the intertextual elements of textiles. See their groundbreaking essay on Quiche Maya texts and textiles (Tedlock and Tedlock 1985). Their input is evident in my dissertation and subsequent published works on textiles (Zinni 2014). The knowledge gleaned from my M.A. thesis advisors, the noted ethnomusicologist Professor Charles Keil and oral historian Michael Frisch, can be found in my works on Italian American musicians (such as Zinni 2012).

16. The subhead above was inspired by *Spring, Summer, Fall, Winter, and . . . Spring*, the title of a very moving film by Kim Duk (2007) about the life of a Buddhist monk on a small island.

17. A blog created by students who participated in the 2012–15 Study Abroad programs in Greece and Turkey that I organized through SUNY/Brockport in collaboration with the Athens Centre can be found at www.atasteofgreece.wordpress.com. I am grateful to Professor Vincent Parrillo and Professor Mario Toscano for the opportunity to exchange ideas with Italian scholars at William Paterson University and at the University of Pisa. Zinni (2010) evolved out of a talk at a conference on Democracy in the 21st Century that they organized in Tuscany. This experience helped me develop my research on social justice, ecology, and common land issues.

18. According to the cosmology of the Haudenosaunee, Skywoman fell through the hole in the sky that formed after a Celestial Tree was uprooted in the Skyworld. This action, based on the fulfillment of a dream, set in motion life on the back of Turtle Island, as it is known today (Mohawk 2005b).

19. See www.ganondagan.org for more information on this historic site and related events.

20. The Two Row Wampum Belt is a written record of the oldest treaty between Europeans and Native American peoples and uses two lines of purple wampum against a background of white wampum beads to convey its metaphor of two paths: the Indian canoe and European ship sailing side by side down the river of life. The metaphor of parallel lines on the belt affirms the sovereign relationship of the Haudenosaunee. On another level, the design and placement of the beads encodes a deep spiritual message about the covenant between the two peoples and the natural world—a message about how the two lines converge in gratitude.

21. Wikoff (2013): "'This trip is to honor the two wampum treaty to protect the earth, and to travel together in peace down this river of life,' said Chief Oren Lyons,

traditional Faithkeeper of the Turtle Clan and member of the Nation Council of Chiefs of the Six Nations of the Iroquois Confederacy. 'We need to take away from the corporate powers that currently are in charge of the direction of this earth and return it to the people where it belongs.'"

22. http://honorthetworow.org/jake-edwards-talks-to-raven-redbone-about-two-row-fracking-and-the-future. Accessed 8/16/14.

23. See in particular his trenchant analysis of neo-liberal policies and the workings of multinationals.

24. Once again I am grateful to John Mohawk for expanding my awareness and introducing me to Vandana Shiva's work. Mohawk, Shiva, Lyons, and LaDuke have been actively engaged in the Bioneers, an innovative nonprofit educational organization that serves as a "fertile hub of social and scientific innovators with practical and visionary solutions for the world's most pressing environmental and social challenges" (www.bioneers.org). As all who loved and heard him know, John Mohawk's effectiveness stemmed in great part from his ability as a storyteller. Some of his words and approach are conveyed in *John Mohawk, Survive and Thrive* (www.youtube.com/watch?v=t6kOA-KtPxw) recorded at a 2005 conference talk for the Bioneers. Time and time again in his public talks, seminar lectures, and personal conversations John sounded the call warning that human-created societies are inappropriately distanced from the physical realities of the world. His warnings have come to pass.

25. See also "The Hopi and Haudenosaunee: Sharing Prophetic Traditions" and "Enduring Seeds" in Barreiro (2010: 14–20, 27–29).

26. On the role of Janet McCloud in spreading the word about the prophecies see the video *Emerging Activist Leadership Conference (2010)* (Indigenous Women's Network 2014) produced in collaboration with Agnes Williams and Cynthia Pérez of the Indigenous Women's Network.

27. The documentary *Koyaanisqatsi* (1982; the Hopi word for "crazy life, life out of balance"), directed by Geoffrey Reggio with music by Philip Glass, takes up these issues.

28. I am writing this on the eve of the pope's visit to the United States. For more on his encyclical see http://www.nytimes.com/2015/06/19/world/europe/pope-francis-in-sweeping-encyclical-calls-for-swift-action-on-climate-change.html.

29. One of the many articles containing the Dalai Lama's talks on the environment has been published on-line by the Alliance of Religions and Conservation: http://www.arcworld.org/faiths.asp?pageID=64.

WORKS CITED

Akwesasne Notes, ed. 2005. *Basic Call to Consciousness*. Revised ed. Summertown, TN: Native Voices Press.

Barreiro, Jose, ed. 2010. *Thinking in Indian: A John Mohawk Reader*. Golden, CO: Fulcrum Press.

Del Giudice, Luisa. 2009. "Ethnography and Spiritual Direction: Varieties of Listening." In *Rethinking the Sacred: Proceedings of the Ninth SIEF (Société Internationale d'Ethnologie et Folklore) Conference in Derry 2008*, ed. Ulrika Wolf-Knuts, 9–23. Department of Comparative Religion, Religionsvetenskapliga Skrifter. Turku, Finland: Åbo Akademi University.

———, ed. 1993. *Studies in Italian American Folklore*. Logan: Utah State University Press.

Duk, Kim. 2007. *Spring, Summer, Fall, Winter, and . . . Spring*. DVD. Producers: Karl Baumgartner and Lee Seung-jae (1 hour, 46 minutes).

Eliot, T. S. 1943. "Little Gidding." In *Four Quartets*, 59. New York: Harcourt.

Frisch, Michael. 1990. *A Shared Authority: Essays on the Craft and Meaning of Oral and Public History*. Albany, NY: SUNY Press.

Gabaccia, Donna. 2000. *Italy's Many Diasporas*. Seattle: University of Washington Press.

———. 1995. *From the Other Side: Women, Gender, and Immigrant Life in the U.S., 1820–1990*. Bloomington: Indiana University Press.

Gardaphe, Fred. 1996. *Italian Signs; American Streets: The Evolution of the Italian American Narrative*. Durham, NC: Duke University Press.

Giunta, Edvige. 2002. *Writing with An Accent: Italian Women Authors*. New York: Palgrave.

Goertz, Monsignor Victor. 2009. *Meandering through the Mystery*. Austin, TX: Diocese of Austin.

Goldstene, Claire. 2012. "The Politics of Contingent Academic Labor." *NEA Higher Education Journal* 28: 12–15.

Grinde, Donald, and Bruce Johansen. 1995. *Ecocide of Native America*. Santa Fe, NM: Clear Light Press.

———. 1991. *Exemplar of Liberty: Native America and the Evolution of Democracy*. Native American Politics Series No. 3. Los Angeles: American Indian Studies Center, UCLA.

Hogan, Linda. 1995. *Dwellings: A Spiritual History of the Living World*. New York: W. W. Norton and Company.

"The Holy Road." 2014. *Lakota Country Times*, August 14 (http://www.lakotacountrytimes.com/news/2014-08-14/The_Holy_Road/Rosalie_Little_Thunder.html).

Indigenous Women's Network (IWN). 2014. *Emerging Activist Leadership Conference (EALP) 2010*. Video. Produced in collaboration with the IWN through a Ford Foundation Grant running time (60 minutes).

Jacobson, Matthew Frye. 2013. "Where We Stand: US Empire at Street Level and in the Archive." *American Quarterly* 65, no. 2: 265–90.

Keating, Thomas. 2007. *Fruits and Gifts of the Spirit*. Brooklyn: Lantern Books.

Kodell, Abbot Jerome. 2009. *Musings from the Monastery*. Collegeville, MN: Liturgical Press.

Koyaanisqatsi. 1982. Film. Directed by Godfrey Reggio. Produced by Francis Ford Coppola (1 hour, 27 minutes).

LaDuke, Winona. 2005. "What Is Sacred?" In *Recovering the Sacred: The Power of Naming and Claiming*. Cambridge, MA: South End Press, 1–15.

———. 1999. *All Our Relations: Native Struggle for Land and Life*. Cambridge, MA: South End Press.

Lyons, Oren. 2008. "Looking toward the Seventh Generation." American Indian Studies Program, University of Arizona, Tucson. 2008. Presentation April 17 (https://nnidatabase.org/video/oren-lyons-looking-toward-seventh-generation).

———. 2005. "Preamble." In *Basic Call to Consciousness* (1978, 1981), 13–25. Summertown, TN: Native Voices Publishing Press.

———. 1994. *Voice of Indigenous People: Native People Address the United Nations.* Edited by Alexander Ewen. Santa Fe, NM: Clear Light Press.

———. 1992. "Haudenosaunee Faithkeeper": Chief Oren Lyons addressing delegates to the United Nations Organization at opening of "The Year of the Indigenous Peoples" (1993) in the United Nations General Assembly Auditorium, United Nations Plaza, New York City, December 10. Audiotape transcribed by Craig Carpenter. https://ratical.org/many_worlds/6Nations/OLatUNin92.html.

Lyons, Oren, Donald Grinde, and Curtis Berkey. 1995. *Exiled in the Land of the Free: Democracy, Indian Nations, and the U.S. Constitution.* Santa Fe, NM: Clear Light Press.

Madigan, Shawn. 1998. *Mystics, Visionaries and Prophets: A Historical Anthology of Women's Spiritual Writings.* Minneapolis, MN: Augsburg Fortress.

Meyerowitz, Ruth, and Christine Zinni. 2008–9. "The Medium and the Message: Oral History, New Media, and a Grassroots History of Working Women." *Journal of Educational Technology Systems* 37, no. 3: 305–18.

Mohawk, John C. 2005a. "Introduction." In *Basic Call to Consciousness*, 9–12. Revised ed. Summertown, TN: Native Voices Press.

———. 2005b. *Iroquois Creation Story.* Buffalo, NY: Mohawk Publications.

———. 1986. "Epilogue." In *White Roots of Peace* by Paul Wallace, 117–56. Santa Fe, NM: Clear light Publishers.

Norris, Kathleen. 2001. *Dakota: A Spiritual Geography.* New York: Mariner Books.

Parrillo, Vincent. 2010. *Strangers to These Shores.* 10th ed. New York: Prentice Hall.

Saverino, Joan. 2011. "Italians in Public Memory: Pageantry, Power and Imagining the 'Italian American' in Reading, Pennsylvania." In *Italian Folk: Vernacular Culture in Italian American Lives*, ed. by Joseph Sciorra, 153–70. New York: Fordham Press.

Sciorra, Joseph, ed. 2011. *Italian Folk: Vernacular Culture in Italian American Lives.* New York: Fordham Press.

———. 1993. "Multivocality and Vernacular Architecture: The Our Lady of Mount Carmel Grotto in Rosebank, Staten Island." In *Studies in Italian American Folklore*, ed. Luisa Del Giudice, 203–44. Logan: Utah State University Press.

Shantideva. 2006. *The Way of the Boddhisattva.* Trans. Padmakara translation group. Revised ed. Boston, MA: Shambhala Press.

Shiva, Vandana. 2000. *Stolen Harvest: The Hijacking of the Global Food Supply.* Boston, MA: South End Press.

Swamp, Chief Jake. 1995. *Giving Thanks.* New York: Lee and Lowe Books.

Sweet, Charlie, Hal Blythe, and Rusty Carpenter. 2013. "Teaching Creative Thinking and More." *NEA Higher Education Advocate* 30, no. 4: 6–9.

Tedlock, Dennis. 1983. *The Spoken Word and the Work of Interpretation.* Philadelphia: University of Pennsylvania Press.

Tedlock, Dennis, and Bruce Mannheim. eds. 1995. *The Dialogic Emergence of Culture.* Urbana/Champaign: University of Illinois Press.

Tedlock, Dennis, and Barbara Tedlock. 1985. "Text and Textiles: Language and Technology in the Arts of the Quiche Maya." *Journal of Anthropological Research* 41, no. 2: 121–46.

Wikoff, Naj. 2013. "Two Row Wampum Historic Paddle: Renewing the Two Row Wampum." *Adirondack Almanack,* August 27. http://www.adirondackalmanack.com/2013/08/historic-paddle-renewing-two-row-wampum.html#more-38118.

Zinni, Christine. 2014. "Stitches in Air: Needlework as Spiritual Practice and Service in Batavia, New York." In *Embroidered Stories: Interpreting Women's Domestic Needlework from the Italian Diaspora*, ed. Joseph Sciorra and Edvige Giunta, 74–98. Jackson: University Press of Mississippi.

———. 2012. "Play Me a Tarantella, a Polka or Jazz: Italian Americans and the Currency of the Piano Accordion." In *The Accordion in the Americas*, ed. Helena Simonett, 156–77. Urbana/Champaign: University of Illinois Press.

———. 2010. "The Relevance of a Commons in Greece, Italy and the United States: Democracy, Social Justice and Ecology." In *Per la democrazia e l'integrazione sociale*, ed. Mario Toscano, 175–88. New York: John D. Calandra Italian American Institute.

———. 2009a. "*Cantastorie*: Ethnography as Storysinging." In *Oral History, Oral Culture and Italians*, ed. Luisa Del Giudice, 83–100. New York: Palgrave Macmillan.

———. 2009b. "The Maintenance of a Commons." In *Uncertainty and Insecurity in the New Age*, ed. Vincent Parrillo, 199–216. New York: John D. Calandra Italian American Institute.

———. 2007. "Interweaving: Memory through Machines." Ph.D. dissertation, State University of New York at Buffalo.

———. 1997. *Backyard Angels*. Video. Passatempo Productions (30 minutes).

———. 1995. *La vita nuova*. Video. Passatempo Productions (30 minutes).

Three

WALKING BETWEEN THE WORLDS

Reflections on a Life of Scholarship

SABINA MAGLIOCCO

BETWEEN TWO WORLDS

Throughout my life, well-meaning people have asked me: "Where are you from?" "Are you more Italian or more American?" And my favorite: "What are you?" I expect that they do not actually mean to annoy me, but nonetheless I struggle to answer these questions. The answer to the first requires a long story that I suspect most don't want to hear: I am not from one place but from many, and no single one can I call home. The second question has always struck me as unanswerable; from the time I was a child, it was obvious to me that someone could be both Italian and American and that the answer depended on context. And the last question, with its silly assumption that identity can be reduced to a single category, makes me want to respond with an equally absurd quip: "An alien" or "A lizard."

Certainly the greatest formative influence on my personal development was growing up between the cultures of Italy and the United States. Yet, unlike the typical immigrant experience, which is one of loss of the homeland with its landscape, language, and culture, my family shuttled back and forth in a yearly seasonal migration, spending the school year in the American Midwest and summers in Italy. This pattern allowed us to maintain strong bonds with our culture of origin, so that we children grew up bilingual and bicultural. But belonging to two cultures and shuttling between them also creates feelings of disjuncture, of always being marginal and temporary, of belonging at once to both cultures and fully to neither. My aunt used to call me her little platypus: I was an awkward child who was sometimes unsure as to which set of cultural rules applied. I grew to be very observant and extremely adaptable, learning to identify the markers of being a cultural insider—idiomatic expressions, dress codes, inside jokes—and imitating them in order to not be excluded by the other children. To this day, I am so sensitive to linguistic differences that if I spend time with people whose accent is different from my own, I will begin to mimic it subtly and unconsciously. Sometimes my strategy worked; other times it did not. Especially in the context of my American schooling, I grew up feeling marginalized and liminal. Eventually, I came to feel comfortable in the margins, sympathetic to other cultural, ethnic, and racial outsiders, as well as toward anything that was excluded or stigmatized by the dominant paradigm. I find the margins and hedgerows, where belonging is more of a negotiation than a given, more interesting, varied, and lively than the carefully tilled fields. There I have found my home.

Moving between my two cultural worlds put me in a permanent state of "betweenness," a state that anthropologist Victor Turner has called "liminal." Typically, liminality is a temporary characteristic of people undergoing rites of passage in which they are separated from other members of society, trained, and tested and then reintegrated into the larger society through ritual (Turner 1968). Some categories of individuals, however, live permanently in a liminal state: they include ritual specialists, shamans, and sorcerers who communicate with the spirit world as well as those whose personal characteristics place them between social categories. Permanent liminality contradicts notions of identity as fixed and ascribed, but it also gives access to other kinds of liminal and marginal categories. In his landmark work *The Ritual Process*, Turner (1968: 57) describes being "betwixt and between" as analogous to "being in the womb, to invisibility, to darkness, to bisexuality, to the wilderness, and to . . . places and entities that are uncanny and 'other.'" As I reread Turner's work in the process of writing this essay, I found this passage eerily predictive of the sorts of themes that I have chosen to pursue. My permanent state of betweenness has affected many aspects of my life's journey, from my choice of profession to the kinds of subjects to which I have been drawn.

Among modern Pagans, one of the communities with which I have done research, this ability to straddle multiple worlds is called "walking between the worlds." Those who walk between the worlds are a conduit between the spirit world and the everyday world of human beings, moving back and forth and communicating between them while fully belonging to neither. In this essay I use the trope of "walking between the worlds" as an extended metaphor for the many acts of mediation that have informed my scholarship and personal development: Italian and American, folklorist and anthropologist, scholar and practitioner. It also suggests a journey—one that has been meandering and peripatetic, a state of boundary-crossing not without its difficulties. Nevertheless, all these identities belong to a single tapestry, woven by the weft of heart-held principles and ideals and the warp of scholarly enquiry.

A HISTORY OF BETWEENNESS

Belonging to and negotiating among multiple worlds is part of my defining family heritage, so let me begin there. My family's transnationalism is inter-generational: my mother was born in Egypt between the two world wars, part of an international colony of Europeans who built businesses around the burgeoning Suez Canal during the first part of the twentieth century. Her grandmother was an Alsatian Jew from Paris; her grandfather, Giulio, was the youngest son of a family active in the *Risorgimento* and so firmly in favor of a republican form of government for Italy that they named one of their sons Lincoln after the U.S. President. Giulio De Castro had left home as a teenager, shipping out on a freighter to Bombay, where he swept floors in a bank and eventually worked his way up to owning it. He sold that business and sailed to Port Said, where he opened a ship's chandlery that sold coal and other supplies to vessels going through the straits. My great-grandparents had a summer home in Grottaferrata, outside of Rome, where my mother spent summers, so the yearly international shuffle was part of her life experience as well. When World War II broke out in 1939, my mother and her family were evacuated from Egypt, then a British colony, and returned to Italy.

My father's father, Vincenzo Magliocco, was a pioneering aviator who lost his life in Italy's east African campaign and as a result became a national hero. His death plunged his widow and children into penury. Because my grandmother had to go to work full-time to support her family, she sent my father to a military boarding school at the tender age of eight. The act of leaving behind their home and country had a different meaning for my parents than it did for many Italians in the twentieth century: it was not unimaginable but rather an integral part of life, what people did to survive, over and over again.

The Second World War had a searing effect on both my parents. For my mother, it meant the end of a privileged colonial lifestyle and a period of growing deprivation and anxiety, as the war intensified and Italy began its anti-Semitic campaign. The family suffered through the food and fuel shortages that marked the period of the war for most Romans, although during the early years their wealth permitted them to obtain food and other essentials on the black market. Through some kind of jerry-rigged geneal-ogy, the family was able to prove it had Christian ancestors and avoid imme-diate deportation. But suspicions remained, preventing my great-uncles from finding employment outside the family business, which was crushed by the war. During the German occupation of Rome from 1943 to 1944, the family hid Jews and Italian army deserters in their home. Knowing that everyone would be executed if the Nazis discovered them, the family sent my mother and her young cousins to board in a convent, where the nuns sheltered many children of Jews and dissidents. As a teenager, my father returned home from boarding school and began to attend the Liceo Giulio Cesare in Rome. During the German occupation, he ran guns for the Italian Resistance, stealing weapons from the Nazis to give to the partisans. Before my parents had even graduated from high school, they had experienced the terror of Allied raids, the destruction of their everyday landscape, the death of schoolmates, and the execution of relatives and friends. Unlike some survivors, my parents spoke openly about their wartime experiences and did not shield us from them. These stories of my family's past and war-time survival formed the connective tissue that bridged the gaps of culture and geography in my life. While seemingly far from my sheltered reality as a child growing up between Rome and the suburbs of Middle America, I was also deeply marked by them. To this day, Nazi soldiers are an ever-present and recurring terror that haunts my nightmares.

Given that stories played such a vital role in my childhood, it is not sur-prising I chose to become a folklorist, a professional who studies stories and other forms of expressive culture. A number of family stories connected me to a long line of explorers, adventurers, and outspoken cultural critics. I learned how my five times grandfather on my father's side, Vincenzo Di Bartolo, a merchant sea captain, was one of the early navigators between Palermo and Boston in the 1830s and was the first to sail from Palermo to the island of Sumatra. My four times grandfather Francesco Mario Magliocco, a Palermitan lawyer whose portrait hung above our fireplace, was known as "the prince of the forum" for his impassioned public speeches against the Bourbon monarchy, which then controlled Sicily, and in support of the Unification of Italy. He paid a great price for his convictions, losing his lands and being exiled to the Lipari Islands. My mother's paternal grandfather Giuseppe Manente had been a well-known composer of music for marching bands and is sometimes known as the John Philip Sousa of Italy. My maternal grandmother was a gifted storyteller who would spin fantastic tales that blended elements from popular romances with details from our own lives, making it seem that the heroes and heroines were children just like us. My paternal grandmother was eternally caught up in her personal tragedy; after my grandfather's death, she became involved with spiritualism in an attempt to communicate with him. At the same time, she held out hope that perhaps my grandfather was still alive somewhere in Ethiopia, waiting to return to his family at the opportune moment. As a very small child, I believed this tale wholeheartedly and waited each day for my grandfather to walk in the front door of my grandmother's flat as we were eating *pranzo* (the midday meal) around the table. From photographs I knew just what he would look like: a tall, dark man wearing a tattered military uniform. He had been missing since my father was a little boy, and it did not occur to me that perhaps he might have changed his clothes in the intervening thirty years. He would be wearing garlands of exotic flowers around his neck. He did not have any grandchildren in Africa, so I was pretty sure that he would have adopted some along the way and that they would be coming to join our family too: several black- and brown-skinned children holding his hands, who would soon be our brothers and sisters in that small apartment on Via Lima. I held onto that fantasy for an entire summer, but my grandfather never came.

I was also nourished by my mother's love of literature. She was trained in classical languages and literature and named us from of the works of the Latin authors. From the time I was small, she read me children's versions of classical Greek and Roman myths, folktales, and stories of King Arthur and his Knights of the Round Table. My love of stories was reflected in my child-hood games, in which I created elaborate cultures and folktale-like scripts for my troll dolls or acted out stories that I read in books, such as Emilio Salgari's novels of pirate adventures in distant corners of the world. These worlds, with their own customs, stories, and traditions, became both a way to negotiate my cultural disjunctions and a refuge from the difficulties that I suffered in my family and school life.

My father, however, read me books about nature and science. He was a physician, and his wish was that I follow him into that noble profession. From a young age, he trained me in the methods of scientific observa-tion: every weekend we would look at slides of various materials under my great-grandfather's old brass microscope. Some were slides that his grand-father had made as a young field veterinarian in Sicily, which my father had kept and brought to the United States; others we made ourselves, looking at onion skin, pond water, cork, and other things from the natural world. My father taught me to keep a field journal with meticulous notes, com-menting on each aspect from the collection of materials to the nature of the cells that we looked at. When I was a little older, he introduced me to the library at the university where he taught. I began to do research there for my school papers. He also schooled me in the gentlemanly arts; not having a boy in the family, he treated me as a son, teaching me to ride horses, shoot, and fence, thrusting and parrying back and forth across the linoleum floor of the family room. My foil, a fine Italian grip, was almost as long as I was tall. My father was a formidable character: tall, dark, elegant, and smelling deliciously of fine tobacco and expensive cologne. I admired him tremen-dously and wanted more than anything for him to love me. But he was riven with conflicts from the horrors he had endured during his own aborted childhood. He had towering expectations of me, was unpredictably violent, and meted out severe punishments even for minor infractions. I will always be grateful to him for never treating me like a girl or expecting less of me because of my gender. But as I grew older my loyalty to him was eroded by my emergent independence; I became rebellious, incurring his wrath more often, all leading to a chilling of our relationship.

We did not live in an Italian American neighborhood and had little con-tact with other Italian Americans. We were an oddity to the other children in the midwestern suburban neighborhoods where we lived. We spoke sev-eral languages, had no television, and ate strange foods. My parents might as well have been Gomez and Morticia of *The Addams Family*. School was no refuge; I loved learning and excelled academically, but socially I stood out like a wild orchid in a field of daisies. My schoolmates teased me for "talking funny" and made fun of my pronunciation. My clothes also set me apart: they were thoughtfully provided by my grandmother, who was trying to help my parents financially as my father started his career, but were so different in style from those American children wore that they too made me the target of playground taunts. My lunches were perhaps the most egregious evidence that I did not belong. At the time, it was still difficult to obtain Italian ingredients deep in the interior of the American continent. So what my mother could not mail-order from Manganaro's, the famed New York deli, she made at home. I tried to trade her frittata on focaccia for my schoolmates' bologna sandwiches on Wonder Bread and Hostess Twinkies, only to bring further derision upon myself. When it somehow emerged that my parents allowed me to drink *caffelatte* (warm milk with coffee) and water mixed with wine, the school dispatched a social worker to chastise them for stunting my growth and turning me into a juvenile alcoholic. Throughout elementary school, I experienced prejudice from schoolmates and teachers alike, culminating in a period during which I endured daily bullying and physical assaults.

I found haven in reading and imaginary play. I loved the works of Mary Renault, Rosemary Sutcliffe, and Mary Stewart, which re-created the worlds of ancient Greece and Roman Britain. As I grew older, my interests extended to the Iron Age cultures and literatures of the Celts; in addition to *The Mabinogion* and *The Táin*, I read their adaptations by Lloyd Alexander and Evangeline Walton, and of course the fantasy literature of J. R. R. Tolkien and Ursula K. Le Guin, to name just a few of my favorite authors from that time. Whether along the Italian Maremma or in the creeks and ridges of the Ohio Valley, I spent long hours by myself in the woods, exploring nature and getting to know the rhythm of the seasons intimately. I developed a strong empathy for animals; I was always bringing home some rescued creature: tadpoles from the creek, white mice from science class, and once a clutch of baby black snakes, which my mother immediately made me release into the woods. Music became another refuge and an area in which I excelled. I learned to play the guitar and fell in love with the ballads of Joan Baez, imitating her style of singing and playing. Then I discovered English folk-rock groups like the Pentangle, Steeleye Span, and

Fairport Convention, learning to play their songs by ear. While my parents did not discourage my musical talent, they were not pleased with my aesthetics; they would have preferred me to play superior classical music, not the music of peasants and pop performers. I was already beginning to move against my family's privileged background.

In Italy I was a fish out of water for different reasons; especially as I grew older, my American sense of egalitarianism increasingly put me at odds with my maternal grandmother, who continued to live a life of privilege. I found her imperiousness insufferable and her criticism of my manners, dress, and personality stinging, so I took refuge with her Sardinian housekeeper, Bettina. Bettina was no Mary Poppins, but she had a dignity that I could not help but admire, even at a tender age: in her relationship with my grandmother, she knew her place but managed to interact without compromising her integrity. Bettina was powerless to discipline me, however. Knowing that I could get away with it, I teased her mercilessly, attaching clothespins to her apron strings just before she was to serve important guests at table, creeping into her quarters during the siesta hour to chant naughty words, spitting off the kitchen balcony onto unsuspecting pedestrians on the sidewalk below, and pestering her for stories about her distant hometown in Sardinia, which seemed to me a kind of fairy-tale realm where children ran wild on the mountain, rode donkeys, kept pet lambs, and cooked dinner over a fire every night. Some afternoons she would visit with Giovanna, a woman from the same village who kept house for my great-uncle in the apartment upstairs. Together the two women would thrill me with legends about ghosts, giants, witches, and other supernatural terrors that roamed the Sardinian countryside.

When I reached my teens, I became radicalized through contact with my father's side of the family, whose sympathies ran decidedly left of center. This coincided with the "hot years" of the 1970s, a period of great political ferment in Italy, marked by strikes, demonstrations, and riots. With my cousins, I attended rallies where radical young seminarians indoctrinated us in liberation theology and taught us to make Molotov cocktails to use against what they called the "fascist" power structure, which, according to them, was waiting to crack down on us. During this period I actively turned against my maternal grandmother and everything that she represented; our interactions frequently culminated in shouting matches. Conscious of the burden that her privilege placed on her staff, I began to resist depending on them in every way I could, from washing and ironing my own clothes to relying on public transportation instead of asking the chauffer to drive me places. These were small acts, but they symbolized my growing sense of social justice and solidarity with the underdog.

COLLEGE AND GRADUATE SCHOOL

By the time I entered college at Brown University in 1977, I was an ideal-istic young woman with six years of Latin and two years of ancient Greek under my belt; I could speak Italian, English, and French fluently, sing over a hundred ballads and lyric songs by heart, and recognize most of the plants and animals in the Ohio Valley and the Italian littoral. But I had very little sense of how the world actually worked. While I began the university with the idea that I would study medicine, it quickly became apparent that I had more of an aptitude for humanistic disciplines. I wanted to write fiction and poetry. But as a college student I had little life experience to draw on, and I was better at expository writing anyway. In my anthropology and folklore classes, I discovered a vocabulary for expressing the cultural disjunction that I felt growing up bicultural as well as methods of analysis that made use of my scientific skills. I was also strongly influenced in my career choice by an aunt by marriage who was a cultural anthropologist at the University of Bologna and by Margaret Mead, a close family friend. Mead and my father had met when he was working at the Menninger Clinic in Topeka, Kan-sas, where she was a frequent lecturer. I was powerfully drawn to the idea of fieldwork—living for long periods in unfamiliar cultures and engaging in participant-observation. In the end I chose to specialize in folkloristics because I was more interested in European cultures and traditions than in those of Third World peoples and because I was deeply invested in so many of the genres within its purview, including supernatural legends, foodways, folk crafts and architecture, and folksongs (I enjoyed a stint as an amateur folksinger from my teens to my mid-thirties). I loved the methodology of cultural anthropology, and folklore was the thread that tied together all of my interests, including my emergent sense of social justice and attraction to the cultural productions of everyday people. I majored in anthropology with an independent concentration in folklore; my undergraduate thesis was a structural analysis of British fairy legends.

During my senior year I applied to a number of graduate programs in folklore studies. I did so with some hesitation, though. While I had greatly enjoyed my studies in anthropology and folklore at Brown, I yearned for greater adventures and wondered whether I was doing something I actually wanted to do by pursuing an academic path or was conforming to family expectations. I had enjoyed my study of historical archaeology, including a course in which we had worked on collections at the Haffenraffer Museum, so I applied for a number of entry-level museum jobs. I also felt tugged by my love of music: I had been performing at local clubs and coffeehouses with some degree of success and felt drawn to the romantic idea of becoming a wandering bard, though I knew myself well enough to know that the instability of a musical career did not suit my temperament. In the end the economic reality made the decision for me: I received funding from several of the graduate programs to which I applied and got no job offers in the depressed market of 1980. I entered Indiana University's folklore Ph.D. program that fall. From the moment I arrived in Bloomington to begin my studies in folklore and met my fellow students in the program, I felt a sense of acceptance and belonging that I had never felt in any other social milieu until then.

My entrance into the program coincided with the death of its distinguished director, Richard M. Dorson, from a heart attack on the tennis court. This unexpected event plunged the Folklore Institute into confusion, and the years in which I was actively taking classes were challenging from an administrative point of view. The effect this had upon us as students was to drive us closer together. While we had many fine teachers and mentors, we grew to rely on each other for support, critiques, and guidance as we made our way through classes, internships, and our first appointments as teaching assistants. I got involved with the student journal *Folklore Forum*, an experience that proved invaluable in my academic life. I loved the collegiality that existed among us; of course, we also competed with one another, but the sense of competition was tempered by affection and loyalty. This model of collegiality became an ideal that inspired the kind of atmosphere that I tried to cultivate among my own graduate students as well as among my departmental colleagues once I attained a permanent position. But that day was still a long way off.

Several folklorists and anthropologists have noted that folklore is often involved in a search for home—for the meaning of that elusive term (Behar

2009; Lawless 2011). As graduate students at Indiana University's Folklore Institute, we were similarly engaged in a search for home. We had common interests in various folkloric and literary genres and shared a sense that the small, the forgotten, the marginalized, and the underappreciated were in some ways worthier and more interesting than the great works valued by mainstream disciplines. For the first time in my life, I felt as though I had found my people; folklore became for us a home.

FIELDWORK: SARDINIA

From the time I began my folklore studies at Indiana University, I was keenly aware of the need to choose a field site on which to base my dissertation. I had originally wanted to work in Ireland or one of the Celtic countries and in fact studied Gaelic for a time; but my graduate advisor Linda Dégh, who came from the Hungarian school of European ethnology, persuaded me that it would be best to work within my own culture, by which she meant Italy. She introduced me to Italian ethnologist Carla Bianco, who had studied both Italian peasants and Italian American immigrants (Bianco 1974), in hopes that she could help me identify a possible field site and subject. I chose to work in Sardinia because of my strong attachment to Bettina, the woman who had worked as a domestic for my grandmother, and her stories of her village in the Sardinian highlands. I imbued it with romantic pastoral ideals that were intensified by the general scorn with which the region was regarded by my urban bourgeois family; already drawn to the marginal and rejected, I became even more determined to go there one day. After my grandmother's death, Bettina retired to her village, where I visited her in the summer of 1983. I like to say that Sardinia got into my blood that summer: I knew then, with a strange feeling of destiny, that I would do my doctoral fieldwork there. I chose to study traditional religious festivals and socio-economic change because this phenomenon was on the lips of so many of the people I met that first summer. It was the summer festival season, and young people were driving from town to town each weekend to attend them. At the same time, I heard from their parents and grandparents about how things had changed during the course of their lifetimes—how festivals were no longer as they had been "in the good old days." The themes of tradition, modernity, and socioeconomic change fit well with issues in Mediterranean ethnology in the 1980s. From a pragmatic standpoint, I knew that I would not have trouble getting my advisor or committee to accept a dissertation on this topic.

Yet even spending part of my childhood in Italy could not have prepared me for the culture shock that I experienced when I first went to live in the village of Bessude with my old nanny and her family in 1986. There were all sorts of tensions, beginning with those of social class and extending to gender expectations and political conflicts. I grew up in a privileged, cosmopolitan family; Bessude was a highland community of shepherds and agriculturalists. I was both resented and regarded as an outsider by most of its inhabitants. What I knew about rural Mediterranean life came from academic books. Even the languages were different: I grew up speaking standard Italian. While Sardinians learned Italian in school, for them it was always a second language; their first language was Sardo, a related Romance language that nevertheless differs significantly from Italian. I had a lot to learn. I eventually forged very strong bonds with a group of young women also in their twenties, who lived at home in the village and either attended the university in Sassari or worked at various jobs. Through them, I gained access to other village networks as well as the organizing committees of the festivals that I was studying. I also became aware of local political tensions and how they came to be expressed through the festivals. The results were reflected in my ethnography *The Two Madonnas: The Politics of Festival in a Sardinian Community* (1993/2005), a book that is quite sensitive to tensions between the categories of tradition and modernity as they were expressed in the margins of Europe in the 1980s and early 1990s. Because of my gender and position as a fieldworker, it offers unprecedented insights into the dreams, ideals, and struggles of village women, showing them to be cultural and political agents in the context of globalization.

Ironically, the very processes that had helped me understand the links between festival organization and political power led to the emergence of a crisis in my relationship with my field community. After I left the field, the political situation in Bessude became so volatile that my efforts to publish *The Two Madonnas* in Italian got caught up in the internecine conflict. I had friends on both sides—a delicate situation, given local expectations that political allegiance should follow family lines. Members of the local administration, which at first had supported my project, felt that the results did not portray their community as they would have liked; they thought that my book made them look backward and old-fashioned. The mayor took out her anger and disappointment on Bettina and her family, because they had hosted me, by taking away a part of their land in order to build a road—a road to nowhere, as it turned out. They had relied on this land to grow vegetables and pasture sheep, so the loss hurt them economically. I was mortified by this outcome. As an anthropologist, I am bound by a professional code of ethics to put the good of the people I work with before my own, and I felt responsible. The last thing I had ever wanted was to cause lasting harm to the very person who had nurtured me like a second mother and who had made possible my doctoral dissertation research and the career that I hoped would come from that. I took it as a personal failure on my part. For a time I did not want to return to Sardinia for fear that more harm would come to the people I loved as a result of my presence. This coincided with a period of instability in my professional and domestic life in which I had neither the funds nor the possibility to return to Italy, so I began to cast about for a new research topic. Since I had examined women's roles in ritual and politics, I hoped to find another venue in which to explore that theme closer to home. I was also painfully aware that American academic publishing was becoming less interested in European ethnography; several colleagues advised me to find something more relevant to study.

SALAD DAYS

My graduate education in folkloristics solidified my desire to pursue an academic career. But an academic position in the fields of folklore or anthropology was getting harder to find. Many fellow graduates with no prospects of a full-time position lived on the edge in Bloomington doing a variety of menial jobs, unable to pay off student loans. I was lucky to have received scholarships throughout most of my studies, but I too was anxious. Our advisors though kept telling us that a raft of retirements in the early 1990s would open up dozens of positions that our generation was poised to fill. Yet when I received my Ph.D. in 1988 the economic boom of the 1980s had not resulted in more funding for public education, but marked only the first of successive waves of draconian cutbacks. I was working two part-time jobs, one in the Department of Anthropology at Indiana University— Purdue University Indianapolis and another at the Mathers Museum. But neither offered tenure-track opportunities, which were also not available anywhere else in the country.

My situation was even more complicated because I was involved in a serious relationship with another academic. I had met him when he was a graduate student at Columbia University and had been invited to guest-teach at Indiana University. Since then he had completed his doctorate and gotten a full-time position. His field was even more esoteric than mine, and the hope of us landing tenure-track positions together at the same institution was slim. Yet we were in love and seemed well suited to one another. He was also a "halfie," a walker between worlds, and I believed that we understood each other's cultural dilemmas well and could share our betweenness. Hoping that we could somehow forge a life with careers for us both as well as a family, we married in 1988, shortly after my dissertation was completed.

We could not believe our luck when the University of Wisconsin advertised a position for a tenure-track line in anthropology with a specialization in folklore as well as a position in my husband's field in a different department. We decided to apply for the positions. Unbelievably, we both were interviewed. He got the position, and I was offered a lectureship in the folklore program. We both had postdocs in Europe at the time, but we accepted enthusiastically and arranged to move to Madison in the spring of 1990. It seemed an ideal arrangement; we were ecstatic, and could not wait to get started on the rest of our lives together.

But what at first seemed ideal did not work out ideally in the long run. During our years in Madison our marriage deteriorated. At the end of the spring of 1994 the university cut back my position at the same time that my husband served me divorce papers. Realizing the severity of my predicament, I put out an email to all my friends and contacts in the professional world, letting them know I was available to work anywhere in the coming year. Joseph F. Nágy of the Folklore and Mythology Program at UCLA came to my rescue: Robert A. Georges had just retired, and they needed someone to teach his classes for a quarter. I threw my books, guitar, and cat Pinky into my car and drove cross country to California, beginning a new chapter in my life and leaving the Midwest behind.

The position at UCLA began my period as a journeyman in my professional career. I had already taught for several years at Indiana University—Purdue University Indianapolis and four years at the University of

Wisconsin—Madison. Now I jumped around even more often: after ten weeks at UCLA, I got a visiting assignment in the Department of Anthropology at the University of California—Santa Barbara. The following fall Alan Dundes invited me to be a visiting professor in the University of California—Berkeley's Department of Anthropology. During this time I continued to apply to a variety of academic positions in folklore, anthropology, and related disciplines. I was desperately anxious about my future, but at the same time the years I spent teaching in different universities and programs were some of the most exciting and rewarding of my career. I mentored many brilliant graduate students who have now become colleagues in their own right as well as friends. I was in my mid-thirties at the time, which made me fairly close to their age, more like a comrade than an advisor. Having to prepare new courses every term pushed my interests in stimulating new directions, stretching me in ways I had not anticipated. Witnessing the ways in which various academic departments were led, as well as the results in terms of student success and departmental climate, provided key lessons that influenced the way I later approached academic leadership. All these lessons were to pay off once I accepted a tenure-track position at California State University, Northridge, a regional comprehensive university in the San Fernando Valley just north of Los Angeles, in 1997. I eventually gained tenure and promotion there, served as department chair, and continue to teach to this day.

CALIFORNIA AND PAGAN RESEARCH

Perhaps most importantly for my professional development, the move to California gave me the opportunity to expand a new research project that I had recently begun on ritual in modern Pagan religions. I had started the project in the early 1990s, after the debacle in my Sardinian field site, when I was teaching a course I had developed called "The Supernatural in the Modern World" (which I still teach today). It looks at vernacular traditions that make reference to magic and the preternatural against the context of an Enlightenment construction of modernity. Among the topics I covered was modern Paganism, a movement of religions that reclaim, revive, and experiment with pre-Christian polytheistic worship. I became aware of a modern Pagan Witch named Selena Fox who was a graduate student in the School of Social Work at the University of Wisconsin—Madison, where I was teaching. I invited her to come speak to my class about her traditions. She, in turn, invited me and my students to an Earth Day ritual at Circle Sanctuary, a nature preserve that she ran with her husband, Dennis Carpenter, near Mt. Horeb. On a sunny, cold Saturday I drove there with some students from the class. The ritual was like nothing I had experienced before. It was held on a tall mound encircled by birch and oak trees, with a view of the valley below. Selena, a powerful woman with flowing dark hair and a strong, deep voice, called on the four directions, invoked the names of goddesses and ancestors, and advocated for a spiritual connection to the land and political action to protect it. It seemed to me then that I had found a possible topic—that modern Paganism might be another way for me to explore the connections between gender, power, and ritual in a new context.

I thought that my new topic was timely and potentially more interesting to American academic publishers than peasant culture on the margins of Europe; in fact I was encouraged to pursue it by several senior colleagues. I did not at first realize how controversial this new area would be among academics. But I have always followed my heart and intuition in research, and this was no exception. As in the case of Sardinia, I felt a sense that fate was drawing me toward this project.

At first one of the things that drew me to study modern Paganism was, paradoxically, a longing for my field site in Sardinia. I missed the friendships that I had formed there with other girls my age; I longed for the sense of community, the connectedness of things, and the rhythm of the year's ritual cycle. In modern Pagan festivals, I could experience some of the same feelings: jumping over a midsummer bonfire, for example, at the same time that I knew my friends in a village half a world away were doing the same thing. Eventually I formed the same kinds of close bonds with my Pagan interlocutors that I had with my Sardinian ones, and the new project took on a life of its own. At a ritual in 1995 I experienced a vision of the goddess Brigid melting my heart in her forge and shaping it into a new one, which she put into my chest while saying, "This is your heart, and fire shall make it whole." I interpreted it as a confirmation that my field methodology, my particular way of working, was valid and would heal the wounds that I still felt as a result of what had happened in Sardinia.

The year following this extraordinary experience, I received a John Simon Guggenheim Memorial Fellowship that allowed me to remain in

Berkeley and immerse myself fully in the modern Pagan milieu, doing fieldwork that would serve as the basis for my scholarship in the following decade. From this fieldwork came my books *Neo-Pagan Sacred Art and Altars: Making Things Whole* (2001), *Witching Culture: Folklore and Neopaganism in America* (2004), and the film series *Oss Tales* (with John M. Bishop; 2007), as well as numerous articles and book chapters. In these works I embraced what has become my signature writing style, which alternates passages from my field notes written in a very personal, embodied, immediate style with more substantial portions of ethnographic and analytical text. This way of writing represents the process of walking between the worlds on the page and takes readers through it, showing them multiple perspectives in succession. Even the film that I made includes passages in which both John Bishop and I reflect on our participation in the filmmaking process. My writing was influenced by the reflexive turn in ethnography begun by James Clifford (1986) and George Marcus (1998) as well as the work of feminist ethnographers who have written "vulnerably," as Ruth Behar (1996) calls it, including Behar (2013, 2009, 1996), Lila Abu-Lughod (1993), Kirin Narayan (1997, 1989), and Jone Salomonsen (1999).

On the whole, my work was well received both by other academics and by Pagans. However, some reviewers of *Witching Culture* criticized me for writing vulnerably about my experiences, perhaps even for having them, assuming that they had somehow changed my beliefs and clouded my ability to be objective about modern Paganisms. This point of view is problematic on a number of counts. The first error—assuming that my beliefs changed as a result of initiation and participation—is understandable, because for people coming from a Christocentric perspective, as most Westerners unconsciously do, belief is seen as the central feature of religion. But, like the majority of world religions, modern Paganisms are not primarily religions of belief; they are religions of practice and experience. My beliefs have not fundamentally changed as a result of the experiences I had during my Pagan fieldwork. Instead I have a deepened, enriched understanding of a religious culture and its performative art forms that helped me portray it in a more holistic way.

The second way that the critics are mistaken is in assuming that it is possible to give an objective account of a different culture. The postcolonial, postmodern critique of the social sciences has effectively eliminated the idea of "objective" research—the notion that the researcher operates as a completely neutral observer who can deliver the "truth" about another society. As James Clifford (1986) stated so eloquently, all ethnographies are only partial truths, because we all bring unique points of view and prejudices with us wherever we go. Those viewpoints and prejudices influence what we see, how we see it, what we think is important, and how we convey it. In that sense, as Clifford (1986) wrote, all ethnographies are "fictions," in the sense of carefully constructed documents, rather than pure, unadulterated facts. The important thing is to admit to ourselves and our readers where our blind spots might lie, so they can better evaluate the texts we produce— something that I tried to do in the introduction to *Witching Culture*.

I am far from the only scholar of mystery traditions to have undergone initiation in order to understand them better. Karen McCarthy Brown (1989), who studied Vodou among Haitian immigrants in Brooklyn, was initiated as a practitioner and "married" to the *lwa* (spirit) Dambala as part of her work. Paul Stoller (1987) underwent initiation as a sorcerer among the Songhay of Niger. Jeanne Favret-Saada (1980), studying witchcraft in rural France, found herself having to participate in the world of magic to some degree. As she found, there is no "outside" when it comes to magic; either you are an insider or you won't learn anything at all. Unusual, even extraordinary, experiences are to some extent inevitable when becoming involved with magic and ritual; that is the whole point of these events as art forms. Many anthropologists before me have had these experiences, and some have written about them. The best-known is probably Edith Turner (1994), who saw a spirit in the shape of a dark cloud rise from the body of a patient who was undergoing a healing ritual among the Ndembu, but others include Bruce Grindal (1983), Raymond Lee (1987), and David Young and Jean-Guy Goulet (1994).

My decision to become deeply involved in Pagan religions was in part intrinsic to the way I approach the people that I study—with an open heart, as one of my interlocutors and friends in Bessude once said to me. But I also find that trust and rapport flourish in this open-hearted atmosphere, and they are ultimately essential to the work. As a folklorist and anthropologist, my job is to access other cultures to try to understand them and bring those insights back to my own culture. My methodology involves participant-observation. It is very difficult to learn much about another culture or religion if one is not willing to participate, and religious rites require some basic level of participation as a show of respect. When I began to study

Paganisms, I discovered that modern Pagan rituals are highly participatory events; there is no outside from which to be an undetected observer (Salomonsen 1999). This is especially true of mystery traditions such as Wicca. So I did what any anthropologist or folklorist worth her salt should do: I found a group with which I felt comfortable, attended their rituals for a year, and eventually underwent initiation. I also attended dozens of rituals from other Pagan traditions. In some of these contexts I had extraordinary experiences; had I *not* had them, I would have missed the whole point of what my interlocutors were experiencing: I would have failed to understand one of the primary reasons why they found their religions compelling, powerful, and important.

Reviewers and critics often wonder whether I feel a sense of split allegiances as a result of studying religions in which I am an active participant or, worse, whether I "went native," violating one of the central taboos of anthropological fieldwork. Feminist scholars, minority scholars, and scholars who are "halfies" of one sort or another all face this dilemma and must carefully negotiate between their belonging to a community and their study of it. Yet the very act of studying something forces us to distance ourselves from it, to be reflexive about our participation in it, and thus changes our relationship with it. There are no true "native ethnographers." In the same vein, anthropological notions of "going native" are based on old-fashioned ideas that served to separate Western anthropologists from the colonized peoples they studied. They also assume that identity is fixed and unchanging. We now understand the fluid, evolving, and contextual nature of identity. Who we are and how we choose to identify depend on many different factors, including whom we are with. That means that either-or constructions of identity are inaccurate and unhelpful.

The key to doing anthropology or folklore research effectively lies in successfully negotiating between the cultures one is studying and the culture of the academy. It is a form of "walking between the worlds." One must learn to move between them with grace and reflection. It is necessary to go deep, participate, get close to people, feel what it's like to be one of them—then pull away and reflect on what just happened, using analysis and theoretical language to frame one's thoughts. Then one goes back and does it all over again. Because I grew up shuttling between two cultures, this process is as natural to me as breathing, and just as automatic.

GIFTS

In both traditional and modern Pagan worldviews, those who walk between worlds are healers: they carry gifts of the spirit back from the otherworld into the human realms—gifts that help make things whole. While I hesitate to claim to be a healer, it is time to reflect on what gifts, if any, I might bring to the various communities among which I move. The idea of giving back to our field communities in gratitude for the ways they help achieve our career goals is ubiquitous in both folkloristics and anthropology; this impulse is what motivated me to publish my study of festivals in Bessude in Italian, despite the damage that it wound up causing. Since then I have become wary of simplistic notions of "giving back" to the communities with which I work, while at the same time my commitment to doing so has grown stronger. In my Pagan fieldwork, one of the principal ways I give back is by maintaining ongoing relationships with people in the community, presenting my research findings at Pagan conferences, and informing the academic and nonacademic communities about this group of religions through teaching and public presentations in the media and online. I fill the role of interlocutor, representing each community to the other and serving as a messenger of sorts between them. In addition, I donate the royalties that I earn from my academic publications to causes that benefit my various field communities, from a fund to support the local heritage association in Bessude to scholarships supporting young Pagans who want to further their education.

A more interesting question, perhaps, and one that is more difficult to answer, is how my Pagan research has informed the work that I do in the academy. This is manifested in both specific and general ways. On the specific level, my work with ritual and festival in a variety of contexts has made me very sensitive to its importance for various social functions, from marking special occasions such as commencement or the beginning of a new academic year to creating a sense of community among students and faculty. Observing and participating in the creation of rituals has given me expertise in this area that extends to academic life, garnering me the joking moniker "Ritual Girl." If there is a special event to be organized, my colleagues know they can call on me. During my service on the Executive Board of the American Folklore Society, for example, I helped develop a new model to memorialize departed colleagues. Another specific way in which my research has affected my professional work is through my increased sensitivity to religious minorities in a pluralistic society. Again, this has many benefits in a diverse working environment such as a large university in a major metropolitan area. One of my goals when I teach intro-ductory courses in the anthropology of religion is to sensitize students to religious diversity and to develop not just tolerance for other religions, but an engaged pluralism that will allow them to interact with individuals with a wide range of religious practices over the course of their lifetimes. To that end, I often design exercises that draw upon my fieldwork experiences— for example, allowing them to experience trance-inducing music, guided meditation, and divination in a safe classroom environment. On a more general level, my lifetime of scholarship on religion and folklore has made me more aware of and sensitive to alternate ways of knowing, more willing to trust my intuition about personal and professional matters. Finally, I am more aware than ever of the spiritual nature of scholarship: on some level, all scholarship is not only a seeking of knowledge but also a spiritual quest to achieve a better understanding of our own nature and how we fit into the larger patterns of the universe.

WORKS CITED

Abu-Lughod, Lila. 1993. *Writing Women's Worlds*. Berkeley: University of California Press.

Behar, Ruth. 2013. *Traveling Heavy: A Memoir*. Durham, NC: Duke University Press.

———. 2009. "Folklore and the Search for Home." *Journal of American Folklore* 122, no. 485: 251–66.

———. 1996. *The Vulnerable Observer: Anthropology That Breaks Your Heart*. Boston: Beacon Press.

Bianco, Carla. 1974. *The Two Rosetos*. Bloomington: Indiana University Press.

Brown, Karen McCarthy. 1989. *Mama Lola: A Vodou Priestess in Brooklyn*. Berkeley: University of California Press.

Clifford, James. 1986. "Introduction." In *Writing Culture: the Politics and Poetics of Ethnography*, ed. J. Clifford and George E. Marcus, 1–26. Berkeley: University of California Press.

Favret-Saada, Jeanne. 1980. *Deadly Words: Witchcraft in the Bocage*. New York: Cambridge University Press.

Grindal, Bruce. 1983. "Into the Heart of Sisala Experience." *Journal of Anthropological Research* 39: 60–80.

Lawless, Elaine. 2011. "Folklore as a Map of the World: Rejecting 'Home' as a Failure of the Imagination." *Journal of American Folklore* 124, no. 493: 127–46.

Lee, Raymond. 1987. "Amulets and Anthropology: A Paranormal Encounter with Malay Magic." *Anthropology and Humanism Quarterly* 12, nos. 2–3: 69–74.

Magliocco, Sabina. 2004. *Witching Culture: Folklore and Neopaganism in America.* Philadelphia: University of Pennsylvania Press.

———. 2001. *Neo-Pagan Sacred Art and Altars: Making Things Whole.* Jackson: University Press of Mississippi.

———. 2005 [1993]. *The Two Madonnas: The Politics of Festival in a Sardinian Community.* New York: Peter Lang. 2nd ed.: Long Grove, IL: Waveland Press, 2005.

Magliocco, Sabina, and John M. Bishop. 2007. *Oss Tales.* Film. Media Generation Productions.

Marcus, George. 1998. *Ethnography through Thick and Thin.* Princeton, NJ: Princeton University Press.

Narayan, Kirin. 1997. *Mondays on the Dark Night of the Moon: Himalayan Foothill Folktales.* New York and Oxford: Oxford University Press.

———. 1989. *Storytellers, Saints and Scoundrels: Storytelling and Hindu Religious Teaching.* Philadelphia: University of Pennsylvania Press.

Salomonsen, Jone. 1999. "Methods of Compassion or Pretension?: Fieldwork in Modern Magical Communities." *Pomegranate* 8: 4–13.

Stoller, Paul. 1987. *In Sorcery's Shadow: A Memoir of Apprenticeship among the Songhay of Niger.* Chicago: University of Chicago Press.

Turner, Edith. 1994. "A Visible Spirit from Zambia." In *Being Changed: The Anthropology of Extraordinary Experience*, ed. David E. Young and Jean-Guy Goulet, 71–95. Peterborough, Ontario: Broadview Press.

Turner, Victor. 1968. *The Ritual Process.* Ithaca, NY: Cornell University Press.

Young, David E., and Jean-Guy Goulet. 1994. *Being Changed: the Anthropology of Extraordinary Experience.* Peterborough, Ontario: Broadview Press.

Four

PREDESTINATION?

MARY ELLEN BROWN

The baby book that my mother kept says I was baptized by my paternal grandfather, but my maternal grandfather—a missionary in China—might well have done the deed if he had not been far away in Jiangsu Province. And for that matter, my father, like my grandfathers a Presbyterian minister, might well have baptized me himself. My family is strongly anchored in the Presbyterian Church—and the list of those three ministers does not exhaust the clergy in my genealogy and does not include the women in my family who today might perform baptisms as clergy themselves. My grandmothers were active church women, one a teaching missionary who went to China as a "maiden" lady, married, bore children, and died there when my own mother was only four. All were Presbyterians, women and men, born and bred, new world descendants of the Reformed tradition of John Calvin, John Knox, and Scotland, where my father did postgraduate work. Had China (not the People's Republic) been accessible and Chinese language study readily available, perhaps I would have chosen that country as locus of my research. Instead, following my father—and maybe even John Knox, but not explicitly specific Presbyterian "beliefs"—I chose Scotland, an "exotic" county far away from home. That country and its Presbyterian inheritance have implicitly guided me in ways that I certainly could and would not have anticipated. In what follows I seek to suggest just how.

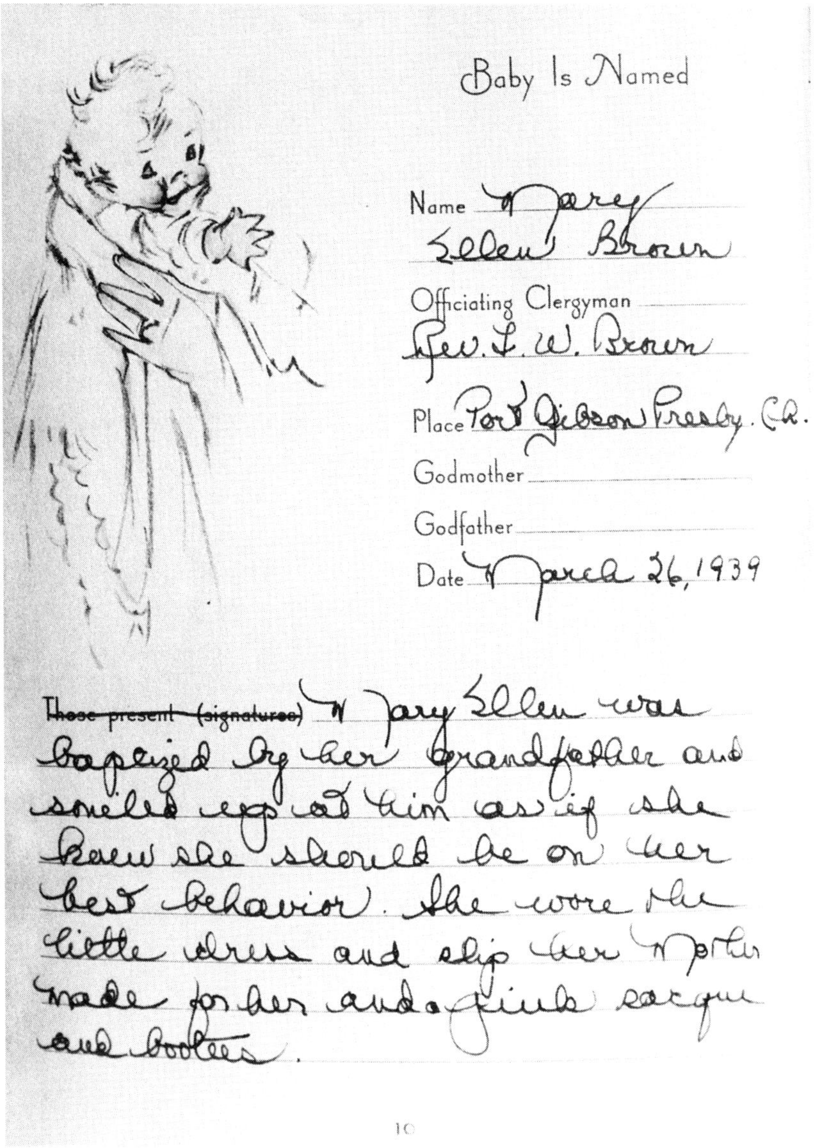

Baby Is Named

Name Mary Ellen Brown

Officiating Clergyman Rev. F. W. Brown

Place Port Gibson Presby. Ch.

Godmother

Godfather

Date March 26, 1939

Those present (signatures) Mary Ellen was baptized by her grandfather and smiled up at him as if she knew she should be on her best behavior. She wore the little dress and slip her mother made for her and finds sacque and booties.

10

FIGURE 4.1 Mother records my baptism.

We did not talk about religious tenets at home, though we strove to follow many of them: always church on Sunday, always Sunday School on Sunday, always youth meetings on Sunday—following the biblical description of creation and the designation of the seventh day for rest—often identified as a time for worship. We lived a modestly Sabbatarian life, for our Sundays were dominated by the church and worldly things were put aside, even doing homework. My mother would mitigate our keeping the Sabbath with stories of her childhood: we were horrified and simultaneously amused when she described her attempt to play "hide and seek" if she said the Lord's Prayer each time she and her companions returned to home base—a failed attempt to subvert the rigid Sabbatarianism that had even led my maternal grandfather Stevens to refuse giving out famine relief in China on the Sabbath, though he subsequently interrogated his behavior. The Bible and the hymns, heard and sung at church more than at home, and prayers, especially before meals and certainly at church, gave language a heightened meaning and provided recognized patterns that infused the way we lived. Of course, I heard many, many sermons, but listening to my father talking from the pulpit most often triggered random thoughts about nothing very religious—a twenty-plus minute recess for personal reflection. Twenty minutes was short: early in the nineteenth century sermons might last two hours; I was lucky. But biblical phrases and poetic lines from hymns and prayers provided the surround, the foreground, of religious encounters and remain both familiar and comforting, embedded in my very being. Witness the lines from Numbers 6: 24–26 (NRSV) used frequently by my Father as a benediction: "The LORD bless you and keep you; the LORD make his face to shine upon you, and be gracious to you; the LORD lift up his countenance upon you, and give you peace." Implicitly I learned of God's sovereignty, the authority of the Bible as revealed through interpretations (especially narratives from the Old Testament), of God's gift of salvation to us all through Jesus Christ. These ideas were expressed in terms of the debated topic of predestination—that actions in our lives are preordained or foreordained by God and, in orthodox belief, that God preordains some to heaven and some to hell. I certainly embraced the educated ministry and the democratic church governance that incorporated ministers and laypersons. I accepted the importance of spreading the good news of Jesus throughout the world as my grandparents did in China early in the twentieth century. Today I might interrogate the missionary assumptions of

First World hegemony. Yet at base the missionary activity sought to spread what they perceived as "the good news" and through that to achieve a more just and equal world. Yet the very structure of the mission field then—male evangelists, female teachers and helpers—suggests the inherited assumptions of male dominance that I studied and taught about and even helped to administer as director and professor of Women's Studies in the late 1980s. As a child and young person I accepted the imperfect reality in which I lived but seem not to have accepted the gender imbalance in thinking of my own future. I belonged to church, so central to my family, and took from it, without knowing that I did, certain notions about how to live.

I learned other things at home: to love classical music and reading and to value education. I cherish the memory of the Metropolitan Opera broadcasts on winter Saturday afternoons, with the summaries and descriptions provided by Milton Cross; and on Sundays the radio was often on again for listening to the New York Philharmonic. Mostly this was beautiful sound. I really did not learn much about the narratives or the composers or anything about the finer points of opera or symphonic compositions: but I loved the musical surround, often as background to reading. We were definitely a reading family; we went to the library and brought home armloads of books, mostly fiction. In fact, we would sit together, each reading our own books quietly, sometimes with music in the background: for me this was and is the ultimate in companionability. The love of reading suggests something else about my family: the great value and emphasis placed on learning, on education. All four of my grandparents were college graduates, two with postgraduate degrees in divinity; my father had a Th.D.; my sisters and I have graduate degrees. Each of these qualities or attributes might well be connected to the church: the resonance of good church music (Johann Sebastian Bach)—organs and choirs; the reading of the Word, the Bible; the value placed on each congregant's learning and reading of the Bible; the educated clergy.

The church, the music, and the reading/education were simply givens, a part of our shared worldview. Pierre Bourdieu (1997: 20) would call this a habitus, a "semi-learned grammar[s] of practice." This concept was especially useful for me when I was working on the Scottish poet, journalist, and ballad editor William Motherwell, as I tried to understand what guided his behavior. I came to believe that the fear of change dominated his work as journalist, poet, and ballad editor. He was against the Reform Bill of 1832, which enfranchised him; his poetry often looked to the past, as in his Scandinavian inflected "The Sword Chant of Thorstein Raudi" (Brown 2001: 65–67); as ballad editor he sought to record oral vernacular poetry that he saw as becoming passé: "The changes every day effects on the domestic habits, tastes, pursuits, manners, and modes of living of all ranks of society in the present generation seem decidedly inimical to the preservation and transmission of Oral Song" (Brown 2001: 22). I studied these evidences of his life and time, seeking to suggest his habitus. Using Bourdieu's formulation I wrote that habitus refers to

> systems of how to be that derive from social origin, education, and economic position and that constrain an individual within a particular social location or class. A *habitus* comprises a range of ideas/beliefs—that is, aptitudes, attitudes, tendencies—held by a group of people occupying similar social space and inclines agents to act and react in certain ways; the *habitus* structures perception and serves as a generative principle; it reflects and reinforces itself. (Brown 2001: 9)

I too was shaped and partially formed by a habitus infused with unstated beliefs and practices that reflected my Presbyterian heritage, my learned appreciation of classical music, and my love of learning. This habitus led me unconsciously to Scotland (or to things Scottish), that home of Presbyterianism, and to a heightened awareness of poetry and language, especially connected with religion. I began with poetry, initially with oral poetry and subsequently with those who used that material as poets or editors. I sought to understand why these men, and they have all been men, did what they did with poetry/language/words, with inspiration and religion being a related drawing card as I explored the lives of the men whose lives became my focus. It was not that the church or religion in general played an outsized role in their lives but that in studying them I was drawn to anything—big or small—that hinted at their involvement in any way in the life of the Presbyterian Church. Such a presumed connection, I think, enabled me to feel a personal connection, at least for a moment, with someone whose life really was quite different from mine and was certainly distant in time. The familiar drew me into their lives; it was an anchor that provided me with a sense that I could understand their worldviews, their cultural contexts, their habitus—however misguided that might have been in reality.

If the church and religion underlay various choices I made—such as whom to study—I have been drawn to the works of men of words, to their poetry or their studies of poetry, especially of vernacular materials like the ballad, folksong, and related forms. I have sought to understand the intellectual history of these vernacular poetic forms. Their brevity and stanzaic patterns, even repetition of certain phrases and clauses, seemed familiar to me, different from but parallel to the stanzaic patterns of hymns with their repetition and in some ways parallel to the Psalms, especially when in metrical form. Perhaps Bible passages from the King James Version (KJV)—the first Bible I knew and one that was in fact sponsored by James VI of Scotland, who became James I of England and Ireland—gave me a love of poetry, of a language infused with beauty whose meaning was enormous, beyond what I could understand, but brief:

> I will lift up mine eyes unto the hills, from whence cometh my help.
> My help *cometh* from the LORD, which made heaven and earth.
> He will not suffer thy foot to be moved: he that keepeth thee will
>   not slumber.
> Behold, he that keepeth Israel shall neither slumber nor sleep.
> The sun shall not smite thee by day, nor the moon by night.
> The LORD shall preserve thee from all evil: he shall preserve
>   thy soul.
> The LORD shall preserve thy going out and thy coming in from
>   this time forth, and even for evermore. (Psalm 121, KJV)

What an amazing statement of the Lord's all encompassing power. Such poetry has dominated my life, drawing me to poets of the past and to poetry and song by the prolific Anonymous—the ballads, the vernacular poetry, often not fully told, elliptical, and occasionally bearing lines of surpassing artistry.

As an academic, I was attracted to balladry, especially examples gathered together by Harvard University's first professor of English, Francis James Child, in *The English and Scottish Popular Ballads* (1882–98). In reading the multiple versions of the 305 ballads in that five-volume work, I have been drawn to individual texts. Sometimes I was attracted by hints of morality and belief, things that seemed familiar, as in Child 9, "The Fair Flower of Northumberland," which first appeared in print in 1633 in Thomas Deloney's *Pleasant History of John Winchcomb*. My attention was drawn to an English rather than a Scottish version. A knight from Scotland, taken prisoner in Northumberland, is overheard bemoaning his fate by the earl's daughter, "the fair flower of Northumberland." Thinking he would marry her, she effects his escape; when they are in view of Edinburgh, he tells her that he is already married and that she should return home. Two English knights rescue her and return her to her father. The ballad concludes with the warning:

> All you faire maidens be warned by me,
> Scots were never true, nor never will be,
> To lord, nor lady, nor faire England. (Child 1882–98: 1:114)

Did such "warnings" echo the lists of "thou shalt nots" that passed as behavioral guides at home? Anyway, this "fair flower" returned home intact, her perfidy against her own father forgotten. I would not have overtly tried to subvert my own father's behavioral principles, but I understand the will to subvert, to question, to make my own decisions and undoubtedly ignore covertly and forget some of the "thou shalt nots," of which there were many. Early on I learned to do and think what seemed right for me, against the background of behavioral rules at home and in church. And I admired the Scottish knight: he got out of jail and returned safely to Edinburgh. I once attended a Halloween party of English graduate students with ordinary street clothes and a placard around my neck on which was written "Child 9," my minimalist costume: no one, of course, guessed who I was!

The language, the words, the mental mellifluousness of such brief poetic narrative renderings and their recurrent verse forms spoke and speak to me. I met them first as printed words, often recorded in the seventeenth and eighteenth centuries, and that is how I personally prefer them—privately read, not collectively heard. My all-time favorite is Child 58, "Sir Patrick Spens." In the A version, taken from Thomas Percy's *Reliques of Ancient English Poetry* (1765) but sent to Percy from Scotland, I see the skipper as caught in a web of fate, having to respond to the king's command but knowing that the result will be his death—a skewed view perhaps of predestination. The exquisite beauty of the words and the repeated stanzaic pattern explain my attraction to this artistic gem, as illustrated in stanzas 3–6 and the concluding one:

> The king has written a braid letter,
>   And signd it wi his hand,
> And sent it to Sir Patrick Spence,
>   Was walking on the sand.

> The first line that Sir Patrick red,
>   A loud lauch lauched he;
> The next line that Sir Patrick red,
>   The teir blinded his ee.

> O wha is this has don this deid,
>   This ill deid don to me,
> To send me out this time o' the yeir,
>   To sail upon the se!

> Mak hast, mak haste, my mirry men all,
>   Our guid schip sails the morne:
> O say na sae, my master deir,
>   For I feir a deadlie storme.

> Haf owre, haf owre to Aberdour,
>   It's fiftie fadom deip,
> And thair lies guid Sir Patrick Spence,
>   Wi the Scots lords at his feit. (Child 1882–98: 2:20–21)

The commonplace stanza 4, even repeated and thus familiar from other ballads, seems at once unique here, so incredibly perfect and apt, describing as it does the skipper's simultaneous assessment of the situation—amusement and dread—an accurate predictor of the outcome, alas. The text draws me in: it does not tell me the reason for the king's command; nor does it tell me where the ship will go. It focuses simply on the command—ours is not to reason why, ours is but to do or die, as Alfred Lord Tennyson later made famous. Of course, editors have tried to uncover the historical event that may have spurred the ballad's creation—perhaps a voyage to Norway to bring back the princess—but knowing that seems irrelevant to the exquisite poignancy of the command. Spens is a very human hero: given a task, he strives to succeed. Like all humans, he does not always achieve his goal, but he dies trying. I live with Spens: a print on the wall perhaps depicting the site of Arthur's Seat, the Salisbury Craigs, is dominated by the sea and emblazoned in the lower right corner with the lines "Waiting for Sir Patrick Spens/Come sailing to the land." Titled "landfall," this print by Robert Adams plays ironically with a landfall never made. My Scottish Fold cat is named Spens.

This ballad, this poem, is a work of art. It nourishes my own need for beauty, as does the final verse of Child 162B, "The Hunting of the Cheviot":

> God saue our *king*, and blesse this land
>   with plentye, ioy, and peace,
> And grant henceforth *that* foule debate
>   twixt noble men may ceaze! (Child 1882–98: 3:314)

This ballad is 64 stanzas long, a detailed account of a battle with the commonplace:

> For when his leggs were smitten of,
>   he fought vpon his stumpes. (Child 1882–98: 3:313)

This does not reach the artistic heights of "Sir Patrick Spens," but the concluding stanza is pleasing and repeatable and expresses so simple a belief in God and a hope for a peaceable kingdom on earth. Like hymns and memorable biblical verses, these lines from ballads connect at once with my aesthetic sense and my worldview.

But the men whose lives and work have dominated my scholarly research show more explicit connections to my world, though separated by time and location. They, like me, have focused on vernacular poetry, though that poetry, read, has seldom been predominant in my efforts to understand the lives they lived. Robert Burns, Scotland's national poet, would be my primary exhibit. I was led to his life and work by the folksongs, the vernacular poetry he had edited, rewritten, sometimes remembered, much of which was published in the *Scots Musical Museum*. Yet those folksongs actually reveal little about his lived reality. Biographical facts and his more narrative poetry, though, suggest various ways in which Burns's life and my own have some points of connection.

Burns was born in 1759 to an older father who, like my own parents, valued education and secured for his son as much as he could afford. Burns acquired more through reading and study of English and Scottish literature and history. As a young man, Burns was punished by the Presbyterian Church as a fornicator, suggesting the role of the church in social control of relatively small, homogeneous communities where everyone might know exactly what a person was up to. Of course the public rebuke and display in church on the cutty stool did not stop Burns from fathering a number of children by numerous women over the course of his life (he died in 1796). I would have been surprised at the role of the church and the power of the church session if I had not actually run across parallel situations among transplanted Presbyterians in the United States when I was a graduate student. I had focused on ministers and sessions (governing boards) in late eighteenth and early nineteenth century western Pennsylvania, reading their written records preserved at Philadelphia's Presbyterian Historical Society. The session had enormous control at the time, overseeing not only the church but the community. Membership in the church itself was serious business and joining quite explicitly exposed people to judgment—public criticism and punishment were especially prominent for fornication and immorality, excessive drinking, various violations of accepted behavior, and even the practice of witchcraft! I thought then that I was glad such ecclesiastical control was of the past. But this research made me cognizant of the typicality of Burns's experience, something that he seemed to put behind him as he lived his life. He did just what he wanted, the church be damned. Still, he had a weapon to use in getting back at the church—his own poetry. "Holy Willie's Prayer" takes aim at Willie's hypocritical behavior, hiding behind his predestination as one of the elect. I have always thought that it was amazingly effective, at least from a sociological perspective, if not from the poetic point of view. The poem was not a direct response to his own experience but to an occurrence that happened to a friend of his, suggesting how frequent unmarried pregnancies were in the pre–birth control days. Yet it might be read implicitly as Burns's response to his earlier censure. It begins with the acknowledgment of predestination:

O THOU that in the heavens does dwell!
Wha, as it pleases best thysel,
Sends ane to heaven and ten to h-ll,
   A' for thy glory!
And no for ony gude or ill
   They've done before thee.—(Kinsley 1968: 1:74)

Burns uses a wonderful verse form, the so-called Standard Habbie, and has "Holy Willie" describe his own position:

Yet I am here, a chosen sample,
To shew thy grace is great and ample:
I'm here, a pillar o' thy temple
   Strong as a rock,
A guide, a ruler and example
   To a' thy flock.—(Kinsley 1968: 1:75)

While of the elect, already predestined to find his way to heaven, Willie openly admits that he has done things that he should not have done:

But yet—O L——d—confess I must—
At times I'm fash'd wi' fleshly lust;
And sometimes too, in worldly trust
   Vile Self gets in;
But thou remembers we are dust,
   Defil'd wi sin.—(Kinsley 1968: 1:76)

Willie admits to fornication, to being *fou* (drunk), but turns his attention to others whose "sins" seem less pronounced than his own and urges the Lord's vengeance on them. The conclusion of the "prayer" asks for a blessing:

But L——d, remember me and mine
Wi' mercies temporal and divine!
That I for grace and gear may shine,
   Excell'd by nane!
And a' the glory shall be thine!
   Amen! Amen! (Kinsley 1968: 1:78)

Burns's treatment here of predestination in its extreme form, the exclusion of good works as a mechanism for salvation, may have prefigured James Hogg's devastating treatment in *The Private Memoirs and Confessions of a Justified Sinner* (1824).

Burns took a different approach to religion in "The Cotter's Saturday Night," an account of a poor cotter (small farmer) awaiting the return home of his children, all working elsewhere, to share Saturday evening's meal and family worship, once a regular part of the weekly round of practices and something that my great-grandmother Thompson fostered as well. Such worship reminded the children "to obey," to do their work well, not to joke and play, to fear the Lord and avoid "temptation's path" to "gang astray." After a simple meal—"Scotia's food"—the father brings out the "big *ha'Bible*" which had once belonged to his own Father, proclaiming with "solemn air" "*And let us worship God!*"

> They chant their artless notes in simple guise;
>   They tune their hearts, by far the noblest aim:
> Perhaps *Dundee's* wild-warbling measures rise,
>   Or plaintive *Martyrs,* worthy of the name;
> Or noble *Elgin* beets the heaven-ward flame,
>   The sweetest far of Scotia's holy lays:
> Compar'd with these, *Italian trills* are tame;
>   The tickl'd ears no heart-felt raptures raise;
>   Nae unison hae they, with our Creator's praise.
>
> The priest-like Father reads the sacred page,
>   How *Abram* was the Friend of God on high;
> Or, *Moses* bade eternal warfare wage,
>   With *Amalek's* ungracious progeny;
> Or how the *royal Bard* did groaning lye,
>   Beneath the stroke of Heaven's avenging ire;
> Or *Job's* pathetic plaint, and wailing cry;
>   Or rapt *Isiah's* wild, seraphic fire;
> Or other *Holy Seers* that tune the *sacred lyre.* (Kinsley 1968: 1:149)

These stanzas show Burns's deep knowledge of the religious currents of Presbyterianism in eighteenth-century Scotland—the mention of well-known tune names, the references to biblical characters. And as the children go to bed or return to their places of work, the "Parent-pair their *secret homage* pay," requesting that the Heavenly Father—he who can stop the clamor of the ravens and make the lily bloom—provide for their children, "But chiefly, in their hearts with *Grace divine* preside." Leaving the couthy environment, the poet perhaps, standing back proclaims:

> From Scenes like these, old Scotia's grandeur springs, That makes her lov'd at home, rever'd abroad: Princes and lords are but the breath of kings, "An honest man's the noble work of God." (Kinsley 1968: 1:151)

I love this poem, have always been pulled in by its honesty as well as its simplicity, and on some level have wished that I had grown up in an environment where such family worship in the home occurred. It describes and praises. And it contrasts so definitely with "Holy Willie's Prayer," both written in the same year. Here I think we see multiple views of the church, the Presbyterianism that both Burns and I inherited, and it is hard, really, to reconcile such opposite perspectives. Burns's poetry and songs offer a range of perspectives, only a few of which resonate with the church. Yet he probably knew more of the intricacies of belief and practice than I ever acquired. Through his poetry, excerpted from his own life and many of his poetic works, I can sense a man responding to the worldview that he inherited. Witness three stanzas from the Ninetieth Psalm, a beginning of a metrical treatment so common in eighteenth- and nineteenth-century Scotland in a sacred use of the 4 3 4 3 scanning pattern used in many ballads:

> O Thou, the first, the greatest friend
>   Of all the human race!
> Whose strong right hand has ever been
>   Their stay and dwelling-place!
>
> Before the mountains heav'd their heads
>   Beneath Thy forming hand,
> Before this ponderous globe itself
>   Arose at Thy command:

That Pow'r which rais'd and still upholds
    This universal frame,
From countless, unbeginning time
    Was ever still the same.

Or we might look at several of the blessings that Burns wrote, perhaps similar to the ones that the cotter used during the Saturday night worship service and that I taught my own children when they were young. Thus Burns and his religiosity became parts of our daily life:

O, Thou, who kindly dost provide
    For every creature's want!
We bless thee, God of nature wide,
    For all thy goodness lent:
And, if it please thee heavenly guide,
    May never worse be sent;
But whether granted or denied,
    Lord bless us with content!
      Amen!!! (Kinsley 1968: 1:475)

Some have meat and cannot eat,
  Some can not eat that want it:
But we have meat and we can eat,
  Sae let the Lord be thankit.

    [Some hae meat and canna eat,
And some wad eat that want it;
But we hae meat, and we can eat,
    And sae the Lord be thankit.] (Kinsley 1968: 2:820 and
      traditional)

Yet much of Burns most acclaimed poetry deals not with Presbyterianism—either the good or the bad of it—but rather with the valorizing of traditional culture, an alternate world, including even a belief in witches in "Tam o' Shanter." Taken together, then, his work presents a varied perspective on the cultural climate of his time. It was this traditional aspect of Burns that led me to him initially: he was a poet and song-wright and embedded aspects of vernacular, traditional culture into his poetry. Because as a man he was amazingly charismatic, he was also made a part of traditional culture—through narratives told as well as through a calendar custom, the Burns Supper. None of these things have to do with Presbyterianism or the church, though some of his poetry does. And in some ways I believe that these expressions and descriptions of religion solidified my interest in him because they provided me with a connection and opened up for me something that hinted at the ethnographic reality of his world—albeit from a male perspective.

When I was studying and writing *Burns and Tradition*, however, I was not myself in a particularly religious frame of mind. I did not go to church. When my parents would ask me why—or ask for some kind of explanation that would make sense for them of what I was doing or not doing as the case may be—I would proclaim that I believed in the church spiritual, but not the church political. I had seen petty politics at work, had seen how it affected my father and thus my natal family. Of course, this was really human nature at work; still it had disgusted me, a response not dissimilar to Burns's in "Holy Willie's Prayer" and no doubt one of the reasons I so appreciated that poem. Over time, with perhaps a degree of maturity, I realized that I needed the church, if not the church of my childhood then a church. When I was a freshman in college, our choirmaster had persuaded several of us to sing in the boy choir at the Episcopal Church: in a bit of "sacred" deception we would go to the balcony and meet the boys there after they had processed. This was my first foray outside of Presbyterianism: I was taken by the liturgical tradition, with the Book of Common Prayer, with the pattern of worship. Forever after—except when I am in Edinburgh—I have gone to an Episcopal church, though I miss the democratic structure of the Presbyterian church. And I have continued to feel a connection with eighteenth- and nineteenth-century Scots whose work and lives have been my focus at least in part because something about their worlds seems to click with my natal habitus.

When I began to study the ballad collecting work of William Motherwell, I suspect that I just assumed there would be at base a commonality. He was, after all, Scottish and I presumed that he too was Presbyterian. Even as a graduate student I had been attracted to the introduction of his 1827 edition, *Minstrelsy: Ancient and Modern*. There he had offered an *avant la lettre* description of oral formulaic composition, a theory of ballad origins suggesting that a singer, for example, would hold in his or her memory not a word for word song, but an outline. In performance it could be filled in and out with learned tropes or commonplaces—like the ones I mentioned earlier in Child 58 and 162. Motherwell too was from the west of Scotland, Paisley and Glasgow, not far from Burns's birthplace in Ayr, though slightly later in time: 1797–1835. Again, though, it was not really Motherwell's collecting and editing of balladry that connected with the church, but rather his lived experiences and those of some of his friends, even those who helped him provide tunes for the ballads in his *Minstrelsy*. Andrew Blaikie was a precentor at the Paisley Abbey Church as well as session clerk; R. A. Smith, whom Motherwell knew in Paisley, ultimately became the music director, the choir master at St. George's Edinburgh. Smith's own settings of the metrical psalms can be found in *The Scottish Psalter*. He was also a fabricator of traditional tunes. In other words, Motherwell was definitely connected with individuals who were a part of the church.

Politically, late in life as the editor of the *Glasgow Courier*, Motherwell wrote about the Irish Catholic question; individually, he joined and became a functionary in the Orange Society. Put simply, he was against tolerance for the Irish Catholics who had emigrated to Scotland, in particular Glasgow, his city. They were not Scots; "they represented a 'hypothetical' dilution of ethnicity, of Scottishness, as well as a putative dilution of religion, the established church" (Brown 2001: 49). Catholicism was anti-Scotland; thus Motherwell's actions link religion to the nation, Presbyterianism to Scotland.

Most of Motherwell's life, however, had been spent in Paisley. As a young man he had recorded in a commonplace book that religion, philosophy, and literature were life's lasting pleasures. Perhaps by religion he meant professing certain beliefs and attending church. Surely religion and the church were a part of his lived reality. At least once in 1818 he went from Paisley to Glasgow to hear Thomas Chalmers, a leading churchman of the nineteenth century who became a leader of the Free Church after the Disruption of 1843. When Motherwell heard him, Chalmers was at the Tron Church and well known for amazing (and very long!) sermons. Perhaps the Glasgow experience had stimulated Chalmers's extreme concern for the urban poor and disadvantaged; he sought ultimately to develop small parish contexts where all could be educated and cared for—and perhaps condemned, as Holy Willie had condemned members of his own congregation. Motherwell, whether or not an attender of church, seems not to have been publicly denounced for being an unwed father, which he was, something that Burns had endured.

Both Burns and Motherwell were young men whose forays into vernacular poetry I admired and continue to admire. The more I learned about them as members of society, however, the more I became aware of their beliefs and actions, the more I saw their human "failings." My original feelings of having been connected through our shared Presbyterianism seemed to dissipate, to seem less like glue and more like sociological behaviors that on some level I found distasteful, even if very human. In other words, I began to judge them as individual human beings and to like them less. Perhaps I, too, have played the role of Holy Willie, however attenuated. And surely, in these judgments, I have violated the "Judge not, that ye be not judged" (Matthew 7:1 KJV) that I heard so frequently in my youth.

In truth, of course, we never know another, certainly not those so distanced in time and place; we strive to understand through the materials available. Still, our avenues into any other life are limited: how accurate, for example, is poetry to tell us about a man's beliefs and practices? How useful are commonplace books from youth in revealing someone's true identity? We grasp at bits and pieces of information, hoping to understand more, to know better. Perhaps I have become better, over time, in acquiring information, in building up knowledge and, as I have become older, in allowing the human failings that I once found unacceptable just to be, to exist as part of a cultural context that I can no longer access. And my own experience moving away or out from Presbyterianism has led me to an interest in more general religious expression and behavior. Certainly that has been my experience in studying the work and life of Francis James Child (1825–96). And I have felt more confident in my responses to his life when I began to study it as part of a much larger study of the making of his lifelong work, *The English and Scottish Popular Ballads* (1882–98), a classic edition of 305 ballads in as many versions as Child could locate through manuscripts, printed books and magazines, and broadsides as well as from oral tradition. This work has been central to my study of balladry, my attempts to understand the intellectual history of this vernacular material. I did not leave Scotland or religion completely in working on *The English and Scottish Popular Ballads*, produced by a Harvard English professor, because some of his primary predecessors like Motherwell, whose manuscript was essential to Child's work, and subsequent correspondents and collaborators were Scottish. One of them, the Scottish legal clerk William Macmath, helped to tilt Child's coverage to Scotland.

The data for my history of *The English and Scottish Popular Ballads* came largely from letters, especially ones that Child received from British and continental scholars and enthusiasts. While he was the primary editor, charting the path his work would take, he relied on his correspondents for ideas, for materials (texts especially), for advice, and even for discovery. In that way his work was genuinely collaborative and his research technique was epistolary. For him, the discovery and publication of the texts of 305 ballads was primary, though he would have liked to explore the larger history of the ballad as a vernacular form. As a step toward that he noted parallel texts in cognate language traditions and benefited from correspondence with scholars likewise studying national literatures and the vernacular component. He did not live long enough to publish a revised second edition or even to formulate an introductory explanation of the criteria that he used to select texts for inclusion. That has been left for subsequent scholars, who have sifted through the abundance of manuscript documents organized by his literary executor, George Lyman Kittredge, and now housed at Harvard's Houghton Library, in addition to caches of letters elsewhere, most especially at the Hornel Library, Kirkcudbright, Scotland. This consists of the trove of carefully organized and preserved materials that reflect all the work undertaken by Macmath on Child's behalf in addition to all the letters he received from Child. Going through the massive manuscript and published work led me to suggest Child's unstated criteria for selecting ballads for inclusion: "great age, initial wholeness, traditionality, and mutability" (Brown 2011: 235), but together these qualities are far from definitive.

No doubt, looking back over my work, I am aware of my tendency to view the figures/men I have studied as all knowing, bigger than life and their works as extraordinary. All the five volumes and multiple versions of 305 ballads in *The English and Scottish Popular Ballads* represent an amazing feat—even with all its limitations. Almost from the beginning some have called it a canon. That it is not. But it is what Child sought for it to be—a critical edition, using all available sources in the nineteenth century yet failing to delimit the criteria and characteristics or to articulate his ideas about origins or mechanisms of transmission.

As I have said, the bulk of the data for my work on Child involved letters, especially letters that he received but also letters he sent. While the primary content of the epistolary data involved work on the ballads, the letters sometimes contain references to his life and beliefs, especially when he was writing to friends away from Cambridge. I began to note recurrent events and thoughts about his family, his children and their animals, meetings with colleagues, his dislike of marking themes, the family's health, his friends, his passion for roses, and even politics. Sometimes only a line or two, a brief thought, would depart from the project at hand. But other letters were multifaceted, touching on many subjects. Published collections of letters to James Russell Lowell and Emily Tuckerman provided me with something that I believe is necessary: more knowledge of past figures and present acquaintances. The letters, collectively, have given me greater access to the man—Frank Child—and to his lived reality. A number of manuscript collections have expanded my growing understanding, especially letters to friends Charles Eliot Norton and Charles Guild as well as those to his wife, both before and after they wed (particularly collections at the Houghton Library, the Harvard Archives, and the Massachusetts Historical Society).

I brought with me to this exploration of Child's life another kind of connection: we were both academics. I could empathize with some of his experiences and concerns as they have sometimes been mine: poor classes, disagreements with colleagues, the need for books and especially for the always missing intangible—time. I found myself far less judgmental, more accepting; and I liked him in all his humanity.

Child really spent his life at Harvard, in the academy, graduating in the class of 1846, though he had spent his childhood years in Boston, especially in the West End, near the sailing ships that used sails like those his father made. At Harvard he excelled. In one of the speeches that he gave as part of the graduation ceremonies, he identified four possible professions for the graduates, himself included: law, medicine, the church, and education.

> Thus may we be able to preserve for lifetime much of the freshness, the ingenuousness & the hopefulness of youth—to be industrious without becoming mechanical, & enterprising without worldliness, to ennoble small things & to alleviate drudgery by a great purpose[,] to be gentle, but not effeminate, philanthropic without affectation— to keep alive a faith in God, and in man, to unite a genuine patriotism with a true love for the human race (Brown 2011: 16).

In the early years after his graduation, in addition to serving as a tutor, Child may well have spent a year studying theology. He became close friends with one of his classmates, Charles Eliot Norton, whose father Andrews was a Unitarian theologian who was against Calvinism and Trinitarianism (essential beliefs from my natal habitus), suggesting the potential for ideological struggles like the one between Michael Servetus and John Calvin in the sixteenth century (see Goldstone and Goldstone 2002). Child spent many hours at the Norton household and perhaps Andrews's Unitarianism rubbed off on him. He assumed the goodness of all and was concerned for others, throughout his life giving to beggars at home and abroad; seeking to improve the situations of the black Americans in the Freedman's Aid Society; sending blankets for Civil War soldiers; supporting the Sanitary Commission (taking care of wounded soldiers) with performances of his pastiche opera *Il Pesceballo*; and publishing a small book of *War-Songs for Freemen* and sending copies to soldiers. In a word, Child was concerned for others and participated in a variety of philanthropic activities.

Child was outside the Presbyterian world of my habitus. But I too had moved on, at least in part. As I have become older, I have thought more deeply about belief and practice and have perhaps become more tolerant of the variety of religious traditions, as I have sought to piece together a way of life, rooted in belief, that enables me to live what I might describe as a better life. In this context, I have found Child's expressions of religious beliefs and practices appealing; some of them are similar to mine. And each time I noted a saying or an expression or a thought on religion I have felt that I knew him better, understood a bit more about where he was coming from, and was drawn closer to the man. I saw that as a young man he was searching for a full expression of belief and understanding, a process that he continued throughout his life. He had listened to Andrews Norton. When he went to Europe and studied for a term in Göttingen, he attended lectures on early Christian theology and the Bible as well as German literature, Aeschylus, and Roman political antiquities (no doubt in preparation for going to Italy). He wrote friends who were also in Europe what he identified as his "10th epistle to the Berliners" (Brown 2011: 20), perhaps building on his study of the Bible and Saint Paul's letters to various communities among whom he had preached.

Child was skeptical of the Roman Catholic Church, which he found especially in Italy; he thought it was constricting. Yet he noticed the art that decorated the churches, especially the Renaissance buildings. A visit to any church, at least in my experience, awakens some religious feelings. Child noted, of course, the religious subjects and interpretations of the art; this was a far cry from the simplicity of the church buildings that he had known in Cambridge. Some churches and cathedrals like the Pantheon were actually repurposed from pagan origins, suggesting a time depth that his country did not have. And the religious art, the visual expression of materials that he had only read, opened his eyes and mind to another way of worship, another way of knowing—at least implicitly. The twenty-two months in Europe were a kind of postgraduate education and like so much in Child's life gave him a feeling of being uniquely blessed. He wrote to Charles Norton: "I am lost in grateful wonder in some illumined moments in which I see a part of the vast design of the spirit that works alike in things great & small & designs to include me in its foresight & providence" (Brown 2011: 33). Was this not an expression of "predestination"?

As Child later returned to Europe and England and Scotland for his health and for research, he would attend churches, noting the beauty of the music and the prayers though critiquing other qualities. Yet going to churches offered something. Back at Harvard, he may even have taught a course in the Bible—at least one student alluded to having studied it with him.

I have found Child's more personal musings, dropped into letters, more telling of his frame of mind. When Mrs. Lowell (James Russell's wife) died, Child allowed that he was consoled by Lowell's faith, which would see him through. When Lowell himself died, Child wondered if he had been reunited with his wife, saying: "For the chief article of my faith is that there is nothing so good that we can conceive that God will not better it—in due time" (Brown 2011: 62). As he grew older, thoughts of mortality came unbidden. During sleepless nights and when he was awakened by gout, he would pick up Henry Drummond's *The Greatest Thing in the World*, probably led to it by Drummond's having given the recent Lowell Lectures, which Child had given twice, once on ballads. He was especially taken with the exegesis of 1 Corinthians 13 (NRSV) with the poignant passage on love:

> Love is patient; love is kind; love is not envious or boastful or arrogant or rude. It does not insist on its own way; it is not irritable or resentful; it does not rejoice in wrongdoing, but rejoices in the truth. It bears all things, believes all things, hopes all things, endures all things.

What was Child's response? I like to think that Drummond's book was reassuring because it seemed to exemplify the virtues for which Child strove—"patience, kindness, generosity, humility, courtesy, unselfishness, good temper, guilelessness, and sincerity" (Brown 2011: 64). Drummond himself was a Free Church Scottish clergyman interested in the reconciliation of religion and science. Perhaps Child had met him when he gave the Lowell Lectures and decided to read his book. This biblical passage is resonant for me, and I recently was called to read it in a wedding service, where it is often used. I may have been drawn to read Drummond's book myself because it contained the words and thoughts of a Scot and a Presbyterian, although an offshoot branch from "my" Presbyterianism.

Child had never been particularly healthy, always suffering from one ailment or another. He read Drummond toward the end of his life when he knew that death would find him soon. Likewise he wrote of attending an Episcopal funeral for a friend of his son, telling Emily Tuckerman that his only consolation was that "present grief may be reconciled with love" (Brown 2011: 66)—perhaps influenced by Drummond and 1 Corinthians 13. He found the funeral particularly affecting, noting that "thanks are offered for those who have finished their course and rest from their labors" (ibid.); he was definitely thinking of his own mortality too. The words on the tombstone in Stockbridge, Massachusetts, seem appropriate:

> what doth the Lord require of thee, but to do justly, and to love mercy, and to walk humbly with thy God? (Micah 6:8 KJV)

Child's few reflections provide me with a kind of solace that comes from knowing that my own thoughts and even experiences were shared by him—and have been shared, of course, by many. Of all the men on whom I have worked, his life and work have touched me more deeply than have those of the others—as exemplary in their own days and times as they were. Still, I have focused on men and their work.

Like the church of my grandparents and parents, their worlds were filled implicitly with gender stereotypes of a kind only moderately changed when I was born. I was not myself explicitly aware of these stereotypical assumptions until I was hired as a faculty member; and my early days in the academy were filled with political conflicts, gender inflected. As I became more cognizant of the effects of stereotypes on women and various minorities, I worked for Affirmative Action and later directed the Women's Studies Program. I sought, personally, to set an example, largely rejecting any stereotypical assumptions. Yet in my research on the past I have focused on men because they were the persons of record who asked questions that interested me. I have always searched to know about the women in their lives, even though their stories were largely invisible, as victims of a world different from the equality I would prefer. My own study of the past has been somewhat out of sync with the contemporary fieldwork focus. I have, whatever else, chosen to work on what interests me rather than adopting more fashionable and contemporary approaches.

I began these thoughts with my baptism, with natal family, with the Presbyterian Scottish heritage that seemed to pervade my life—at least for the first number of years. This habitus has actually served me well; it has not constrained me but rather given me a place from which to begin the process of living a life, enabling me to recognize the value of religious belief and to see it working not only in my life but in the lives of those whom I have studied. The choice of studying in Scotland, to focus on Scottish poets and ballad and folksong enthusiasts, or to examine those who also have used the Scottish materials as primary in their own works—as Child did—seems quite natural to me. Perhaps too their various religious responses and reactions have been a part, however limited, of my own explorations of religion, of beliefs and practices.

Finally, a great deal more goes into the academic study of a subject than initial attraction and ongoing personal connections with those materials. Yet I would maintain that those connections enriched my understanding of these men and the contexts in which they lived. I have seen religious responses as a special kind of key to understanding the men and their works while at the same time calling me to interrogate my own religious situation. I might even maintain that their religious thoughts have stimulated my own unconscious thoughts about religion. But I stand at the end of a process of study that began over fifty years ago, so these musings may only be my own attempt to make sense of what I have done with some of my time: among everything else, I have focused on a vernacular poetic form and been fascinated by attempts to define and delimit it, to collect it, to publish it. I have been extremely interested in the intellectual history of the study, seeking to put the men and their work that I have studied into their own societal contexts but also to explore how they fit in with others who were working at similar times, if not in the same places. I have sought to reveal a vibrant aspect of cultural traditions, often overlooked. Like Child, I cannot write an intellectual history of the poetic form, the ballad, but I see, as he surely did as well, some of the steps that have been taken to understand what the ballad is, where it may have come from, and how it lives and continues to thrive (see Brown 2007, 2006).

All our lives are a jumble of influences and false steps as we seek to make a living, raise families, and interact with friends and colleagues. In the final analysis, beliefs and practices, however vague, have come to mean more to me personally as I always negotiate how to live. And I am content to perceive that some of what I have done may very well have been predestined, that I am a product of a Presbyterian habitus, and that, finally, it has served me well.

WORKS CITED

Bourdieu, Pierre. 1997. *Outline of a Theory of Practice*. Cambridge: Cambridge University Press.

Brown, Mary Ellen. 2011. *Child's Unfinished Masterpiece: The English and Scottish Popular Ballads*. Urbana: University of Illinois Press.

———. 2007. "Balladry: A Vernacular Poetic Resource." In *The Edinburgh History of Scottish Literature*, edited by Murray G. H. Pittock, Ian Brown, Susan Manning, and Thomas Clancy, 1:263–72. 3 vols. Edinburgh: Edinburgh University Press.

———. 2006. "Placed, Replaced, or Misplaced?: The Ballads' Progress." *Eighteenth Century* 47 (2006): 115–29.

———. 2001. *William Motherwell's Cultural Politics 1797–1835*. Lexington: University Press of Kentucky.

———. 1991. "Robert Burns." In *Eighteenth-Century British Poets, Dictionary of Literary Biography*, edited by John Sitter, 33–53. Detroit: A Bruccoli Clark Layman Book/ Gale Research.

———. 1984. *Burns and Tradition*. London: Macmillan/Urbana: University of Illinois Press.

———. 1968. "Folk Elements in Scotch-Irish Presbyterian Communities." *Pennsylvania Folklife* 18 (1968): 21–25.

Child, Francis James. 1882–98. *The English and Scottish Popular Ballads*. 5 vols. Boston: Houghton Mifflin.

Drummond, Henry. *Drummond's Addresses*. New York: Hurst, n.d.

Goldstone, Lawrence, and Nancy Goldstone. 2002. *Out of the Flames*. New York: Broadway Books.

Kinsley, James, ed. 1968. *The Poems and Songs of Robert Burns*. 3 vols. Oxford: Clarendon Press.

Five

MAKING DEAD BONES SING

Practicing Ethnography in the Italian Diaspora

LUISA DEL GIUDICE

> *The dead are not dead,*
> *The dead are never gone:*
> *they are in the shadows.*
> *The dead are not in earth:*
> *they're in the rustling tree,*
> *the groaning wood,*
> *water that runs,*
> *water that sleeps;*
> *they're in the hut, in the crowd,*
> *the dead are not dead.*
>
> —Birago Diop, "Les souffles" (1960)

STATEMENT OF (LIFE) PURPOSE

"The dead are not dead," asserts Senegalese poet and storyteller Birago Diop in "Les Souffles" (1960). This poem inspired Bill Viola's video *Three Women* (2008), which I, in turn, consider an evocative visual meditation on ancestral time. We watch entranced, as three women—in my view representing the three ages of Woman (Maiden, Mother, Crone)—walk toward us in very slow motion, through a veil of water. The first and oldest woman emerges, turns, stretches out her hand toward the younger woman behind her, and pulls her through. Together they turn once more, bringing forth a young girl. Then one by one each returns, receding behind the watery threshold.

The youngest looks toward us one last time, wistful, seemingly reluctant to leave. It is that suspended parting moment and that ambiguous, questioning gaze that best capture my own sense of the dialogic rapport with our past: what do the ancestors want from us as they float in and out of our fluid consciousness?[1] And what do we ask of them? How do we call our ghosts forth toward this side of the watery veil into living memory? How do we make their dead bones sing?

As a practicing folklorist/ethnographer and oral historian, I am keenly aware of the many ways in which ancestral memory is spoken, sung, and embodied by those who carry oral traditions, cultural practices, history, and spiritual knowledge across the generations—sometimes only in the realm of memory. But despite toiling in the discourses of personal memory for decades, I had never given Time (with a capital "T") more careful consideration until I attended the conference of the International Society for the Study of Time, held in the Monteverde cloud forest of Costa Rica, in 2010. That is, I had recorded life histories and cultural practices handed down through the generations but had never engaged with more abstract notions of Time. I began reflecting on the conference theme, "Origins and Futures," specifically on ancestors and descendants. How might our link to our ancestors help us envision, create, and negotiate the future? That meditation on ancestors also merged with earlier writing, "Ethnography and Spiritual Direction: Varieties of Listening" (Del Giudice 2009), a personal reflection on my own evolution as an oral history and oral culture scholar as well as a trained spiritual director[2]—someone, that is, who had practiced a good deal of listening to others and to myself. My writing here is best read in conjunction with that essay as well as with the introduction to this volume. This blended essay engages in a general discussion on ancestry and time, while returning to take a "second look" at, or reflect upon, my own personal and academic engagement with these areas of study.

Origins—all our "in the beginning" stories (personal, scientific, and mythic)—have a special fascination, are symbolically charged, and seem to hold hidden, essential truths about ourselves, our cultural identities, and perhaps our destinies. At least, we imbue them with such primacy and power. The need to know how we got here, who we are, and where we fit into the greater scheme of life appears to be a fundamental human impulse. Romanian ethnologist Gheorgita Geana (2005: 349) reminds us, in fact, that it is foundational for historicity; that the cult of the ancestors is "one of the most elaborated responses to the human perception of being-in-time." A return to origins is a fundamental way in which we narrate and make sense of our lives. Indeed, an inaccessible or broken dialog with our personal and collective past (for example, due to genocide, slavery, or displacement) may compound these traumas in ways that trauma workers and neuroscientists have only recently begun to understand more fully. Sometimes archaeologists or geneticists can identify the bones and help recover such traces and at other times oral historians can give voice to silenced or hidden stories inside those bones. Recent UN legal parameters have even been put in place to ensure this human right to know our past—thanks, in part, to the Argentine Grandmothers of the Desaparecidos, women who had lost sons and daughters to a murderous regime's Dirty War and whose grandchildren had often secretly been given over to the very members of that military. All traces of such adoptions had been hidden, until genetic testing made it scientifically possible to complete some shocking puzzles of identity often aided by the Grandmothers' own family narratives.

We are all engaged, with greater or lesser degrees of urgency, in the task of knowing ourselves. As an ethnographer, part of that self-knowing for me has involved knowing my own cultural heritage as it intersects personal and family history. Through bibliographic investigation related to these topics, as well as fieldwork with first-person oral testimonies, I have attempted to arrive at what nonetheless remain only partial and incomplete narratives. For me, this process of cultural knowing has been an intensely personal project of self-knowing, besides a professional vocation. In fact I have been haunted by the ancestors all my life, as I collected their faded pictures, listened for their voices, and tried to understand what they were saying by piecing together immigrant lives ruptured by displacement, including my own triangulated one involving Italy, Toronto, and Los Angeles. Italian migrants who left small villages in the immediate postwar years also left behind communal life and shared identities, suffering geographic as well as psychic displacement. Their descendants inherit this legacy. In small groups, they once told stories, sang songs, shared reflections on passing time. Such occasions and places for shared cultural expression in intimate settings underwent significant disruption, and that heritage became less readily accessible to subsequent generations. Further, many who carried much of that information have passed, so we are left trying to piece together a coherent understanding of what they themselves often preserved only as

FIGURE 5.1 *(top)* My paternal grandfather, Giovanni Del Giudice, and grandmother, Luisa Palmacci Del Giudice.

FIGURE 5.2 *(left)* My mother's cousin, Vetulia Caracuzzo.

FIGURE 5.3 *(right)* Wedding photo of my parents (Liliana Caracuzzo and Alberto Del Giudice) on the front steps of the cathedral of Terracina.

FIGURE 5.4 *(above)* My paternal great-aunt, Luigina Del Giudice, faith healer, in her shop in the medieval quarter of Terracina in the mid-1980s.

FIGURE 5.5 *(right)* Interviewing my maternal uncle, painter Mario Caracuzzo (January 5, 1917–December 7, 2012).

FIGURE 5.6 Playing the *tamburello* (frame drum) in the music of neo-*tarantismo*, the *pizzica* at the Italian Cultural Institute in Los Angeles (with Luigi Chiriatti, Kedron Parker, Lorenzo Buhne) in October, 2000.

faded memory. In my case, I have specifically focused on the cultural life of peasant Italy before World War II, a cataclysmic event and a watershed for traditional societies throughout Italy, as well as the transformations of that culture in the postmigration lives of that generation and its descendants.

My practice of ethnography has to some degree become an act of conjuring those ancestors for myself on this far Pacific shore, in Los Angeles, where I have resided since 1981. It has been through intense acts of remembering, research, and embodiment that I have recovered a sense of belonging, a sense that I have found them and have been found by them. My mother has many times narrated a five decade–long recurring (postmigration) dream of having lost a small child on the streets of Terracina, frantically knocking on neighbors' doors, asking if anyone had seen her, and waking in a state of deep agitation. The lost child, I presume, is my mother anxiously trying to get her bearings. Apparently, after all these years as a diaspora Italian in Toronto, finding a sense of place and belonging, is a task that has eluded her, because the lost child continues to inhabit her dream life. In some curious way I seem to have inherited my mother's dream (and

FIGURE 5.7 Foraging for wild food (snails), part of a Slow Food program that I organized in 2001.

anxiety) regarding a sense of place. I too became a wandering lost child, knocking on doors, trying to find my way home. Given new research on the epigenetic influence of trauma on children and grandchildren, this may not be altogether merely imagined or intuited.[3]

To find that place in time, I have engaged in reintegrating fragmented memorial bits (a phrase or name here, a personal anecdote or village event there) into a personally meaningful narrative, while also conducting broader ethnographic research in Italy and the diaspora. I began formally listening to this past as a graduate student, beginning in the mid-1980s while at the University California, Los Angeles, through a dissertation on folksongs. This listening project opened an "inner ear" whereby I began reconciling on many fronts,[4] my own as well as a collective diasporic past. And I have been honing those listening skills in dialog with the known, imagined, and reconstructed past ever since.

My goal was to personally transform that past into lived memory and sometimes embodied practice, by singing the songs, playing the instruments, dancing the dances, foraging for wild foods, preserving and cooking them, enacting ritual cycles of fasting/feasting, adorning the body, and so forth. By directly experiencing, at times reclaiming, traditional practices, I hoped to access broader cultural truths that might illuminate deeper mind/body consciousness. A direct experience of ethnic practices such as these, as well as research and writing about them, literally and metaphorically helped me inhabit my life more fully, integrate worlds of knowing and self-knowing, and affect transformation in my private and academic life.

FIGURE 5.8 I have worn a *cornetto* (small horn), a talisman against the evil eye and marker of southern Italian identity, around my neck for over a decade. I have recently added this gold rosary as well.

I was especially interested in the deepest sort of knowing, which I describe as "spiritual archaeology," much of it specifically through women: family ancestors as faith healers, ballad singers in Brallo (Pavia), musical genres such as lullabies, and the dance ritual of the spider's bite in the Salentine folk revival movement known as neo-*tarantismo*, as well as communal rituals of abundance and of hospitality in the St. Joseph's food altar tradition (for example, Del Giudice 2001, 2010, 2014b). The cultural practices in which I felt most invested were not, strictly speaking, those from my own Lazio regional heritage but meandered throughout northern, central, and southern Italy as well as its diasporas. I approached these cultural practices as a participant-observer through fieldwork, through bibliographic and archival research, and through deeply incorporating them into my own personal and family life, allowing them to sink deeply into my psyche. I have shared my gleaned learning with others in the academy and the public sector, in publications, recordings, conferences, and public programs (such as conferences and festivals of the Italian Oral History Institute [IOHI]). Some of this activity has also become the basis of my social activism (for example, the Watts Towers Common Ground Initiative: Del Giudice 2014c).

In short, I searched for a usable past that might help me understand and navigate life as a first-generation transnational diasporic Italian. I perceived the urgency of sharing this process with my cohort of Italian migrants, especially those with similar class and ethnic experiences. I firmly believed that a collective ancestral wisdom deeply rooted in lived lives, in a historic thread that had withstood the test of time, might better guide us all, even as we adjusted it for our own times, geographies, and personal trajectories. Indeed, throughout these many years of research, each new project seemed to illuminate specific life experiences for me: research on lullabies helped me navigate motherhood (including its dark patches); tragic ballads, erotic metaphor, and the spider dance clarified a gendered perspective on sexuality and marriage; gastronomic utopias instead brilliantly illuminated a class history of hunger, deeply embedded in various ritual food practices; a discovery of female faith healers instead helped me recover my own family spiritual lineage (and perhaps calling).

Indeed it seemed that the cultural history of my own family and ethnic tribe had profoundly shaped my worldview in negative and positive ways. It was my task to understand these origins and root causes, evaluating what to keep and carry forward and what instead to discard. By no means did I deem all of it worthy of transmission, but all of it was nonetheless valuable to perceiving the cultural lights and the cultural shadows. For example, Roman Catholicism might have been expected to determine my sense of the sacred, but it did not. A powerful patriarch dominated my family of four sisters, as well as my benignly passive mother, making me acutely aware of the male-worshipping culture of Italians, which I firmly rejected. How could I, as a feminist, not form a front of resistance against cultural and religious patriarchies in my life? Could I compound this cultural tradition by subscribing to an equally unacceptable (and for a woman self-destructive) patriarchal Catholicism, which placed a Supreme Male God (a Father *and* Son!) on an altar, all managed by a pope and an all-male, sexist hierarchy? (I did, though, retain Mary as a representation of the Nurturing Mother in my personal iconography of the Female Divine.) Of the four sisters, I challenged the hardest, denounced the loudest, and abandoned most completely. (I was, by the way, also the only one not to have married an Italian.) My own variety of Christian practice instead focused on what I consider to be a decidedly female approach to the divine, focused on the domestic, on food, on woman-centered practices (see Sered 1994; Bynum 1987).[5] My sense of the sacred, in other words, focuses on "god as hospitality," on gathering family and community around a table (often my own), on celebratory feasting, on cultural practices of redistributing wealth as food (such as St. Joseph's Tables), and on food justice (Del Giudice 2014b). These were activities in which women seemed to be invested (or to which they had been assigned), at which they excelled in most cultures across time and geography. They created networks of shared food and love at a capillary community level, which frequently provided opportunities for leadership extending from those intimate "home places" out into the larger world (Belenky, Bond, and Weinstock 1997).

My acts of deep listening in the Italian diaspora have presented their own challenges for someone removed from family of origin in Toronto and from my birthplace in Italy. This physical separation has likely heightened the need to create (sometimes virtual) communities of belonging as well as an awareness of my own personal responsibility in the chain of cultural transmission. That is, I needed to remember, preserve, enact; and I needed to keep returning, whatever the costs, if any of this heritage was to live in and through me. These multiple dislocations have also contributed to an existential state of being perpetually "between and betwixt" (see Magliocco, this volume), common to biangulations and triangulations (see Del Giudice 2014a) as well as determining the many bridging roles that I would play in life. Being multicentered has made me resistant to boundaries, curious about seeing the other side of the wall, eager to break it down and connect. I have come to embrace these intersections as liberating and expansive and this "space between" as one of heightened creativity. This existential state creates a buffer zone where it is easier to see clearly, evaluate, compare, decide what to keep and what to discard, and perhaps how to recombine these and those cultural forms for a particular purpose.

This space of heightened self-reflection, where boundaries, identities, and temporalities merge, has also helped me see the "shadow" sides of my own culture, that is, the areas that might require healing and integration, as we sort ourselves out from one generation to the next. Historic traumas may leave their legacies in individual bodies and psyches (as in my mother's dream), as well as in collective cultural neuroses and hauntings (see Stuhmiller 2003). In memory work (such as recording life and cultural histories) the interviewee's desire to forget sometimes trumps the researcher's desire to remember. And sometimes witnessing trauma becomes hazardous to the listener's emotional and physical health. But remember and witness we must.

For instance, as I happened upon one Italian tradition after another, it seemed to me that the collective trauma of hunger had been insufficiently acknowledged, even as it continued to inform many foodways as well as personal and folk narratives among diaspora Italians. The centuries-long search for a mythic place, Il Paese di Cuccagna (the Land of Cockaigne), a gastronomic utopia where rivers ran with wine, mountains were made of cheese, and no one went hungry, became conflated with America for immigrants. In America they indeed conquered hunger but not the fear of hunger and hence frequently indulged in excess, in the hoarding of food in wine cellars, kitchens, and freezers, in the obsessive search for abundance. But the memory of hunger also led to practices of radical hospitality and feeding of the poor (such as in St. Joseph's Day Tables), expressing the idea that everyone—even the strangers among us—must receive hospitality (see Del Giudice 2010).

I have more recently become aware of the disorders that can afflict those engaged in the very projects of memorializing ancestors, including ethnographers, archivists, personal and family historians, and other first-hand collectors. That is, the accumulation of words, images, sounds, artifacts, and memorabilia can become obsessive and oppressive, resulting in physical and mental clutter. The stuff of the past can literally overwhelm our closets and our psychic space (compare Foer 2002). I can attest from personal experience that such deliberate and constant attentiveness is exhausting and can become a psychological burden. How much time and effort, I ask myself, ought anyone spend in this seemingly evanescent enterprise of living in the remembered and even partly embodied past, simultaneously recording and analyzing it, while making space for the emergent present?

For those engaged in writing the history of a people largely without a written history (Italian peasants and their descendants), the project is also somewhat fugitive. These ancestors leave scant material or oral culture behind and can no longer speak into a recording device, so their lives remain sketchy at best. We may only possess a grandmother's rosary beads, another's prayer book, a great-aunt's favorite recipe, one single anecdote about a grandfather, to illuminate an entire life. The rest we must piece together with the help of others' testimonies. But often we are unable to gain information about their specific lives and find only general information about a cohort, a group, a village with whom they shared similar family, regional, or occupational experiences. We reconstruct wider historic and cultural contexts, attempting to understand them by studying their built domestic environments, occupational technologies, and oral traditions, as transmitted through the generations. How I wish I had their direct oral memoirs to give me greater insight into their actual lives, just as my husband enjoys written memoirs from ancestors on both sides of his family.

I have done my best to understand key aspects of their regional ethnicity and class experience, while creating and sharing narratives in academic and public settings. I have taught Italian oral traditions within Italian literature departments, but it has not been easy to create compelling reasons to include oral culture within literary paradigms, even if I did focus on song, narrative, proverb, and other genres that might generally be more acceptable therein (rather than material culture or belief). Building appreciation for such cultural expressions, often class-specific, has been a real challenge. Often these genres are not considered worthy of serious study and are viewed as out of place within literary studies. Of course, this has not been my challenge alone, and it has not been limited to Italian folklife studies and oral history. There continue to be vast swaths of the world's populations that remain "silent" and "invisible," for which a public space cannot be found—although I agree with Arundhati Roy: "There's really no such thing as the voiceless. There are only the deliberately silenced, or the preferably unheard" (http://sydney.edu.au/news/84.html?newsstoryid=279). We must lend them our voices; better yet, it is our responsibility to create the venues and means by which the submerged and silenced may speak for themselves. My own self-appointed task has been to speak these silent ancestors into the future, trusting that this effort of remembering will be of use to our descendants, even if we cannot know for whom and when. It is my way of keeping faith with my ancestors while perhaps encouraging those who come after to do likewise.

But why do we invoke these voices of the past? Anthropologist Eric Gable (1996: 104) reminds us: "Ancestors, after all, are mute and intangible. Somebody has to want to give them voice, or embody them." We engage them for a variety of reasons in our own private and collective history-making: to reconnect with the "earth that knows our name" (to paraphrase the title of an exceptional book on the importance of gardens in immigrant cultures: Klindienst 2006); to learn vital information for living our present; to find moral guidance. In many parts of Africa where ancestor cults are common, ancestors are sometimes invoked to resolve land disputes in a sort of tribunal managed by the living elders speaking for the ancestors. The past, as oral historians such as Alessandro Portelli (for example, 2007) tell us, is firmly rooted in the present. The question is: why do we remember, forget, or misremember what we do, as subjective memory and history interplay? Why do we choose specific stories to tell? To a large degree, we create our own past. Michael Lambek (2015: 93) states: "spirits are vehicles for memory rather than the frozen remnants of memory." Or put more cynically perhaps: "We arouse and arrange our memories to suit our psychic needs" (Kammen 1991: 9).

How do we embody these ancestors, spirits, avatars (that is, gods in earthly guise)? In our cultural practices, the language we speak, the gods we worship; in the constructed and natural landscape; in the archaeological remains of the past. Societies develop cultural mnemonics, techniques for remembering (for example, genealogical charts in Japanese shrines, recitations of the ancestors and their deeds in African oral epic, photo galleries in our living rooms, written memoirs). We commemorate them in public places of remembrance (such as gravesites and monuments); invoke them in seasonal rituals (for example, the Mexican Day of the Dead and Memorial Day); or install them on home altars. They communicate in rituals of possession and ecstatic dance, in shamanic journeys, in dreams—all those "thin places," as the Irish call such "portals for the passage of the dead to and from our world" (Bill Viola, as cited at https://sunwalked.wordpress.com /2007/09/21/%E2%80%9Cthe-self-is-an-ocean-without-a-shore-bill-viola).

But ancestors, of course, are also inherited in our very bones, in our gene pool. That is, we physically embody them: a father's nose, a mother's anxious disposition, a grandmother's mystical tendencies. DNA testing is advancing at a staggering pace, helping us to access recent and remote ancestors. These new technologies show great promise, for example, in forensic science and law and in medicine (helping to identify genetic predisposition to disease), but anthropologists also warn of the dangers of such reductionism with regard to complex phenomena such as cultural identity and ethnohistory. Many disciplines are now devoted to this area of overlay between culture and genetics (such as neuroanthropology, neuroculture, and behavioral genetics). Some are making bold and even counterintuitive claims: for example, Ernest Rossi's *Psychobiology of Gene Expression* posits that humans can remake their own genetic composition through their own thoughts and actions. The hypothesis that we can actually influence and remake the genes that we pass on to our descendants is mind-boggling to me.

My curiosity nonetheless got the better of me a few years ago when I requested a National Geographic's Genographic Project Geno 2 kit (a variation of other enterprises such as 23 and Me or Ancestry.com) as a Christmas gift and cautiously embarked on that adventure with a mere swab of

FIGURE 5.9 A representation of my mother's paternal grandmother, Giacinta, painted by my mother's half-brother, Mario Caracuzzo, in 1935.

my inner cheek. I learned that I am 55 percent Mediterranean, 23 percent Northern European, and 19 percent Southeast Asian, with a 1.6 percent Neanderthal component. What does this mean, and what impact does this knowledge have on my own understanding of my identity and narrative of ancestry? I am not quite sure except that it does confirm the Mediterranean identity in which I feel most invested. But while it tells me something about my matrilineal genetic pool, it will take another mouth swab from one of my now-deceased father's brothers (and several hundred dollars) to complete the picture. Frankly, I don't really feel compelled to know more. The timescale is so vast and so remote that it seems to have little to narrate about ancestors linked through human memory.

Our ancestors therefore are linked to us genetically; they influence us through many historical legacies (including class struggle and migrations);

they leave traces in our oral/aural cultural inheritance (such as folksongs, tales, and proverbs); and they hand down forms of material cultural and ritual practices to us as well—often with the express intent of passing on important skills, historic lessons, and moral truths.[6] I have spent most of my professional energies trying to record and decipher them. As a result, ancestors' voices seem to speak more clearly now, as they inhabit many parts of my life. I have also become more acutely aware of my own role and responsibilities as cultural "medium," as I imagine the ancestors speaking through me (or I ventriloquizing them). As Lambek (1981: 78), a scholar of trance in Mayotte ritual, simply states, "to become possessed is to open new channels of communication." But there is little "shamanic" about this process, in my case. It is to a large degree an imaginative act. The more I learn, the more confident I feel about speaking my ancestors' truths in a way that my generation might understand. It does, though, create a tendency toward hyper-embodiment, symbolic enactment, and more conscious performance and staging of tradition.

As I have stated elsewhere (Del Giudice 2009: 16), recently I began feeling oppressed by these ancestors, by the weight of the past, and by moral obligations to family, class, and culture. How many generations did it take to get past collective traumas literally out of our psyches and our bodies, I wondered? We make peace with our own past as best we can, each of us assessing how much space to allot it in the present. I concluded that perhaps I had repaid my debts and should now be released from ancestor hauntings.

On second thought, today I recognize and accept that there may be one last (and more comprehensive) task for me to accomplish. I must now narrate my own life, both as it does and does not relate to my cultural past. That is, I must write my memoirs—the memoirs I might have wished my ancestors had left behind for my benefit, communicating the inner meanings of their lives. I imagine this process as both a literal and metaphorical clearing out of closets, as I evaluate what goes into the heirloom box and what instead goes into the thrift shop recycling bin. From the bits and pieces of memory, I hope to create a synthesis, a more coherently whole life history. And then, finally, I will travel more lightly, having put the ancestors (in me) to rest.

In the meantime, though, I have found many ways to put them to work in new ways, seeking their guidance and applying their knowledge in the service of a more expansive global consciousness and purpose. Whenever and wherever possible, I engage in social action for the common good,

FIGURE 5.10
My mother in the
same posture over her
needlework taken, in
2013, seventy-eight
years later.

in intercultural, interfaith, interspiritual work, highlighting and using the
best parts of my cultural heritage to do good in the world. For example,
I redirect significant aspects of Italian foodways and cultural history (food
altars, food utopias)—much of it emerging from trauma and displacement—toward food justice and current migration issues (see Del Giudice
2014b). We have much to share with others about these two urgent issues in
contemporary society.

FIGURE 5.11 Our
ancestor Lucy, "Mother
Africa," in the Ethio-
pian Ethnographic
Museum of Addis
Ababa (taken in 2010).

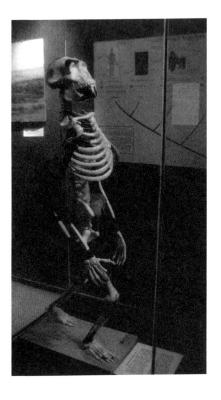

Common ground. There is a poignant scene in the Genographic Project documentary *Human Family Tree* (2009), where New Yorkers who
have undergone DNA testing are placed into groups according to common
genetic heritage and regrouped again according to earlier genetic subgroup-
ings, retracing their global migrations, until in the end all find themselves
standing in the same circle, literally on the same patch of ground. That is,
each and every one returns to Mother Africa, where it all started. On the
one hand, such genetic migratory maps offer a stunning visual reminder
of humanity's millennial and incessant global migrations. With rare exceptions (southern African Bushmen),[7] every human ancestor has experienced
migration somewhere along the line. Even though we relish the thought of
being rooted firmly in this place, and belonging here, it is frequently only
a chronologically thin fiction. Such scientific projects also help us understand how race and ethnicity—identities that we cling to so dearly—are
sometimes only a single generation deep.

Therefore, just as the mystical traditions have always maintained (and genetic science has confirmed), we are one family and share a deep ancestry on earth. Take a further step back into cosmological time, and we discover a yet more expansive and mind-bending truth—that all life is made of the very same stuff of the universe: stardust. Brian Swimme, mathematical cosmologist, states it best: "It's really simple. Here's the whole story in one line. This is the greatest discovery of the scientific enterprise: You take hydrogen gas, and you leave it alone, and it turns into rosebushes, giraffes, and humans" (Bridle 2003). If that does not affirm a mystical sense of the ultimate oneness of all life, I don't know what does.

Back to earth. We can engage many discourses of origins (cosmological, theological, genetic, historical, geographic, cultural) to help us understand who we are and also to help us reflect on what we must do to co-create our future. We can imagine that meeting place—the here and now, a sort of temporal ground zero between origins and futures—as a moment of creative possibility from which to take transformative and hope-filled steps forward. Wisdom gained by living within our lineages, choosing what resonates deeply with us, may help us transmit what we know to be good and beautiful and true (precisely because it has withstood the test of time), while giving it our own creative spin as we live our lives, impart our own lessons, and become ancestors in turn.

PROFESSIONAL PATHWAYS

Now that I have briefly articulated my own statement of purpose and the depth of my commitment to this autoethnographic vocation, let me step back to reflect on how I have labored in this field and on the specific challenges, successes, and travails that I have experienced in my scholarly and professional life.[8] To a large measure, this work has been relegated to the margins in the academic environments in which I found myself (Italian Studies departments). Hence, with few and sporadic exceptions, I have labored as an "independent scholar"[9]—that is, either on contract as a visiting professor or as a short-lived founder-director of the Italian Oral History Institute, working alongside but not part of academic and cultural institutions. My identity as an independent scholar (or outsider academic?), a scholar unmoored, will likely remain with me to the end. My entire "career" has been (for the most part) monetarily unremunerated. Therefore, from a strictly economic perspective, my work has been free academic labor.[10] I have volunteered away my life, like a typical 1950s housewife—like my mother, I am shocked to admit. It is not that I have not sought gainful employment as an academic but that many restrictions prevented me from achieving it. At first, family life and early motherhood limited time and energy for employment. When I was ready to explore employment after those early parenting years, the job market in my field had become remarkably difficult, especially since my search was geographically limited, in order to remain a hands-on parent in Los Angeles. When we became "empty-nesters," I searched much farther afield but without success, despite an impressive résumé. Positions that "had my name on them" (as colleagues assured me) as far as expertise in diaspora studies were concerned did not even elicit a confirmation of application received, let alone a personal interview, despite my academic work and experience bridging town and gown— as many job descriptions purported to want. I was stunned by these rejections. I felt invisible once again.

My husband's employment as a tenured UCLA faculty member has been a blessing and a curse. Our contiguous fields (Italian dialectology and Romance philology for him, Italian ethnography and folklore for me) may have prevented me from becoming a full-fledged member of any shared department (due also to a general resistance to such spousal academic arrangements, no doubt). But a series of other issues also came into play in our specific case: personality conflicts between my husband and another male faculty member (of which I became a casualty), the Italian department's male chauvinism, more generally, and a resistance to my areas of expertise. Add these to the usual range of factors (cronyism, "open" job searches that are not open, gender bias, ageism, and so forth), and we might more clearly understand my specific case. While family economic stability has permitted my research, conference-going, and publishing to flourish, geographic limitations and closed gates everywhere on campus and elsewhere in the California southland have at the same time proved a crushing blow to my own academic employment and sense of professional identity.

But there are other factors to consider in my journey, which are more subtle and perhaps difficult to articulate, even to myself. It was a culturally induced attitude toward dutiful motherhood that likely also contributed to my not pursuing employment as a young mother. Unarticulated cultural and moral parameters around motherhood, I now realize, limited my own choices as I attempted to align with family expectations—particularly those of my husband's educated, upper-middle class, professional family. The well-being of children seemed to take precedence and to dictate a mother's self-sacrifice, at least during their earliest years. It had for my mother-in-law too. It also seemed to be expected that highly educated mothers were the best suited to provide this early-childhood care and education. On the other hand, I was never warned that diaper-duty might negatively impact the psyche of a highly educated and professionally ambitious woman like myself. I was too inexperienced, perhaps did not understand, and was unable to articulate the deep conflict that this created for me. I could not know then how damaging nonpursuit of a career would be to my own sense of self. Oddly enough, it was my working-class family (my sisters, in particular) who did not approve of my full-time mothering, after so many hard years of study. And why, they insisted, had I remained unemployed for as long as I had? I felt caught between cultures: Italian working-class immigrant and Anglo-American professional. Somewhere between these polar opposite worlds, I lived as neither fish nor fowl. I must have achieved a compromise: I continued to labor as a full-time but unremunerated scholar while being a hands-on mother, providing all the advantages that an educated mother could give: fully participating in elementary to high school lives, arranging after-school lessons and time in the library while providing all the other perks that a stay-at-home mother could give: home-cooked meals, fun in the kitchen, handmade children's clothes, carpools.

I clung to scholarly work of the mind to stave off "existential death." I kept telling myself that I was too young to die! And I continued to struggle with the (self-)justification that this *was* work, just unpaid work. But I derived great satisfaction from knowing that I had not retreated to a life of leisure, society, and philanthropy—although my daughters and I did learn about social teas through a mother-daughter charitable organization. I justified that personally unenjoyable experience by reasoning that I was providing my daughters with another social language, which they would require in their future roles as leaders. Being among a bevy of similarly unemployed but educated and competent women (many of whom seemed to relish their lives of leisure and "charity") caused much inner turmoil. I recognized that I had, in the end, "volunteered away my life" in so many ways through social charities but also in the form of service to academic societies, scholarly publishing, and nonprofit public educational work. As it turned out, I managed to do philanthropic work through an academic avenue. I am still sorting out these contradictions and complexities of my life.

What I firmly know, however, is that I constantly struggled to maintain an academic identity, working overtime as a hyperproductive (if noninstitutional) scholar, certainly because I had the time and means to do this but also perhaps to compensate for not being a full participant in any institution. In any case, by the mid-2010s, having founded a nonprofit educational institute and carried it along at great personal effort, I had reached an impasse, a sense of profound emptiness and defeat. My years of dedicated service seemed to have run their course. I was now experiencing compassion fatigue, having grown weary of carrying this labor of love on my shoulders. Finally, I suspended the Italian Oral History Institute's activities in 2006 and dissolved it in 2007. This was also the same year my father passed away. In retrospect, this may not have been coincidental, recognizing that things were coming to an end—my father's life (which I conflated with an entire generation's) and the institute. Perhaps I had completed my debt to the ancestors and therefore my personal raison d'être for the IOHI had also passed.

Once the institute had been dissolved, my own sense of loss, compounded grief, and rage over thwarted professional ambitions sent me into a tailspin. I became sick at heart and in body and was on all accounts in a state of deep crisis—an existential crisis of (non)presence, of nonbeing or belonging in the world (compare Ernesto De Martino's concept of "crisi della presenza"; for example, in De Martino 1948), like the defeated peasants in Nuto Revelli's *Il mondo dei vinti* (the world of the defeated; 1977), like the *tarantate*, women suffering an inexplicable ennui after being "bitten" by the spider. I felt invisible, an outsider, an exile, and began to wander, literally walking the city of Los Angeles. I also traveled as something of a "spiritual tourist" to near and far-flung retreats whenever possible.[11] I needed to find myself and/or be found. I wonder: how many even close colleagues could have known the extent of my own sense of exile and defeat? The more marginal I felt, the more I marginalized myself. I needed to belong fully not partially. I did not want to be the house guest invited in on Thanksgiving or other special occasions (as a visiting lecturer or a visiting professor). I too wanted to be part of the household.

I abandoned research and writing and ceased my academic activities of attending conferences,[12] all the while withdrawing from colleagues and institutions (especially the people and sites associated with defeat). The pain literally became unbearable. And I began reflecting on and earnestly sorting out the past, possibly retraumatizing myself over and over as I examined my open wounds, pondering the deeper meaning of it all. But more poignantly, I asked myself: Where to now? What was I to do with the rest of this "one wild and precious life" ("Summer Day": Oliver 1992), and how was I to "save the only life I [could] save?" ("The Journey," also by Oliver).

It was my professional crisis as an ethnographer and folklorist, therefore, which ushered me into a "discernment" process regarding life's callings and vocation. (Was I meant to do something else with my life, after all?) Ethnography, in other words, had brought me to the door of spiritual direction. But it was spiritual direction that led back to a closer examination of my role as an ethnographer—which, I concluded, was in need of some revision. I needed a more spiritually sustaining way to be an ethnographer. The fact is, there had always been many intersections of ethnicity and spirituality at the core of who I was and what I did in life, but I did not explicitly take a step toward integration until I encountered *At the Heart of This Longing: Reconciling a Spiritual Hunger and a Feminist Thirst* by Carol Flinders (1998), later followed by *Enduring Grace: Living Portraits of Seven Women Mystics* (1993) and more recently *Enduring Lives: Portraits of Women and Faith in Action* (2006), a further meditation on integrated contemporary women, mystics, and social activists. In that first encounter I read of Flinders's exploration of her own warring inner life (feminism and Zen Buddhism, and their integration). It was revelatory. Why had dual realities in my life, hidden in full view, escaped my attention? Why had I only reluctantly recognized this truth for myself?

I am convinced that it was partly a perceived sense of the academy's disdain for and mistrust of spirituality and religious sentiment that was to blame—most pronounced among my own progressive colleagues on the left, with whom I naturally aligned with regard to cultural and political ideologies. In my view and experience, though, hardcore leftists of the atheist, antiestablishment variety had created a veritable temple around nonspirituality and nonreligiosity. This blind spot, in other words, shut down discourse around matters of the spirit. But it could not shut down spiritual experience. Such a schizophrenic split between academic and religious life (between university and church) seriously hampered my ability to openly live an integrated life of head and heart and had likely done the same for more than one academic. We seemed to be living existentially fragmented lives as disembodied heads, rather than as balanced human beings, integrating the life of the mind, heart, and hands—and we did so at our own peril.

Frankly, it was only when I took a break from scholarship (however short-lived) to take care of my broken heart and examine my own academic experience that I could see things more clearly, intuitively trust my sense that something was fundamentally wrong, and ultimately return to my life of learning with renewed energy and sense of socially engaged purpose. That is, I confirmed in my own bones that I am indeed a woman of learning and always will be. That is what I was trained to do and that is what I do best. It was during this hiatus that I received two confirmations that others thought I was too. In fact it was enormously important to my sense of self-worth to have had my scholarly work in the academy and my non-profit work in the public sector recognized through two awards, each highly meaningful to me: in 2008, I was named an honorary fellow by the American Folklore Society and I was awarded a knighthood (named a "Cavaliere") by the Republic of Italy. This proved to be a decisive turning point. It confirmed that, although it often seemed to me as though my work was for naught, I had not been invisible after all; my work had been valued by colleagues and by my own tribe of Italians. I felt affirmed and could now feel less anxious, easing into a period of more balanced, less frenetic activity.

Today, as a result of having weathered the storm, I understand my complex and nonlinear professional life with greater equanimity. I have gained greater wisdom about enduring existential questions, including who I am and what my deepest purpose is. I also believe that I have become a more consciously integrated academic able to "see with new eyes" (the epigraph from Richard Rohr in the introduction). I imagine this task of self-reflection and life review to be especially urgent to all of us during the second half of life as we reflect upon and adjust our life's direction, reintegrating the split-off parts and achieving greater balance. It is never too late to complete the process of "composing our lives" (Bateson 1989 and 2010), of achieving and adjusting our life's purpose. Once we find that equilibrium, it may also be time to contemplate our place in Time, sharing what life lessons we might have learned with others.

This task of life review coincided and was infused with another sort of learning, as I trained as a spiritual director. Spiritual direction is a practice sometimes defined as "an ancient ministry of listening to sacred stories," "spiritual companionship," or simply "holy listening." In effect, much of this listening seemed a more nuanced extension of what I had already been doing as a folklorist and oral historian. Honing skills of listening on all fronts, listening to others and to myself, helped me pay attention to the movement of spirit in life, teaching me how to align with that spiritual core (for example, Palmer 2000).[13] I became keenly aware of how I had been attempting to tune my ethnographer's ear empathetically all along to "listening with the heart" to cultural practices of faith and spirit, listening for expressions of longing, suffering, loss, wonder, and celebratory joy. Ethnography had become a form of spiritual practice. And in some real sense, I may also have become my own spiritual director.

I reviewed the evolution of my listening. Although deep listening requires stillness and my own path was always imbued with a profound need for silence, my own (ethnospiritual) autobiography began with cacophony. As a bilingual and bicultural child, living in a multifamily immigrant household, I listened attentively to get a better grasp and negotiate the various linguistic and social milieux that I inhabited, within and beyond the family foyer. But overall I was not being much heard or seen and sought out quiet whenever possible. As a curious child, I listened intensely. Although formal stories from children's books were few and far between (my family had no books), my older sisters brought home the few books to which I was exposed (for example, C. S. Lewis's Narnia series), opening a rich world of the imagination. Instead I was drawn to stories from my family's oral repertoire and later from the oral traditions I encountered as a scholar: folktales and personal narratives that told of oppressed peasants and class struggle, wronged women, unrequited love, tragedy, and separation. Many derived from the "immigrant repertoire," heavily based on both traditional and on popular Neapolitan song. All of this helped me to understand my own family and our culture more fully; personally, it was cathartic and spiritually transformative.

As the director of the IOHI, I consciously crossed over into the public sector, convinced that this material might be equally vital to others and therefore must travel beyond the academic inner sanctum. I opened myself to a wider public through programs and festivals, engaging with museums, cultural associations, and community arts institutions. But in this growing public role, coinciding with a greater virtual presence (through email and websites), I also often felt like the village pump, accessible to any and all.

My Inbox was filled with many questions that I was expected to resolve—from the practical to the abstract. I provided genealogical tools, bibliographies, discographies, and archival collections; I referred musicians, journalists, and other professionals connected to the Italian community; and finally I created www.ItalianLosAngeles.org to help provide a wide range of information to a wider public on all local things Italian. I also became increasingly aware that my urge to serve others had its very real dangers—as it does for women in general, I might add, acculturated to being "handmaidens" serving this or that cause, this or that community. Vigilance to balance service to others with self-preservation is critical.

The desire to share knowledge, to teach others, has been a strong driving force in my scholarly life. I am an effective teacher, I enjoy the task, and it has been a great personal loss not to have been given the opportunity to do more teaching. As a university teacher, the highest form of gratification has come not merely from providing new information to students eager to learn but from learning that I have affected positive personal transformation in them. This has occurred most directly through university teaching, but also through publishing, lecturing, and public programs. These days I seem to operate in more of a vacuum, because as a writer alone at my computer, I do not always come face to face with my interlocutors. I trust that there is a readership of colleagues and students for at least a portion of what I write. I work in good faith, believing in the intrinsic value of what I do, but ultimately I live with uncertainty about how I affect others.[14]

Today I no longer eschew the language of hope and compassion. The work in which I engage is the sacred work of sharing love, affecting positive transformation, and helping to achieve the common good. I can only wish that more of us could be encouraged to pursue such work; that academics might exit their solitary perches and engage with the world beyond—no matter how hard, no matter how messy. But I do not believe that it is only academics, often exiled from the life of the heart and soul (exiled from themselves), who live in existential danger. All those who live one-dimensional and self-centered lives must constantly be reminded to turn inward and then outward toward community.

At the core of my being is a deep and abiding sense of restless longing as well as a need to belong. I sometimes imagine this existential state to be akin to the longing felt by migrants leaving their homes in search of more hospitable lands, frequently spurred on by talk of utopias (see Del Giudice 2001). They dream and they speak Utopian. I have known this feeling intimately, in personal and professional life, and I have spent a lifetime searching for places to belong—as a young schoolgirl, as a young adult at college, and as an older adult, negotiating families, cultures, social class, and professional affiliations. The persistent feeling that I did not fully belong anywhere has followed me like a shadow. I experience the frequent urge to move, to move on, to move out—to continue searching. I have also learned to create the communities to which I could belong, institutions that might reflect my own purpose. My modus operandi across years of institutional homelessness has been to create "home places." Today I embrace this capacity to create community as a mark of visionary leadership, giving form to what is not yet and could be, the freedom and confidence to invite others to do the same. (Not invited to the "big house party" of mainstream institutions, I have learned how to throw many parties of my own—literal and metaphorical!) And so too does this publication, emerging from experiences of exclusion, wandering, and transformation, seek to gather together women of learning and heart, as a community of wayfarers reflecting on their own journeys, sharing lessons learned, and helping envision a better future. Perhaps together we can create a transformed academy that is not so punishing to us women.

In conclusion, I see how, like my own tribe of diaspora Italians washing up on many shores, I continue to build places of belonging with my own hands, making much with little, finding a way to express my purpose, sharing and celebrating life with others. On second thought, this is what the ancestors have taught me. Therefore, I must concur with Birago Diop: "The dead are not dead/the dead are never gone."

NOTES

This work is dedicated to my daughters, Elena and Giulia. Parts of this work have been read at conferences since 2004, under various titles: "Ethnography as Spiritual Practice," "Ethnography and Spiritual Direction: Varieties of Listening" (Del Giudice 2009), and "Living Memory, Embodied Ancestors: Practicing Ethnography in the Italian Diaspora."

1. As in another Viola video, *Ocean without a Shore* (from a twelfth-century Sufi poem: "The Self Is an Ocean without a Shore"), these collective images seem to comment on spirits of the dead, on ancestors, and on the porous border of consciousness between the dead and the living as well as our ability to call the spirit/ancestors forth into being.

2. I completed three years of training in "The Art of Spiritual Direction" with Stillpoint: Center for Christian Spirituality, which explored topics such as creativity, dreams, shadow, suffering, loss, grief, eroticism and sexuality, mysticism, social responsibility, oppression and injustice, self care, and ethical practice.

3. I wish to thank Kerry Noonan for encouraging me to see the dream within the context of this emerging field of research. In the popular press, see Shulevitz 2014 for Cambodian survivors and Thompson 2015 for Holocaust survivors.

4. It also trained me to appreciate melodies and to memorize song texts. Regina Bendix (2000: 36) identifies the "pleasures of the ear" in folklore scholars as frequently having had to do with the deep and often emotional and sensory attraction to folksong, narration, and craft but believes that they have also created a habit of screening out emotional vocabulary, the "affective linkage between scholar and subject," together with the corporeal and the sensual. She notes the "scholarly fixation on text and textualizing" and how any mention of heart and soul instead "came to be commonly labeled and dismissed as evidence of romantic exuberance." What a culture itself listens to, how it listens, and how it shares this emotional experience all seem relevant to an "ethnography of listening," according to Bendix.

5. I thank Kerry Noonan for calling my attention to the scholarship of Susan Starr Sered and Carolyn Walker Bynum in her own work on Dianic Witchcraft (Noonan 1998: 151): "Caroline Walker Bynum, in *Holy Feast and Holy Fast: The Religious Significance of Food to Medieval Women*, argues that food was the primary metaphor in women's spiritual expressions and experiences in the late Middle Ages. One reason for this is that food fell within women's domain. 'To prepare food is to control food. Moreover food is not merely *a* resource that women control; it is *the* resource that women control—both for themselves and for others' (Bynum 1987: 191)." In *Priestess, Mother, Sacred Sister: Religions Dominated by Women*, Susan Starr Sered (1994: 133) claims that "emphasis on food and food preparation is one of the clearest and most common themes of women's religions. Cross-culturally, food is an especially sacred symbol because it is ingested—incorporated into the body of the believer."

6. As Kathryn Coe, Nancy E. Aiken, and Craig T. Palmer (2006: 36) state, when considering the narrative tradition of Aboriginals in Australia and their "Dream Time," the traditional nature of these tales "magnifies the role of stories in human existence, because it allows a story to influence the social behaviour of countless generations of descendants." It is a tradition that encourages generosity, cooperation, restraint, and sacrifice crucial to social relationships and crucial to survival.

7. Apparently only few peoples on earth, such as southern African Bushmen, having stayed put throughout the millennia, can claim a territorial rootedness through human time. I have wondered how "ancestral time" might actually be experienced in such places.

8. This second half of the essay draws heavily on "Ethnography and Spiritual Direction: Varieties of Listening" (Del Giudice 2009).

9. I have had a hard time with academic definitions, given my precarious and nontraditional mode of being an academic. The term "independent" scholar suggests being gainfully employed and supporting oneself as an independent contractor, which is not my case at all. Had I not had a gainfully employed professor-husband, I likely would not have continued on this path. Conversely, I was able to forge this specific area of study largely because I did not need to support myself doing it (as few Italian departments would have encouraged such an area of study and teaching). It is a paradox that in the final analysis it was Italian Studies (via my linguist and dialectologist husband) that materially made my work in Italian diaspora ethnography viable.

10. This has been a vexed question in my adult life: the issue of tangible versus intangible compensation for my labor, the nuanced distinctions between vocational (uncompensated) versus employment (compensated) "work." Is an uncompensated "labor of love" still labor? In a materialistic society such as ours, how does monetary compensation measure self-worth and how does self-esteem suffer, despite the fact that someone's labor may be valued (yet uncompensated) by others? Does a long list of academic "products" in my résumé compensate sufficiently? Sometimes it seems to, and other times it does not. I have become particularly sensitive to the issue of academic exploitation, however, especially requests for unpaid work from paid academics—yet another form, in my view, of internal colonization. This can take many forms: the request for articles and essays ("raw goods") that might then be converted into prestigious "finished products" (collections, anthologies, encyclopedias, journals, conferences, programs) by pedigreed academics and institutions. Or it may involve requests to assist students, or bibliographic and consulting requests from the academy and the general public. And I have also come to understand, alas, the paradox of calling myself an "independent" scholar.

11. I participated in many sorts of gatherings in many spiritual and faith traditions. Here too I recognize my scholarly ways, applying a "scientific method" to matters of spirituality. I could draw my own conclusions only after reading widely and personally experiencing—that is, after "researching" several spiritual, cultural, and faith traditions—so that I could arrive at my own fundamental truths: be open, respect the sacred in all, in whatever form touches us personally, practice mindfulness, and intentionally apply our work to the greater good. And that would be enough. The rest was merely a matter of style and cultural history.

12. At most I could manage to sit through a panel or two. I had been attending as much for the collegiality and friendship (and cultural tourism) as for the academic exchange itself.

13. For a more focused discussion of ethnography and spiritual direction, the practice, language, and metaphors of spiritual direction, as well as how deep listening affected my own understanding of ethnography, see Del Giudice 2009.

14. Compare the controversy regarding the recently published letters of Mother Teresa and her apparent crisis of faith. She went on acting selflessly, encouraging others to believe, while she herself lived with constant "dryness," "darkness," "pain," and little consolation or certainty about the presence of the divine in the world. Was she of little faith, therefore? We might argue, on the contrary, that she was a woman of great faith precisely *because* she continued her action for good in the world, despite abiding doubt about ultimate reality. In a recent sermon, the Reverend Susan Klein,

rector of St. Alban's, elucidated this subtle question of faith and concluded that faith that expounds certainties is not faith but something else.

WORKS CITED

Bateson, Mary Catherine. 2010. *Composing a Further Life: The Age of Active Wisdom*. New York: Knopf.
———. 1989. *Composing a Life*. New York: Grove Press.
Bauman, Zygmunt. 1998. "The Holocaust's Life as a Ghost." *Tikkun* 13, no. 4: 33–38.
Belenky, Mary Field, Lynne A. Bond, and Jacqueline S. Weinstock. 1997. *A Tradition That Has No Name: Nurturing the Development of People, Families, and Communities*. New York: Basic Books.
Bendix, Regina. 2000. "The Pleasures of the Ear: Towards an Ethnography of Listening." *Cultural Analysis* 1: 33–50.
Bridle, Susan. 2003. "An Interview with Brian Swimme." *Enlightenment Magazine* 19: http://www.thegreatstory.org/SwimmeWIE.pdf.
Bynum, Caroline Walker. 1987. *Holy Feast and Holy Fast: The Religious Significance of Food to Medieval Women*. Oakland: University of California Press.
Coe, Kathryn, Nancy E. Aiken, and Craig T. Palmer. 2006. "Once upon a Time: Ancestors and the Evolutionary Significance of Stories." *Anthropological Forum* 16, no. 1 (March): 21–40.
Del Giudice, Luisa. n.d. *In Search of Abundance: Mountains of Cheese, Rivers of Wine and Other Gastronomic Utopias*. New York: Bordighera Press (forthcoming).
———. 2014a. "Evolving Triangulations in the Canada-Italy-USA Borderlands." Read at the Italian American Studies Association, University of Toronto, Canada, October 16–18.
———. 2014b. "Feeding the Poor—Welcoming the Stranger: The Watts Towers Common Ground Initiative and St. Joseph's Communal Tables in Watts." In *Political Meals (Politische Mahlzeit)*, ed. Regina Bendix and Michaela Fenske, 53–65. Wissenschaftsforum Kulinaristik (Forum Culinaristics). Münster, Germany: Lit-Verlag.
———, ed. 2014c: *Sabato Rodia's Towers in Watts: Art, Migrations, Development*. New York: Fordham University Press.
———. 2010: "Rituals of Charity and Abundance: Sicilian St. Joseph's Tables and Feeding the Poor in Los Angeles." In *California Italian Studies*, ed. Lucia Re, Claudio Fogu, Regina Longo (http://escholarship.org/uc/item/56h4b2s2).
———. 2009. "Ethnography and Spiritual Direction: Varieties of Listening." In *Rethinking the Sacred: Proceedings of the Ninth SIEF Conference, Derry 2008*, ed. Ulrika Wolf-Knuts, 9–23. Religionsvetenskapliga Skrifter. Turku, Finland: Department of Comparative Religion, Åbo Akademi University.
———. 2001. "Mountains of Cheese and Rivers of Wine: Paesi di Cuccagna and Other Gastronomic Utopias." In *Imagined States: National Identity, Utopia, and Longing in Oral Cultures*, ed. Luisa Del Giudice and Gerald Porter, pp. 11–63. Logan: Utah State University Press.

De Martino, Ernesto. 1948. *Il mondo magico: Prolegomeni a una storia del magismo.* Turin: Einaudi.

Diop, Birago. 1960 [1984]. *Leurres et lueurs: Poèmes.* Paris: Édition Présence Africaine (http://www.biragodiop.com/index.php/extraits/79-leurres-et-lueurs/109-les-souffles). Translated in *Death: An Anthology of Ancient Texts, Songs, Prayers and Stories*, ed. David Meltzer. San Francisco: North Point Press, 1984.

Flinders, Carol Lee. 2006: *Enduring Lives: Portraits of Women and Faith in Action.* London: Penguin.

———. 1998. *At the Heart of This Longing: Reconciling a Spiritual Hunger and a Feminist Thirst.* New York: Harper Collins.

———. 1993. *Enduring Grace: Living Portraits of Seven Women Mystics.* New York: Harper Collins.

Foer, Jonathan Safran. 2002. *Everything Is Illuminated.* Boston: Houghton Mifflin.

Gable, Eric. 1996. "Women, Ancestors, and Alterity among the Manjaco of Guinea-Bissau." *Journal of Religion in Africa* 26, fasc. 2 (May): 104–21.

Geana, Gheorghita. 2005. "Remembering Ancestors: Commemorative Rituals and the Foundation of Historicity." *History and Anthropology* 16, no. 3 (September): 349–61.

Human Family Tree. 2009. Video. National Geographic Society, Genographic Project (1 hour, 32 minutes).

Kammen, Michael. 1991. *Mystic Chords of Memory: The Transformation of Tradition in American Culture.* New York: Alfred Knopf.

Klindienst, Patricia. 2006. *The Earth Knows My Name: Food, Culture and Sustainability in the Gardens of Ethnic America.* Boston: Beacon Press.

Lambek, Michael, 2015. "The Past Imperfect: Remembering as Moral Practice." In *The Ethical Condition: Essays on Action, Person and Value*, 86–104. Chicago: University of Chicago Press.

———. 1981. *Human Spirits: A Cultural Account of Trance in Mayotte.* Cambridge: Cambridge University Press.

Noonan, Kerry. 1998. "May You Never Hunger: Religious Foodways in Dianic Witchcraft." *Ethnologies* 20, nos. 1–2.

Oliver, Mary. 1992. *New and Selected Poems.* Boston: Beacon.

Palmer, Parker. 2000. *Let Your Life Speak: Listening for the Voice of Vocation.* San Francisco: Jossey-Bass.

Portelli, Alessandro. 2007. *Storia orale: Racconto immaginazione dialogo.* Rome: Donzelli.

Revelli, Nuto. 1977. *Il mondo dei vinti: Testimonianze di vita contadina.* Torino, Italy: Einaudi.

Rossi, Ernest L. 2002. *The Psychobiology of Gene Expression: Neuroscience and Neurogenesis in Hypnosis and the Healing Arts.* New York: Norton.

Sered, Susan Starr. 1994. *Priestess, Mother, Sacred Sister: Religions Dominated by Women.* Oxford: Oxford University Press.

Shulevitz, Judith. 2014. "The Science of Suffering: Kids Are Inheriting Their Parents' Trauma: Can Science Stop It?" *New Republic*, November 16: http://www.newrepublic.com/article/120144/trauma-genetic-scientists-say-parents-are-passing-ptsd-kids.

Stuhlmiller, Simon. 2003. "Ethnography as Exorcism." Presented at the Annual Meeting of the Society for the Study of Symbolic Interaction. Atlanta.

Thompson, Helen. 2015. "Study of Holocaust Survivors Finds Trauma Passed on to Children's Genes." *Guardian*, August 21: http://www.theguardian.com/science/2015/aug/21/study-of-holocaust-survivors-finds-trauma-passed-on-to-childrens-genes.

Viola, Bill. 2008: *Three Women*. Video (http://www.billviola.com/ordering.htm).

———. 2007. *Ocean without a Shore*. Video (http://www.billviola.com/ordering.htm).

———. 2002. *Emergence* . Video (http://www.billviola.com/ordering.htm).

Six

CHICANA ART HISTORIAN
AT THE CROSSROADS

CHARLENE VILLASEÑOR BLACK

I compose this essay—part personal reflection and part activist's call for change—from a position of *nepantla*, the Nahuatl (Aztec) word for a state of in-betweenness. That is, I write from the intersection of the Chicana/o community and academia. As an art historian who works both on the colonial world and on contemporary art, I feel compelled to ground the term historically. "Nepantla" can first be documented in several colonial Mexican sources, including two early dictionaries, by Andrés de Olmos (2002 [1547]: 112) and Alonso de Molina (1970 [1571]: 69r), where it is defined as meaning *en medio* (in the middle) (Maffie 2013: 13–14). A fuller and more suggestive definition is found in Dominican friar Diego de Durán's *History of the Indies of New Spain* (1994 [1581]). In a passage recounting how he reprimanded an indigenous convert whom he suspected of secretly continuing his Pre-Columbian sacred practices during a Catholic celebration, the convert replied: "Padre, no te espantes pues todavía estamos nepantla" (Father, don't be afraid, since we are still nepantla) (Durán 1867–80: 1:268). Durán glossed the term to mean that the indigenous converts were *en medio*, between their Pre-Columbian world and the newly imposed Spanish Catholic one, and furthermore that they were *neutros* (neutral). Nepantla shares some characteristics with the better-known anthropological term "liminality," meaning in between or ambiguous (Turner 1964). According to Durán, nepantla is "el lugar de nada (no estar ni en un lado ni en otro) y el lugar de todo (estar a la vez en dos lugares incompatibles)": [the place of nothing (to be neither on one side nor on the other) and the place of everything (to be in two incompatible places at the same time).] It is this last gloss of "nepantla," as a place of both nothing and everything, of being neither on one side nor on the other, of being in two incompatible places simultaneously, that seems best to explain where I am now in the middle of my life and career as a Chicana, a professor of art history and Chicana/o Studies, and a single mother.

MY PATH IN NEPANTLA

My path to the Ph.D. was not a typical one. As a Chicana from a working-class background, it sometimes seems like a miracle that I was able to earn my doctorate and am now a tenured professor at a major research university. My unusual journey allows me to tell the students I mentor, with honesty and heartfelt conviction, that there is more than one path to achievement in life. So how did I arrive at this crossroads, this place of nepantla?

When I was a child, it was clear to my grade school teachers that I was bright, if from a poor family, and I am grateful for their respect. Indeed, I received positive attention in school as a result, even though a high school teacher whom I later befriended as an adult commented that he and others fully expected me to end up "barefoot and pregnant." I was certainly a rebellious teenager—the result, I now realize, of being insufficiently challenged academically. With little guidance from my family, I finished high school as class valedictorian and went on to the University of Michigan on scholarship and financial aid, entering the School of Music. Being a musician was the other half of my life, begun belatedly, at the age of twelve, when I began playing the French horn. After hearing a public address announcement in seventh grade that the junior high school band needed members, I volunteered to play the French horn, after the band director informed me that it was the most difficult instrument. I was intrigued by the challenge and threw myself into this new musical life, even working professionally within a year. Music satisfied my need for emotional intensity, and I lost myself in something larger—the community of musicians and the music itself.

My college plan was to train as a high school band director, ensuring me a steady job. But somewhere along that path I changed tracks, switching to the riskier major of music performance. A prime motivation was the ability to free up my schedule, eliminating no longer required music education classes, so that I could take all the history and language courses that I wanted. That was an initial clue to my future career path.

I graduated from the University of Michigan, despite holding down multiple jobs and always being on the edge of financial disaster, and began working as a performer and music teacher. Although I never had a bad day teaching, I felt increasingly intellectually frustrated as well as discouraged by what I perceived as a personal lack of success and a lack of meaning in my life. Yes, I had a regular position in a regional orchestra, with plenty of freelance work and numerous private students, but something was seriously missing. A challenge? "Success"? Was I making a difference in the world? Unsure of what to do, I applied to graduate school in my home state of Arizona, accepted a scholarship to complete my master's degree in music performance at Arizona State University, and moved back. Within months I made the heart-wrenching decision to quit music altogether. The emotional fallout felt akin to divorce. Unsure of what to do, I took a job as an assistant manager at a clothing store, while I considered what to do with my life.

I was fairly certain I belonged in academia.

I took classes as I worked in the store, helping women choose suits and pantyhose, as I tried on various fields of study myself. I seemed to be good at languages, and I did love history. Even though music history seemed the logical choice, returning to music school seemed too painful. Frankly, I could not face the feeling of failure at leaving performance. But then I took my first art history class and was enthralled. To tell the truth, I had not even been aware that such a field existed before attending the university— but this discipline somehow seemed a natural transition from music. Both fields involved creative expression and periodization (which I had learned in music history)—medieval, Renaissance, baroque, modern—periods that were easily applicable to art history. Art history also combined my love of languages, a natural outgrowth of a musician's keen auditory sense, and history.

An event occurred when I was fifteen, which I consider in hindsight to have been a premonition of things to come. While I was on tour in Mexico as part of a performing group, we stopped in the colonial city of Taxco,

FIGURE 6.1 Santa
Prisca church,
1751–58, Taxco, Guer-
rero, Mexico. Credit:
Gianni Dagli Orti/
The Art Archive at
Art Resource, New
York City.

Mexico, for a day of rest and tourism. While my teenage friends shopped
for silver (for which Taxco is famous), I spent the day visiting churches.
One church in particular left me breathless—the perfectly preserved colonial church of Saints Prisca and Sebastián, a dazzling, ornate, and soar-
ing structure built between 1751 and 1758, during the great Mexican silver
boom. The church's tall towers and elevated, tile-encrusted dome rise dra-
matically amid the surrounding mountainous village. Its interior is perfectly preserved, a quintessential example of the emotional style of Mexican
ultrabaroque architecture. When I look back on that encounter, I realize
that was the moment I became an art historian and a specialist in the art
of the baroque. Today my students literally gasp when I show them that
church; and then I tell them my story.

I thrived in graduate school. Still searching for my own identity,
I began to seek out classes on Mexican art, at a time when there were none

FIGURE 6.2 Santa Prisca church, interior, Retablo Mayor (main altarpiece), eighteenth century, Taxco, Guerrero, Mexico. Credit: Album/Art Resource, New York City.

at my university. In fact the subject was being taught at very few institutions in the late 1980s and early 1990s. So instead I took a course on the Spanish baroque, a seemingly logical preparation for modern Mexican art, the topic I was actually interested in. But I was sidetracked by the baroque, overwhelmed by its drama and passion, and profoundly moved by its religious art, which looked so familiar to me, having been raised Catholic. That course was a turning point in my journey. After taking a year of preparatory coursework, I applied to graduate school in art history at the University of Michigan to work on Spanish baroque art and was accepted on a fellowship. I eventually became a specialist in the gender politics of Spanish religious art, writing a dissertation on ideals of Hispanic masculinity as manifested in depictions of St. Joseph and the Holy Family (Villaseñor Black 2006, 1995). I consciously chose *religious* art as an affirmation of my Catholic upbringing, Mexican heritage, and working-class roots. While I had never entered an art museum until I was in high school, I had seen and lived with plenty of art, in the form of images of Mary, Christ, and the saints in churches and in my home. We had a statue of the Sacred Heart of Jesus from Nogales, Mexico, in our living room, whose glass eyes—I swear—followed me around the house. (It was only later in graduate school, upon reading Michel Foucault's *Discipline and Punish*, that I realized that this plaster statue functioned as an all-seeing panopticon, disciplining my behavior [Foucault 1995: 195–228].) Catholic imagery became my subject of study. I soundly rejected suggestions that I work on royal patronage or elite portraiture or anything else that I associated with privilege.

I finished my M.A. and Ph.D. and went on the job market (terrified of being unemployed, having experienced poverty both as a child and as an adult). Fortunately, I was offered several academic positions, ending up first at the University of New Mexico and then at the University of California, Los Angeles. Both were close (but not too close) to home and family in Arizona. And both were in parts of the country where I felt comfortable. I longed for the desert landscape of my childhood, the sharp smell of creosote after the rain, looming mountains, and the lilting cadence of Mexican Spanish. While graduate school classmates hoped for jobs on the east coast, I had my sights set on the other side of the country.

Because I myself am the product of public schooling, from Head Start to a Ph.D. from the University of Michigan, I had a strong commitment to the mission of the public university—to make a first-rate education accessible to all, including first-generation and underrepresented students. In fact, I specifically looked for jobs at *public* institutions, wanting to pass forward the benefits I had myself enjoyed: I would not even be a professor had it not been for affordable, accessible public education. It has always been my goal to offer the advantages of private education—access to faculty, thoughtful mentoring, an emphasis on critical thinking—at the public university.

I am now in the middle of my career as an art historian at UCLA, with a joint appointment in art history and Chicana/o Studies, with publications on both early modern/colonial art and contemporary Chicana/o art. And I recently turned fifty. There is clearly something about this milestone that causes us to review and reevaluate where we have been and where we are headed. Increasingly, I feel an unresolved tension between my two contradictory halves—being Chicana and being an art historian—as well as a rift between my professional life and the life of my family and community. I concede that this may be exacerbated by living in Los Angeles, where more than half the residents speak Spanish, the city with the largest Mexican population outside of Mexico City. Perhaps it would have been easier to locate to the east coast or Midwest after all, where I might have been able to blend in anonymously.

But this disquiet may also have to do with conflicts between the rarefied and privileged world of art history and the practical, activist-oriented politics of Chicana/o Studies. I am a tenured professor of art history at a Research 1 institution, where I am reminded daily how few other Chicana/o or Latina/o faculty there are at such places. At these moments I take comfort in the inspirational words of César E. Chávez, co-founder with Dolores Huerta of the United Farm Workers movement, which guide me as a researcher and teacher:

> We cannot seek achievement for ourselves and forget about progress and prosperity for our community. . . . Our ambitions must be broad enough to include the aspirations and needs of others, for their sakes and for our own. (http://www.ufw.org/_page.php ?menu=research&inc=history/09.html)

This commitment to community guides my teaching and research. It also leads to friction between me and the art history world. I research and write on Chicana/o art as well as on the seventeenth century. I am attempting to make visible, to *valorize*, Chicana/o art as a valuable addition to the canon of art history. But I am afraid that Chicana/o art historians are losing this battle—the topic is relegated almost exclusively to ethnic studies departments. My colleagues in art history simply do not consider Chicana/o art to be "art" of high enough "quality" to merit inclusion within the hallowed canon of art history (Villaseñor Black 2015). In my writings on seventeenth-century religious art of the Iberian Empire, which are often comparative studies of Spanish and Mexican art, I seek both to valorize religious art (an art form frequently designated as the art of ordinary people) and to confront the Roman Catholic Church on a variety of issues (Villaseñor Black 2014, 2010, 2006, 2003, 2001a, 2001b, 1995). In my analyses of the gender politics of religious art, for example, I have sought to demonstrate the power of religious imagery as well as the propagandistic and coercive potential of this art in historic context. I have also researched how artists subverted Inquisition guidelines for the "proper" depiction of sacred imagery and how devotees' agency functioned in their own uncircumscribed reactions to this art. When I speak to popular audiences about my research, often in parish halls, sometimes in English and sometimes in Spanish, women frequently come up to me to tell me that "their eyes have been opened."

One day I am holding forth on the beauty of Michelangelo's David and his Pietà or of Leonardo da Vinci's *Last Supper*, as I teach an introductory survey course on Renaissance and baroque art. On other days I am engaging with contemporary Chicana/o artists and activists, while teaching protest art. The controversial artist Alma López has been a regular visitor to my classes. I have also invited "hacktivist" artists, Ricardo Domínguez and Electronic Disturbance Theater, known for their acts of Electronic Civil Disobedience (virtual blockades, virtual sit-ins) to campus to talk about their work and meet with students. Thoroughly trained in European art, and able to teach students to date, attribute, and analyze works from the seventeenth century, I nonetheless also challenge them to answer questions such as "What is the current state of activist art?"

My political commitments are reflected in my teaching but also in my role as mentor, particularly in my relationships with students of color as well as working-class and first-generation students. Let me repeat: I am in the middle of my career, and yet I have never successfully mentored another working-class Chicana/o at the Ph.D. level! I wonder what this says about racial and class attitudes in the academy and in particular about attitudes toward Chicana/os at my own institution and in Los Angeles—the city with the largest Mexican-descended population in the world after Mexico City. It is not that students do not apply to work with me; it is that they are never admitted into the Art History Department in the first place. Instead they go to other prestigious and more progressive universities on full fellowships. Increasingly, in order to mentor Chicana/o students, I have begun teaching more of my courses in Chicana/o Studies rather than in art history. I have also begun mentoring more undergraduate students, even as I maintain my graduate program. Perhaps in the future these working-class Chicana/o undergrads will be accepted into graduate programs in art history at institutions such as mine and change the humanities from within, demanding that it expand to include underrepresented voices and viewpoints.

My increasing mentorship of Chicana/o students has led to its own series of problems, however. An upper-level university official recently advised me that such mentoring was "holding me back professionally." I objected to his observation, which assumed that I had not published as much as my colleagues (not the case: I have, in fact, published as much or more). But the image of the nurturing female faculty member of color "wasting" her career away, selflessly mentoring underprivileged students, is clearly a vibrant and living stereotype at my institution. I hope that the undergraduates I mentor do go on to graduate programs and into universities where these attitudes do not prevail. Despite these setbacks, I remain committed to fostering access to higher education for all, regardless of their backgrounds. And I remain optimistic or at least hopeful. And yet a Chicano colleague in another department who has taught at my institution for thirty years tells me that things are not any better for students of color now than they were when he began.

On a more hopeful note, allow me to recall a second quotation from César Chávez, which encapsulates my teaching philosophy: "Students must have initiative; they should not be mere imitators. They must learn to think and act for themselves—and be free" (César E. Chávez Foundation). These two tenets about initiative and freethinking are critical to my own teaching philosophy. Freethinking is important: unless students can think for themselves, they will accept society's stereotyped ideas about who they are and accept these externally imposed limitations. Furthermore, the ability to think critically is fundamental to democracy. Without the ability to think, look, or listen critically, citizens are vulnerable to tyranny. By modeling academic rigor and dedication to service in the classroom, it is my hope that I may help prepare our students—whether art historians or not—to be become truly thoughtful and critical individuals, full participants in democracy, and politically aware persons not afraid to think for themselves. And, yes, to be free sometimes implies resistance to authority (another trait that I value deeply). Had I not resisted authority, I would not be a university professor. I frequently ponder a favorite saying from the colonial Americas: *Obedezco pero no cumplo* (I obey but I do not comply). The saying originates with colonial administrators chafing against the control exercised by the motherland, but I find it useful to negotiate the halls of academia.

Thus I find myself in the land of nepantla, between and betwixt art history and Chicana/o Studies, between academia and my family and community. Some days I hold forth on Michelangelo, Leonardo, and Raphael in my introductory survey course; other days I join in worker strikes, write letters of protest to the chancellor, and speak passionately about art and activism. Or I visit with family in rural Arizona, work with members of my community here in Los Angeles, and volunteer as a translator for asylum cases.

This feeling of nepantla also characterizes another area of my life, as a single parent of a teenage son. Since his birth, I have felt torn between love of my profession and my dedication to parenting. I've tried to find ways to make the tensions productive. Becoming a mother turned my attention to scholarly issues involving maternity, and I wrote essays on ideals of motherhood and female holy persons as I nursed him and raised him. Single motherhood affected my parenting in other concrete ways. My son has never been on what he describes as a "real vacation," but he has been to archives in Spain and Mexico, waited patiently in the refectory of a fifteenth-century monastery as I worked in its library, and seen countless cathedrals and churches from the inside. He has created artworks under the guidance of artist Alma López as well as master printers at Self Help Graphics in East LA. He has attended protests and strikes. And despite my best attempts to discourage his early interest in music—due to my own unresolved conflicts here—he became a talented opera singer. Eventually I realized that mothering was my most effective model for mentoring my students, that my goal was to nurture, support, and teach them, as I prepared them to become independent of me.

I began this essay puzzling over the colonial definition of "nepantla." With other colleagues, I note that it has been retheorized and rethought by several Chicana writers, including Gloria Anzaldúa, Pat Mora, Laura Pérez, Alicia Gaspar de Alba, Laura Medina, Emma Pérez, and by various artists such as Yreina Cervantez and Santa Barraza (Román-Odio 2013: 51–74). Anzaldúa (2009: 180) writes: "*Nepantla* is the Náhuatl word for an in-between state, that uncertain terrain one crosses when moving from one place to another, when changing from one class, race, or sexual position to another, when traveling from the present identity into a new identity." Nepantla is like a bridge: "Bridges span liminal (threshold) spaces between worlds, spaces I call *nepantla*, a Nahuatl word meaning *tierra entre medio*. Transformations occur in this in-between space, an unstable, unpredictable, precarious, always-in-transition space lacking clear boundaries" (Anzaldúa and Keating 2002: 1). AnaLouise Keating (2006: 6), writing about Gloria Anzaldúa, describes *neplanteras/os* as threshold people: they move within and among multiple, often conflicting, worlds and refuse to align themselves exclusively with any single individual, group, or belief system. This refusal is not easy; nepantleras must be willing to open themselves to personal risks and potential woundings which include, but are not limited to, self-division, isolation, misunderstanding, rejection, and accusations of disloyalty.

It is this recent retheorizing of nepantla as a space of transformation, potential innovation, and new perspectives that I find inspirational, that builds upon and improves the colonial definition of "nepantla" as in-between, in the middle, or even neutral. It is this definition that I now willingly embrace after many years of struggle. Yes, nepantla can be painful, but it can also be a productive space. I will always be in between communities, both literally and figuratively bilingual, bicultural, and biracial (half white and half Chicana). There is a word, in fact, to describe people who are half white and half Mexican, still in use in contemporary New Mexico: *coyote*.[1] Like the wild wolf-dog, half-breeds are wily and clever, able to move stealthily between worlds as tricksters and rule-breakers. I will always have footholds both in the rarefied worlds of art history and classical music and in the working-class, activist Chicana/o community. It was my early life experiences of nepantla, in fact, that deeply molded my personal life and professional work. Professionally, I am a border-crossing early modernist, working across geographical and chronological borders. My time at UCLA, and in Los Angeles, poised between Latin America and the Pacific Rim, has had a profound impact on my research, teaching, and service—I became more politically aware in this evolution. The opportunity to grow intellectually, as I cross through between regions and disciplines, has forged my perspective as a scholar.

In this scholarship I have been at the forefront of changing my field from its focus on a single country to one that looks beyond national, territorial, and maritime borders as well as one that investigates continuities of artistic production beyond strict chronological frames. Personally, I also cross many borders. In my forties I literally found my voice again as I began singing as a classical musician, thus combining these two parts of my past lives. As a single parent, I move between being an effective mother and trying to be a father to a teenage son. Spiritually, I have moved for many years between the Roman Catholic Church and the Episcopal Church, which I joined as an adult, in revolt against Roman Catholicism's intolerance and discrimination, embracing a more inclusive, loving, and tolerant spirituality. In the final analysis, nepantla has not always been a comfortable space in which to dwell, but it is the one I can inhabit. And thus I offer this *testimonio*, this eyewitness account as an unofficial report, a form of resistance at the margins, in lieu of the standard narratives of the lives and résumés of women in academia.[2]

NOTES

1. *Coyote* has been in use as a racial term since at least the 1700s in Mexico. See its slightly variant meaning in colonial Mexico, as documented by Katzew (2004: 44).
2. See these discussions and theorizations of the emergence of *testimonio* as an alternative form of history in Latin America in the 1970s and 1980s: Yúdice (1991) and Zimmerman (2004: s.v. *testimonio*): "Testimonio is generally defined as a first-person narration of socially significant experiences in which the narrative voice is that of a typical or extraordinary witness as a representative voice, and therefore at one remove from actual oral testimony . . . or protagonist who metonymically represents others who have lived through similar situations and who have rarely given written expression to them."

WORKS CITED

Anzaldúa, Gloria. 2012. *Borderlands/La Frontera: The New Mestiza*. 4th ed. San Francisco: Aunt Lute Books.

———. 2009. "Border Arte: Nepantla, el lugar de la frontera." In *The Gloria Anzaldúa Reader*, ed. AnaLouise Keating, 176–86. Durham and London: Duke University Press.

Anzaldúa, Gloria, and AnaLouise Keating. 2002, eds. *This Bridge We Call Home*. New York: Routledge.

Black, Charlene Villaseñor. 2015. "Introduction: Teaching Chicana/o and Latina/o Art History in the Twenty-First Century: P'adelante, P'atrás." *Aztlán: A Journal of Chicano Studies* 20, no. 1: 115–25.

———. 2014. "Paintings of the Education of the Virgin Mary and the Lives of Girls in Early Modern Spain." In *The Formation of the Child in Early Modern Spain*, ed. Grace Coolidge, 93–119. Farnharm: Ashgate.

———. 2010. "Inquisitorial Practices Past and Present: Artistic Censorship, the Virgin Mary, and St. Anne." In *Art, Piety, and Destruction in the Christian West, 1500–1700*, ed. Virginia Raguin, 173–200. Burlington, VT: Ashgate.

———. 2006. *Creating the Cult of St. Joseph: Art and Gender in the Spanish Empire.* Princeton: Princeton University Press.

———. 2003. "Images of St. Anne and Maternal Archetypes in Spain and Mexico." In *Colonial Saints: Discovering the Holy in the Americas, 1500–1800,* ed. Allan Greer and Jodi Bilinkoff, 3–25. New York: Routledge.

———. 2001a. "Love and Marriage in the Spanish Empire: Depictions of Holy Matrimony and Gender Discourses in the Seventeenth Century." *Sixteenth Century Journal: The Journal of Early Modern Studies* 32: 637–67.

———. 2001b. "The Moralized Breast in Early Modern Spain." In *The Material Culture of Sex, Procreation, and Marriage in Premodern Europe,* ed. Anne L. McClanan and Karen R. Encarnación, 191–219. New York: Palgrave.

———. 1999. "Sacred Cults, Subversive Icons: Chicanas and the Pictorial Language of Catholicism." In *Speaking Chicana: Voice, Power, and Identity,* ed. D. Letticia Galindo and María Dolores Gonzales, 134–74. Tucson: University of Arizona Press.

———. 1995. "Saints and Social Welfare in Golden Age Spain: The Imagery of the Cult of St. Joseph." Ph.D. dissertation. University of Michigan.

César E. Chávez Foundation. http://www.ufw.org/_page.php?menu=research&inc=history/09.html. Accessed 10/20/2013.

Durán, Fray Diego. 1994 [1581]. *History of the Indies of New Spain.* Trans. Doris Heyden. Norman: University of Oklahoma Press.

———. 1867–80. *Historia de las Indias de Nueva España y islas de Tierra Firme.* 2 vols. Ed. José Fernando Ramírez. Mexico City: Ignacio Escalante.

Foucault, Michel. 1995. *Discipline and Punish: The Birth of the Prison.* Trans. Alan Sheridan. New York: Random House.

Gaspar de Alba, Alicia. *Codex Nepantla.* http://codexnepantla.blogspot.com/p/tlaltocal-lesbofeminista-13082011.html.

Katzew, Ilona. 2004. *Casta Painting.* New Haven and London: Yale University Press.

Keating, AnaLouise. 2006. "From Borderlands and New Mestizas to Nepantla and Nepantleras: Anzaldúa's Theories for Social Change." *Human Architecture: Journal of the Sociology of Self-Knowledge* 4 (Summer 2006): 5–16.

Maffie, James. 2013. "Pre-Columbian Philosophies." In *A Companion to Latin American Philosophy,* ed. Susan Nuccetelli, Ofelia Schutte, and Otávio Bueno, 9–22. Malden, MA/Chichester, West Sussex, UK: Blackwell.

Medina, Lara. 2006. "Nepantla Spirituality: Negotiating Multiple Religious Identities among U.S. Latinas." In *Rethinking Latino(a) Religion and Identity,* ed. Miguela A. de la Torre and Gastón Espinosa, 248–62. Cleveland, Ohio: Pilgrim Press.

Molina, Alonso de. 1970 [1571]. *Vocabulario en lengua castellana y mexicana.* Ed. Miguel León-Portilla. Mexico City: Porrúa.

Mora, Pat. 1993. *Nepantla: Essays from the Land in the Middle.* Albuquerque: University of New Mexico Press.

Olmos, Andrés de. 2002 [1547]. *Arte de la lengua mexicana.* Ed. Ascensión Hernández de León-Portilla and Miguel León-Portilla. Mexico City: Universidad Nacional Autónoma de México.

Pérez, Laura E. 2007. *Chicana Art: The Politics of Spiritual and Aesthetic Altarities.* Durham and London: Duke University Press.

Román-Odio, Clara. 2013. *Sacred Iconographies in Chicana Cultural Production.* New York: Palgrave Macmillan.

Troncoso Pérez, Ramón. 2012. "Crónica del Nepantla: Estudio, edición y anotación de los *Fragmentos sobre la historia general de Anáhuac*, de Cristóbal de Castillo." Ph.D. dissertation, Universitat Autònoma de Barcelona.

Turner, Victor W. 1964. "Betwixt and Between: The Liminal Period in *Rites de Passage*." *Proceedings of the American Ethnological Society*: 4–20.

Yúdice, George. 1991. "*Testimonio* and Postmodernism." *Latin American Perspectives* 18, no. 3, *Voices of the Voiceless in Testimonial Literature*, part 1 (Summer 1991): 15–31.

Zimmerman, Marc. 2004. s.v. "*testimonio*." *The SAGE Encyclopedia of Social Science Research Methods*. Ed. Michael S. Lewish-Beck, Alan Bryman, and Tim Futing Liao. Thousand Oaks, Calif.: SAGE Publications. http://srmo.sagepub.com/view/the-sage -encyclopedia-of-social-science-research-methods/n1006.xml.

Seven

WHEN I'M TIRED OF WALKING, *I FLY*

KAREN GUANCIONE

Sometimes I feel like a foreigner in my own home. From an early age I felt the desire to run, flee, move far away. My mother said that when I was two years old she opened the front door and I raced like a speeding dog down the steps and down the street, gleefully exclaiming in a quasi-Italian accent "I gotta fasta feet." She was fast too, but I was almost at the end of the block before she could reach me.

Not only have my "fasta feet" taken me down the street, but in later years they carried me to other continents, for years at a time. They transported me into the worlds of art, music, dance, community, language, teaching, political action, and arts advocacy. These activities have shaped every aspect of my life and work. Everything I do as an artist and world citizen is stimulated by inner convictions that influence external action in the larger world. Immigration stories, family lore, the influence of folk traditions and devotional practices sometimes unexpectedly reappear in the small details of my everyday life. Gender, birth order, class, historical circumstances, and time and place of birth affect personal choices and life's path. The intersection of internal and external worlds is the stepping point from where I begin. I began with "fasta feet" and continue to run with my convictions and profession sometimes at dizzying speed.

I am a visual artist who creates interdisciplinary works—often integrating mixed media constructions, handmade books, sculpture that incorporates household objects, printmaking, dance elements (with performers moving within an installation and calling upon viewers to join them), live music, ritual, and video. My work focuses on women's work and ethnicity, issues of identity and class, as well as forms of resistance that challenge injustice and inequity. Large-scale installations, often spanning hundreds of square feet, have been created around the topics of prostitution, domestic work, the environment, immigration, labor, and faith. My life, labor, and travel experiences have all profoundly influenced the way I see the world— and, as a result, have shaped the art I create.

For most of my life I have recorded these experiences and observations in richly collaged journals that now number in the hundreds. The

FIGURES 7.1–2 *When I'm Tired of Walking, I FLY* (2006): details from site-specific installation with the artist (on ladder), over 15,000 pieces of handmade and hand-painted paper, torn prints, and other found materials hand sewn and suspended beneath a two-story-high illuminated skylight and throughout the space at the John Cotton Dana Library, Rutgers University, Newark, NJ. Viewers were literally surrounded and touched by pieces of the hanging installation, the first time a work of this scale has transformed an entire area of the Dana Library. Photo by Ed Berger.

FIGURE 7.3 *Bolsas de Mandado* (detail) (2012): ongoing series, mixed-media installation, machine-sewn recycled plastic bags from around the world; detail shows sewn plastic bags collected by Iraqi friends in Baghdad shortly after the United States invasion and small *bolsas de mandados* (Mexican market bags used for daily chores), size: 900 square feet. Photo by Bruce Riccitelli.

FIGURE 7.4 *Market Value* (2008–9): installation, thousands of machine-sewn recycled plastic bags from around the world and shredded U.S. currency, 4725 square feet. Photo by Bruce Riccitelli.

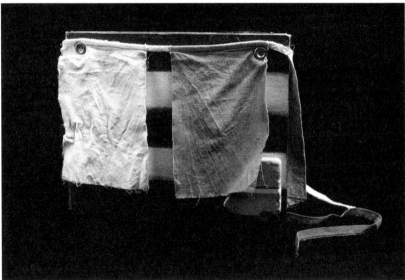

FIGURE 7.5 *Bolsas de Mandado* (2012): ongoing series, mixed-media installation, machine-sewn recycled plastic bags from around the world, exhibited at the Long Beach Island Foundation of the Arts and Sciences, 900 square feet. Photo by Bruce Riccitelli.

FIGURE 7.6 *Livre de l'été, aôut 2009 (Nice, France)*: mixed-media, found tile shard and weathered prayer flags, grommets, acrylic paint on outside and inside covers, 100 pages collage, drawing, painting, width: 12½ × height: 9¾ × depth: 2½ inches, August 2009. Photo by Bruce Riccitelli.

FIGURE 7.7 *Trash (Accordion Plastic Bag Book)*: mixed-media artist book, sixty scanned collage images, five connectable machine-sewn segments, and removable plastic bag covers using plastic bags collected from many countries, paper and other recycled materials, grommets, open size variable, closed: width: 9½ × height: 6¾ × depth: 6¼ inches, 2005. Photo by Bruce Riccitelli.

vocabulary of my work has continued to expand, reflecting new paths and experiences, including community art projects as well as an immersion in performance and the language of ritual. To explore the questions surrounding women's work and the value placed on labor, I often employ traditional, labor-intensive methods such as painstakingly cutting, tearing, sewing, assembling, and disassembling materials; arranging tens of thousands of singular pieces; and methodically reconstructing them. This repetitive process mimics those found in piecework and domestic tasks—associations that I intentionally bring into an art environment. I continue to be interested in work that reveals the art of labor and the labor of art.[1] I often use found materials and intense applications of color that share a sensual delight in "the stuff of life." The ever present aesthetics of accumulation and excess resonate in my world.

BEGINNINGS

Growing up female in a working-class environment led to personal freedom. Outwardly, the world I lived in appeared to be fraught with limitations. But I came of age in an era that offered at worst benign neglect and at best opportunity and the possibility to do what I wanted. Years before I became a multimedia artist, teacher, and traveler, I had to contend with the start of adolescence, that terrible moment when girls and boys introduced new words and definitions daily into my life: "blow job," "pussy," "cunt," and "fucking" readily come to mind. We shared the newfound terms at our desks, in the playground, and at the corner store after school. At the same time, I went to catechism and had acquired a large black Bible, part of the required ecclesiastic paraphernalia purchased from the church before receiving the sacrament of confirmation. I had heard, probably from older Catholic school students, that the Bible had lascivious words and stories, so I was interested in exploring it for myself. Ever an eager researcher, to my amazement I learned in those pages of necrophilia, bestiality, incest, and other abominations. Sex with daughters, sisters, animals, and corpses seemed bizarre. I marked the pages and shared the findings, certain that I had uncovered major pertinent and unusual information. There was a free and sordid exchange among sixth-grade classmates, and our autograph books were filled with smut. My autograph book was stashed away with the Bible, the First Holy Communion purse and gloves, rosary beads, and other mementos in my white French provincial desk with a hutch.

I was the neighborhood as well as family archivist. As the oldest child in the extended family, I listened to everything and remembered it all in great detail. This meant that I knew everything that was going on in the tribe, often before the other adults did. My opinion counted. Maybe it was because I read all the time, did well at school, and was considered "the smart one." Since I had an active imagination, I was able to entertain myself for hours on end, drawing, reading, stitching, never being bored making things. I suspect that this allowed me unobtrusive access to all conversations, whether I was in the room or listening from afar. I remember being aware that the adults had no idea how much material I was mentally gathering, particularly about the maternal side of my father's family, an enormous Neapolitan clan that started life in America in Newark, New Jersey, and soon after populated nearby Montclair and the environs with hundreds and today literally over a thousand cousins. They were fun-loving jokesters who formed civic and community organizations, volunteered, and celebrated with parties, camping trips, picnics, parades, and other gatherings. Everyone seemed to be related, and we all helped one another. Sometimes I felt a sense of belonging and protection from the larger outside forces. At the same time, the constant tensions between my father and his siblings made me feel like an outcast. I wondered why my father's immediate family was so miserable, so unlike the rest of the big jovial clan. Years later I learned that my grandmother lost her mother at a very young age and did not know maternal affection. Her husband ruled over the family's dry cleaning and tailoring business, beat her, went with whores, and once ran off to Florida with a *gooma*.[2]

In most ways my mother, Mary, was a product of her times and circumstances. Yet when she was seven years old her mother, Anna, left her Sicilian husband and large extended family in Easton, Pennsylvania, and came to work in the Newark, New Jersey, sewing factories. Mary was a first and only child. All her other siblings, including twins born prematurely, never lived beyond a few days or weeks after being incubated in warm shoeboxes near the stove. Anna worked in the sewing factories and lived with Mary in a cold-water flat in Newark.

My maternal great-grandmother, whom I never knew, learned to sew at the age of seven at the turn of the twentieth century. It was simple then: you sewed, the work was examined, deemed unworthy, ripped out, and you started anew, until you got it right. My mother told the story matter-of-factly, and without much judgment, but I cannot help but reflect on how the need for perfection and artistry has persisted in all of us. The need for flawless craftsmanship resurfaces in everything: sewing, cooking, housekeeping, manner of dress, arrangement of drawers and closets, and countless other tasks. The Old World work ethic was passed on. Much of my work honors the skilled handwork, the intense beauty, and the delight that comes with its creation.

In Anna and Mary's finely tuned household operations, there was no waste. Plastic bags were washed and hung on the line; the last bits of tomatoes in the can were rinsed with a bit of water or wine and added to the gravy pot; garbage was carefully sorted and neatly arranged in a compact package on the curb once a week, decades before recycling became mandatory. A rare paper towel was dried and reused; the last drops of liquid dish soap were mixed with water; bleach water sanitized first a dish towel then a tomato-stained enamel container then the sink. Clothes were hung to dry in strict order of drying time; old paper was burned in the fireplace; excess vegetable juice was drunk; tea bags were used twice; coffee cans were saved, and the grinds were dumped in the garden. My aunt soaked her kitchen dish drainers in the chlorinated swimming pool: "It's just bleach after all." None of this was miserly nor compulsive. There was an efficient order, a natural thrift and resourcefulness that were undoubtably passed down through generations of domestic habit. Today this constant use and reuse is an integral part of my entire process of art-making and every large installation that I create.

Early feminist art often referenced the anonymous handwork created by women. It speaks of the work of all women and has personal resonance for me because of the immigrant great-grandmothers, grandmothers, and mothers who passed their experiences on through the generations. As an artist, I painstakingly rearrange small objects and vast quantities of pieces into massive installations that require countless hours of labor. When my mother helped prepare thousands of plastic bags for several of my installations, she perfectly washed, sorted, and folded every one of them before I sewed them together on my grandmother's 1940s industrial sewing machine, salvaged from a Newark coat factory. I later created an edition of letterpress printed books that paid homage to these multigenerational skills. The text on one of the pages reads: "By eye and without measuring my mother could sew perfectly straight lines. Mine are intentionally crooked" (Guancione 2007: 1). My mother viewed one of these massive installations consisting of several thousand hand-printed etchings pinned together, which hung in the gallery from floor to ceiling in long overlapping strips over two stories high. As viewers exclaimed at the lushness and beauty of the work, my mother, with serious concern, mentioned to me that one of the panels near the ceiling was crooked and needed adjusting.

The Newark Riots, a time of protest and social change, initiated change for me too. Traditional class barriers were breaking down. I was the first in my family to go to college. No adult or peer in our surroundings knew anything about education except that, theoretically, it was a good thing. I was free to orchestrate my path of learning on my own, including negotiating

FIGURE 7.8 *Contro il Malocchio (Against the Evil Eye) Number 3* (2003–4): ongoing series of mixed-media installations with handmade paper, etching, beeswax, pins, baled and loose shredded money, pinned dollar bills, width: 15½ ft. × height: 20 ft × depth: 9 ft. Photo by Bruce Riccitelli.

generous scholarships. There were no immediate role models or guidance, as few people in the working-class neighborhood ever left. My small group of renegade artistic friends were hellbent on fleeing our environment as soon as possible. The Manhattan skyscrapers were visible from our street. From a very young age we would take the bus to Broadway plays, performances, and museums. My father took me in his big lime green truck to Soho, where he bought industrial pressing machines and boilers that he installed in sewing factories. Artist gentrification had barely begun, but I knew on all levels that I wanted out. I would be an artist, live in a studio, and get as far away from the sordid environs of Newark, New Jersey, as I possibly could.

Despite the constraints of the working-class environment, there was also, for me, a great aperture. My family loaded the station wagon, and we traveled like vagabonds on cross country or southern road trips every summer. I sat in the front seat with maps and the Rand McNally atlas and navigated as my father drove, while my brother, sucking his thumb, sat in the back seat close to my mother. My parents assumed that it was normal for me to organize the trip and take the lead. I prepared by reading ahead of time about national parks and other places to visit and kept extensive travel journals. I began my first one at age seven, and the practice continues to this day.

VAGABONDAGGIO: THE MAKINGS OF AN ARTIST

When I was nineteen, in the mid-1970s, I left the United States and completed my last year of art school at Hornsey College of Art in London at the height of punk. The desire to run, to escape the known and discover other places, was strong. Not feeling quite at home in my country of origin— a participant without a tribe of my own—was a stimulus for art-making, a gateway into the diverse world community of which I was quickly becoming a part. I witnessed privilege and disadvantage through the many people whose paths I crossed.

Hornsey, situated in a large rundown Victorian building called Alexandra Palace at the top of a hill in northeast London, was famous for its student takeovers. I was the only American there, and fellow students commented on my strong foreign accent. Most of the art students were pierced, coiffed, booted working-class punks from northern England. They had been on the dole, working in pea-packaging factories or at other menial jobs, or had come from unemployed poor families. Mixed in were a few rich kids from Kensington. Drinking nonstop and reveling in nihilism unified us all. The punk ethic felt deliciously destructive. From early teatime onward the art students and their teachers spent most of the day in the famed Panorama Bar located directly below our school, with late afternoon intervals of work upstairs in the studios (when all pubs by English law were forced to close for a few hours).

I lived in unheated flats with lots of friends. For food I discovered the prime pickings in the refuse of nearby markets. At the end of the day a huge selection of discarded damaged vegetables lay on the ground, free for the taking. It was practically an urban garden. I filled big burlap sacks with booty and made vats of delicious "garbage soup" that could feed fifty people. The skinny English kids never ate anyway. And we didn't take much care about hygiene either. I was just as filthy as my fellow art students. Once a week or so we went to the public baths where, for twenty-five pence, we could enjoy an entire tub of hot water.

By the end of the school year I could no longer afford rent and instead found various places to sleep at night. Sometimes I would climb up wrought-iron bars onto a roof and climb through a window to squat in the storeroom of a former church, or stay in a friend's "council flat" in the East End, or wherever else I could in the big city. I hitchhiked to Ireland for the weekend with no money at all and ended up walking, wandering, and hitch-hiking through Ireland, Scotland, and Wales for months. I slept in ancient underground crypts, graveyards, barns, and bushes or snuck into unlocked cabs and tour buses, fought off lechers and psycho "bachelors," and picked strawberries for money. It rained every day for months in Ireland, so there were bountiful wild nettles and berries to pick. I cooked them in a tin can on an open fire and bin-picked leftover chips. When someone offered me tea, I ate everything in sight and took away the extra sugar. It was glorious, even though the sugar-filled diet was boring cavities into my teeth. I drew constantly, everyone I met. The Irish, who were even poorer than the Eng-lish, insisted "draw me next," buying me pint after pint in payment. I drank too slowly, and the pub table around me filled up with pints that I'd never touch. What I really wanted was some food or coffee, which was nowhere to be seen.

I planned to hitchhike to Asia, despite being aware that I would be a woman traveling in a world of men. I knowingly took huge risks but always carried a weapon in my pocket—a blunt, rusty iron spike, about the size of a railroad tie. I also wore another heavy wrought-iron piece on a shoelace around my neck, once a decorative part of a fence, now a handy weapon. They were useful on several occasions and saved my life when I was brutally attacked when hitchhiking alone in the mountains of northern Spain.

In 1979 I found myself in the south of Morocco, planning to go fur-ther south into Africa. As a woman alone, I traveled on buses and ran-dom pickup trucks for a while with Eric, a savvy Swiss in a well-worn wool djellaba, a seasoned traveler whom I met on the road. We were barely friends, but Western women in Morocco often did not want to be seen as single female travelers, in order to avoid harassment and attacks. Once we arrived at our destination, Eric and I parted ways and each pursued our own interests. Somehow I ended up in a very remote village with one dusty dirt road, no electricity, and no running water. Here I discovered African music. Although it was probably obvious that I was a woman alone, it at least looked like I was with a man when I arrived with Eric.

Everything at this outpost seemed to exist in a complete suspension of time. The hashish, the desert rimmed with distant mountains, a wide-open sky dotted with brilliant stars in complete darkness—all punctuated by candlelight and gas lanterns as we hauled water from wells—gave the feel of a life from a thousand years ago. Hassam, an energetic hash-smoking man from Mauritania, rented rooms to foreigners. I drew him in his white djellaba with jeans, sinewy arms, sharp features, a dramatic head, and nose almost too big for his small body.

All through one day and long into the night we prepared for a feast. We cooked big vats of couscous and vegetables in clay tajines. We spent endless hours rubbing handfuls of hot couscous to fluff it up, in a repetitive ritual. A large number of Moroccan and Sub-Saharan African musicians played music and danced through the night. The drums and trance-like rhythms filled our bodies. I was the only woman and, as always, drew portraits of everyone. Drawing had become the magic key to entering all worlds and was also the means of self-protection. Like Scheherazade, saving her life through the telling of stories, I drew one person after another, quietly, intently, uninterrupted. Men lounged, their bodies motionless in rooms filled with smoke from *kief* mixed with strong black tobacco. People liked to watch me draw. I was not invisible but was unobtrusive. The drawing worked like a charm, temporarily eliminating harassment, groping, and sexual propositions. As the night wore on, the rhythm intensified and the room of men became one massive, ecstatic explosion of energy. We felt connected to the heavens, unified through pure sound and movement, as we danced until daybreak.

After dawn I returned to my room and went to sleep. At eight in the morning armed police arrived, looking for foreigners. Men entered the darkened rooms with flashlights. We were awakened and rushed into small trucks, our passports confiscated. The authorities drove in silence for hours on mountain roads to the nearest police station. We were detained for an entire day, searched, and moved from place to place, never knowing why. Finally, with no explanation, our passports were returned and we were told to leave the area. I changed my plans to go deeper into the desert and the rest of Africa and headed north.

The cold and nonstop rain in the north, together with my lack of money, convinced me to head for Italy. I made it back to Barcelona, sleeping under café tables and using the little money I had for the boat to Genova.

LA CAMPAGNA: THE COUNTRYSIDE

Ultimately, I arrived in Fiorenzuola d'Arda, a provincial town in Reggio Emilia where everything felt familiar. At Bar Roma, the main gathering place for everyone in town, located in the main square, I met dozens of the town's lively cast of characters, including Guido, one of the most memorable. Known as Guidoni, Il Lama Tibetano di Fiorenzuola, he resembled a cross between a Roman emperor, a rotund Buddha, a prizefighter, and the beautiful Italian saint statues from my childhood. He talked about Tibet, and in full public view smoked and shared a steady stream of enormous elaborately hand-rolled paper chillums of Afghani hash and tobacco that were practically the size of small ice cream cones.

I also met Emanuele, who had moved out of town into the nearby countryside to Travazzano, where medieval castles stood between groves of chestnut and fruit trees. The rolling hills were covered with grapevines, and the last vestiges of rural life continued as it had for centuries. There were small farms, horse traders, cows, sheep, and fields of corn and wheat still tended by traditional farming families who spoke the Piacentine dialect,[3] a strange mix of French and other languages that were unfamiliar to me. Emanuele's restored stone farmhouse was old and magical, with stone and terracotta tiled floors, wood-burning stoves, rough-hewn exposed beams, and rustic antique furniture. Everything was simple, practical, and very beautiful. A stone barn, a *cantina* (winecellar and winemaking area), and a big hayloft were attached to the house. Emanuele grew everything by hand without the use of machines or heavy farm equipment, bartering for everything and buying absolutely nothing, while using organic, biodynamic farming methods. He kept horses and other animals that he treated humanely, and he did not eat meat. Emanuele was timeless; even his looks were from another era and place: Moorish, Hindu, Sicilian—something far away but familiar, somehow buried in my own distant roots.

I had plans to discover Italy, go south, and then work my way towards the east. I thought I would go to Egypt, work on a kibbutz in Israel, travel overland through Afghanistan and other countries, and eventually make it to India, the mecca of the times. In Travazzano I unexpectedly found calm in the gentle hills and foggy winter vineyards. The early weeks there unexpectedly became a slow, comforting rhythm of cooking, making bread, chopping wood, drawing in tiny *osterias* (taverns) filled with old men, and speaking with a minuscule vocabulary that I developed in farm women's kitchens, which later developed into fluent Italian. Little by little, I was getting to know the many inhabitants of the area, in addition to neighbors. Winter turned into spring, and I was firmly planted in the rich, blossoming earth. But secretly I was torn: Should I stay or travel onward?

Carolina, our closest neighbor and the matriarch of her farm, told me what herbs and plants to make into poultices or what teas to use for minor ailments or injuries. She was considered a *stregona* (witch), and people came to her for healing and help with various sorts of maladies and problems. The farmers calculated animal gestation periods and planting according to the cycles of the moon. Emanuele used biodynamic farming methods that advanced many of these old traditions and more. Sowing, planting, pruning, and harvesting were done in relationship to the moon, which was believed to affect growth as it does the tides and the rise and fall of water.

We started going to town with a horse-drawn carriage or on horseback. It took hours to get anywhere, but time unfolded slowly, completely determined by the seasons and daylight. Before sunset I'd ride my horse Nina past castles and old chapels, in woods and through fields. Sometimes we rode long distances at night after a day's work, galloping in the dark by a sliver of moonlight. We rode horseback to friends' summer parties in the medieval village of Castell'Arquato. Returning home late at night, we trotted through woods and countryside, as though in a fairytale. We found our way on old unused paths overgrown with trees, sometimes going steeply downhill in darkness, seeing absolutely nothing ahead of us. Stargazing on horseback in total blackness, with no idea where the trail might lead, brought on an ecstatic state and a feeling of suspended time, heightened by the music created by the rhythmic sound of horses' hooves. Riding by moonlight took even longer than usual. In a quiet stretch I dozed in the saddle, drowsy from wine.

By now we had a small cow and calf, a few horses, a pony, and several goats to pasture, which meant more tree-cutting and fence-making so they could run free and not be confined to a barn, as were all the other animals in the area. All the farmers' animals supported the farm economy, including the barking dogs who guarded everything and scrawny cats who killed mice. We quickly learned that it required entire seasons of back-breaking labor and a significant percentage of land and lake water to grow enough hay and grain to feed just a few animals. The reality of self-sustaining agriculture without pesticides and heavy machinery was far from images pictured in storybooks and proved to be another significant chapter in my learning about labor. In this case I became intimately acquainted with the cycles of nature and its attendant workings.

In late June it was time to harvest the wheat. In winter we had sowed and raked the seed into the ground by hand; as we pruned the old branches and bound the grapevines, I watched the steep hills turn green with tender sprouting wheat. At the time, raking seed meter by meter into the entire field had seemed extremely difficult, but it was nothing compared to the quantity of heavy work that we were now doing. Each new task became more physically strenuous, as if in preparation for the next and more arduous project. Preparing for the harvest was loaded with pastoral and mythical symbolism and was the most physically exhausting and repetitive labor that I had ever experienced.

The hills were covered with beautiful thigh-high golden stalks. Careful observation of the weather and size of the grain determined the best moment for the harvest. That required several steps and long days of hot, dusty labor. We would use a tractor-drawn apparatus to cut the majority of the wheat but had to cut a very wide path around the entire perimeter of the field by hand using a scythe and sickle. The cutting tools were sharpened with a whetstone that was stored in a cowhorn. The enormous quantity of wheat and stalk was left to dry in the sun then tied into an endless number of sheaves, loaded into cart after cart, and carefully transported up the hills so that no piece of wheat would break or fall off. All the fallen kernels left on the ground had to be gathered up bit by bit. Rain, hail, or an unexpected storm could damage everything. After that long process, *la trebbiatrice* (a huge thresher) would separate the wheat kernels from the stalk and bale the excess straw.

The anticipated day for *la trebbiatura* (threshing) finally came at the end of June. It was a crucial event when everyone in the immediate area worked together. We started at seven in the morning. Very old farm men and women, young people, relatives, and neighbors carried big bales on their backs. Emanuele, Luisa (the neighbor's older married daughter), old Angiolina (four and a half feet tall), and I stood atop giant mounds of wheat furiously loading the grain onto a moving shoot that carried tons to the top of the thresher. An infinite din from the thresher, tractors, cows, dogs, chickens, and people continued until noon, all in nonstop motion, howling and sweating in the hot sun, the air heavy with dust and flies.

To make money I decided to pick tomatoes on a large nearby farm. The women's conversation while picking fruit was usually about sex or totally mundane household matters like "What color are your bed sheets?" Marita talked and laughed loudly and incessantly pulled two big breasts out of her shirt. She offered them to the fields: "Qui vuole latte? Who wants milk?" The ensuing conversation was all about bothersome bras that bind and make one sweat. She announced: "Today is the first day I went without one; I took it off in the car." Everyone started pulling at their bras, exposing breasts, laughing while still picking ripe fruit. I added: "I never wear one." Marita, suddenly astonished, turned quiet and serious: "Ma mai? Neanche, la domenica?" (But never, not even on a Sunday?).

La vendemmia (the grape harvest) was by far the biggest event of the year, and everyone was called upon to help. Sexual innuendos peaked as conversations between the rows grew animated. Friends, family, and neighbors snipped the fruit as quickly as possible. Timing mattered; different varieties of grapes ripened days apart. Somehow, by working long hours, there were enough hands to gather abundant yields in time. In spite of the quantity, we handled each bunch with loving care, making sure that no leaf entered the big baskets and removing any damaged, bitter grape berries. References to men's scrotums in relation to the size of clusters and to a woman's *figa* (vagina) increased as the days stretched on.

The farmers had become my friends and willing models. Whenever possible, I drew and photographed them and documented our work. I had few materials but made a makeshift darkroom in the winecellar or cantina and slowly developed the black-and-white film. At the end of the grape harvest all of the locals gathered at the fattest, wealthiest *padrone* (landowner) farmer's house. I presented a slideshow of their portraits, chronicling the inhabitants of La Costa Nicrosi di Travazzano (myself included) at work in all seasons. Everyone drank, laughed, and screamed out hilarious commentary in dialect.

This was a radically changing period in Italy in the late 1970s, when farmers in the hills and mountains still worked the land using old methods unchanged for generations. In the flat plains large-scale agro-business was the norm, but we were living in a world straight out of Pier Paolo Pasolini's films about post–World War II Italy.[4] What we did not know at the time was that within the span of a few years that traditional life would vanish completely. The change was visible in a younger generation of teenagers, the farmers' children who hoped to find jobs and move to nearby towns or provincial cities like Piacenza. These places were not far away geographically but were worlds apart with their fashionable clothing, discotheques, and consumer goods. The young people's expectations were not unusual; they were rural teenagers with limited experience who wanted an easier future. A small country school, exposure to Italian television, gossip magazines, comic books, and an occasional trip to the city may have fueled the desire for something new, but even without those influences who could possibly want to do the back-breaking work of parents and grandparents when there was another choice? No romantic notions were attached to working the land, as I too had experienced firsthand.

The contrast between the parents who looked and lived like nineteenth-century peasants and their daughters was striking. The young bleach-blonde women in designer sunglasses, skintight dresses, and jeans drove sporty cars fifty feet from house to field and walked through the mud and rocks in spiked heels, while smoking cigarettes and eating packaged ice cream cones. They had money from jobs as schoolteachers, shop clerks, dental assistants, and nurses. They had boyfriends but lived with their families and never missed a home-cooked meal. Their mothers' fastidious ironing ensured that their pants were creased and shirts crisp and clean. Some enjoyed participating in Miss Italia pageants and, in step with the times, shooting heroin in the pastoral, age-old surroundings.

The clash between old and new evolved slowly and naturally, Italian style. No one espoused radical change; neither did anyone resist progress or want it otherwise, as people happily adapted to the incrementally small novelties. The gravel and dirt road was paved by the state. Instead of hearing approaching vehicles grinding on the rocks from afar, the vehicles now slowly glided by, barely affecting the sleepy, quiet atmosphere of the countryside. The pathetically slow mail service remained pathetically slow. When telephone service came to the area, we had a single old phone installed next to the rustic outside door. A tiny satellite dish appeared on the terrace of the more modern and prosperous farmer across the way. Farmers started replacing beautiful wooden vineyard poles with regular long-lasting metal or cement ones. And people all kept working every day as they had done for a lifetime.

CHANGING WORLDS

I have often radically changed worlds, living in diametrically opposed corners of the globe. At one point in my life I went directly from years of living off the grid in a village with fifty people on the Libyan Sea in southern Crete to lobbying for artists in New York City and Washington, D.C., meeting with the United States Justice Department, negotiating collective bargaining contracts, crafting tax and intellectual property legislation, and organizing demonstrations. During the late 1980s and early 1990s I served as national president of the Graphic Artists Guild and legislative director of SWAN (Self-Employed Writers and Artists Network). During this time I was instrumental in spearheading Artists for Tax Equity, a coalition of seventy-five organizations representing approximately one million artists. We lobbied to change onerous provisions of the 1986 Tax Reform Act that would compromise the livelihood of all creative professionals working in all forms of media, including film, photography, visual arts, and writing.[5] The coalition consisted of the Graphic Artists Guild, Volunteer Lawyers for the Arts, the National Writers Union, Women's Caucus for Art, the College Art Association, the Society of Illustrators, Women in Film, and the American Federation of Teachers, to name a few. Sometimes these schizophrenic, soul-wrenching changes left me feeling unmoored or like a fish out of water. I was waves ahead with a vast array of unique experiences, yet at that time I was out of sync with regard to the deep waters that I had abruptly entered. I had always searched for adventure, insatiably seeking out new life and work experiences, and each and every one of these experiences I lived fully, passionately, as though nothing else existed besides what I was doing at the time. I completely immersed myself in the moment. As I grew older these experiences melded together into a more integrated whole.

My involvement in Artists for Tax Equity was my first major political involvement in the United States. Our activism was obsessive, heady, and strangely successful. It was one of those rare moments when varied forces came together and actually produced change. Because we succeeded, I could

FIGURE 7.9 *Rebozos/K'uanindik'uecha* (2009–12): silkscreen on rebozos (traditional handwoven shawls made by Mexican women), flannel cloths, and woven rags used for domestic chores. The final installation consisting of hundreds of printed pieces, drawings, video, and a traditional loom was created and exhibited at El Centro Cultural Antiguo Colegio Jesuita, Pátzcuaro, Michoacán, and traveled to Casa de la Cultura Uruapan, Uruapan, Michoacán, for La Semana Santa celebrations and other public venues in Mexico. The title is also in Pure'pecha, the indigenous language of Michoacán. Photo by Suzanne Reiman.

see how individuals with enough energy, effort, and luck could accomplish big things.[6] From that point onward, political action influenced how I saw and functioned in the the world and became an essential part of my art. Although I deal with politically charged topics, all of my work also has an underlying beauty and joy; the thread that runs through creating, teaching, curating and everyday living is beauty and abundance. In my installations and performances joy is often addressed in connection with its ambiguous opposites; both sides of a story are told, the joy and "the great struggle that tends to precede joy" (Smith 2013: 4–5). Celebration and transcendence are intertwined with exploitation and collective struggle. Ultimately they are one.

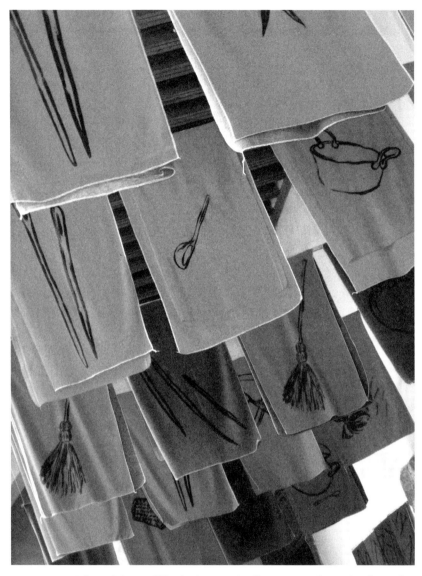

FIGURE 7.10 *Rebozos/K'uanindik'uecha* (2009–12): silkscreen on rebozos (traditional handwoven shawls made by Mexican women), flannel cloths, and woven rags used for domestic chores. Vernacular household objects such as needles, scissors, thimbles, thread, brooms, combs, braids, bobby pins, pots and cooking utensils from local women's kitchens were depicted. The final installation consisting of hundreds of printed pieces, drawings, video and a traditional loom was created and exhibited at El Centro Cultural Antiguo Colegio Jesuita, Pátzcuaro, Michoacán, and traveled to Casa de la Cultura Uruapan, Uruapan, Michoacán, for La Semana Santa celebrations and other public venues in Mexico. The title is also in Pure'pecha, the indigenous language of Michoacán. Photo by Suzanne Reiman.

FIGURE 7.11 *Contro il Malocchio (Against the Evil Eye)*, performance (2001): southern Italian music, drum, dance, and ritual. Photo by Gary Guancione.

DEMENTIA

Nothing in my varied and adventurous life prepared me for the drudgery and deadening grind of caring for my demented aging mother, Mary. I write this while under "house arrest" between diaper changes and the sound of television movies that barely hold my mother's interest. After refusing to live an ordinary life, I find myself, begrudgingly, camping out in my mother's house, the home where I was born and raised. I have been transformed into a domestic servant, as the dutiful oldest Italian American daughter of the family—yet another and uniquely female category of labor. My present life is filled with all those things that I had managed to avoid for a lifetime: domestic servitude; conversations about ShopRite supermarket specials and Dollar Store deals; other people's stories of nieces, nephews, and grandchildren; lottery ticket numbers; rotten relationships; and recipes. Most of my art valorizes the lives and stories of ordinary people, yet I am longing to flee the interminable conversations with the various devoted women who are trying hard to help me care for my babbling, good-natured, incontinent mother who never, ever sleeps.[7]

Let me allude to some of the challenges and tedium of my labor as a caregiver. My mother can barely walk, but that does not stop her as she totters between tables and chairs strategically placed to prevent the inevitable falls. The walker is too alien and complex for her to comprehend, so the only time I have a few minutes to myself is when Mary is meticulously folding towels, pants, pajamas, bras, and shirts. When I look away for what seems an instant, the tidy piles miraculously have been moved to another corner of the house, difficult to find when a sudden diaper and clothing change is urgently needed. If we cook together and I avert my glance, the only sharp knife in the house inevitably vanishes, stashed away in a purse or distant drawer. My mother was a fervent housekeeper, and even as her brain fades away those deeply assimilated motions continue. She can barely walk, yet when I leave the room for the bathroom I find her unlocking the door and going outside or else climbing on a chair to rearrange the objects on top of the refrigerator, never knowing how she gets to those steps or heights.

I sleep on a twin bed near her hospital bed, now prominently fixed in the living room. The colorful, comfortable afghans and pillows do nothing to entice her to sleep, and the retractable railings on the sides of her bed (to prevent falls) have become an obstacle that she is determined to overcome. Her few hours of sleep at dawn are short. When I am finally able to lie down—also at dawn—I can soon expect wails, the rattling of bars, and a morning escape attempt, her eyes still closed, diaper full. I don't know which is worse, sleep deprivation or total lack of silence, freedom, privacy, or time to think.

My mother has lived in the same house since she moved here with her mother in 1950. She cared for every inch of it with ceaseless vigor, and it was always in a state of complete and immaculate perfection. Her work habits were relentless. She was a happy maid. She possesses the heart and soul of an artist, so her labors were self-imposed and ever varied.

I am trying to enable my mother to live in her home for the rest of her life, hating the idea of nursing homes and tearing her from her familiar surroundings in old age. It is a deeply and culturally engrained value that elders should be cared for by family. The idea of handing her over to strangers and then having to spend hours a day visiting her in a nursing home goes against my own beliefs as well. Upholding these beliefs means

FIGURE 7.12 *the art of labor* (detail) (2003): from 2,000-square-foot mixed-media installation: mono-prints, handmade paper, folded clothing, linen, antique fabric, pins, sewing, prints, and projected images, size variable. Photo by Bruce Riccitelli.

that I must make an enormous sacrifice. I curse daily being an Italian elder daughter, resenting my brother's life in sunny Key West, the one who continues to bestow all caregiving responsibilities on me. I am deeply angry that a similar sense of ethical duty does not enter the psyche of my only other sibling, a younger male, whom my mother had doted upon all his life. Were the unspoken expectations so different?

Far too often a guilty thought crosses my anxious mind: that I care more about my tomatoes than my mother. To escape the grinding monotony of caregiving, my salvation seems to be in my obsessive gardening in a small backyard and narrow strip of earth alongside my mother's house—where I am now reluctantly marooned, leaving only to teach, shop for food, or on rare occasions hastily deliver (infrequently made) artwork. Every season, every moment, day or night, when my mother naps, I race outside and dig, weed, hoe, compost and cultivate a paradise between the ugly aluminum-sided houses and excessive urban cement. My ear is atuned to hear her whimpers or moans, and I drop everything to run inside and dance with the next disaster. This is a monumental triage, prioritizing which crisis will take precedent over another. Sometimes I get her in the hospital bed, which I have outfitted with attractive unclimbable padded bars (everything must be aesthetically pleasing for her to accept it), and I can work uninterrupt-edly for brief spells and forget everything. All I care about is pounding in stakes, tying the eggplant, maniacally growing tomato vines, and harvesting the ripened bounty. Sometimes I hear her stirring and I finish a task, know-ing that those extra few minutes can mean catastrophe. It's a domino effect: one omission can mean an overflowed diaper, a puddle of piss, a complete change of clothes and bedding, and loads of laundry (sheets, blankets, pil-lows, and padding), or far worse—a fall down the steps or a crash through the glass front door. Caregivers are warned to not feel guilty about these mishaps. When I have totally had enough and simply can't come running fast enough on the first cry, inevitable damage occurs and guilt quickly turns to pure seething rage.

Eleanor Cooney wrote in *Death in Slow Motion* (2003: 119): "She can't help it, you tell yourself. She can't help it. But neither can you." The incred-ibly honest story of Clooney's mother's dementia and caregiver reality mir-rors my own experiences. These three short lines are manna in a desert of well-meaning advice. If I read one more blog, book, or article extolling the blessings of caregiving, while in the same breath describing its toll, I will blow up this bag of Depends. Perhaps those blogs or books were written *after* the loved one had passed away, when sleep deprivation and anxiety had given way to mourning, to relief, or to other nostalgic longings. But, unless one is extremely wealthy with a full staff dedicated to the care of the frail, ever demanding, endlessly needy elders who are increasingly popu-lating our world as lifespan lengthens, one can truly forget such blessings and instead curse, curse, curse. The only real blessing of caregiving is not having to deal with nursing homes. The steady stream of hospice nurses, aides, physical therapists, occupational therapists, pet therapists with dog in tow, social workers, chaplains, babysitters, and other helpers, sometimes devoted and well-meaning, sometimes deranged and harmful, almost always demands more energy than my mother does and creates far more work for me than doing the caregiving myself. Yet I desperately need them.

The constant, well-meaning advice given to caregivers is to take care of yourself, get rest, get help, do something special. I try meditation, continually repeating a mantra, chanting for a moment. Against all such advice, when five free minutes present themselves, instead of breathing, doing a yoga stretch, or washing my face, I normally run for a cigarette, the vile habit I resumed after years of nonsmoking, when caregiving duties overwhelmed me. How can I rest when just brushing my teeth becomes a major feat or a quick sponge bath, in a house with no shower and sixty-year-old plumbing, means a mad dash, climbing over the baby gate and other intentional obstacles that restrain my mother and flying up the barricaded stairs to the abandoned upstairs bathroom, all the while anxious that the next crash will happen while I'm naked and wet.

My occasional other mantra (self-created) is this:

This is life . . . how can you, a privileged, spoiled brat, complain, when compared to most of the world, you are warm and fed, not fending off rape or other atrocities just to stay alive another day? In the scheme of things, this is small, and you've had a good run up until now, so stop whining and just clean your mother's ass. She's done it thousands of uncomplaining times for you.

I have been maniacally prolific, making art installations and exhibiting constantly for so long that without realizing it I came to define myself through these large, complex works. For the sake of my career, I have been hesitant until now to acknowledge my predicament publicly, letting only close friends rather than colleagues, curators, or collectors know—as though this was my private shame. The relentless need to make art has driven every action in life. The radical change in roles, from artist to eldercare giver, makes me feel like a fraud. By lessening production, I irrationally start to believe that I am an artist not making art, a caregiver no longer caring. Ironically, the role reversal means putting art-making aside to care for my mother who lovingly cared for me so I could be a whole, self-realized, and active artist. To put life's work on hold, albeit temporarily (but who knows for how long) creates a private anxiety, dread, and shame.

FIGURE 7.13 *Sutra* (2013): site-specific installation at the Noyes Museum of Art, made of hand-typed recycled library catalogue cards, shipping tags, thread, width: 23 feet × height: 11 feet. Photo by Bruce Riccitelli.

The critical standard, relentless rigor, ancestral perfectionism must go, to be replaced by a new absence that I had never before felt. Author Nell Lake (2014) calls this process a "slow loss."

When the Noyes Museum of Art invited me to create a site-specific installation to be prominently displayed for over a year, I was well into this endless, exhausting, all-consuming caregiving hell. Normally it takes months to create a piece and marathon days of around-the-clock work to hang an installation in a public space, but I could not leave my mother's living room. I contacted librarians, who helped me obtain tens of thousands of long discarded and forgotten hand-typed library catalog cards that I wanted to recycle for this installation. While caregiving around the clock, I was able to work near my mother and string together the thousands of pieces of paper—a repetitive, meditative act that enabled me to continue making art. The process revealed what I already knew, that I could not do any single task for more than fifteen minutes without interruption. I named the installation: *Sutra*. "The Sanskrit word *sutra* literally means a thread, string or

FIGURE 7.14 *Stripes (Number 2)* (2007): mixed-media installation, machine-sewn handmade paper, paint, grommets, pins, fabric, aluminum rods, at Ben Shahn Galleries, William Paterson University, width: 10 feet × height: 12 feet × depth: 2 feet. Photo by Bruce Riccitelli.

line that holds things together. It derives from the root *siv-* (to sew), and is related to *suere* in Latin, *sew* in English, and the medical term *suture*. It refers to Hindu or Buddhist texts, sometimes described as threads of wisdom or knowledge strung together" ("Sutra" 2013).[8] Caregiving is a process that requires compassion and, like art, sometimes tests the limits of patience and endurance. As I sewed, I was reminded of the piecing together of segments of the lives of all people, who, depending on individual or social circumstance, may themselves become long discarded and forgotten.

Whispers of sanity are heard at four in the morning when I'm ready to throw a wet diaper, her walker, and myself into a snowbank. Lessons learned from years of teaching yoga resurface.[9] Teachers are taught that our own injuries or limitations can help us better understand the physical difficulties that a student might feel and to use such physical and emotional sensations as a stepping stone to help further a student's practice. We are reminded how we can learn from what we cannot do. By begrudgingly putting my life's work on hold to do my odious but essential duty as a loving daughter, I am experiencing an absence and slow loss that I had never imagined possible. After a lifetime of no limitations, constant motion, and freedom, I am now forced to learn humble patience and compassion—kicking and screaming all the way. This too has become part of my life's journey. I am learning how to stand still while believing I can fly.[10]

NOTES

The title *Quando sono stanco di camminare, VOLO (When I'm Tired of Walking, I FLY)* was originally written for me by the Italian poet Roberto Dossi as text for a limited edition of letterpress books that I created in 2004, printed and published by Edizioni Pulcinoelefante in Osnago, Lecco, Italy. The books accompanied a series of exhibitions/installations of my work with the same title that were exhibited widely in the United States and Italy over several years.

1. *the art of labor* was a series of installations and ongoing performances giving recognition to the repetitive and hidden work often done by immigrants. The interdisciplinary project explored issues of ethnicity/immigration in the lives of textile workers and the changing role of women's work by collaborating with textile union workers of Latino/a heritage; the final piece was installed during Women's History Month at the Paterson Museum, a former factory. During a six-month residency at the American Labor Museum (in a building that was an important landmark in the 1913 Paterson silk strike), funded through the Mid Atlantic Arts Foundation, I researched historical and contemporary immigrant textile workers of Latino/a, Asian, Arab, European, and African American heritage and created a public presentation that honors the work often done by those newly arrived in this country. The installation, approximately 2,000 square feet in area, was created daily on the site over the course of one and a half months, incorporating photographs, stories, and objects related to workers in the sewing trades brought by workers and visitors. The materials included antique silk scraps, fabric, garments, silk thread woven in Paterson textile mills, typography from early twentieth century strikers' posters, archival photographs transformed into hundreds of prints, projected images, video, taped sounds of factory looms, music selected by textile unionists, and factory machinery (such as the 1940s industrial sewing machine that my grandmother used in a Newark coat factory, operated on site by myself and community workers). To reveal the art of labor and the labor of art, the installation displayed the process of creation, revealing an active changing display of art-making, and allowed for constant interaction between the maker and the viewer. A limited edition artist's book, *the art of*

labor (printed in letterpress and published by Edizioni Pulcinelefante) also reflects the spirit of this project.

2. *Gooma* is the Italian American pronunciation of *comare*, the Italian word for god-mother or close family friend. In Italian American culture the word often refers to a mistress or girlfriend.

3. Piacentine (*piacentino*) is "a variety of the Emiliano-Romagnolo minority language," itself a Gallo-Italic language (http://en.wikipedia.org/wiki/Piacenza), "spoken west of the River Taro in the province of Piacenza and on the border with the province of Parma. The variants of Piacentino are strongly influenced by Lombard, Piedmontese, and Ligurian" (http://en.wikipedia.org/wiki/Emilian_dialect). Accessed 02/28/14.

4. Pasolini's films often spoke of the culture of the rural past, depicted conflicting values, and criticized mass consumerism. See also John Berger's trilogy *Into Their Labours*, which tells intimate stories of rural inhabitants at a time when the encroaching globalized, industrial world radically changed peasant life.

5. See Malarcher (1988).

6. Margaret Mead once commented: "Never doubt that a small group of thoughtful, committed citizens can change the world; indeed, it's the only thing that ever has" (http://www.brainyquote.com/quotes/quotes/m/margaretme100502.html).

7. Micaela di Leonardo (1987: 442-43) uses the term "work of kinship" to describe the work that women do to keep families together, such as hosting family dinners, food preparation, ritual holiday celebrations, gift-buying, correspondence, and maintaining cross-household links. Kin-work, like housework, childcare, and care of the elderly, is most often shouldered by women. "It differs from these forms of labor in that it is harder for men to substitute hired labor to accomplish these tasks in the absence of kins-women."

8. Spiritual teacher Sri Swami Satchidananda describes each Sutra as "being the barest thread of meaning upon which a teacher might expand by adding his or her own 'beads' of experience, example, etc. for the sake of the students" (*The Yoga Sutra of Patanjali* 1990: xi–xii).

9. I am certified through Integral Yoga Institute to teach hatha and prenatal yoga and have taught throughout the United States in a wide variety of settings.

10. Mary Sarah Guancione (née Platia) died on February 23, 2015, peacefully and fully aware in her own home at the age of ninety-one and a half. Her death occurred almost two and a half years after I began writing and editing this essay. Her last months were filled with grace and consciousness; the dementia seemed almost gone. This essay is dedicated to her, my ancestors, the late Giancarlo Mastroianni, and the many treasured friends and family members whom I consider life's gifts.

WORKS CITED

Cooney, Eleanor. 2003. *Death in Slow Motion: My Mother's Descent into Alzheimer's*. New York: Harper Collins.

Guancione, Karen. 2007. *Stripes*. Osnago, Lecco, Italy: Edizioni Pulcinoelefante.

Lake, Nell. 2014. *The Caregivers: A Support Group's Stories of Slow Loss, Courage, and Love*. New York: Scribner.

Leonardo, Micaela di. "The Female World of Cards and Holidays: Women, Families, and the Work of Kinship." *Signs* 12, no. 3 (Spring 1987): 440–53.

Malarcher, Patricia. "Artists' Coalition Seeks Tax Relief." *New York Times*, May 15, 1988.

Smith, Zadie. 2013. "Joy." *New York Review of Books*, 60, no. 1.

"Sutra." Wikipedia. 2013: http://en.wikipedia.org/wiki/Sutra.

The Yoga Sutras of Pantanjali. 1990. Translation and commentary by Sri Swami Satchidananda. Buckingham, VA: Integral Yoga Publications.

Eight

RISING AND FALLING AND RISING

JENNIFER GUGLIELMO

At our own pace, without speed or aggression, we move down and down and down. With us move millions of others, our companions in awakening from fear. . . . Right down there in the thick of things, we discover the love that will not die.
—Pema Chödrön, *When Things Fall Apart*

I dreamt last night that I was six months pregnant. I wrapped my arms around my large, round protruding belly and loved the feeling, but I was surprised. There was no turning back. This baby was coming. I awoke wondering: what am I birthing?

Pregnancy dreams seem to come at particular moments in my life, signaling something new that is gestating, growing within. There is so much mystery to human existence, so much that we don't know. But there are a few things we do know for certain. One is that we inhabit a body that is alive, an organism whose imperative it is to live, heal, and survive. We also know that we are born, we live, and we die. The creative cycle of life-death-life emerges in dreams and is reflected all around us too, in the sun's journey through the day, the changing of the seasons, the phases of the moon, the menstrual cycle, and so much more. All around us is the evidence that growth is not linear or hierarchical but cyclical.

My work as a teacher, writer, and scholar emanates from and is inspired by this understanding—that the body and spirit move according to a creative cycle that is connected to the dynamic flow of all life. I have learned that with spiritual practice the cycle of life, with its periods of gestation, birth, maturation, decline, death, fallowness, and regeneration, can become a spiral toward greater consciousness. Barbara Ann Brennan (1993) describes this process in her book *Light Emerging*. As we delve more deeply and come to know the specific ways in which we are unconscious (motivated by our fears, traumas, and other conditioning), we also uncover "the original positive creative force that was distorted into the negative aspect that we now wish to change." This then "brings us the gift of our original, true, clear, and loving self" (Brennan 1993: 93). In this way each of us is like a little universe with the ability to expand inwardly and outwardly as we evolve over time. These understandings have led me to ask a question that guides much of my work today as a historian and college professor: what would it mean to align academia with this process, to infuse such work with the practice of becoming more conscious as we connect with and live from our deepest selves?

The answer to this question seems to arise each day in the quiet of my own daily practice. This morning I awoke in the way I love: slowly, gently, and naturally, as my spirit was ready to come back into my body and I had the rest I needed. This dream of pregnancy stayed with me as I wondered about this new aspect that is being born. I counted the months and realized that the ninth month coincides with the start of a new school year after a year-long period of leave and sabbatical. I wondered: what new part of myself am I birthing to guide this ever-expanding cycle?

The life that I have built enables periods of quiet reflection because it is the only way I know to connect within. Being in nature is also at the heart of my spiritual practice because it invokes a meditative state: the summertime hum of crickets lulls me to sleep and the birds' songs bring me into each new day. Some days I sit in the garden in my backyard right after I awake, in the shade of a giant maple tree, surrounded by tall majestic trees moving with the gentle breeze. Today I sat for an hour, breathing with the trees, calling my mind back to my breath whenever I felt it begin to wander toward some preoccupation or another, back to the breath, rising and falling and rising. And I pray, asking my highest self, my innate essence, to manifest more fully and guide me, in service of my highest good and the highest good of all.

This is the ground of my sacred practice, to which I've been deeply committed for the past two decades, and it informs every aspect of my life, including my academic work. I meditate regularly, though not in any formal way. Mostly I do so when I wake and before I go to sleep, sometimes seated, sometimes lying down, as a way to check in with my body, and connect more deeply with my own core of being. Throughout the day I try to do so as well, for a moment here and there, returning to my breath and again asking my truest self to incarnate more fully and guide me. In this way I try to create some time each day to be aware of myself, my body, my heart, my thoughts, and my surroundings and to notice whatever judgment or resistance might arise. In this way, I try to attend to the various parts of me that are calling for my attention, the dark and the light.

After many years of being overly focused on work, I now devote considerable time to that which makes my heart sing. I consider this to be fundamental to cultivating a connection with my deepest self, whether it is delicious and healthy food, peace and quiet, solitude, daydreaming, bubble baths in the middle of the day, dance, being in the company of warm, wise and down-to-earth folk, or just moving with the ebb and flow of life. And I have witnessed how nourishing myself can create space for others to do the same for themselves. We are in so many ways tuning forks for one another.

My relationship to the sacred also flows from my commitment to heal from trauma and to contribute in some way to collective healing in my lifetime. My intention as a teacher, mentor, and scholar is ultimately to facilitate healing and connection to spirit and creative power. I see the work that I do as a writer and teacher of history in particular as fundamentally a spiritual vocation. Saidiya Hartman (2007: 18) writes of this in her history of the Atlantic slave trade, *Lose Your Mother*: "I am a reminder that twelve million crossed the Atlantic Ocean and the past is not yet over. I am the progeny of the captives. I am the vestige of the dead. And history is how the secular world attends to the dead." Each of us on the planet bear the psychic scars of slavery, colonialism, capitalism, patriarchy, white supremacy, and imperialism, though from different locations, each with our own stories, our own set of ancestral and present-day relationships to oppressive power and to collective suffering and resilience. To tell these stories, to write and teach them, especially from the perspective of those "deemed unworthy of remembering," is to "attend to the irreparable," as Hartman (2007: 16) notes. It requires being as present as possible to the horrific, not as a spectator but as a witness, and allowing oneself to be "arrested and disturbed by another's suffering."[1] As we attend to our own wounds we are more capable of bearing witness to one another. Individual and collective healing requires this level of reckoning, and the study of history, like any endeavor, is an opportunity to cultivate greater consciousness.

To do this work in the realm of higher education feels necessary, especially since this arena seems so desperately in need of more heart, more spirit, to plunge more deeply than the intellect can go. So I come to this profession with the understanding that writer, scholar, and Jungian psychoanalyst Clarissa Pinkola Estés articulates so powerfully:

> We do not become healers. We came as healers. We are. Some of us are still catching up to what we are. We do not become storytellers. We came as carriers of the stories we and our ancestors actually lived. We are. Some of us are still catching up to what we are. We do not become artists. We came as artists. We are. Some of us are still catching up to what we are. We do not become writers, dancers, musicians, helpers, peacemakers. We came as such. We are. Some of us are still catching up to what we are. We do not learn to love in this sense. We came as Love. We are Love. Some of us are still catching up to who we truly are. (Estés 2013)

This sense that we are already whole, already wise, already gifted (though sometimes we need to get out of our own way) and that life can teach us to become more of who we truly are guides all of my work.

I came to this practice out of necessity, out of desperation, and I have been fortunate to work very closely with several spiritual teachers/counselors—wise women elders—for most of my adult life. I consider these apprenticeships to be my most significant work in this lifetime, as it feeds all that I am and do. So much of what I share here reflects the practices and understandings that they have taught me. While I have learned a great deal from reading key spiritual texts, I have found that nothing can replace working one-on-one with someone highly skilled in the art of healing and consciousness. My practice has transformed a great deal over the years, enabling me to evolve with the dynamic process of life. I have tried in this essay to convey something of this arc, from the origins of my experience of the sacred to the ways in which it shapes my work as a scholar-teacher today.

✤

The wisdom of my ancestors, passed down in my family and rooted in Italian American cultural and spiritual traditions, provides a strong foundation for my practice. As Angie Pontani (2014), a burlesque dancer and choreographer from Trenton, New Jersey, says so well in a recent interview on how she approaches where she's going in her profession: "I don't know where I'm going and I never have. I just keep going and I don't know, I never have a plan. I think the universe has my plan for me. So I just go where the spirit moves me." This she learned from her Italian grandfather, who was both a marine and an astrologer.

My Italian grandparents also taught me to "go where the spirit moves me," even though it took me on a path that no woman in my family had ever traveled. My grandparents were humble, wise, loving, and deeply spiritual. This meant so many things. They honored the long journey from their parents' southern Italian villages—Avellino, Apice, Ferrandina—with stories that brought our ancestors into the room and invoked them as teachers, whether it was through cautionary tales of heartbreak or moments of transcendence. Their determination to pass on the wisdom from past generations, from peasants who were illiterate and impoverished, imbued them with a dignity and authority that I rarely saw reflected in the larger world around me. To be an immigrant was to be despised. To be uneducated was to be ignorant. To be poor was to be pathetic. Yet these stories taught me differently: I saw how those on the margins possessed great insight because they could see power more clearly. I learned the value of humility coupled with courage and strength. Perhaps even more importantly to my young self, I saw how their stories had the power to move across time and space, to heal all of us. Indeed the veil between the living and the dead could be traversed with story. Later I would learn how my own healing could do the same: a few years ago, in a meditation, I felt a ribbon of light move from my heart through each of my ancestors' and all of our burdens became lighter.

I see now that my first cycle of scholarly work was essentially my honoring of my grandparents and those who came before them. Their love saved me as a child, so I felt called to tell their generational stories as I grew older, especially given how the world around us devalued them in so many ways. When I was just five years old, they stepped in and cared for my two younger brothers and I when our mother died from cancer at only twenty-eight years old. She passed away after a year-long sudden and debilitating illness, leaving us in the care of our father, who like many men of his generation was ill prepared to be the sole caretaker of small grieving children while also caring for his own devastation. Several additional traumas immediately following my mother's death also shaped my life, including neglect and sexual abuse. My grandparents came to our rescue as much as they could, given that they had eleven children of their own, as they were devoted to doing whatever they could to help us survive with our spirits intact.

I see now how my mother's death and all that followed was the beginning of a long spiral down into the depths of my spiritual journey in this lifetime. In order to survive I had to learn how to turn within for love, guidance, and security. This took me a long time to cultivate, in close work with many gifted healers, and it has become a lifelong practice. For much of my childhood and early adulthood, all I felt was my mother's absence, a loss so huge that it haunted me. I did not even speak aloud the sexual abuse that happened when I was five and six years old until I was twenty, when the toxic combination of self-destructiveness and unrelenting anxiety forced me to go in search of help. When I began to connect with the depths of my own suffering, I was certain that it would swallow me whole. I was fortunate to have close friends who were also survivors, and we walked the road together. I also followed my intuition to find the right counselors with whom to do this important work. As I began to heal, others in my family and community joined me on this path as well. We who walk the earth without mothers in physical form comprise a sort of tribe, especially those of us who experience their deaths as children. And those of us dealing with the trauma of childhood sexual abuse form yet another tribe of survivors. Healing is the work of spirit. We can never know why things unfold as they do in our lives, but it does seem as if everything can become a catalyst for awakening.

I learned the craft of history as I learned the art of healing, and each has inspired the other. My first book, *Living the Revolution: Italian Women's Resistance and Radicalism in New York City, 1880–1945* (2010), and the essays that have emerged from this body of research all feel like a series of altars in honor of my ancestors. As a young woman, I turned to my elders for guidance and I soon felt compelled to tell their stories because so much of what I learned from them was both life-giving and completely absent from the historical record. I would come to see that there is a direct correlation between the two.

I figured that if *I* needed their stories so badly, I was probably not alone. This was confirmed every time I ventured out into the world to share my findings, at various gatherings, communal and professional. Over the years I found and drew around me a community of those similarly committed to passing on these "medicine stories," whether as historians or poets, singers, painters, or filmmakers (Levins Morales 1999). Knowing that I was not doing this work of recovery alone, that I had companions to which I could turn, and that my work was part of a much larger collective healing process, a much larger circling back around to attend to the past, connected me more viscerally to the web of life.

I see now, on the cusp of entering my fiftieth year, that my work with herstory/history and healing has taught me what it means to be human. It has helped me to incarnate more fully, to bring spirit into flesh, to cultivate an inner core strong enough to bear witness to myself and the world around me, and to participate in a healing that ignites and transforms us all.

I see now how I began this work as a child. When I was not communing with the trees and rocks and flowers, I was writing stories. I first drew and then wrote about witches, oracles, and prophetesses as a girl. I stacked together paper, used staples to create the binding, and made a series of little books with hand-drawn pictures about women who were powerful and knowledgeable and could cast and break spells. One by one they shattered curses, allowing new worlds to emerge.

As I grew into a young woman I continued to love such stories. I studied them while working at the local public library as a teenager and then in college classes and archives. When I was fortunate to cross paths with wise women, I listened closely. What they have taught me has transformed my life. They have revealed how trauma can invoke a vicious pendulum swing in which we vacillate between two poles: repression of our most difficult emotions (but this means that they only collect and build) inevitably followed by their rising up to take possession of us. And they have provided me with another way, a practice of cultivating the observer self: *she who bears witness, who holds space, who has infinite compassion and love.* Learning not to over-identify with any particular aspect of myself, and to be steadfast in my commitment to allow for all aspects to reveal themselves, has transformed my entire life. This is my life's work, and my hope is that it infuses all of who I am and what I do.

My grandparents were my earliest spiritual teachers. Both of them culti-vated a sacred practice in their own way. My grandfather Angelo hung an old sepia-toned portrait of the Sacred Heart of Jesus at the top of the stairs on the second-floor landing and knelt before him every morning in quiet reverence. He also loved to go for long walks by himself and often strolled clear across Queens. In the days before his death he began to open his heart in new ways to release the pain that he had carried in this lifetime. One afternoon, as we sat together in the kitchen, he began to weep. This was the first and only time that I ever saw him cry. My brothers and I instinctively encircled him, holding him gently in our arms, his once strong body now frail from stomach cancer. He told us a story we had never heard, of his younger brother, who died when they were children. They were out playing and he was in charge of watching his brother. But something happened. They were swimming and his brother drowned. Grief rippled off my grand-father's body in waves as he sobbed. It had taken him to the end of his life to bear witness to his own pain. But he did it.

My grandmother attended mass regularly and prayed to the saints. She did the things she loved—she read, painted, gardened, wrote letters and occasional journal entries, and considered all of this to be the heart of both her spiritual practice and her life. As she aged, especially during the last part of her life, her devotion to her own joy, serenity, and spiritual growth was unwavering, especially after having lived the first fifty or so years com-pletely in service to her family. She was only forty-seven when I was born, so I was able to witness her third act in life. I watched very closely. As a result, I redefined my own act two, the period in a woman's life cycle typi-cally focused on motherhood (and sometimes marriage) that has shaped women's lives for generations. I chose not to marry or to have children in my twenties, thirties, and most of my forties and instead focused my ener-gies on mothering myself. No one in my family ever questioned my choice, and certainly not my grandmother. She was proud I had chosen another path and knew that she had helped facilitate this.

My grandmother Grace was in so many ways my earliest role model. She was born Mariagrazia in the Bronx in 1920, the youngest of fourteen, though she shortened and Americanized her name to Grace as she became a woman. Like my grandfather's family, her parents eked out a living doing heavy physical labor far from their rural village in the hills beyond "Nabola" (the way she said Napoli or Naples). Her parents both died when she was a child. Her mother Antonia passed away from complications with pneumonia when my grandmother was only twelve. Soon thereafter her father passed away as well.

One of the few remaining photos of her parents, taken at the end of their lives, shows them standing in their garden, behind the small produce store they owned on East 183rd Street, between Washington and Park near Arthur Avenue, in the Bronx. They lean into one another with visible affection, their heads gently touching, their faces serene. His arm is draped affectionately over her shoulder. Their hands are thick and strong, like the rest of their bodies. She is wearing a simple dark dress with a flower corsage and a beaded necklace. He wears a clean white shirt, old, worn trousers, and suspenders. These touches of elegance in their worn clothes suggest that it was a special day. But what is most pronounced is the love between them.

My great-grandmother Antonia has always been especially vivid to me because my grandmother told me so many stories about her. As a child I repeated her name aloud, feeling the Italian sounds move across my tongue. I learned that she was not literate but was curious about the world around her and often asked others to read aloud to her. She refused to wear the customary black when death came to a loved one because it would have meant wearing it continuously. My grandmother remembered her mother as unconventional, even rebellious, and told stories of her independence with great admiration. Her tone mirrored the way I felt about my own mother, since we both knew our mothers only when we were young children. We revered them like saints and held them in the deepest place in our hearts.

For both of us, our lives after our mothers died had been very rough. "What you had to live through," my grandmother would say to me often, especially in her later years, almost like a mantra, signaling her respect for my resilience. Neither she nor I had been allowed to grieve as children. Some of my grandmother's older sisters were unkind to her, and once their parents died she was firmly in their care. She would tell me often how she grew up feeling as if she was nothing, stupid, invisible, ugly. She had only an eighth-grade education, and when she was in her teens, after her parents passed away, she worked for one sister as a maid, in exchange for room and board. She married at nineteen and, like so many women of her generation, followed a self-sacrificing path that led to her misery.

By the time I was born, my grandmother's life had become unbearable. She suffered a nervous breakdown, fought off cancer, and buried a son—and this is not even the half of it. To heal she began to cultivate a spiritual practice firmly centered on nourishing herself. She connected more deeply with the sacred through a range of contemplative practices. She started making regular trips to the public library and pored over books by Rumi, Thomas Merton, Hermann Hesse, Kahlil Gibran, Jamaica Kincaid, Edna St. Vincent Millay, and Henry David Thoreau.

My grandmother became especially passionate about learning. She got her high school GED and then attended and graduated from Queensborough Community College in her sixties, taking courses in art history, English, history, and women's studies. She collected books from tag sales and thrift stores with titles like *Zen Flesh, Zen Bones, An Introduction to Haiku, The Meaning of Flowers*, and *Women of Faith and Spirit*. She kept St. Theresa the Little Flower and St. Anthony especially close. She meditated in her small but lush backyard garden in Flushing, to which she lovingly attended daily. She pressed the flowers she grew into phonebooks and cookbooks and then, after they dried, glued them carefully to ivory cardstock to frame or send to family and friends. She set up an easel on the front sun porch and began to paint with oils while also experimenting with Japanese reed paintings. She was drawn to landscapes: beaches, trees, gardens, and fields of flowers. She cultivated this craft for many years, and it was not long before her paintings became masterpieces. She rendered sand dunes, waves, clouds, and flowers with such delicacy and richness. Toward the end of her life she converted one small room in her house into an art studio.

On her deathbed at eighty-nine, my grandmother did not request a priest, though she had befriended several in her parish over the years. Instead she drew her loved ones close. Her death was a huge turning point in all of our lives. The center of our world was shifting. She was not feeling well and had a difficult time breathing. Several trips to the doctor and then to the hospital revealed that her lungs were not oxygenating properly. She probably had lung cancer. She had smoked a great deal in her lifetime, knowing full well that this day would likely come. She loved to smoke cigarettes and took great pleasure in each and every drag. For years, before I quit, we smoked together often at her kitchen table, relishing the sensation of the deep delicious inhale and the way the smoke unfurled on the exhale. When I quit, I realized how much smoking had been a way to connect with my breath.

My grandmother refused further tests or any talk of chemotherapy and decided instead to go home. She was ready. We all made the pilgrimage to see her. My drive to her deathbed is still a blur. All I really remember is the moment when I became visible to her in the doorway to her bedroom. The way her eyes searched through the group of people gathered there until she found mine. I don't think I will ever forget how we smiled at one another in that moment or how her sage green eyes were full of light.

She lay in her favorite nightgown, in her own soft sheets, in her warm bedroom, while the house hummed with the life that she had created. In the final days, as our large extended family gathered at her home, she moved in and out of this world, swimming with the currents, joining the spirits and then returning to look us each deep in the eyes and smile. Back and forth she went. Once she startled herself back into the room by calling out "Christ!" She opened her eyes, looked at me, and smiled. "He better be here!" she snapped. We burst out laughing. Hers was a death with dignity, awareness, love, and self-determination. To the very end she was present to herself, and it seemed to me that this was the kind of death that a rich spiritual life can bring.

My grandmother Grace was a woman who came to know and respect her own power. She was loving in a tough no-nonsense kind of way, always vigilant that it did not come at her own expense, especially in her later years. She took great care of herself while tending to all that was meaningful in her life. This was the heart of her spiritual practice, and it became mine.

It was my grandmother who also introduced me to prayer. I remember how inviting the dark, cool, quiet cavernous church of Saint Andrew of Avellino felt, a sanctuary from the bright sun and loud, heavy traffic on Northern Boulevard. The mass was a mixture of Latin and Italian, so I understood very little of it. But I loved sitting in the pew close to her, surrounded by all the older Italian ladies, their rosaries draped between worn fingers as they prayed together, women in quiet recognition of each other. I always dipped my hand in the cool water of the font and blessed myself, in the name of the mother, the daughter, and the Holy Spirit. I revised a lot of Catholicism as a child, to place women at the center because to me they were. I would cross myself when we passed the Blessed Mother everywhere in the neighborhood, just as my elders did, and I felt my mother's presence in her.

When I was older, my grandmother would greet her friends at church by pushing me forward, reminding them that I was her oldest grandchild. She'd tell them how I was going to college, and later how I was a professor, her pride always audible in her scratchy, thick Bronx accent. After mass we'd stop for lottery tickets at the corner store. We'd pick up some sausages from Mike the butcher, cold cuts from the deli, bread and pastries from the bakery, walking past the giant mural to a slain young man. *Rest in peace.* Past the weeping willow that bent over the giant metal fence, its roots pushing through cracked concrete. Back to my grandmother's kitchen that would look so tiny after she passed away but was the most sacred space of all.

How did it feel to be there? It was like entering the warmth of a beating heart. Hers was a working-class kitchen: thin wood paneling on walls painted cream, cheap linoleum on the floor, worn down in front of the sink and the stove, decorations collected from tag sales over the years, postcards from around the world taped up on the front of the pantry door and along the door frame, documenting holidays and all of our travels. There was just enough counter space for the dishes to dry, a coffeepot, and a small radio, so the tiny Formica table was the place where we did everything. That table could barely fit four; but with my grandmother in the seat closest to the sink, it was the very center of all of our lives. We gathered there late at night to smoke cigarettes, drink coffee, pick at leftovers, and talk about the day. In the morning we returned to share our dreams, the sunlight streaming through the one small window that looked right onto the neighbor's house. Sometimes voices were raised across the table's small expanse. Other times we held hands and wept. Mostly we told stories. And boy did we eat. "Did you have enough? Here, have some more. *Eat!*" Followed by laughter. We knew we could be pushy.

I can see the table now packed full of crumb buns and poppy seed rolls, salami, prosciutto, provolone, Swiss, ham, and some cheeses made by Trappist monks that somebody brought to share. "It's made by monks. Try it!" The smell of coffee, tomato sauce simmering on the stove, garlic, parsley, and lemon on the cutting board. Once before a wedding in the late 1970s, when I was around ten, I came into the kitchen to find some of my uncles and aunts, who were then in their early twenties, snorting cocaine. The white lines were arranged neatly on that same table. I didn't really know what they were doing, but I could feel the sacrilege.

I loved when the house was so packed that you could barely fit into the kitchen, but I also loved when it was just the two of us, my grandmother and me. Once, just before she became very ill, I had come for a visit. It rained the entire day so we couldn't sit outside in the garden as we had hoped. "Go look," she insisted, in reverence for the ever-shifting beauty of her garden. I grabbed an umbrella and stood in the center of this tiny plot that she had turned into a sanctuary. The Chinese maple planted soon after I was born, the hydrangeas that we thought would never return, the fig tree that Uncle Michael brought one Sunday, the basil and oregano, already as large as bushes, the special section that my grandmother devoted to my uncle John, who died in her home from AIDS when he was just forty. I had brought a lily. I put my offering in a ceramic pot, filling the edges with soil, and rinsed my muddy hands in a puddle. I stood there for a moment feeling the end of this era creeping in. Soon she would be gone, the house would get sold, and the garden would be paved over.

Our love is so deep. I know that death can't sever it. I know that she's more powerful now. When I imagine her in my mind's eye, I see her this way: shimmering light, radiating all that she is more fully than ever before. I know that I am of her, one of the many creations that she nourished with a full heart. I know that those we love must die and we will too. All of this knowledge does not assuage the pain of not hearing her voice, kissing her face, holding her hands, hearing her stories, looking into her eyes, and being alive together. Thirty-three lives she and my grandfather created. Now, like planets without their sun, we are spinning in a new space, forced to embody spirit even more fully.

The grief that my grandmother's death inspired circled me back down into the depths, back into the abyss. And I wondered: is part of the pain of death that we have to confront our underdeveloped abilities to connect with those we love on the other side? We have to face the limitations of our minds and bodies and feel how unfamiliar we are with the infinite?

⚕

As my grandmother prepared to die I received the page proofs for *Living the Revolution*, the book I wrote to honor her, her mother, my grandfather, and all my ancestors. It arrived just in time for me to show her the mock-up of the cover and my dedication to her and my grandfather, which included a photo of them with their first two children, including my father, the first-born, as well as the photo I love of her parents in their garden in the Bronx.

The book came out in the springtime while we were all still reeling from her passing. All told, the book was an eighteen-year odyssey that had occupied a great deal of my adult life up to that point. I don't think I will ever forget the day the book arrived in the mail. I opened the package on my porch and turned it over in my hands, hardly able to believe my eyes that it was finally in physical form. More than two decades ago I had gathered my books and left a lecture hall at the university where I was a student. As I strolled through dusty streets strewn with scattered leaves, I thought to myself, one day I'm going to write a book. I began to collect writing that inspired me, a collection of treasured texts that now fill several rooms. At that point I could barely craft a properly constructed sentence, much less a paragraph. First Fs, then Ds, and then slowly Cs began to appear on my college essays. But this little dream guided me through all that red ink, essay after essay, until one day, after a long and exhausting week, I arrived home to find my book waiting for me.

As my book went out in the world, I began to ponder. What do I want to create now? I rolled this over in my mind, let it into my heart, and watched it seep into my cells, this acceptance of creative power. I find that the answer comes subtly and quietly each day. Today I feel the garden calling me. Today I'd like to just sit and watch the sky from my hammock. Then I'd like to write down my dreams from the night before and maybe a little poem too. In this way my intention is to begin to perceive what my deepest and truest self, my innate essence, desires to create. I have come to realize that this inner voice speaks in soft tones, so listening requires being quiet and tuning in.

Thankfully, I am finally at a place in my life where I have the ability to work in this way, at my own pace, so I am slowing it all down. I am attending to my spirit more. I am spending more time with loved ones. I am having more fun. I am trusting that any creative/scholarly/professional expression of mine will be more meaningful if rooted in this practice of simply taking care of myself more fully and deepening my connection to myself. To do this feels both necessary and revolutionary.

So much about higher education and the world around us more generally removes us from a depth of being. An overvaluing of the intellect and productivity—doing doing doing and going going going—drives so much of our world, especially in the United States. Jumping through all the hoops that have brought me to this moment in time required a level of striving that was both debilitating and unsustainable. The great writer Sandra Cisneros reflected recently on why she had not published anything since her novel *Caramelo* in 2002, which had taken her a decade to write:

I was so exhausted writing that one I thought I'd never write another one because it took too long. It was like being in a convent or being in jail and I said I'd much rather have my freedom to live and explore it through other art forms. But now I'm being tempted by the idea of a novella (Lane 2015).

This is what it means to go where spirit moves you.

My book arrived in the mail from the press the same week the letter granting me tenure was delivered to my door. Just a few days later the chair of my department impressed upon me how I needed to continue the grind and not let up: promotion to full professor had to be achieved after the next seven years, not to keep my job as had been the case with tenure but to advance at the college. Another book had to be written. I needed to start now. I would also be expected to expand my service to the college in many more ways, mentoring the next generation of pretenure colleagues, chairing my department, serving on a whole host of college-wide committees, and so forth. Yet something deeper was calling me. My sole desire was to create the space to listen and follow my own intuition and guidance about any and all next steps. I had worked so hard for this privilege and was not going to squander it.

I have spoken with many women in the academic profession about this dynamic and many others have written about this as well (Castañeda and Isgro 2013; Gutiérrez y Muhs and Flores Niemann 2012; Seltzer 2015). We work ourselves to the bone, often to the detriment of our bodies, relationships, and spirits. All this sacrifice to acquire what we think will bring security in an insecure world: a livable wage, economic autonomy, and job security. When this striving became detrimental for me, I came to see how it was motivated by fear—fear of poverty, fear of economic dependence on a spouse and the level of vulnerability that this can bring (which I witnessed in so many of the women I grew up around), fear of not living up to my full potential, fear of not living my dreams, fear of not amounting to anything.

Once I began to realize and embody how true security comes from connection within, I began to enjoy life more, including my job, and reorient my inner compass in a more authentic way. The classroom, scholarly work, mentoring and advising, chairing my department, serving on college-wide committees, presenting papers at conferences, giving guest lectures—all the things that make up the professional life of a professor—I now see are among my chosen vehicles to learn this lesson about true security and the true self, the self beyond the titles, roles, activities, identities, accomplishments, failures: the self that is infinite.

Recently a friend who is approaching tenure at her institution wrote to ask me for any advice as she goes through the daunting process of evaluation. I passed on the piece of wisdom that was given to me by one of my wise women at the same time: trust that this job is your own creation. It is not something they gave you. It is something *you* created. Whenever I began to worry about the tenure process/decision I came back to this truth, that I created this because it served my highest good and hopefully the highest good of the all. If it is not meant to be then that is because there is somewhere else I need to be, and I trust that it will be even better than this.

This understanding helped me immensely because it reoriented the authority and power arrangements that undergird so much of our work lives, especially pretenure. We are told that we are in a "probationary period" (the institution's language). We are told that we have to prove ourselves worthy. I found this narrative to be immensely disempowering, but it also did not resonate with my growing spiritual understanding of the universe: that each of us is the co-creator of our lives with the Creator.

The college's wording alone ("probationary") suggests how much the carceral state has infused the language of contemporary life in the United States. The hierarchies of academia mirror those that shape the world all around us, and it takes a conscious effort to become more aware of this and decolonize our minds and beings. Formal educational spaces, especially at elite colleges like the one where I work, have historically been locations of great power, privilege, exclusion, and hegemony (Ahmed 2012; Bousquet 2008; Chatterjee and Maira 2014; Ferguson 2012; Kelley 2016; Wilder 2014). Each semester I see how students and colleagues are struggling to "become subversives in the academy," as historian Robin D. G. Kelley has written (2016), "exposing and resisting its labor exploitation, its gentrifying practices, its endowments built on misery, its class privilege often camouflaged in multicultural garb, and its commitments to war and security." We are attempting to create new educational communities, with the same simple yet mysterious questions: Who am I? Why am I here? What is my life's purpose? What does it mean to be alive at this particular moment in human history?

And we are alive at a momentous time, in a world dying and rebirthing before our very eyes: grave economic disparity, environmental degradation, perpetual warfare, and brutality and violence in the forms of hunger, poverty, exploitation, assault, abuse, mass incarceration, and many other forms of dehumanization are pervasive. As Barbara Tomlinson and George Lipsitz (2013: 1–2) recently summarized so powerfully: "The nation whose history and culture frame American studies scholarship and teaching seems to be unraveling at the seams. Its economy, environment, and educational system are all in crisis because of the cumulative consequences of four decades of neoliberal dispossession, displacement, and disciplinary subordination." When we factor in the less popularly known histories that gave rise to and continue to shape these forces, such as slavery, colonialism, capitalism, imperialism, white supremacy, racial segregation, heteropatriarchy, and nationalism, it becomes clear that our current moment is a culmination of many centuries of violence.

Yet this current state of crisis also brings the opportunity for a rebirth. We have the opportunity to take an evolutionary leap forward as a species. Indeed often it feels to me as if humanity is in a birth canal—chaotic, messy, dangerous, and frightening. Will we emerge? Many of us are afraid. But more and more of us recognize that we each play a pivotal role in this process. Therefore it seems all the more critical that we bring the whole of who we are to our work—our bodies, our spirits, our humanity, our deepest true self—and not leave any part of who we are at the door. The more we come to know and express the fullness of who we are, the more we will want to create a world that is beneficial not only to ourselves but to everyone else.

History offers us powerful guidance for these perilous times. It helps us to understand how oppressive power operates, to unmask it and make it more visible, to know how those who came before us survived enormous hardship, and to trust our capacity as human beings to transform, grow, and evolve. History also teaches us precisely what I learned from my grandparents: that the most visionary ideas of human liberation come from those excluded from formal political power, the stigmatized, outcast, maligned, so-called backward and illegal. We need these stories and their wisdom, especially now.

This sense of purpose and the commitment to build upon past generations' work to create a new world can inspire us. I have been a teacher for over two decades, first at state universities and community colleges in both rural and urban settings and for the last thirteen years at Smith College, a small liberal arts women's college in western Massachusetts. I offer classes on the subjects that I research and write: histories of women, im/migration, labor, race, transnational cultures and activisms, and revolutionary social movements in the United States. As with other educators committed to the radical possibilities of the classroom, I approach this profession with the understanding articulated so beautifully by bell hooks (1994: 207):

> The academy is not a paradise. But learning is a place where paradise can be created. The classroom, with all its limitations, remains a location of possibility. In that field of possibility we have the opportunity to labor for freedom, to demand of ourselves and our comrades, an openness of mind and heart that allows us to face reality even as we collectively imagine ways to move beyond boundaries, to transgress. This is education as the practice of freedom. (see also Freire 2013 [1970])

In aligning with such a practice, I turn to my ancestors and elders for guidance; but I believe deeply in the inspiration that flows from young people, as they bring fresh, creative perspectives to the challenges that face the world today. We need only to look at the world around us to see how the next generation is changing the world with enormous creative vision. Immigrant youth are coming out from the shadows Undocumented and Unafraid to fight for an end to detention and deportation and demand full access to citizenship, including the right to an education. They are forcing a deep questioning of citizenship overall and the right of nations to police and criminalize the historic movements of people across land and sea, sometimes in their own ancestral homelands. They are leading efforts to broaden and deepen understandings around gender and sexuality and pushing LGBTQ social justice movements to go beyond reformist demands such as marriage equality (Costanza-Chock 2014; Mock 2014; Nichols 2013; Truax 2015). They are filling the ranks of the Black Lives Matter (BLM) movement with "a call to action and a response to the virulent anti-Black racism that permeates our society" and rebuilding the black liberation movement by "broadening the conversation around state violence to include all the ways in which Black people are intentionally left powerless at the hands of the state" (http://blacklivesmatter.com/about; see also Herwees 2015). Young people have joined and formed dozens of BLM chapters across the country, in towns and cities, in middle and high schools, where they are cultivating hopefulness among the besieged and developing powerful critiques of structural racism as deeply interconnected with gender, class, sexuality, citizenship status, and dis/ability. Young people are also leading efforts to decolonize education and the larger world around us. As Arizona has attempted to make Chicana/o Studies illegal in public schools, teenagers have taken to the streets, chained themselves to desks during school board meetings, and formed alternative schools with their teachers, to fight for a curriculum that speaks to their hearts and spirits and honors their ancestors (*Precious Knowledge* 2011). They are exploring, expressing and demanding the right to live a deeper life, one not governed by the demands that a largely unconscious society makes of them.

Youth are at the forefront of such movements because they are often the most targeted by repressive state measures, especially black and brown children, whether in the form of "Stop and Frisk" practices and other forms of racial profiling and police repression, immigrant detention and mass incarceration, or vigilante violence. As Robin D. G. Kelley (2013b) has argued in his recent lecture series "The War on Our Youth":

> Problems that were once handled by teachers, principals and parents are now remanded to juvenile or criminal courts or police. Crisis, moral panics, neoliberal policies, racism fuel an expansive system of human management based on incarceration, surveillance, containment, pacification, lethal occupation, and gross misrepresentation.

Young people are "not only trying to stop the violence, they are creating a new community dedicated to a post-racist, post-sexist, post-homophobic, post-colonial world" (see also Kelley 2013a).

As an educator, one of my core commitments is to mentor and support all students, but I feel particularly devoted to first-generation students, working-class and low-income students, and all students of color, because their vision for the future of education is deeply democratic, accessible, and visionary. Having personally experienced exclusion and marginalization on multiple levels, they are asking their schools (which often express rhetorical commitments to diversity, equity, and access) to live up to their ideals and "walk the talk." They are holding us accountable in ways that are necessary and inspiring because they know how education can remain relevant to future generations.

Another core commitment of mine is to teach those histories that have been intentionally repressed in order to justify past and contemporary power arrangements, with the belief that such knowledge empowers, transforms, heals, and makes new worlds possible. This means rooting my courses in more marginalized histories. It also means connecting students with contemporary activists and social movements and supporting student activisms to transform higher education and the larger world. At the college where I work, students are leading efforts to defend dining and housekeeping workers' labor rights at the college and within the larger community. They are working to expand admissions policies and practices to admit, fully fund, and support undocumented students. They are creatively calling into question longstanding practices of racism, classism, and ableism at the college. I have found that as faculty we can play an important role if we listen closely to their visions. For one, we can help bridge the divide between the administration and the student body, to help facilitate conversations that assist everyone in moving beyond an "us/them" framework toward meaningful dialogue but also toward concrete material changes.

For me, such work is sustained by the relationships of solidarity and support that I have cultivated with colleagues at my college and within surrounding communities. When I began my job at this college, I organized a writing group with four other women on the faculty. For over a decade now we have met consistently. All of us work in the humanities and social sciences; all of us teach courses that explore power and resistance across time and space; all of us are similarly situated at the same college (we were all pretenure together and now we are all associate professors and chairs of our departments and programs). In many ways we reflect a new generation of faculty (at least at our college) because of our race, class, and cultural backgrounds and because each of us engages academic life from both an intellectual and activist perspective. And some of us bring spiritual practice into this as well. We supported one another as we wrote our first significant body of published work. We also talked about raising families, our love lives, and all the other things women tend to talk about when we come together, as well as surviving the rigors of academia. We always meet in our homes for at least a few hours, and there is always good food. When I read my book now I can easily mark the places in the text that emerged because of the rich conversations that unfolded among us. These women have become my close friends. They helped me to understand and appreciate my own intellectual ability through our sustained work together and work through the imposter complex that is so common for those of us who are the first to enter into such spaces. These relationships have also become foundational to our organizing work at the college, because we trust and care for one another deeply. Each year we work in multiple ways, sometimes as a whole, sometimes in pairs or smaller groups, to connect faculty, staff, students, alumnae, and community members in the shared project of creating an educational culture that encourages the practice of integrity, wholeness, dignity, cooperation, contemplation, and social justice.

I find that all of this work is a part of and necessitates spiritual practice. There are so many opportunities to get hooked throughout the day as we confront our own unconsciousness and the many ways in which it manifests in the world around us. Our intellects are a powerful tool for liberation, but they are extremely limited. History and the world around us instruct again and again how the intellect can become extremely dangerous when separated from heart and spirit. The world today feels particularly combative and reactive, and a small college campus, like any community, can very easily begin to vibrate to high levels of frustration, stress, anger, alienation, and disassociation. My work thus boils down to trying to be as grounded, nonreactive, and openhearted as possible in each and every encounter I have. I am not always successful of course. The semester can easily feel overwhelming, offering many opportunities to get reactive. But I try to notice when I have become hooked and to come back to my practice. It is always there for me. I need it now more than ever, especially in these deeply challenging times when we are called to remember our collective potential for rebirth and renewal.

NOTES

I am thankful to Melchia Crowne, Sujani Reddy, Angelo J. Guglielmo, Mark Guglielmo, Andrew Fletcher, Edvige Giunta, and Luisa Del Giudice for reading drafts and offering their wise advice and suggestions.
1. Hartman address at Smith College, Northampton, Massachusetts, October 1, 2015.

WORKS CITED

Ahmed, Sara. 2012. *On Being Included: Racism and Diversity in Institutional Life*. Durham, NC: Duke University Press.

Bousquet, Marc. 2008. *How the University Works: Higher Education and the Low-Wage Nation*. New York: New York University Press.

Brennan, Barbara Ann. 1993. *Light Emerging: The Journey of Personal Healing*. New York: Bantam Books.

Castañeda, Mari, and Kirsten Isgro. 2013, eds. *Mothers in Academia*. New York: Columbia University Press.

Chatterjee, Piya, and Sunaina Maira, 2014. eds. *The Imperial University: Academic Repression and Scholarly Dissent*. Minneapolis: University of Minnesota Press.

Chödrön, Pema. 2000. *When Things Fall Apart*. Boston: Shambhala.

Costanza-Chock, Sasha. 2014. *Out of the Shadows, into the Streets!: Transmedia and the Immigrant Rights Movement*. Boston: MIT Press.

Estés, Clarissa Pinkola. 2013. "Simple Prayer." In *How to be an Elder: Myths and Stories of the Wise Woman Archetype* (audiorecording). Sounds True.

Ferguson, Roderick A. 2012. *The Reorder of Things: The University and Its Pedagogies of Minority Difference*. Minneapolis: University of Minnesota Press.

Freire, Paulo. 2003 [1970]. *Pedagogy of the Oppressed*. New York: Continuum International Publishing Group.

Guglielmo, Jennifer. 2010. *Living the Revolution: Italian Women's Resistance and Radicalism in New York City, 1880–1945*. Chapel Hill: University of North Carolina Press.

Gutiérrez y Muhs, Gabriella, and Yolanda Flores Niemann, eds. 2012. *Presumed Incompetent: The Intersections of Race and Class for Women in Academia*. Boulder: University Press of Colorado/Utah State University Press.

Hartman, Saidiya. 2007. *Lose Your Mother: A Journey along the Atlantic Slave Route*. New York: Farrar, Straus and Giroux.

Herwees, Tasbeeh. 2015. "The Motivating Forces behind Black Lives Matter." *Good: A Magazine for the Global Citizen,* July 20, 2015: http://magazine.good.is/features /black-lives-matter-feminism-history.

hooks, bell. 1994. *Teaching to Transgress: Education as the Practice of Freedom*. New York: Routledge.

Kelley, Robin D. G. 2016. "Black Study, Black Struggle." *Boston Review*, March 7, 2016.

———. 2015. "Toward a Decolonial Democracy?" Part Three of "Mike Brown's Body: Meditations on War, Race, and Democracy" Lecture Series, Toni Morrison Lectures, Center for African American Studies, Princeton University, April 13–15, 2015.

———. 2013a. "The U.S. v. Trayvon Martin: How the System Worked." *HuffPost Black Voices*, July 15, 2013: http://www.huffingtonpost.com/robin-d-g-kelley/nra-stand -your-ground-trayvon-martin_b_3599843.html.

———. 2013b. "The War on Our Youth." Race Matters Lecture Series, University of California Center for New Racial Studies, November 21, 2013.

Lane, Tahree. 2015. "Of Two World Views: Sandra Cisneros Promotes Understanding among Different Groups." *Toledo [Ohio] Blade*, April 19, 2015: http://www .toledoblade.com/Books/2015/04/19/Of-two-world-views-Author-Sandra-Cisneros -promotes-understanding-among-different-groups.html.

Levins Morales, Aurora. 1999. *Medicine Stories*. Boston: South End Press.

Mock, Janet. 2014. *Redefining Realness: My Path to Womanhood, Identity, Love & So Much More*. New York: Atria Books.

Nichols, Walter. 2013. *The DREAMers: How the Undocumented Youth Movement Transformed the Immigrant Rights Debate*. Palo Alto: Stanford University Press.

Pontani, Angie. 2014. "Driving Jersey: Angie Pontani." New Jersey Public Television. Airdate February 27: http://www.drivingjersey.com/drivingjersey.com/Angie_Pontani.html.

Precious Knowledge. 2011. DVD. Directed and produced by Ari Palos and produced by Erin Isabel McGinnes. Dos Vatos Productions (70 minutes).

Seltzer, Rena. 2015. "To Find Happiness in Academe, Women Should Just Say No." *Chronicle of Higher Education*, July 19, 2015.

Tomlinson, Barbara, and George Lipsitz. 2013. "American Studies as Accompaniment." *American Quarterly* 65, no. 1 (March): 1–30.

Truax, Ellen. 2015. *Dreamers: An Immigrant Generation's Fight for Their American Dream*. Boston: Beacon Press.

Wilder, Craig Steven. 2014. *Ebony and Ivy: Race, Slavery, and the Troubled History of America's Universities*. New York: Bloomsbury Press.

Nine

REPINING RESTLESSNESS

JOANNE LESLIE

PROLOGUE

It was about 1986. I was working as an international health consultant. On this particular trip I was the only non-African member of a National Nutrition Assessment team in Togo. After traveling hours on mostly unpaved roads in two small jammed-full cars, we arrived in a remote village for the afternoon. For several hours the villagers graciously answered our questions about maternal diet, weaning practices, and child health problems.

The afternoon wore down; all of us wore down. It was time to get in our cars for the long drive back to the provincial capital. As we prepared to depart, one of our hosts politely mentioned that there was a woman in a nearby hut, the *dispensaire* (clinic), who had been in obstructed labor for over 24 hours. They hoped the visiting American doctor might check on her to see what could be done. The request threw me into an uncharacteristic moment of panic. My doctorate is in public health, so I knew I was not going to be much help. Fortunately, one of my colleagues was an experienced Togolese midwife. Eliane and I went into the little hut together.

Already the light was fading and the clinic had no windows. My job was to hold a kerosene lantern while Eliane examined the woman. Pretty quickly Eliane assessed the situation as *pas bon* (not good). She explained calmly but firmly, first to me and then to the woman's family, that both mother and baby would die if they remained in the village.

We offered, insisted in fact, to drive the woman to the nearest hospital. Actually, the nearest hospital was not all that close. It was back in the provincial capital with our hotel—a long bumpy ride, even under good conditions, and these would prove to be not good conditions.

Not only was it getting dark, but, worse, it had started to rain. The rest of our team members squeezed into one car and departed. More than an hour later, following some prolonged negotiation with the woman's family, and after acquiring a niece and some provisions to accompany her, the second car could leave. The driver and Eliane sat in front. The laboring woman sat in back with her niece on one side and me on the other. She grasped a hand of each of us and squeezed extremely hard with every contraction.

By now it was completely dark and the rain was sheeting down blindingly. We prayed we would not encounter other vehicles on the road. As we crept along our driver requested with increasing urgency that we stop, at least until the worst of the rain was over. But knowing that every minute counted, I insisted we keep going. Well past midnight we finally made it to town and transferred the woman into the hands of the not-so-welcoming hospital staff. I never learned the outcome. Eliane, whose judgment I trust, said that it was probably too late for the Caesarean section to save both mother and child. Most likely, the baby died but the mother lived and was able to return to her husband and other children.

This experience in Togo was one of the most dramatic of my international health career. However, it was by no means unique in involving me in life and death situations. What made the trip a spiritual turning point for me was the sense of confidence that my African colleagues, Muslim and Christian alike, expressed in God's presence throughout that day. Speaking with the same matter-of-fact certainty as when discussing medical matters, they assured me that God had sent us to the village to rescue the woman and that God had kept everyone safe during the long, dangerous drive to the hospital.

Then, as now, this does not quite align with my own understanding of how God works. Nonetheless, I finally acknowledged to myself a deep longing to share my colleagues' integrated sense of the HOLY at work in all aspects of their lives.[1] I remained fully committed to the goals of public health, but they no longer seemed like enough to sustain my sense of purpose. From that trip forward, I sought a way to merge my public health work and my reenergized faith life into one path.

First, a caveat. This essay is not an autobiography. Rather it considers how one important thread has woven itself through my personal and professional life. Many people and events, including many that are extremely important to me, have been left out or mentioned only briefly. I trust that no one's feelings will be hurt.

It may seem odd to designate my first forty-five years as the early years. It is only from the vantage point of my early seventies (and preparing for my second attempt at retirement) that I can see how raw and unformed I was during those first four decades. In my family life and career I had been fortunate and reasonably successful, but I had hardly begun any inner exploration. There were spiritual sparks from time to time, but I did little to kindle them.

My journey began on June 9, 1944. I was born in Ottawa, Ontario, to Scottish Canadian parents. All four of my grandparents had immigrated to Canada as young adults from Aberdeenshire, Scotland, bringing to their new lives plentiful energy and ambition but little in the way of money or education. The one partial exception was my maternal grandmother, Grannie Cumming, born Amelia MacDonald, who possessed a Scottish Teachers Certificate, of which she was justly proud. Upon arriving in Prince Albert, Saskatchewan, she taught elementary school for a couple of years, earning enough money to help launch Grannie and Grandpa's farm in the nearby community of Eldred.[2]

As the eldest of three grandchildren (with no cousins and just two younger siblings) I was a frequent and privileged audience for my grandparents' stories, which were formative in how I understood my place and purpose in the world. My maternal grandmother held particularly strongly expressed opinions about how "our kind of people" should behave.

One of Grannie's more beneficial biases was that our kind of people valued books. In the early twentieth century the provincial government of Saskatchewan provided traveling libraries for rural communities. One family would house the library in their home, and my grandparents offered to take on this role in Eldred. Both my grandmother and my mother recalled the excitement they felt over the monthly arrival of a new selection of books and their pride in being the home that others would visit to borrow these books.[3]

Another story, this one from my father's side, has mythic status in our family. Grannie Leslie, born Emma Duncan, came into the world one frigid day in 1887 in Keith, Scotland. Her mother had experienced several previous stillbirths. Apparently my grandmother also appeared to be dead at birth. The ground was frozen solid in January and the Duncan family lived on an isolated rural farm. So my grandmother's infant body was wrapped in a blanket and left in a shed until the ground could thaw enough for her to be buried. Fortunately, a little later someone happened by the shed, heard the baby crying, and brought her back into the warm house. Over the course of her reproductive years my great-grandmother Duncan gave birth to thirteen children, but only six lived to adulthood. Of those six, only one married: my grandmother, who could easily have died in the shed. Grannie Leslie herself had only one child, my father. When I learned about this remarkable series of births, deaths, and almost deaths, I felt simultaneously frightened and destined. The genetic thread had narrowed dangerously, but it never broke; thus my existence was made possible. As a child, this seemed to me miraculous. I believed that it indicated a special purpose for my life.

When I was three, my family moved from Canada to the United States. We lived first near Elizabeth, New Jersey, where my sister and brother were born. Then, when I was seven, we moved across the country to Walnut Creek, California. Despite moving to the United States very young, I did not grow up feeling American. Whether it was because of our annual summer visits to my grandparents in Vancouver, British Columbia, or because we did not change our citizenship, or just perversity on my part, I grew up identifying as Canadian and Californian but not as American.

As a young child I believe that I sometimes went to a Presbyterian Sunday school. However, my first clear church memory is of St. Paul's Episcopal Church in Walnut Creek, where my sister, brother, and I were all baptized. My main memory of my baptism is of feeling cheated because my parents also served as my godparents. I also remember on Sundays my longing to join other people going up to the communion rail, where I was sure something important was happening that I was being left out of. But my most formative childhood memory of church is from the Easter when I was ten years old.

The children had been asked to bring in a flower on Easter Sunday. I had taken a lot of care in selecting a perfect pink and yellow rose from the bushes that grew along our driveway. When we got to the packed church, in front of the transept there was a large, rather unattractive three-dimensional cross, constructed from chicken wire. During the service, perhaps at the offertory hymn, the children were invited to come forward to place their flowers in the chicken-wire cross. It felt like a long walk up to the cross. I was a bit nervous going alone but proud to place my rose in one of the empty spaces. By the time I got back to the pew to rejoin my family and looked again at the cross, it had been transformed into a thing of astounding beauty. The empty chicken wire cross was gone, replaced by a beautiful cross, constructed entirely of vibrant, colorful flowers.

Sixty years later I can still feel echoes of my awe and amazement at beholding the transformed cross. Perhaps, in part, my response was so powerful because I had participated in its creation. At the time I possessed no theological language to relate what I saw to emptiness and hope, death and life, the tomb and resurrection. But there is no doubt; when I was ten years old I had a visceral experience of Easter that marked me for life. That Sunday I felt the presence of the HOLY, and a desire to recapture that sense of connection has never left me.

It was only a couple of years after my Easter cross experience that my family made an unexpected international move. This move came like the answer to a prayer that I had not realized I had been praying. In retrospect I admit that my preadolescent angst may have been mostly born of frustration with a limited school curriculum and a growing disdain for what I perceived as the narrow horizons of suburban California. But I believe there was more than that.

At around age twelve I first became consciously aware of an intrinsic restlessness and sense of incompleteness that remains part of my nature even today. Years later I read and resonated with Margaret Guenther's description of herself (2006: 23): "When I was young, I could not have articulated what motivated me. I simply knew that there was always 'more'—not money, prestige, or power, but an indefinable something more."

I started reading and loving George Herbert's poetry in college, initially not having any idea that Herbert (like Guenther) was an Anglican priest. I felt such relief on encountering in his poem "The Pulley" (Herbert 1995) an explanation for this sense of unfulfilled longing that I could not seem to shake. I have taken my essay's title from this poem. Herbert attributes divine purpose to what he calls "repining restlessness." "The Pulley" describes a generous God who bestowed abundant gifts on his human creatures but decided to withhold the final gift of Rest. These are the final two verses.

> For if I should (said he)
> Bestow this jewel also on my creature,
> He would adore his gifts in stead of me,
> And rest in Nature, not the God of Nature,
>   So both should losers be.
>
> Yet let him keep the rest,
> But keep them with repining restlessness;
> Let him be rich and weary, that at least,
> If goodness lead him not, yet weariness
>   May toss him to my breast.[4]

Returning to events when I was twelve years old, in December 1956 my family had a visit from a college friend of my father's, Cam Williams, and his dark-haired, dark-eyed, Brazilian wife, Iliana, who spoke beautiful English with a musical Portuguese inflection. Cam, Iliana, and my parents sat around the fireplace in our Lafayette living room talking late into the evening. They may have been so absorbed in their conversation that they forgot that I was in the room. For whatever reason, I was not sent to bed and listened with growing excitement as it slowly dawned on me that my parents were actually serious about what was being proposed. Cam was inviting my father to teach in the first graduate program in chemical engineering in Brazil. The idea that my suburban family might pack up and move to Rio de Janeiro sounded unbelievably wonderful to me, like something out of the Enid Blyton adventure stories that had inspired me as a child.[5]

I remember staring into the flames in the fireplace that evening and holding my breath. I was afraid that I would wake up the next morning and discover that it had been just a dream or that my parents would change their minds. But six months later, just days after my thirteenth birthday, my mother, sister, brother, and I boarded the *Del Mar* in New Orleans to sail to Rio de Janeiro to join my father, who had already moved to Brazil to start work in March.

Brazil introduced me to an exotic new world, so different from the familiar rhythms and attitudes of life in either Canada or the United States. I was deeply disturbed by frequent encounters with raw poverty and less sanitary living. I remember my initial shock at seeing disabled children begging alone in the open-air street markets. I also vividly recall being scared out of my wits one night. Unable to sleep, I went to get a snack from the refrigerator and discovered cockroaches swarming on our kitchen floor. The next morning our maid, Dulce, offered me this surprisingly offhand reassurance: "Oh that's OK, the kitchen belongs to us during the day and to the *baratas* at night."

However, along with being distressed by the children and scared by baratas, I was also excited by the vitality and looseness of life that the streets of Rio offered. Perhaps because I quickly became more fluent in Portuguese than my parents, I was allowed a remarkable amount of freedom at age thirteen. I took my younger sister and brother to the American School by bus and rode the jam-packed *bondes* (streetcars) all over Rio to meet my friends or do errands for my mother. One day, while shopping in the open-air market, I was introduced to a delicious, sweet, deep pinkish-red fruit called *caqui*. For me, the intensity of color and flavor, the sheer juiciness of the caqui, symbolized everything that I loved about Brazil. For years I assumed that caquis were particular to Brazil. I was almost disappointed when many years later I was told that they were the same thing as persimmons.[6]

My in-school education during the years we lived in Brazil was not up to the standards of the California schools that we had left behind. The American school in Rio and Queens College, a British boarding school that I attended for a year in Terezopolis, were academically uneven at best, although I loved the adventure and independence of being at boarding school. However, my three years in Brazil provided an incomparable out-of-school education. I quickly learned Portuguese from being immersed in it daily and became reasonably fluent in French, serving as an afternoon companion to a down-on-her-luck Romanian princess.

In Brazil I also came face to face with economic inequality from both sides. On the one hand, I was appalled to see how poor the *favela* (slum) families were compared with my own. Within walking distance of our comfortable apartment, families were living in one-room shanties with no running water or electricity. On the other hand, I learned to feel awkward and embarrassed when I grasped how much wealthier and more sophisticated most of the other expatriate families were compared with mine. My economic horizons were broadened in both directions.

I would have been more than happy to finish high school in Brazil, but my mother was tired of struggling with the unfamiliar environment. My parents thought that my chances of getting into a good college would be better if I completed my last two years of school in California. An additional consideration was that my Leslie grandparents had died while we were in Brazil. It seemed important to return to be closer to my Grannie and Grandpa Cumming while they were still alive. So the summer I turned sixteen, after a wonderful family holiday traveling in Western Europe and visiting long-lost or never-before-met relatives in Scotland, we returned to the house in Lafayette from which we had left three years and a lifetime ago.

Two years later, in 1962, I started at Reed College in Portland, Oregon. My mother did not want me to go too far from home for college and my father had heard that Reed was very strong academically. Fortunately, he had not heard as much about Reed's reputation for free love, atheism, and communism. At Reed I majored in English and French literature, with an unofficial minor in social activism.[7]

From my perspective, I was fortunate to be in college in the mid-1960s. Many Reed students, like their peers across the country, were fervently engaged in the big political issues of the day. One early and particularly vivid memory is of a protest against HUAC (the House Un-American Activities Committee) that I participated in during my sophomore year. My then boyfriend, Peter Bergel, was one of the organizers of the witness and march at Pioneer Courthouse Square. Portland was not the progressive haven that it has since become, and I was nervous on my virgin foray into public social activism.

As I stood passing out flyers on the corner, an angry middle-aged woman began shouting at me about communism and beatniks. Then, coming close to my face, she venomously hissed that she hoped if I ever had children they would grow up to hate me. It felt like the curse of the wicked fairy. Peter, who was standing nearby, flushed red, and the muscles on the back of his neck grew rigid. I could see how much it cost him to stay true to his principles of nonviolence.

Feeling beleaguered together in a worthy cause can forge powerful bonds. At the end of my junior year at Reed, Peter and I decided to marry. This decision was clearly a major disappointment to my father and to a number of my professors, who had envisaged graduate school in my future. They may have known me better than I knew myself. Within a few months of graduation, Peter and I were on the verge of divorce. Part of the problem was a disagreement about going into the Peace Corps. Almost as soon as President John Kennedy established the Peace Corps in 1961, I wanted to join. It seemed, in many ways, a natural follow-up to my experience in Brazil. Before we got married, I somewhat unfairly extracted a promise from Peter that we would stay in Portland an extra year after his graduation so that I could finish and then we would go in the Peace Corps for two years.

In 1966 Peter and I got assigned by the Peace Corps to go to Bechuanaland. We would have begun training as soon as I graduated from Reed. I was very excited, but Peter begged me to find some way to postpone our departure so that we could spend the summer living the hippie life in San Francisco. I managed to get us reassigned to Liberia for September. But again, when the time came, Peter balked.[8] It was clear by then that our incompatibilities went deeper than the Peace Corps. To this day I stay in touch with Peter, and I have enormous admiration for his lifelong commitment to progressive causes. But we were just too young to be married—or at least I was.

The period from the fall of 1966 through the spring of 1968 was among the unhappiest, most hopeless times of my life. It looms gray and endless in memory, and I still have a hard time believing that it lasted less than two years. Initially I supported myself by working for AT&T in Oakland, California, as an overseas operator. This was where the Vietnam War intersected with my life in a more personal way. A typical shift involved at least one or two desperate wives or mothers asking me to try to reach a soldier in Saigon or Da Nang whom they had not heard from in months. During the year I spent working at AT&T I never succeeded in reaching a single soldier in Vietnam. Daily I felt guilt and a growing sense of anger.

In retrospect, it is clear that I was clinically depressed most of the first year after Peter and I separated. I lived in a dingy studio apartment, experimented with drugs, and slept about fourteen hours a day. I could barely drag myself to my job at the phone company. Eventually, however, I emerged from the worst of the depression. With some help from the son of a friend of my mother's, I got a job developing computer-assisted curriculum for elementary school children at the Institute for Mathematical Studies in the Social Sciences (IMSSS) at Stanford University and moved to Palo Alto.

I did not actually enjoy computer coding at IMSSS, but it was certainly an improvement on attempting failed phone calls to soldiers in Vietnam. During my year working at Stanford and living in East Palo Alto, I became part of a wonderful group of friends, especially Lucy, a woman I loved deeply for several years. In 1967 my sister Kathleen jump-started the next generation in our family by getting pregnant when she was nineteen. Kathleen was living in London, and my mother and I decided that I should go to England to be with her for the birth.

Lucy joined me in England soon after my niece Genevieve was born in July. From August 1968 to July 1969 Lucy and I wandered without a set itinerary all over Western Europe and North Africa, hitchhiking and picking up agricultural work when we needed extra money. I still have a much tattered copy of the single book I carried throughout the journey, *Modern Poetry* (Mack, Dean, and Frost 1964), complete with burnt corners from holding it too close to the fire that provided the only illumination in our olive pickers' hut in Provence. That poetry book remains a cherished talisman of a time that feels like the freest year of my life, at least in retrospect.

Eventually I began to feel restless, or at least the aimlessness of travel began to pale. I felt I should be doing something intentional and worthwhile with my life. I was also growing tired of having no money. By the time Lucy and I left Europe to return to the United States in the fall of 1969, I was fairly sure that, more than anything else, what I wanted next was to start a family. By Christmas I had returned to California and reconnected with some former friends and colleagues at IMSSS. That led to an introduction to a young professor of economics named Dean Jamison, who had just begun teaching in the Stanford Business School.

Dean, who was ill suited to a business school, had attached himself to IMSSS, where he was somewhat improbably assembling a team to work on a radio education project in collaboration with the Brazilian Space Agency. The project was seeking Portuguese-speaking curriculum experts to help develop teacher education material to be disseminated by satellite throughout rural Brazil. Dubious as I was about getting involved, I agreed to go to an informational meeting because the idea of returning to Brazil was intriguing.

An hour into the meeting, sitting across the room listening to Dean, who was slouched in his chair in a Pendleton shirt, soft-spoken and given to ironic jokes, I rapidly grew much more interested in the project. On the strength of my language skills and my previous IMSSS experience, I was hired. Over the course of the spring of 1970 I spent a great deal of time with Dean as I was being prepared to be sent as one of two "curriculum experts" to work at the Brazilian Space Agency headquarters in São José dos Campos.

As it turned out, I barely fulfilled six months of my two-year contract. Dean was based at Stanford, and our desire to be together outweighed the attraction of being back in Brazil. Dean and I moved in together in Palo Alto and got married in August 1971. Our first son, Julian, was born in January 1973; and six months later we moved across the country. Eliot, our second son, arrived only eighteen months after Julian. By the summer of 1974 I was somewhat surprised to find myself living as a full-time wife and mother in Princeton, New Jersey.

I spent the whole two years in Princeton pregnant or nursing. Except for one friend from Reed, who was a link to my former self as well as the mother of a young child, I knew no one. We were far away from both Dean's family and mine, and Dean traveled a lot. Despite the loneliness, however, life with two affectionate wee boys in a comfortable house with a big backyard bordered by a small creek had its rewards. I have many sweet memories of that time. The spring that Eliot was learning to walk, the boys and I spent a lot of time supervising the hatching of some robin eggs in a nest in the flowering cherry tree. As the baby birds fledged, I felt in sync with the mother robin.

My own mother very much wanted me to enjoy what she saw as my idyllic life as a suburban stay-at-home mom. However, by the time we were thinking about leaving Princeton, I had began to realize with increasing anxiety that being a wife and mother was not going to be enough for me. With Dean's strong encouragement I decided to explore opportunities for graduate school, although I worried that at thirty I might be too old to return to school.

It took reading a book by Alan Berg (1973) called *The Nutrition Factor: Its Role in International Development* to provide me with a focus for graduate school. Like most of my cohort of young mothers in the 1970s, I was obsessive about eating and drinking the right things during pregnancy. Thanks to Adele Davis,[9] I had consumed impressive amounts of fruit smoothies fortified with brewer's yeast and oyster shell calcium, especially during my first pregnancy. I was equally adamant about breastfeeding Julian and Eliot, something that I enjoyed and could feel virtuous about at the same time.

Berg's *The Nutrition Factor* provided a connection for me between my personal desire to give my own children the best possible nutritional start and my strong but dormant desire to alleviate poverty in low-income countries. Berg's data showing that malnutrition and declining rates of breastfeeding were major contributors to high rates of child mortality in the developing world spoke to the mother in me. However, it was his groundbreaking argument concerning the negative effect of child undernutrition on economic development that really captured my imagination. By the time I finished reading *The Nutrition Factor* during the quiet afternoons while both Julian and Eliot were napping, I realized I had found my professional path. Preparing myself to work on reducing child malnutrition in developing countries offered a chance to address a problem that was morally urgent and that offered a real possibility of having a large-scale impact, both of which were important to me.

Of course there was more to it than merely making a decision. My self-taught nutrition knowledge and the bits of economic development I had picked up from Dean and his colleagues were only a beginning. But now that *The Nutrition Factor* had showed me how the two fit together, I was surprisingly confident that I could and would acquire the other skills and information I needed to make a contribution.

I was fortunate to be accepted by the International Health Department at the Johns Hopkins School of Hygiene and Public Health. My Hopkins education took seven years—longer than we had expected, partly because I started out to get a master's degree and ended up doing a doctorate and partly because I limited the time I spent in school in order to be a hands-on mother. Although the decision to limit the hours that I spent away from home slowed the rate at which I could complete graduate school, surprisingly, at times being the mother of two small boys provided an advantage.

For an epidemiology course my first year at Hopkins, we were required to conduct residential interviews about dietary calcium consumption. I was frustrated by not having adequate time to spend in Baltimore going door to door and by the large number of people who refused to open their doors when I did finally find time. In desperation, one weekend when my mother was visiting, we took Julian and Eliot to Baltimore on a Saturday so I could try to conduct some interviews before we spent the afternoon with the boys at the aquarium. Approaching people's homes with a blond toddler in my arms and a serious-looking four-year-old holding my clipboard proved to be the magic formula. Doors were opened eagerly, and I easily completed my twelve interviews in one morning.

My life, like the lives of so many women of my generation, did not unfold neatly with one stage coming to a close before the next began. The decision to pursue graduate work in international nutrition was rooted in part in a concern about poverty and inequity that dated back to my teenage years in Brazil as well as in my disappointment about not going into the Peace Corps with Peter ten years earlier. The particular focus on maternal and child health grew directly from my own experience of pregnancy and breastfeeding.

An even bigger circling back, and one of the best gifts of my life, was the decision to have another baby when I finished graduate school. By then Julian and Eliot were nine and ten years old. Many friends and family, including most notably my mother, were perplexed by this decision, even disapproving. It seemed to them that two healthy boys happily established in elementary school and busy with soccer and tennis lessons constituted more than enough family for a couple nearing age forty who also had a demanding career in one case and serious career ambitions in the other. But for Dean and me, perhaps because we both came from families of three, having a third child had always been part of the plan. Having weathered some marital challenges and with my dissertation all but finished, the time finally seemed right.

One sparkling winter morning in January 1983 I got my amniocentesis results telling me not only that the baby had no chromosomal defects but also that she was a girl. More than thirty years later I can vividly see the trees heavy with snow and bathed in radiance and feel the joy of hearing the nurse give me the good news. The following June our daughter Leslie was born, nine pounds and full of wonder.

Julian and Eliot were thriving at a highly rated public school located right across the street from our house in Chevy Chase, D.C. When Leslie was about a year old, I got a job I loved at the International Center for Research on Women. It seemed as if all the pieces of my life were finally in place. I was working hard, certainly, juggling a busy professional life and three children, but I had everything I had ever wished for. I knew I should be completely content, and for a while I was.

This time it took several years and some events outside my control for the sense of restlessness to rise to the surface again. During the years when we lived in D.C. I was happy and reasonably successful in my public health career. Most of the time I worked part-time doing an interesting mix of research and program work related to maternal and child health and food policy in developing countries. Both Dean's career and mine involved international travel, which required frequent negotiation and careful scheduling, but we managed.[10] We loved our children, we enjoyed parenting together, and I think we were good, if occasionally erratic, parents.

In 1988, when Leslie was five years old, we moved back to California, this time to Los Angeles, where Dean's mother lived. The move was motivated in part to be closer to family because our parents were growing older. My mother, who lived in Oakland, had begun to develop some serious diabetes-related complications. I wanted to enjoy time with her, to bring the grandchildren closer and to be more available to help.

Dean got a tenured position in the School of Education at UCLA, and after a couple of years I was hired as an adjunct professor in the UCLA School of Public Health. Although my UCLA faculty position lasted for almost fifteen years, it was always part-time and never secure. So I supplemented my teaching with consultancy and nonprofit work, venturing increasingly into research and programmatic work on more local public health challenges such as obesity and chronic disease prevention.

SACRED CALLINGS

Almost as soon as we got settled in Los Angeles, I began seeking a church to attend. For people who are regular churchgoers, this is a normal, expected part of moving to a new place. But at age forty-four I had not attended church regularly since my family moved to Brazil. When pressed, I described myself as an agnostic during those years, although it was not true. My persistent sense of connection to the HOLY was something that I kept private for much of my early adulthood. I was somewhat embarrassed and mystified that I continued to pray. I would occasionally slip off to an

Episcopal church on Christmas or Easter. My husband and friends did not disapprove; they just did not understand.

Once we got to California, my need to be part of a church community felt more urgent. I was also finally willing to come out of the closet as a person of faith. Perhaps, in part, it had to do with growing older, wondering about the meaning of life and facing the prospect of my mother's death. At least initially, however, my need for church felt less like a search for answers to existential questions. What felt more urgent was my need for a spiritual welcome that felt authentic and my desire to be part of a justice-focused community I could trust.[11]

After I had visited but had not felt entirely comfortable in several affluent Westside churches, one of my UCLA students (Katie Derose, who has subsequently become both a close friend and fellow deacon) introduced me to Holy Faith Episcopal Church in the working-class community of Inglewood, California. When I first went there in the fall of 1991, Holy Faith was a vibrant, multicultural, socially progressive congregation with, among other groups, a large number of parishioners from Nigeria. The Nigerians looked, dressed, and talked much like the friends and colleagues I had worked with in francophone West Africa for over twenty years. The priest was smart and personable and engaged my questions seriously. The congregation was welcoming and clearly enjoyed gathering around the table, both at the altar and at the coffee hour. Although it sounds clichéd, when I walked into Holy Faith that first Sunday in the summer of 1991, I knew that I had come home.

For the first few years after I joined Holy Faith, I did not try to integrate the different components of my life. I rather liked the way the three realms balanced each other out, each one refreshing me for the others. I had my busy family life, which included an ambitious house-remodeling project in Pacific Palisades. I had my multifaceted public health career, which encompassed international consultancies, teaching at UCLA, and collaborating with feminist colleagues and students to launch a nonprofit called the Pacific Institute for Women's Health. And I had my church life, rich with sacrament, service, and a growing trust that I was being embraced and supported by something bigger and more mysterious than I could describe.[12] Then things started to unravel.

The story of how Dean's and my twenty-three-year marriage came apart does not need to be told here. The tangled threads that lead to the disintegration of a long relationship can provide an engrossing if painful subject of conversation for those directly involved, but for everyone else—with the possible exception of the therapists and lawyers who are paid to sort through the mess—it is a tedious tale. Suffice it to say that soon after we moved to Los Angeles Dean was offered an opportunity to return to the World Bank to head the team putting together the first ever World Development Report on Health (*WDR93*). This was a major responsibility and required his being in D.C. or on the road for the better part of eighteen months. I stubbornly refused to uproot the children and myself, and Dean stubbornly insisted that this was a prestigious and consequential opportunity that he could not turn down. The resulting *WDR93* (World Bank 1993) was a big success, highly visible and influential in shaping the global health field in the years since.[13] Unfortunately, it also cost us our marriage. But even that painful loss had a silver lining. The divorce led indirectly to my call to ministry.

I clearly recall one of Dean's and my more dramatic arguments as we strode up and down the slate steps in front of our house in Pacific Palisades. Those words I yelled out almost twenty years ago are seared into my memory, although I suspect that he forgot them within the hour. In the time-honored fashion of angry couples, we were busy defending ourselves by hurling accusations at the other as fast as we could. I can see myself standing on the second step from the sidewalk shouting up at Dean in desperate frustration: "You don't know anything about me; why I might want to become an Episcopal priest." Then, as now, I wonder where those words came from. I could not remember ever consciously having thought about religious ordination except for a teenage fantasy about becoming a nun, which I believed was impossible because I was not Roman Catholic. But in my hurt something broke open that day, and the words just spoke themselves.

In the 1990s I made a few forays to bring my public health life and my faith life a little closer together. I began noticing more and more public health studies exploring possible beneficial linkages between personal religiosity, or attendance at worship services, and health. So I cautiously introduced a sociological perspective on religion and health behavior into my UCLA courses. Then in 1998 I stumbled across an opportunity to apply for state funding to start nutrition and exercise promotion at African American churches. I obtained one of the first California Nutrition Network grants for Healthy Active Families through their faith channel. Holy Faith, Inglewood, was a pioneer in the now quite widespread faith-based health promotion movement.

But for quite a while the idea of ordination seemed to me much too radical a step. I wrestled with what I have later learned are common objections of a person discerning a call to ministry: I was not properly qualified (either morally or educationally); my friends and family would be shocked; how could I presume to lead others closer to God when I was plagued by doubts myself? I was also held back by more personal concerns. I did not want to delude myself, mistaking what might be nothing more than a need to feel wanted and useful after my twenty-three-year marriage to Dean had ended for a genuine call to ordination. Last but not least, I did not want to abandon public health. I was not looking for a new career. I just kept feeling that there was something more I was meant to do.[14] Despite my outburst to Dean, however, becoming a priest did not feel like exactly it.

Then my friend Katie, en route to getting her own doctorate in public health, was ordained at Holy Faith into the Sacred Order of Deacons. As I supported Katie's process, I learned more about this ancient order of ministry. Because diaconal ministry focuses primarily on service outside the church rather than on congregational work (although deacons participate in both) I started to see a way in which I could remain in public health and also respond to the call to ordination.

Once again a book came into my hands at just the right moment. Katie gave me a copy of *The Diaconate: A Full and Equal Order* by James Monroe Barnett (1995). Katie's inscription, dated June 1998, reads: "To the newest deacon-to-be, to help you in your discernment." Later that summer, on a consulting trip to Africa, I remember lying on my bed in a small, family-style hotel in Nairobi, Kenya. I finished reading Barnett's book and returned to a paragraph that had particularly struck me:

> Perhaps the most misunderstood idea relating to the diaconate is the fact that its primary significance does not lie in any of its functions, whether pastoral, charitable/societal, or liturgical. The origin of the diaconate and its development in the first centuries reveals above all the deacon as symbol par excellence of the Church's ministry. The deacon illuminates the indelible character of *service* Christ put on his ministry and of *servant* on those who minister.

He is the embodiment of the first principle of this ministry: *sent* to *serve*. (Barnett 1995: 137)

In that moment I accepted that the ordained diaconate was indeed my call. What I experienced went beyond intellectual assent. I felt emotionally and spiritually ready to connect more deeply with the HOLY through service, accepting also that I had no idea exactly where this might lead me.

In the Episcopal Church the process of selection and formation of a deacon is quite rigorous and lengthy. But, as if to balance out my prolonged time of discernment, my formation went quickly and smoothly. I was able to complete most of the required coursework during one ambitious academic year at the Church Divinity School of the Pacific (CDSP) in Berkeley from fall 2000 through spring 2001. This timing coincided with Leslie's first year at college, thus helping me survive what otherwise would have been a bad case of empty-nest syndrome. I was also able to live with my mother in Oakland during the CDSP year. Mom died of congestive heart failure at the end of 2002, and I will always be grateful for the gift of our time together.

On June 8, 2002, I was ordained a deacon in the Episcopal Diocese of Los Angeles. My presenters represented all parts of my life: my sister Kathleen; my soon-to-be husband, Walter;[15] Toni Yancey, a friend and fellow professor at the UCLA School of Public Health;[16] Katie, my friend, fellow deacon, and public health colleague; Ken Adams, the leader of Holy Faith's Social Concerns Committee; and Gary Commins, the priest at Holy Faith who remains one of my wisest friends and mentors. In addition to being precious to me individually, as a group they were a visual testimony that my dream of bringing my public health life, my family life, and my faith life together had finally come true.

I have found many opportunities and avenues to do public health work as a deacon. One of the most meaningful activities took place at my current church, St. John's Cathedral in downtown Los Angeles. For several years a group of us organized foot washing for the homeless men and women who came to our food pantry. As we soaped and rinsed dirt off calloused feet in preparation for them to be examined by a team of nurses, I realized with joy that I was simultaneously participating in worship and public health.

As a more recent example, as this essay was being initially written, I involved our diocese in education and outreach about Covered California.[17]

Through this project the church was able to offer valuable information to its congregants and others in the community about new options for health insurance and improved access to preventive care through the Affordable Care Act. At the same time, by making information available through a trusted institution such as the local church, we were able to reach individuals who were mistrustful or unaware of other sources of public health information. Only through connections in both the public health community and the faith community was I able to broker this partnership. It felt like exactly what I was ordained to do.[18]

CLOSING THOUGHTS

After almost fourteen years of serving in ordained ministry and on the boards of several admirable nonprofits, I again feel stirrings of restlessness and uncertainty about my true north. Working on this essay has provided a welcome opportunity not only to look back but also to imagine forward. I am fortunate, as I begin my seventh decade, that both my husband and I are in reasonably good health. It would be quite possible to begin a new vocation.

I have seriously considered expanding my diaconal ministry into a challenging new area such as some kind of church without walls for those who don't feel welcome coming inside. I also feel drawn to accompanying people who are dying, particularly those who otherwise might die alone. I have thought about finally visiting Botswana (formerly Bechuanaland) or going on a mission trip to Haiti or on pilgrimage to Iona. I could certainly benefit others and myself by improving my quite modest skills in gardening and Spanish. But my remaining decades are few; I am not at all sure that a new goal is what I need.

All my life, immersing myself in a new activity or taking on a new set of responsibilities has been my default way to tame the restlessness. To be honest, I have now spent enough time in therapy and spiritual direction to have learned that new activities will never satisfy my truest longing. At this stage in my life I will be served better by *unlearning* things than by *learning* things. Although it runs counter to my nature (or at least counter to long-established patterns) the time has come for less *doing* and more *being*.[19]

In the Episcopal Church we talk of the three-legged stool of scripture, tradition, and reason on which our faith is grounded. In a sense my life is now based on my own personal three-legged stool of family, public health, and ministry. This personal stool feels quite solid and sufficient. I don't really need or want a four-legged stool. I hope and intend that I will always have time and energy to give to family, public health, and some form of ministry, especially to my growing brood of beloved grandchildren. Now it is my turn to sit on the stool that I have built and tell *my* grandchildren stories.

Much more than when I first read "The Pulley," I grasp the wisdom in what Herbert imagines God saying: "If goodness lead him not, yet weariness may toss him to my breast." Although not exactly weary, I have begun to experience a certain disenchantment with striving, planning, and leading. Resting on the breast of God sounds increasingly appealing.

So for now there is no more need of comment. I wait, with as much patience as possible, for what the HOLY has in store for me next.

NOTES

1. I have adopted the term "the HOLY" from *Living on the Border of the Holy* (Countryman 1999). Countryman uses the term to point to our "non-rational" sense of the divine, an awareness that can never be captured by language. I had the good fortune to have Bill Countryman as a professor when I was in seminary at the Church Divinity School of the Pacific in Berkeley in 2000. Among his many wonderful books, this one was particularly helpful to me as I struggled to situate myself both as an Episcopalian and as part of a larger, more fluid, and more inclusive faith world. Perhaps more important, *Living on the Border of the Holy* helped to show me how accepting a call to ordination could be consistent with firmly believing that all people are called to ministry.

2. In the summer of 1998 my mother took my brother, my sister, and me on a long postponed trip to see where she had grown up. Eldred no longer exists as a town, although you can follow the bed of its railroad tracks. We also managed to get inside the community hall that my grandfather had helped build, which was still standing sturdily in the prairie wilderness seventy years later. By the next summer my mother was confined to a wheelchair. She died in December 2002. We were all grateful to have made the trip when we did. And my mother's impromptu baptism of us in the waters of the Saskatchewan River was a *thin space* experience that all three of us treasure.

3. A year ago my husband and I purchased a small wooden outdoor bookshelf from the Little Free Library organization. We painted it bright blue to match the trim on the house and installed it in our front yard. It started out with our own eclectic selection of children's books, detective stories, E. B. White classics, and books on religion. But since the idea is for neighbors to take, borrow from, and add to the

collection, it continually changes. I love the idea that I am replicating a piece of my own family history in Santa Monica in the twenty-first century.

4. Herbert's poetry is deeply satisfying because it works both poetically and theologically. Herbert writes of our relationship with God with an economy of expression and in a way that almost always rings true for me. In addition to "The Pulley" I find my own experience perfectly described in Herbert's "Love (3)," which addresses the human sense of unworthiness in the presence of the HOLY.

5. The Enid Blyton series that I especially loved was the "Famous Five Series," starting with *Five on a Treasure Island*. These stories, which were sent to me by my Scottish aunts for Christmas and my birthday throughout elementary school, featured four cousins and a dog who spent the school holidays together. They always seemed to find themselves in the middle of a challenging adventure, which they got through with almost no intervention from adults. The oldest cousin was named Julian. I gave this name to my first son, although I did not consciously make the connection to the Famous Five until years later.

6. I actually still find this hard to believe, for no persimmon that I have eaten in the United States tastes remotely like the caqui I remember from Brazil.

7. Years later I met Professor Burton Clark, who very kindly gave me an autographed copy of his book *The Distinctive College*, when he learned that I was a graduate of Reed College. This book focuses on the way in which three colleges (Antioch, Reed, and Swarthmore) acquired and maintained their reputations for academic excellence. Writing of Reed, Clark (1970: 91) observes: "Portland, Oregon, is a long way from the cities and suburbs of the Eastern Seaboard, where the money and sophistication of an established upper class have helped to fashion superior institutions. All in all, Reed rocketed to the top in an unlikely setting." I am grateful to my father for finding the almost perfect college for me relatively close to home, although he may not have realized all of what Reed offered in the way of extracurricular activities.

8. I have had a chance to travel and work in many countries and on all continents since then, even once visiting Liberia, but both Peace Corps assignments remain missed opportunities that I continue to mourn. I tried to continue with the Liberia assignment on my own and was outraged when told that the Peace Corps had a policy against accepting one member of a married couple.

9. My two go-to Adele Davis books were *Let's Eat Right to Keep Fit* (Davis 1970b) and *Let's Cook It Right* (Davis 1970a). They remained the dog-eared Bibles in my kitchen throughout my pregnancies and most of my children's formative years. I no longer have either book, but I am pleased to note that Adele Davis's fan club continues to flourish.

10. I offer a vote of appreciation (to wherever their spirits may reside) for the gift of devoted grandmothers. Dean's mother, Dell, and my mother, Pat, are both now deceased, but my gratitude for the many times they stepped in to help care for Julian, Eliot, and Leslie remains very much alive. I hope that they know how much I love and appreciate them.

11. I recently read with great interest *The Faith Instinct* (2009) by Nicholas Wade. Wade makes (to me) a compelling case for the evolutionary roots of religion. I was particularly interested that he finds the community-binding, group-solidarity aspect of religion to be its root *raison d'être* onto which various creeds and belief systems were

later grafted. This sequence of events seems to be mirrored in my personal faith journey.

12. Again Margaret Guenther's description of her own experience captures mine almost perfectly. In *At Home in the World*, Guenther (2006: 24) writes: "A lifetime of turning and turning and turning again, which is what conversion means, has bit by bit destroyed my bland, two-dimensional images of God and replaced them with a multifaceted Mystery. Something tells me that I am not done yet. *Conversatio morum* is the work of a lifetime."

13. I bear no grudge against the report itself. In fact I am rather proud of my association with it and of the sections on nutrition that I helped to write. As a testimony to the enduring influence of *WDR93*, the influential British medical journal the *Lancet* commissioned and published in December 2013 a twenty-year follow-up entitled "Investing in Health: World Development Report 1993 @ 20 Years."

14. Shortly before I began writing this essay my sister loaned me a book that she thought I would find interesting: *The Third Chapter—Passion, Risk, and Adventure in the 25 Years after 50* (Lawrence-Lightfoot 2009). Sara Lawrence-Lightfoot, the Emily Hargroves Fisher Professor of Education at Harvard University, identifies the years when we are neither old nor young as the Third Chapter, a time of resisting the narrative of decline and allowing deferred passions or burgeoning dreams to lead us in new directions. I found *The Third Chapter* helpful in identifying a broader cultural phenomenon into which my own experience of midlife ordination partially fit.

15. I did not plan to remarry, but the fall after I returned from seminary I went to a church-related social justice conference, where I met a very good looking, recently retired fellow Episcopalian named Walter Johnson. Walter and I hold similar values. We each have three children and we entered the grandparenthood stage of our lives together. The chance to share my church life, my social justice work, and our beloved grandchildren with Walter has made all of it richer. I thank him so much for his support over these fourteen years.

16. Dr. Antronette (Toni) Yancey was a close friend and colleague at the UCLA School of Public Health for over twenty years. It is in large part through my collaboration with Toni that I had an opportunity to do research in marginalized communities of Los Angeles. I learned most of what I know about the social realities of ethnic disparities in health from Toni. It was an enormous loss to me personally, as well as to the world of public health, when Toni died of nonsmoking-related lung cancer in April 2013.

17. Covered California is the name of the state health insurance marketplace established for our state implementation of the Affordable Care and Patient Protection Act. I serve on the board of a nonprofit in Los Angeles called Community Health Councils (CHC). The Episcopal Diocese worked as one of ten subcontractors to CHC on their Covered California education and outreach grant. As of the end of the initial enrollment period (which ended March 31 2014) enrollments surpassed their goal in the state. It feels gratifying to be a small part of the nationwide success of the Affordable Care Act.

18. In 2003 I was interviewed for a book being written by Gary Gunderson, then on staff at the Interfaith Health Program of the Carter Center, entitled *Boundary Leaders*. Gunderson (2004: 9) defines a boundary leader this way: "As a boundary leader

you will flip inside out and upside down, over and above, across and beyond the dominant boundary definitions of our time." My own story did not make it into the final version of the book, but I embraced the term "boundary leader" as part of my self-definition. It fits the diaconal vocation perfectly. Deacons walk with one foot inside the church and one foot outside, which is not a particularly comfortable way of walking.

19. I have been helped to understand this not only by my spiritual director but also by a wonderful book on spirituality for the second half of life by Richard Rohr, entitled *Falling Upwards* Rohr suggests that there are two major tasks of life. The first task is to create a strong *container* or identity and to "build a proper platform for our only life" (Rohr 2011: xiv). The second life task is more spiritual and not arrived at by everyone. Rohr emphasizes that most of the skills we honed for the first task, which necessitate lots of *doing*, don't serve us as well for the second task, which requires more *being*.

WORKS CITED

Barnett, James Monroe. 1995. *The Diaconate: A Full and Equal Order*. Valley Forge, PA: Trinity Press International.

Berg, Alan. 1973. *The Nutrition Factor: Its Role in National Development*. Washington, D.C.: Brookings Institution.

Blyton, Enid. 1942. *Five on a Treasure Island*. London: Hodder and Stoughton Limited.

Clark, Burton R. 1970. *The Distinctive College: Antioch, Reed & Swarthmore*. Chicago: Aldine Publishing Company.

Countryman, L. William. 1999. *Living on the Border of the Holy: Renewing the Priesthood of All*. Harrisburg, PA: Morehouse Publishing.

Davis, Adele. 1970a. *Let's Cook It Right*. New York: Signet Books.

———. 1970b. *Let's Eat Right to Keep Fit*. New York: Signet Books.

Guenther, Margaret. 2006. *At Home in the World: A Rule of Life for the Rest of Us*. New York: Seabury Books.

Gunderson, Gary. 2004. *Boundary Leaders: Leadership Skills for People of Faith*. Minneapolis: Fortress Press.

Herbert, George. 1995. *The Complete English Works*. Everyman's Library Edition. New York: Alfred A. Knopf.

Lawrence-Lightfoot, Sara. 2009. *The Third Chapter: Passion, Risk, and Adventure in the 25 Years after 50*. New York: Sarah Crichton Books.

Mack, Maynard, Leonard Dean, and William Frost, eds. 1964. *Modern Poetry*. 2nd ed. Englewood Cliffs: Prentice-Hall.

Rohr, Richard. 2011. *Falling Upward: A Spirituality for the Two Halves of Life*. San Francisco: Jossey-Bass.

Wade, Nicholas. 2009. *The Faith Instinct: How Religion Evolved and Why It Endures*. New York: Penguin Press.

World Bank. 1993. *World Development Report 1993: Investing in Health*. New York: Oxford University Press.

Ten

FINDING MY FEMALE ZEN ANCESTORS

Is There Such a Thing as a Woman?

GRACE SCHIRESON

How surprised I was, in 1985, when a male Zen Buddhist teacher, recently returned from a North American conference of Zen teachers, offered a nonanswer to one of his female student's questions. She asked: "How many women teachers were included in your conference?" The male teacher answered: "We were all women." A long, confused silence followed. He had offered one of the last patriarchal holdouts within our tradition, and we were made speechless by it. How do you speak to the Buddhist invocation of oneness when it silences you and your personal experience?

I had found Buddhist practice because I believed that women had an equal place in the tradition. I had loved the spiritual feelings that arose for me in the Reform Synagogue I attended. While I was raised in the Jewish tradition, the inclusion of girls in a Bat Mitzvah ceremony was not known to me. Furthermore, I saw no female rabbis or other indication of female leadership in the tradition. When I was introduced to meditation practice by Shunryu Suzuki Roshi in 1966, I saw no obstacles to my full entry as a Zen practitioner. But I was getting an education in Zen's more subtle exclusionary practices.

This particular interaction brought up the tension that I felt between the female students, who were beginning to question the disparity between Zen's *stated* position on female equality and the *actualization* of full inclusion for women within the institution. The Buddhist position on equality of all beings is one of its fundamental tenets. But no matter what the principle, where were the actual examples? At that time there were few female teachers leading Buddhist practice communities (sanghas, retreat centers, and so forth). Most importantly, the woman was daring to question an American male founding teacher about Zen women's representation in the real Zen world, not in the world of beautiful ideas. And she was smacked down with the "Oneness" thing.

The woman's question and the teacher's response also pitted the female student's suffering and insight against the teacher's wisdom and authority. Women exchanged glances and silently wondered: will women ever be empowered to participate fully in Zen or not? And more immediately: can we even ask this question and continue to be accepted in a Zen community in which a male teacher can smugly say that "we are all women"? Do we women not "get" Zen, or does this male teacher not "get" us?

MY JOURNEY

Twenty years ago the women present looked uncomfortably at one another, perplexed at our bind; we did not have the words or the assurance of inclusion to challenge his answer verbally. Today I would cut through the "Oneness" trick by politely asking him: "How many of you women teachers used the ladies' room at the Zen conference?" "How many of you were menstruating during the conference?" Or: "How many of you women chose not to wear your brassieres because supported breasts did not fit well in the priest *koromos* [required formal teacher attire] designed for men?"

It took twenty of my more than forty-five years of Zen practice to go beyond being intimidated by the "Oneness" ruse ("We are all women") and formulate a response to Zen teachers using it to sidestep the possibility that gender discrimination in fact exists within Zen. Doubtless, there is the One. It shows itself as rocks, mountains, and rivers—as well as men and women. But, as stated in the Zen chant book at Berkeley Zen Center: "To understand that all is one is not enough." The One reveals itself through myriad unique formations—even as men and women. Why was it so difficult to talk about women and their place within Zen?

So often the questions we pose about the place of women in the history of a specific tradition are met with defensiveness. Men feel attacked; the questions bring up personal memories of painful conversations with sisters, wives, or daughters. Men may feel the enormity of the discrimination against women in their lives and may feel uncomfortable about their helplessness to solve the conundrum or may even feel guilt.

My own questioning about women in Zen Buddhism arose as a request for more information, not as a complaint about unfairness. But no matter how carefully I posed the question about women and their inclusion in Zen's history (to avoid being met with personal defensiveness) my questions still challenged my teachers' personal authority and the teachings of Buddhism. My questions raised the possibility that mistakes (gender discrimination) could be found in the formation of the Buddhist institution. If there were flaws or mistakes in the Buddhism that our teachers had received from their teachers, then what was the basis of their teaching authority?

Understanding how provocative continued questioning was becoming, I felt that I had to change the course of my inquiry if I wanted to maintain my credibility and relationships within the Zen Buddhist community. I also felt that in order to pursue this particular topic, as a Zen practitioner, I needed to respect Zen's traditional goals and not become overly focused on my personal issues. In other words, I needed to make sure that I was not entangled in myself-clinging as a female Zen person. It was essential that I move beyond my own story, my wound, my sorrow, and my anger about a long history of neglect. And yet, perhaps even worse, I asked whether indeed women had purposefully been eliminated from Zen's history.

My study goals shifted in 1998; I stopped questioning what had gone wrong with Buddhism and why women Zen teachers had been excluded from the historical record. Instead I began to see my function, in the current Zen generation, as a seeker of stories of *actual* not mythical women and their historical spiritual practice from the beginning of Buddhism. I wanted first to find their stories and then to build a conduit for these exemplar women's past practices by which to move them forward so that they might speak anew and finally be heard. I wanted to collect the teachings from our Zen grandmothers and honor their efforts by carrying them to our Zen granddaughters—the women who were still on their way to entering Zen practice in the West. I wanted to find my own practice as a twentieth-century Western woman by finding my place within this community of historical Zen teachers. My studies of my female ancestors revealed their own sense of dual lineage: a formal inheritance from their ordaining teacher, and a matrilineal lineage from their female ancestors. I was finding my own dual ancestral lineage. And I wanted to help contemporary Zen practice find its way to a more balanced perspective that included the voices of male and female Zen masters.

By moving beyond an idealization of "Patriarch's Zen," I sense that I have developed a more mature love of and responsibility for Zen practice. After finding my female ancestors, I changed my focus from why and how female Zen ancestors had been erased from Zen's history. I had learned through my research that early Buddhists placed women teachers in a lower position than male teachers. Additionally, blaming the Buddhist institution for neglecting women's history in the tradition seemed to raise more defensive responses than interest in the subject. Rather, I concentrated my efforts to identify these erased women and put them back into the Zen practice that I love. I believed that their story, once told, would validate their life work and at the same time correct the mistaken tendencies that had silenced their voice. And I believed that they could help me find my own voice. I was not surprised to learn that other women also longed to hear about these female Zen ancestors.

For about fifty years we in the West have been trying earnestly and patiently to follow the directions of our Japanese, Korean, Vietnamese, and Chinese teachers. We have been trying to build an American Zen practice that will guide us to the depth of their understanding. We have followed their instructions for meditation, kept their daily monastic schedule, worn their traditional monastic clothing, answered obediently when called by our new Dharma names in Asian languages, and heartily chanted their untranslated sutras. We have asked one another what these various teachers taught, we have studied their books, and we have transcribed their spoken words. Some of us have even crossed oceans to return to our teachers' home temples in Asia in order to then bring back the Dharma to life here at home. In some cases we have transferred our hopes and obedience to their designated successors, and some of us have even become these successors.

But my mission became finding the traces and scraps of these individual Zen women's stories and piecing them together. How had these women expressed Zen, and what could they teach us? By learning about their complex and contextualized lives, how might my own practice take deeper root in this female body? The search became more urgent for me after my priest ordination in 1998, and even more essential as I took the teaching seat that same year.

What was I supposed to do? Who could I turn to as a role model? My women's peer groups were informal and met rarely, but they were essential for guiding me. The more deeply I entered practice, the more I wished to express my own Zen practice on the most personal level. I did not want to imitate the male masters or my own male teacher. What did I do as a female Zen priest with a husband, children, and grandchildren? These questions led me to research and study my own—*our* own—female Zen ancestors.

THE EARLY BUDDHIST VIEW OF WOMEN AND THE DANGEROUS VAGINA

I had decided to pursue a study of Buddhist women leaders, but I could not ignore the early Buddhist view of women that was still being disseminated through Buddhist scriptures. In the Anguttara Nikaya Sutta, Buddha says: "Monks, a woman, even when going along, will stop to ensnare the heart of a man: whether standing, sitting, or lying down, laughing, talking, or singing, weeping, stricken, or dying, a woman will stop to ensnare the heart of a man" (Hare 1932: 55–57).

The context for this sermon is that the Buddha had just been informed of an incestuous mother-and-son relationship within the Sangha. As a response, the Buddha chose to lecture on the sexual power of women, rather than on these particularly unwholesome family dynamics. The implication here is that the ensnaring woman functions as an outside force to steal a monk's heart/mind and turn him away from his devotion to practice. Through this Buddhist teaching, the view of women as dangerous objects was reinforced, and Buddhist monks were taught to stereotype women and avoid them, rather than to reflect on what arises within themselves during their encounters and relationships with women. Is it only women ensnaring men, or do men too have a longing to belong to, to be part of, the union of male and female energy? The answer is obvious, but the scripture denying such dynamics has nonetheless continued to form the basis for some of our Buddhist practices and institutions.

In another graphic exchange, the Buddha again admonishes his monk Sudinna to eschew woman. Sudinna, previously a married man, had lapsed in his practice of celibacy and confessed this fact to the Buddha. He had engaged in sex and impregnated the wife he had abandoned to pursue a Buddhist monk's life to assuage her grief over her loss of her husband (himself) to the Buddhist order. The monk tried to emphasize the selflessness of this sexual act with his abandoned wife while nonetheless expressing his sense of repulsion toward it. But Sudinna's sense of family duty conflicted with the Buddha's command that he sever ties to his family. The Buddha rebuked Sudinna over this defeat (that is, his failure to observe celibacy in his practice):

> It would have been better, confused man, had you put your male organ inside the mouth of a terrible poisonous snake than inside the vagina of a woman. It would have been better, confused man, had you put your male organ inside the mouth of a black snake than inside the vagina of a woman. It would have been better, confused man, had you put your male organ inside a blazing hot charcoal pit than inside the vagina of a woman. (Wilson 1996: 23)

Thus it seems that, according to the Buddha (or to later Buddhist editorial additions to the canon of the Buddha's discourses), a woman's vagina and sexual intercourse are more dangerous than the harm caused by a poisonous snake or a burning charcoal pit. While it is not so hard to understand why the Buddha warned monks to avoid getting lost in sexual pursuits, this severe admonition carries quite a charge. Far from manifesting a cool, dispassionate, and mindful approach, in this Buddhist teaching dialogue the instructions sound nearly hysterical.

In this early one-sided Buddhist view of male-female magnetism we see once again instructions to steel ourselves against emotions and to avoid and repress feelings. Rather than strengthening the monk's training through observing arising desire and biological impulses, there is an attempt to control the monk's behavior and emotional vulnerability through creating a dangerous object or projection of a hungry woman who will destroy your virtue. This projection labels women as a danger to practice, something to be eliminated. Instead of eliminating contact with or feeling for women, wouldn't it have been more in keeping with true mindfulness practice to experience the sensation, the feeling of longing for intimacy and union with a woman's body, and then transcend it? This would appear to represent a deeper and more wholesome practice of mindfulness for men *and* women. The scripturally based, demonizing practice seems much less likely to develop honest awareness with the experience of your own sensations and impulses.

Didn't the Buddha teach, in every other situation, that desire arises in our own mind? Yet, in this teaching, men's desire is projected onto and then managed through a negative stereotype of the "ensnaring woman." The monks' problems are not solved by seeing the nature of mind, but instead by getting rid of any contact with women or managing male-female relations through this filter and warning label: "Women are dangerous to your practice; women are out to ensnare you." The Buddhist model of the ever-ensnaring female with her sole purpose of capturing and enslaving the male victim is thoroughly dispelled by the many wonderful practice relationships that women enjoyed with male teachers and Dharma brothers. Today we know that these male-female relationships do not necessarily distract from practice but may also enrich them.

The importance of clarifying the Buddha's early teaching on women that advised avoidance, repression, and projection was obvious to the Buddha's faithful follower Ananda. Ananda persisted in questioning the Buddha even as the Buddha was passing away (as chronicled in the Mahaparanibbana Sutta, Walsh 1995: 264). Ananda asked the Buddha how monks should act toward women. The Buddha had divided his community to separate men from women, but Ananda realistically questioned just how monks could avoid all contact with the nuns and women that they might encounter. The Buddha responded at first with his policy of avoiding women and repressing the entire experience of meeting an actual woman: "Don't see them, Ananda." Ananda continued to probe: "But if we see them, how should we behave, Lord?" The Buddha advises further rejection: "Do not speak to them, Ananda." And finally, Ananda asked the Buddha what to do if all previous avoidance strategies had failed to repel the woman: "But if they speak to us, how should we behave, Lord?" Only after this third inquiry does the Buddha allude to a practice for engaged and sexual human beings: "Practice mindfulness, Ananda" (Walsh 1995: 264).

In this passage we see Ananda struggling to clarify the Buddha's teaching relating to women before the Buddha is gone and before his earlier repressive injunctions had become the de facto record. Ananda seems rightly to be concerned about instructions that will guide followers in the millennia to come. He seems to have realized that a policy of avoidance and revulsion was both inadequate and inconsistent with the mindfulness practice that the Buddha taught. Perhaps, on the most advanced practice level, the Buddha is saying that we don't need to see women or men as women and men, as differentiated sexual objects. But even so, what about the arising of human feelings? And what about women's need to be taught, spoken to, and included in practice? What then, Buddha? Ananda's questioning helped the Buddha clarify his teaching that meeting a woman or any object of sexual desire with mindful attention is the essence of understanding and releasing attachments.

MIAOZONG'S VINDICATION OF THE VAGINA

Miaozong and Wanan were both Dharma successors of the great eleventh-century Chinese Zen master Dahui. Wanan persisted in questioning Dahui's female student, Miaozong, and her presence at Dahui's training monastery. Finally Dahui suggested that Wanan visit Miaozong and that he interview her himself. The passage that follows was written by Wanan to describe his experience and interview with Miaozong.

> Miaozong and Wanan in Dharma combat: What is a pure monk like you doing in a place like this?
> [Wanan] relied on Dahui, and served as his Senior Monk (the head monk of the Sangha Hall in which the monks in Chan training lived and studied) at Dahui's monastery on Ching-shan.
> Before Miaozong had become a nun Dahui lodged her in the abbot's quarters. The head monk Wanan always made disapproving noises. Dahui said to him, "Even though she is a woman, she has strengths." Wanan still did not approve. Dahui then insisted that he should interview her. Wanan reluctantly sent a message that he would go.
> Miaozong said, "Will you make it a Dharma interview or a worldly interview?"
> The head monk replied: "A Dharma interview."

Miaozong said: "Then let your attendants depart." [She went in first, and then called to him,] "Please come in."

When he came past the curtain he saw Miaozong lying face upward on the bed without anything on at all. He pointed at her [genitals] and said, "What kind of place is this?"

Miaozong replied: "All of the buddhas of the three worlds and the six patriarchs and all the great monks everywhere—they all come out from within this."

Wanan said "And would you let me enter, or not?"

Miaozong replied: "It allows horses to cross; it does not allow asses to cross."

Wanan said nothing, and Miaozong declared: "The interview with the Senior Monk is ended." She then turned over and faced the inside.

Wanan became embarrassed and left.

Dahui said, "It is certainly not the case that the old beast does not have any insight." Wanan was ashamed. (Levering 1996: 152)

But what was it that made Miaozong present herself stripped naked to Wanan? She had received a message through monastery channels that Wanan would be coming to conduct a Dharma interview. Before he could open his mouth, she stripped naked to encounter him.

Miaozong was a mature and sexually experienced woman when this encounter took place. She must have intuited Wanan's all-too-familiar critical attitude about her, his suspicions about her role as a seductress in the celibate Zen monastery. She chose to confront the attitude directly. Her right to practice with her chosen teacher, Dahui, was at stake. And for all we know, she sensed that she was holding the door open for other women's practice as well. How many enlightened Zen masters in her day would allow women to train in their monasteries? Perhaps only this one—Dahui. She may have taken on this exchange as her spiritual life-or-death struggle on behalf of herself and women to come. Or I would like to think so. Faithful to her teacher's spirit, she held nothing back, in true Zen Dharma combat style.

In this encounter it is clear that Miaozong saw Wanan's intention in more ways than one. His arrival with attendants broadcast his need for formality and his dominance in the Zen hierarchy; his need for a witnessed meeting spoke to his rigid adherence to the rules. The Buddha had long ago established that monks were never to be alone in a woman's room. The need for the chaperones was obvious on that count. Attendants also signaled Wanan's high status in the monastery.

Miaozong, a master of strategy, taking control of the meeting before it even started, asked: "Will you make this a Dharma interview or a worldly interview?" When Wanan asserted that this was to be a Dharma interview, Miaozong suggested that he dismiss his attendants and that she would dismiss hers too. Her request, consistent with the understanding that communicating Dharma is intimate, insisted that he engage directly, removing conventional armor and/or status symbols. Without attendants or position, the Dharma flows unimpeded by such extra baggage.

Miaozong called for a clarification of venue—Dharma or worldly—the Dharmic version of a duel. "Choose your weapons and proceed at your own risk," she seems to be saying. A Dharma interview is no ordinary discussion. Everyday conventions of politeness, propriety, and half-truths are thrown out the window. A Dharma interview's sole purpose is to make clear the whole truth, in *this* very moment, in the most direct, pertinent way, with as few words as possible. Ultimate truth and this particular moment appear in one seamless response. Dharma interviews are not discursive. They cut to the chase: no need to talk about the weather, use little polite gestures, or engage in conversational ploys assuring mutual appreciation. And so Miaozong did!

Miaozong saved Wanan the time and trouble of stating the problem that he had with her presence at the monastery. She presented the problem as directly as possible by exposing her utterly naked body, in spread-eagle fashion. Without speaking a single word she enquired of the troubled monk: "It's this, isn't it, it's my actual female body right here in your male monastery. Isn't that the heart of your objection? I give you my arms, legs, belly, breasts, and my vagina. Nothing is hidden; my female organ is neither dressed nor wrapped in convention. How do you wish to engage the problematic existence of these female body parts in your monastery? Point to the part of this body which is the direct cause of your disapproval."

To his credit, Wanan did not faint or back down at the outrageously unconventional behavior of this "well-brought-up lady" from a respectable family. Her behavior went well beyond the conventions of Sung Dynasty China, where women were sequestered behind a wall. Even worse, her behavior was in direct opposition to the explicit Buddhist rules against a woman being alone with a monk in monastery. Being naked with a monk in her room may even go well beyond our own liberated and far-fetched twenty-first-century student responses to a Dharma interview. "Unless a student is interested in seducing her teacher, which one of us has enlightenment so deep that naked exposure of this particular body would pose no problem?"

This may have been the first time in his adult life that the celibate monk Wanan was in the presence of a nude woman. Wanan held his own by asking: "What kind of a place is this?" while pointing to her genitals. He got right to the point, and we can imagine his unspoken words:

> What the hell do you think you're doing with that thing, here in this monastery, missy? Of everything you have shown me, what is the meaning of that particular place, your sex organs? What is the meaning of you bringing that female part into our monastic setting? How will you make sense of that place in Zen practice?

Aha! Now Wanan has clarified his disapproval; he directly pointed to the problem between himself and Miaozong. The problem is the fleshy entryway between her legs. Miaozong has made it easy for him to choose the exact problem. Quickly and silently she processed the nature of his objection to her participation in the monastery:

> Oh, it's this, my female sexuality, right here in my body. This is the crux of your problem! I brought my female sex organs right into your holy monastery! This isn't about my personality, my physical appearance, my ability, or my marital status, is it? My dear Mr. Enlightened Head Monk, it's *this* place, my vagina, which is bothering you and your deep understanding of the Buddhadharma.

What an accomplishment! Everything is now out in the open. Without repressing, bemoaning, or defending Wanan's disapproval, without rationalizing or apologizing for any inconvenience or hardship that her vagina had caused by accompanying her inside the monastery, without acting out hurt feelings or imagining what the problem might be, the issue could now be addressed with a Zen mind.

Both participants openly and honestly showed themselves. We can guess that by this point in her Zen career Miaozong was tired of explaining or defending her right to practice, tired of saying that the Buddhadharma had nothing to do with male or female, tired of the hypocrisy between the supposed equality and poor treatment of women, tired of worrying about disturbing the holy male monk's composure with her female appearance, and tired of arguing about the necessity of bringing her female genitalia into the male monastery.

Miaozong taught me that there is nowhere to hide if women want to find and maintain a respected place in Zen Buddhist practice. I will need to be strong, strategic, bold, unashamed, and visible, in order to practice deeply and to invite other women to practice with me.

MY FINDINGS

I learned that when I collected the stories of my own female Zen ancestors I encountered women like myself who were trying to balance their love of family with their love of spirit. Unlike their male monastic counterparts, who believed in cutting all family ties, women maintained their connection and love for family. More often than male monks, these women developed projects to feed, teach, and tend to their communities. They adapted Buddhist practices to accommodate women who lacked education. Their spiritual practices were rich, deep, connected, flexible, and varied. In short, their practice resembled the adaptation of Buddhist practice in the West. Today serious and committed practitioners offer their skills to various communities, live at home with families, and are developing a devoted, sincere, and original practice.

The Buddha's teaching has moved across cultures for centuries, taking time to sink roots in new soil wherever it has spread. It took five hundred years for Buddhist practice to be transplanted from India to China and another five hundred for Buddhism to take root in China. In Japan it again took approximately five hundred years for Buddhism to be expressed in its own Japanese way. We are still within the first hundred years of Buddhism's Western inception, and we are watching Buddhism adapt even as we are adapting it. Clearly one of the biggest changes in Western Buddhism is the affirmation of equality of its women teachers. Yet all of the West's founding Asian teachers have been male. Exploring and learning about the female side of the practice widens our view of the history and evolution of practice worldwide.

Now that so many men, and indeed so many women, are teaching Zen in America, some of us are beginning to see that the traditional Zen that we are trying to follow does not quite fit who we are and therefore requires adjustment. Put simply: Zen needs to grow if it is to serve its Western practitioners. If, when raising this concern, we fear being disloyal to our Zen ancestors, we must remember what our teachers themselves have told us. As much as we love and live the practice, there is always more to uncover, and we need to make this Asian practice our own. Being intimate with the whole of our lived reality is actually what our teachers asked of us.

One reason the Zen literature that we have studied does not quite fit is that it is based entirely on the tradition of *male monastic training*. From the perspective of our Asian mentors, a Zen teacher was necessarily male; all teachers who have been most esteemed through liturgy and literature were male monastics. The classic Zen literature *only* contains male masters. One of my Japanese friends reported that she had asked about female Zen teachers when she was in high school in Japan and was told that there were none. Given that women compose half of American Zen practitioners and that a few of us are monastics, we must consider whether such a tradition can lead us to an authentic American Zen practice, no matter how long or how closely we follow it.

Most Zen teachers in America understand that we need to find a balance between following traditions and changing them, but some are concerned that some essential qualities of Zen will be lost in the flux. "Let's not throw out the baby with the bathwater!" is often heard regarding our need to adapt Zen practice for modern Westerners. We need not throw out either. At the risk of overly extending the metaphor, let me suggest that we use a bigger bathtub, fill it with more bathwater, and put male and female babies in it.

For the past twenty years I have been deepening my relationship with female Zen ancestors. I wanted to know who they were, what challenges they faced, and how they were taught. When I began to teach, I also wanted to know how they taught Zen as they lived it to their students. How could I relate to them and their practice across the divide of time and place? I put myself in their place and pondered how they faced decisions about caring for their families, husbands, lovers, and students.

And I asked them many specific questions that related to my own practice: How did it affect them to be taught by men? What did they feel trying to fit into this male practice environment, and how did their Zen training help them navigate their feelings? Did their practice lives and relationships differ from those of their male teachers? Did they express the Dharma in their own way specifically for other female students? Was their teaching consistently different from that of male ancestors?

Because I wanted to know so much about these women and their experiences, both personally and from the perspective of their sociocultural context, I needed to know where they came from and what they needed to do to enter a male-dominated Buddhism. What I learned about their lives has deepened my practice and my intimacy with my roots. These women adapted their Zen practice to their lives and their lives to their practice. Some of them maintained relationships with their families. Some of them used traditional skills—cooking and sewing—to take care of the indigent in their communities. Some of them created orphanages to raise and teach abandoned children—children they missed having in their nun's life. They formed institutions to meet their needs and take their practice out into their wider communities. Women started a temple for abused women; the formerly abused wives became nuns (temporarily) and were allowed to divorce their husbands. Women kept their female relatives alive by forming small convents during times of war. They found ways to support themselves and their institutions financially. They offered classes in traditional crafts, barber shops, hospitals, and pharmacies. In short, they faced many of the issues that Westerners now face in establishing Zen Buddhism in our environment.

MY FEMALE ANCESTORS

I discovered my Zen mothers, aunties, and Dharma sisters tossed aside in one historical account after another. Some showed up only incidentally, as students of great male masters; some were found in the accounts of male monks; some were remembered fondly by modern-day teachers; but most were discovered by female Buddhist scholars. The present-day feminist movement reaches backward and forward in time to help us discover our capacities as women. I found women who were beaten, pushed aside, and refused entry to Zen training and women who kept on their path no matter what. Some were saucy and some were proper, but each one found herself in Zen practice, and each one shared her strength with me. I surrounded my office with their art, their poetry, and their teaching words as I gathered research materials for my book about them, *Zen Women: Beyond Tea Ladies, Iron Maidens, and Macho Masters* (Schireson 2009). They held me and guided me. I have since visited many Zen Centers and authored many chapters in books and magazine articles on the subject of women's Zen. I also helped to introduce a list of female ancestors that was accepted by the national Soto Zen teachers as a recommended document or chant. This newly approved document is now being used in many Zen Centers across North America for empowerment ceremonies designed to recognize accomplished lay practice, priest ordination, or independent teacher status.

By studying the lives of my Zen sisters, I found my place among them and developed a stronger community of contemporary Zen women. I learned to dive deeper; I learned to accept the minor hardships that bothered me so much. My perceived slights paled next to their own obstacles. Many lost their children, families, and livelihood, but they continued to pursue Zen. Some burned their faces, and others stripped naked to make a point, while still others practiced without a single encouragement from anyone. Each one handed me a gift, moving me forward: You can do this, and you can do this as your true self, as a mother, wife, and grandmother. And you can do this as a woman who loves clothes, her home, babies, and Zen ceremonies.

The Zen women also taught me, and teach all of us, that spirituality is not only about following rules, emulating a silent Zen master, or living as a hermit in a monastery. Each one of us must be thoroughly honest and go deeply into whatever it is that we love. Each one of us, in fact, has her own path, and as we follow it we are not alone. We hold hands with our female ancestors and beckon forward the generation that follows us.

WORKS CITED

Hare, E. M. 1932. *The Book of the Gradual Sayings*. Lancaster, UK: Pali Text Society.

Levering, Miriam. 1996. "Stories of Enlightened Women in Chan." In *Women and Goddess Traditions*, ed. Karen King, 137–76. Minneapolis: Fortress.

Schireson, Grace. 2009. *Zen Women: Beyond Tea Ladies, Iron Maidens, and Macho Masters*. Boston: Wisdom Publications.

Walsh, Maurice, trans. 1995. *The Teachings of the Buddha: Long Discourses of the Buddha*. Boston: Wisdom Publications.

Wilson, Liz. 1996. *Charming Cadavers*. Chicago: University of Chicago Press.

Eleven

THE ARC OF BECOMING

WILLOW YOUNG

There are truths glimpsed early on that needed a whole lifetime to be redis-covered and authenticated.
—Marguerite Yourcenar (1981)

Tell me, what is it you plan to do with your one wild and precious life?
—"The Summer Day," Mary Oliver (1992)

These last lines from Mary Oliver's poem "The Summer Day" continue to awaken in me a sense of wonder, curiosity, and awe. In particular, the words "your one wild and precious life" resonate and reverberate within my soul. They call me to value this one wild and precious life that is dear to each of us. I reflect here on the threads that have been interwoven into my life and life work, the pattern of which was not consciously planned or rationally scripted. My life's work has unfolded as I have become more myself and increasingly comfortable with myself. Certainly there have been periods of challenge, of unknowing and despair, of confusion, and all the entanglements that spur one toward greater consciousness and clarification around the quest of exactly what it is that I am supposed to be doing with my life. It has taken many years to glimpse and understand the full meaning and the full beingness also referenced by Mary Oliver (1992): "You only have to let the soft animal of your body love what it loves" ("Wild Geese").

"If life has a base that it stands upon . . . then my [life] without a doubt stands upon this memory" (Woolf 1984: 5) of black dark Vermont earth and little carrots weeded in late spring plantings; goslings and early spring.

Of water in many forms—icicles, snow cups with maple syrup poured over, crunch of morning snow, spring brooks, the powerful force of the rivers, springhouses from which people filled water jugs. As well, the Vermont seasons of dark nights and the clear arc of the Milky Way high above alternate with images of spilt milk in spring mud. How is a life made from these experiences and images that smell, feel, and captivate the imagination? How does our ever-present psyche respond in the young life of a child to not only the experience of being alive on the planet but to the experiences of accompanying parents and other family members on their errands and engagements to the bank, farmer's market, town meetings, hardware store, church socials, and long walks of one sort and another from here to there and back again?

My early childhood memories are contained within the experience of living in relative isolation on a farm five miles off a country road near Corinth Corners in rural Vermont. My parents had come to Vermont in the mid-1940s from Reed College in Portland, Oregon, to found an economic cooperative movement based upon the International Cooperative Alliance birthed in Manchester, England, in the late 1800s.[1] My father had studied at the economic cooperative schools in Manchester, taught the subject in Copenhagen, Denmark, in the late 1930s, and was initially a participant in the Conscientious Objectors camps facilitated by Lewis Mumford and Stuart Chase in Vermont.[2] My mother's intellectual foundation and dedication to progressive exploration combined with training and skill in Swiss handicrafts and her love of the written word.

FATEFUL ENCOUNTERS

I use the word "fate" to describe the inexplicable confluence of events and occurrences encountered in the process of becoming as well as to indicate that forces other than will and intention propel us forward to our becoming.

> [W]e know there is no human foresight or wisdom that can prescribe direction to our life, except for small stretches of the way. . . . Fate confronts [us] like an intricate labyrinth, all too rich in possibilities, and yet of these many possibilities only one is [our] own right way (Jung 1977 [1917]: 48).

The term "Individuation" best describes the process of becoming one-self, wholly individual, and integrated with the collective norms. Individuation "is a process of differentiation, having as its goal the development of the individual personality" (Jung 2008 [1938]: 118). And it is the process of becoming our essential selves by separating ourselves from others through an articulation of the significant elements unique to oneself and often experienced as inner promptings from the unconscious. This constitutes a fundamental conception of psychology. C. G. Jung (1950 [1935]: 79), in *The Tavistock Lectures*, distinguished the personal unconscious (characterized by contents that are of a personal origin and make up the personality) as a whole from the collective unconscious, which consists of

> another class of contents of definitely unknown origin, which cannot be ascribed to individual acquisition. These contents have one outstanding peculiarity and that is their mythological character. It is as if they belong to a pattern not peculiar to any particular mind or person, but rather to a pattern peculiar to mankind in general, and are therefore collective in nature.

My Pacifica Graduate Institute colleague Lionel Corbett has described these inner promptings as the messages the Self sends to the ego, from the unconscious to the conscious part of our selves. The Self is defined as the inner God force in humans. Individuation then could be considered the process of incarnating the inner God into the flesh of human beings. The Self is incarnated or contained within each human being, and individuation is the fulfillment of the Self in the individual. The idea is that the incarnation occurs slowly over time, unfolding both consciously and unconsciously. I have experienced the process of my becoming, as prompted by the unconscious, through the symbolic language of soul, dreams, dream images, and intuitions.

"Much of our adult life is busy with differentiation. St. Paul considered discrimination a valuable virtue. Jung defined individuation as a process of differentiation: differentiation of consciousness, differentiation of self from the collective" (Hillman 1999: 79). In reflection or "on second thought," this essay is an exercise in differentiation. I distinguish the parameters of the life I was born into and the historical context of the times and the pursuits of my parents, which have had a defining impact on my experiences and my values, and the outer influences from the inner impulses and forces, which have provided their own compelling experiences and impact on my life.

I have been visited by dreams from a young age and consistently throughout my life. Had I not been, mine might have been an altogether different life. I might have been quite happy to be a social worker in Boston, which was my fantasy when I was eight and nine years old. At that time my imagination was fueled by a short novel (title forgotten), which described a young red-haired graduate, working in the tenements of South Boston. Her smart, capable, sexy personality riveted me. She was full of heart and sensibility. Her big city adventures and encounters with various characters further revealed a passion for human life and experience. But the wellspring of living waters lapped at the shores of my young life with a recurring dream.

I dreamt I was out by a pond. The air was exceptionally clear, the sky a remarkable blue. Huge cumulus clouds billowed above and were reflected on the surface of the pond where two swans glided idly. Then I saw a cross-sectional view that included the sky, the clouds, the swans, the still water of the pond, and the murky waters below the surface. At the bottom of the pond was a gnarly little man in a rough hooded outfit, who threatened the swans.

I was terrified of this figure and would awake feeling very shaken. I thought of this man as a "burlap man," gnome-like, in his hooded coat. The dream ceased recurring somewhere around the age of nine or ten. In late adolescence the feeling of the dream would recur—I would feel overwhelmed by the presence of the burlap man, as though he were the size of Gulliver in *Gulliver's Travels*. I worried that I might be going crazy and "held on for dear life." Years later I would come to appreciate how dear life held onto *me*.

It would be years before I developed enough of a relationship with the psyche to understand that the fierce calling of the unconscious required a deep appreciation of even the most frightening figures. I learned this in Jungian analysis, which I began at the age of twenty-four. With the valuing of the unconscious came a change in the attitude of the inner figures themselves. The burlap man appeared more frequently as a helpful figure, not unlike the ancient forms of the Phrygian Cabiri or the Greek Telesphorus, who is depicted as the companion of the Greek god Asclepius, the father of modern medicine.[3] An inner figure of this sort may serve as a bridge to the unconscious, if the right attitude is cultivated. In befriending this inner figure I relied upon the practice of active imagination, engaging him

FIGURE 11.1 Statue of Telesphorus found in southern France and now in the Archaeological Museum of Nimes. Wikimedia Commons, Creative Commons Attribution-Share Alike 3.0 Unported License.

FIGURE 11.2 A Roman diptych of Asclepius and Hygeia with Telesphorus, ca. 400/430 AD, Museum on Merseyside, Liverpool. Hellenica at www.mlahanas.de, GNU Free Documentation License.

in dialogue, leaving him offerings on my altar, and engaging in attempts to externalize him, to give him form in clay and paintings. I argued with him, exhorted, made pronouncements, cajoled and teased him, gave ultimatums, set limits and boundaries, and eventually humbled myself in the face of his wise counsel. In my mind, he was both a terrifying figure and a small god who must be honored, tended to, and loved.

In my eighteenth and nineteenth year I rented a room in a wonderfully spacious apartment that backed onto the National Zoo in Rock Creek Park, Washington, D.C. From my bedroom facing the park I could hear sounds of the zoo animals at night and early in the morning. The photographer who owned the apartment kept a large library. There on the shelves were the impressive eighteen volumes of the black cloth-bound *Collected Works of C G. Jung.* I would look at the illustrations and read a paragraph here or there. One day I selected volume 9, *Archetypes and the Collective Unconscious.* I loved reading it and would lie about, reading and napping, drifting in and out of sleep, and then reading some more. It was an odd experience. I finished the book and wondered, "How can it be that I so deeply loved reading this book and yet I don't understand a word of it?" So I read it a second time. I still could not make rational sense of it. A couple of months later, after reading Jung's purported autobiography, *Memories, Dreams, Reflections*, I again read *Archetypes and the Collective Unconscious*; with the rational context of Jung's life in mind, I finally grasped the work in a rational way. Thankfully, the experience of the first readings continued to resonate.

In my late teens and early twenties, when I lived near the beach in Ocean Park, California, in a compound of five houses neighbors would gather in the common garden, cups of tea or coffee in hand, chat, and tell our dreams. One neighbor casually mentioned that the Jung Institute was some miles up the road. I had been trying to decide on a career path and needed to talk with someone other than my friends and contemporaries. So the journey of analysis began. Little by little a conscious awareness of my life and of life around me began to develop. I slowly found my personal containment and orientation within the collective and became more consciously engaged in my life, making more conscious decisions about its direction. Through the creative commitment to the expressive arts of sculpture, painting, and writing, I ever so slowly began to emerge from the unconscious and murky terrain of the burlap man, which had held me captive since I was a child. A memory of my paternal grandmother, who aspired to be and became a woman of society, is of her telling me that I was a "pygmy Aborigine." Dark from being in the sun and often dirty from playing outdoors, crawling around in the underbrush, and climbing trees, my wild childhood appearance may have resembled her idea of Aborigines. She had seen me when I was very little running around naked in the summer sun with the goats at my parents' farm in Vermont. I probably did look like a little Aborigine. Perhaps she sensed something of the presence of the primal "burlap man" in me. I felt cast out of the acceptable family strata and carried an identification with those less fortunate and culturally different. Family photos confirm the difference. There the clan is assembled in best dress. My parents and the three of us children look remarkably different in handmade clothes and moccasins, which were in contrast to the store-bought clothes of Aunts, Uncles and Cousins. I was born into the black sheep strata of the family. My parents, in their way, encouraged our individuality. A natural ethical orientation developed in me, one that guided and sustained me for many years. Even as in my early teens I was actively working in the Civil Rights Movement, for example, serving lunch to committee members of the Congress on Racial Equality. I attended Martin Luther King Jr.'s March on Washington in August 1963, and was present for his "I Have a Dream" speech. I felt a natural and powerful connection with the tide of humanity that I experienced there.

The Ethnic Arts Program (now called the World Arts and Cultures Program), an undergraduate multidisciplinary degree program at UCLA, hosted my interests in world cultures and provided the ground and support for my education of the archetypal as it surfaced in world mythologies, dance, theater, music, folklore, and art. I felt deeply content during those years of study. It was not an easy path to navigate. In the logos-dominated world of the university, I functioned intuitively and thus experienced deep feelings of alienation and inferiority. The struggle to persevere was aided by the engaged process of active imagination in a dialogue with the self-critical voice, which would prefer that I stop the preposterous activity of education altogether. For a year, between classes, with the support of analysis, I sat on a knoll, writing dialogues with my inner critic. Only in this way was I able to get through the demands of course work. The benefits of being in analysis were inwardly valuable and were becoming outwardly evident. I felt it was saving my life. I felt supported and valued. My interest in the cultural life of the Hopi and Navajo led me to study the Snake Dance Ceremony. I traveled three times to participate as an observer of the ceremony with Katie and Sandy Sanford, Jack and Linny Sanford, and others. Experiencing enactments of the archetypal world of the Hopi was deeply meaningful for me. Feelings of being at home in the world of archaic pueblo life and feeling I was also of the contemporary urban world led me to express the experience in a painting (now lost) that featured an infinity strip lying on its side with images representing the two worlds contained within the circles. It became for me a living mandala of evolving consciousness.

With a desire to formalize my education, I volunteered at the Craft and Folk Art Museum in Los Angeles, which well suited my eclectic and multidisciplinary background. A President's Grant from UCLA supported my research on masks, mask-makers, and festivals in Guatemala. The image of the red-haired Bostonian social worker came to mind during this time. Upon my return from Guatemala in 1979, the museum hired me as the producer of the annual Festival of Masks. This began a ten-year period of intense involvement with many ethnic communities in southern California and with their many cultural traditions. This profound work took my colleagues and me to the heart of the city's cultures, peoples, and neighborhoods and into the heart of the living wisdom tradition of each culture. I was born with a natural interest in people and drawn to the way and presence of being that was pervasive in each cultural group. The World Arts and Cultures program deepened my knowledge and respect for the people I encountered and their ancestors, while the Craft and Folk Art Museum provided an extraordinary container for the development of community relations that evolved as different cultural groups encountered and learned from each other. The deep respect that each group felt for its ancestral culture was extended to the others. It was this sense of deep respect that enabled many to endure the tensions that would arise in the course of the multifaceted relationships that would develop and were sustained year after year.

The range of cultural diversity and the people I encountered were all concerned with meaning and well-being, whether someone was tending a personal ancestor shrine or tending the judging mask of his tribe; or, as the Dalai Lama does, tending the living religious tradition of his country; or cultivating the expressive hearts of the children in the stateside Hawaiian community as Auntie Mary did; or cultivating bamboo and gourd gardens that ran out along the unpaved alleyways of Mar Vista, like the Filipino lantern maker. The expressive arts of the cultural groups and people that I worked with communicated the interior experience of being alive. As a result of the focus, a dedication and imaginative engagement intimately expressed the felt sense of being alive as communicated by each artisan. In some ways the community work in the arts was a religious experience shared by many.

The National Endowment for the Arts selected the museum as the regional organizing hub of an international cultural exchange program. I was for many years involved in what was known as Arts Management and Community Leadership. I became a multicultural facilitator and worked as a consultant with many cultural organizations in Los Angeles, Chicago, San Francisco, and Fresno.

Although I continued in Jungian analysis for a number of years, I was so busy that I felt disconnected, exiled from my own inner process. I needed contact with a community of people who strove to relate consciously and were engaged in that commitment. In 1982, I found that group in James Kirsch's Monday evening seminar.[4] The respect for the nature of the psyche that prevailed during these sessions was renewing for me. I participated in this group for a number of years, until my work schedule became too demanding.

Marriage in 1985, the birth of my daughter in October 1986, and the experience of motherhood initiated a profound personal shift for me. I took an extended leave from the museum, which coincided with a respite from analysis. I wanted to sink into my mothering experience, wanted my instincts, intuition, and gut responses to have free rein. I was beginning to trust myself and was both returning to and arriving at a deep way of observance and quietude. I read the writings of body-worker Bonnie Bainbridge Cohen and engaged in bodywork and in writing the internal experiences of my body-mind journey.

My family tradition was steeped in psychology. My maternal grandfather had been a psychiatrist, my uncle a psychiatrist and mental health director in the state of California, and my mother a counseling psychologist. For years I had been dancing around the edges of the field. I struggled with the meaning that psychology had for me personally, as distinct from my family's multigenerational involvement in the field. I reentered analysis, first with James Kirsch and then with Maud Ann Taylor. In 1989 I had a dream that evoked a strong response in me. I decided, finally, to pursue the study of depth psychology and explore work as a therapist. I had continued to read Jung and the writings of his students and colleagues and had been attending the Friday night lectures sponsored by the Analytic Association for several years. In the spring of 1990 I attended a three-day symposium dedicated to exploring the myth of Hera with James Hillman. The symposium coincided with the dedication ceremony at Pacifica Graduate Institute's new site. It was as though I had found a new home. My psyche appreciated the experience.

I enrolled at Pacifica in September 1990, completing my course work in 1992. Eventually, after a hiatus for healing from cancer, I completed my thesis, "In the Care of Artemis: Nurturing a Girl's Journey." I received my MA at last in 1995 and was licensed in 1999. I began working as a staff psychotherapist at Devereux in Goleta, California, treating severely emotionally disturbed children and adults and those with pervasive developmental disabilities, while establishing a small private practice, all of which was a complex process. I learned to integrate object relations theory, self-psychology, and cognitive behavioral approaches into my Jungian background. This was like learning to speak different languages. Further, I began a private practice internship. The work with my clients has been deep and engaging. I have learned from them. I earned my MFT license in 1999.

While studying for the licensing exam I dreamt: I was at James (Kirsch's) house. It was around the Christmas season. There was a knock at the door. I opened the door and saw James Hillman standing there. He handed me a bunch of sealed envelopes to deliver to the analysts and one unsealed one, stating: "This one is for you." The exchange was formal. He turned to leave and I shut the door. I looked in my envelope and found the most beautiful collection of ancient seeds and beans. As I was setting out the envelopes on a counter in the garage, facing a window, I looked out and saw him on the stoop of a house three doors down, leaning back and grinning at me.

The atmosphere of the dream and the numinosity of the collection of seeds and beans reminded me of my relationship with the archaic and ancient life of the psyche. With the presence of the dream I felt the affirmation that I could integrate my two worlds: the timeless world of the psyche and the contemporary world of life and work. I facilitated a small dream group hosted in my private practice office in Santa Barbara. It became a place for me to share my background in the arts and expression of world cultures, my developing understanding of the archetypes of the personal and collective unconscious and of psychology more generally. Working on dreams involves reading the dream aloud. As we do so, we listen to the dream figures, observe the specificity of the dream images, make note of the dream atmosphere, and become aware of the feelings present in the dream. In this way we hear the symbolic language of the psyche. The emphasis is not on the interpretation of the dream so much as it is on the living experience of the dream and its exploration, as we elucidate personal associations and cultural amplifications. Inevitably, meaning emerges through this process.

My dream of Hillman at James Kirsch's house and my viewing of the Fraser Boa film *The Way of the Dream* (1988), with its focus on Marie Louise von Franz as she worked with dreams, reawakened my desire for additional training in dream work. I applied and was admitted to the Analytic Training Program at the C. G. Jung Study Center of Southern California. I selected it over other graduate programs because it was known that the Study Center analysts continued to engage in personal and transpersonal work with their individual psyches as well as the collective psyche. As I had hoped, the Study Center supported my process of cultivating consciousness and encouraged my developing relationship with the psyche. For me, the diploma in Analytical Psychology and the Analytic Certification serve as an ultimate acknowledgement of the long journey toward consciousness, which was constellated in the unconscious and which I eventually consciously chose and cultivated. The relationship, conscious and unconscious, that I have with psyche has been an enduringly private and sacred journey over deeply personal and meaningful terrain. I dove into the training and hence continued a long and meaningful journey, which has supported my work as an analyst, educator, and organizational leader.

More recently, I serve as chair of the master's in counseling psychology program at Pacifica Graduate Institute in Carpinteria, California, where I tend the educational development of students who are in training to be psychotherapists and engage in the building of a solid programmatic infrastructure that supports the process of individuation for faculty, staff, and students. I integrate my training and work with psyche as I support the mission of Pacifica and the hopes and dreams of the students. The outer world challenges continue to provide the material with which my own individuation is forged. I was accustomed to working with my own complexes, navigating my way through personal psychic material. It is much more difficult to encounter the complexes of others. I have found myself repeatedly exploring the territory of my own shadow and power complexes while encountering those of my colleagues and have experienced the intolerable and painful heat of an inner forge. Somewhere between work that is guided by mission-centered core values and the organizational shadow that naturally exists we stand, holding and enduring the moving tension of the multifarious opposites while breathing, consciously and easily breathing.

The process of lifelong learning continues for me, as well, as I attend seminars and presentations by analytical colleagues and prepare to teach seminars to analytic candidates at the C. G. Jung Study Center in Culver City, California. As it is, I am in leadership positions that further ask for and require deeply considered responses. I learn from coworkers and from each situation as it asks something uniquely specific in response to the core demands made on us.

The struggle continues: to live the truth of my being, to stand on my own ground, consciously *choosing* a life in relationship with the psyche and not just live abducted by it—as I did as a child, adolescent, and young adult. At that time, I did not feel "called"; rather I felt kidnapped and invaded.

I had no choice in the matter. The wrangle to live an engaged life in relationship to the multiplicity of opposites expressed in psyche and therefore the world we inhabit has been made possible through whatever gift of strength and endurance the struggles have forged. It is a gift to tend the living image of the psyche as it makes its presence known in my dreams and in those of my patients, students, and colleagues. If I feel called at all, it is to learn more deeply the language of the psyche, to enter deeply into an engaged relationship with psyche as I live my life. To become ever more conscious as a companion to the people I work with in a more knowledgeable and present way. I remain awed and humbled by the poetry, the beauty, the terror, and the archetypal images of psyche. It is the forever-profound process through which we cultivate "one wild and precious life."

NOTES

1. Most scholars recognize the business of the Rochdale pioneers of England as the first cooperative. In 1844 this group of twenty-eight men (weavers and skilled workers in other trades) formed a cooperative society. They created business principles to guide their work and established a shop in which to sell their goods. Increased pressure from the changing market system was a driving force in their decision to move toward cooperation (Birchall 1997). See more at http://www.culturalsurvival.org/publications/cultural-survival-quarterly/none/cooperatives-short-history#sthash .GLTy2ZkA.dpuf. Accessed 12-27-13.

2. Writer Lewis Mumford was an early advocate of American participation in World War II, in which his son Geddes lost his life. Stuart Chase was a noted economist and writer who wrote the first "popularization" of general semantics, *The Tyranny of Words* (1938). Chase included *Science and Sanity* as one of the top three books in a national magazine article, noting the most influential developments of the first half of the twentieth century.

3. The chthonic gods of the eighth century BCE Phrygian archetypal Great Mother were referred to as Cabiri, also spelled Cabeiri and Kabeiroi. In the Greek myths they were identified as the sons of the blacksmith Hephaestus and therefore associated with metallurgy, handicraft, and dexterity. From this they are associated with alchemy, transformation, and the psychological process of individuation. The Cabiri are also said to have originated the Orphic mysteries. They were associated with the Dactyls, a race of divine beings associated with the Mother Goddess and Mount Ida, a mountain in Phrygia sacred to the goddess. In the Samothrace mysteries the Cabiri are depicted as small boys who served the Great Mother. The fairy tale "Snow White and the Seven Dwarves" exhibits similar archetypal patterns.

4. James Kirsch was a Jungian analyst and founding member of the Los Angeles Jung Institute. He held a Monday evening seminar in his home, reading line by line the various volumes of Jung's *Collected Works*.

WORKS CITED

Birchall, Johnston. 1997. *The International Co-operative Movement*. Manchester, UK: Manchester University Press.

Boa, F. (producer-director). 1988. *The Way of the Dream: Dr. Marie-Louise von Franz in Conversation with Fraser Boa*. Toronto, Canada: Windrose Films Production (10 hours, 39 minutes).

Chase, Stuart. 1938. *The Tyranny of Words*. New York: Harcourt, Brace.

Corbett, Lionel. 2007. *Psyche and the Sacred: Spirituality beyond Religion*. New Orleans: Spring Journal.

Hillman, James. 1999. *The Force of Character and the Lasting Life*. New York: Random House.

Jung, C. G. 2008 [1938]. *Children's Dreams: Notes from the Seminar Given in 1936–1940*. Princeton: Princeton University Press.

———. 1977 [1917]. *Two Essays on Analytical Psychology*. In *The Collected Works of C. G. Jung*, ed. H. Read et al., trans. R. F. C. Hull, 48. 2nd ed. Vol. 7 Princeton, NJ: Princeton University Press.

———. 1950 [1935]. *The Tavistock Lectures*. In *The Collected Works of C. G. Jung*, ed. H. Read et al., trans. R. F C. Hull, 79. 2nd ed. Vol. 18. Princeton, NJ: Princeton University Press.

Kerenyi, Carl. 1959. *Asklepios: Archetypal Image of the Physician's Existence*. New York: Pantheon Books.

Oliver, Mary. 1992. *New and Selected Poems*. Vol. 1. Boston: Beacon Press.

Roosevelt, Eleanor. 1969. *You Learn by Living*. New York: Harper and Bros.

Woolf, Virginia. 1984. "A Sketch of the Past." In *The Virginia Woolf Reader*, 5. New York: Harcourt.

Yourcenar, Marguerite. 1981. *Fires*. Toronto: McGraw-Hill Ryerson.

Twelve

SACRED MEDICINE

My Healing (R)Evolution

ANNALISA PASTORE

Nearly fifteen years ago, while on the verge of completing my doctorate in medicine, I contemplated the words of Kahlil Gibran, which had articulated my path toward doctoring as a spiritual endeavor:

> Life is indeed darkness save when there is urge
> And all urge is blind save when there is knowledge
> And all knowledge is vain save when there is work
> And all work is empty save when there is love
> And when you work with love you bind yourself to yourself, and
>   to one another, and to God. (Gibran 1998 [1923])

I first read those words in 1997, after my first year of study at Albert Einstein College of Medicine. I happened upon Gibran's *Prophet* in the ship library during a family cruise to Alaska. We were celebrating the remission of my uncle's lymphoma. I wondered at the healed state of both his physical body and spirit. It occurred to me that, in fact, his spirit had paved the path for his body to heal. It was that awareness that first prompted me to cultivate an ever-growing respect for the healing process that would transform and define my work as a physician.

Armed with that respect and deep faith, I found that my clinical years in the hospital did not scar me with the cynicism that afflicted many of my medical student peers. Through the obvious challenges of clinical clerkships, my mother often reminded me that doctoring was a vocation. As with other callings, it was possible to transcend the dysfunctions of the system, by remaining ever present, transmitting love and compassion to those being served. I revisited Gibran's words as I prepared my application to residency programs, pondering where I might be taken next.

Today, years later, my work as a physician has undoubtedly evolved toward Gibran's climacteric description of "working with love." As such, medicine is an expression of my sacred contract. It binds me to my (higher) self and, by the nature of the woven web of creation, binds me to all others and to God, the divine weaver of that web. As Caroline Myss (2003) explains, our sacred contracts are assignments taken on before birth such that the events in our lives unfold toward the fulfillment of those contracts. This is the story of those events, evolving and revolutionizing my relationship to medicine.

URGE

The "urge," alluded to by Gibran, to understand more about dis-ease of the physical body, dates back to my elementary school years. At the age of nine, it was a more primal need, prompted by the unraveling of the nest that was my family. Early in the summer after fourth grade, specialists examined both my father and grandmother. My father, Franco Pastore, a ship captain who left Italy when he married my mother fifteen years earlier, had been slurring his words. His co-workers suspected he was inebriated. Of course he was not. The slurring was caused by a grave malfunction of his brain circuitry. During his examination, the neurologist witnessed a seizure that prompted an emergency brain scan. At the same time, my mother's mother, Ida Luisi, a strong matriarch who migrated with her family from Italy in 1958, was seeing an orthopedist for a large ulceration on her thigh. Hers was a more overt expression of physical decomposition. That day quickly went from seemingly ordinary to staggeringly consequential as they each heard the word "cancer." As a family, we plunged from the lightness of summer pleasures into the deep and murky waters of fear, loss, and suffering. Yet, as the Zen Buddhist monk Thich Nhat Hanh puts it, "We need the mud in order to make the lotus." *No mud, no lotus.* My lotus had found fertile terrain.

Cancer, by its very nature, is an assault of the body against itself. Most conventional treatments are assaults, right back, on the very same battle-field of the body. The strategy for my father was a blind ammunition shower against a widespread metastatic cancer involving his brain and liver. His primary site of involvement remained unknown. So the indiscriminate assault included whole brain radiation therapy and unselective chemo-therapy. My grandmother's battle wound was a limb amputation. My father succumbed to his fight in our home on September 18, 1983, just two and a half months after his diagnosis. He was forty-two. For nearly three years my grandmother suffered debilitating phantom limb pain, an experience common to many amputees. My mother and aunt cared dutifully for their mother, an armored female warrior by nature, now fighting to stay rooted in this world, even if on one leg. She became dependent on narcotics for pain relief yet suffered greatly nonetheless. There was no analgesia for her torment. She finally gave up her life in April 1986. Bearing witness to such deterioration and loss during those formative years was my initiation into the sacred contract of medicine woman.

KNOWLEDGE AND WORK

I took all the necessary steps toward fulfilling my call to medicine. I com-pleted my premedicine track at Yale University and started medical school soon thereafter in 1996. I remember little about my academic life between elementary school and medical school. It was as if I had been in a state of suspension. But once at Albert Einstein I was profoundly aware of my knowledge quest, the conduit to my eventual spiritual work. Einstein him-self, one of society's most revered scientists (and the namesake of our institu-tion), spoke often of spirituality. He did not belong to a particular group, but described his religion as "a humble admiration for the illimitable superior spirit that reveals itself in the slight details we are able to perceive with our frail and feeble mind" (Bucky and Weakland 1992: 86). Interestingly, most people are unaware of Einstein's veneration of Spirit. Instead much effort has gone into exploring the structure of the physical brain that he humbly described as "feeble." Scientists postulate its theoretical workings, as though the qualities of his genius could be isolated in his vacated physical anatomy.

My own brain had always been quite adept at storing bytes of information. This skill allowed me to perform at the highest academic levels. In medical school I was acknowledged by the Alpha Omega Alpha Society for my mastery of the curricular material. However, there was no medical school curriculum for developing a noncognitive, intuitive understanding of the patients and illnesses that I confronted. We were not encouraged to experience the condition of another human being in any way that evoked a feeling or "knowing" about their maladies. We were urged instead to think and differentiate from a set of known diagnoses, in order to arrive at the correct "match." It appeared that the more mechanistic a person could be, the better. Much of my time in medical school involved the most restrictive and least expansive parts of my mind. Yet, unknowingly, the evolution of my work was happening just as Gibran had prophesied. The "knowledge" I was amassing was giving further orientation to my "urge," something that had emerged more than ten years earlier in the tumult of surviving trauma and loss. A nonemotive intelligence was traversing the depths of the water from which that emotive lotus was initially seeded. Ongoing fulfillment of "my contract" would require many more years of labor, utilizing my cognitive skills *before* I could blossom those intuitive, untaught abilities. In caring for a few remarkable patients, even in the capacity of a student, I had glimpses into the expansive and sacred nature of medicine. I experienced the capacity of human connection to touch the spirit and offer healing even when the physical body's failure was inevitable. I recognized the blessedness of sharing in the timelessness of the final moments of a patient's life. Larry and Christina were my teachers of these lessons.

Larry was a middle-aged black man who succumbed to cancer after years of cigarette smoking and asbestos exposure. When I met him in my third year of medical school, he had been hospitalized for breathlessness. He knew, in his wasted state, that his body could not be cured. His mother was his witness during this time of sickness. Decades after birthing him into this world, she was *the* constant presence who would usher Larry out of the physical world. Honored to observe their process of approaching death, I shared with them Kahlil Gibran's poetic reflection on the matter (Gibran 1998 [1923]):

What is it to cease breathing, but to free the breath from its rest-
    less tides,
that it may rise and expand and see God unencumbered?
Only when you drink from the river of silence shall you indeed
    sing.
And when you have reached the mountain top, then you shall
    begin to climb.
And when the earth shall claim your limbs, then shall you truly
    dance.

Eventually, Larry's mother took him home, and there he was released from his corporeal life. Christina was a Filipino adolescent whose mother carried her onto a plane to the United States desperately seeking a cure for her daughter's sarcoma. By the time I met her, Christina was an amputee (just as my grandmother had been). I met this little soul sister not through my clerkships, but through my mother, who assisted her family with immigration issues. She was alone in the United States except for her mother and biological sister, so I spent hours of my free time with her. I served as witness to her dreams and visions, too painful for her mother to bear. While Christina was not long for the physical world, these aspirations were no less a part of her soul's language. She frequently spoke to me about exploring the splendors of the universe. Notwithstanding her outer world, which for months was confined to a hospital room, her inner world encompassed the cosmos with all its brilliant stars and elements. She passed away in August 1999, soon after I became engaged to my husband-to-be George, then a fellow medical student. We were in Greece meeting his family when my mother called with the news. I knew it mattered little that I was not nearby when Christina died. As I looked up into the starry sky illuminating the otherwise dark Greek village, I was aware that Christina had transcended physical space and time.

The "thread" of consciousness and the cosmic energies that allowed my path to cross with Larry's and Christina's are like a silken, surprisingly resilient thread woven by our common creator. These nonphysical cords are often perceptible to the intuitive mind. A quotation often attributed to Einstein expresses deep appreciation for this more subtle yet powerful aspect of our mind: "The intuitive mind is a sacred gift and the rational mind [its] faithful servant. We have created a society that honors the servant and has forgotten the gift." The remainder of my (r)evolution in medicine consisted in remembering this gift. Love—the force that engages so powerfully in creation and procreation—was the vehicle by which my inner wisdom found greater expression. It was motherhood, my greatest expression of love, that allowed me to deepen my understanding of healing.

LOVE LESSONS FROM TASO

I conceived Taso, my first son, during my second year of residency training at Columbia Presbyterian, a strongly academic institution where my rational mind was honed ever more rigorously. For many years, I had considered a subspecialization in oncology. In fact my encounters with cancer patients and their anguished families called most to my heart. But I rationalized that I would be perpetually challenged by the task of separating myself enough to be present for the family I had already begun. Thus, at the end of my chief residency, I elected a fellowship in critical care medicine. It was similarly intense, intellectually challenging, and infused with ethical considerations surrounding life and death. Yet, as shift work, it had self-imposed boundaries regarding patient care, with a clear beginning and end to the doctoring role. I took (false) reassurance in this containment, somehow feeling less exposed.

I began my critical care fellowship at Columbia when Taso was nineteen months old and I was already pregnant with my second son. Three months into my fellowship, Taso was being seen by a developmental pediatrician. A neighbor (and preschool teacher) had brought it to my attention that Taso was not responding consistently to his name or sustaining eye contact. He often covered his ears or closed his eyes, struggling with information from his external world. How had I *not* been attuned to Taso's symptoms after years of mind-pruning in medical school and residency? Self-doubt inundated me as I disbelievingly answered an intake question about Taso's favorite activity: spinning wheels on his strollers and cars. This is a typical symptom of autistic children. How had I *not* suspected the diagnosis myself? After a two-hour visit, the specialist diagnosed Taso with an autism spectrum disorder and further suggested that the son I was expecting had a 15 percent chance of being autistic as well. Every expectation that I had about the next few years of my family and work life crumbled.

In deciding how I was going to pick up the pieces and reformulate my life, my mind yielded to the callings of my heart. I left the fellowship. This was beyond the realm of comprehension for most of my colleagues. How could a recent chief resident and leading physician among peers at a prominent academic institution forego her career to mother her child? But my commitment could be to nothing other than this labor of love: fostering Taso's emergence from the darkness that veiled his mind and young life. What I learned from Taso—that no fellowship program could have taught me—was that the heart's intelligence yields rewards far richer than the mind's. Inevitably, when we move from the heart, we engage love in our work and more strongly *desire* a favorable outcome. I felt pride and self-gratification when Taso was eventually integrated into a mainstream education program with very little residual from his initial diagnosis. My ego, however, would learn its next lesson in humility from an as-yet unborn soul orienting the rudder on my lifeboat in another direction.

LOVE LESSONS FROM ADREANNA

When Taso was three years old, aging out of early intervention services and entering preschool, and Francesco, my second born, was nine months old, I was still considering the option of returning to my critical care training. I had spent over a year away from it. Now confident that Taso was on a better path, I was ready to return. During that time, I had worked two or three grueling overnight shifts a week as an intensive care unit hospitalist physician: I kept my skills sharp at resuscitative/invasive ICU procedures, while also teaching residents. My children saw me as a full-time mother because I only worked while they slept. Once Francesco, seeing a picture of me in a white physician's coat taken during my chief residency, asked if the picture was from when I "*used to* be a doctor." I clarified that I *was still* and *would always* be a doctor. Yet during that time, which turned into five years (much longer than expected), I allowed my identity to be mostly that of a mother. Each attempt I made to return to the fellowship was thwarted and, even though my husband and I had made no plans for additional children just yet, Adreanna was conceived.

While still nursing Francesco and on the pill, I sustained the unfortunate occupational risk of a needle stick. I was working an overnight shift and another hospitalist physician/mother asked to be relieved early from her shift. Relating to her desire to get home to her family, I agreed. She shared the updates on her service, asking me to follow up on the respiratory status of a patient well known to her—a morbidly obese, drug-addicted woman, who frequently came in with compromised breathing. My colleague was confident that the patient was already improving on a breathing mask and would continue to do well overnight. My sense of responsibility urged me to check on the patient soon after the other physician had departed.

What I found was quite different than what had been related: the patient was semicomatose, with a very low blood pressure for the last twelve hours. The nursing staff had alerted the other physician numerous times, but she had not intervened. The patient required immediate resuscitation, through both intubation and catheterization of a large, central vein. After intubation, the patient became increasingly belligerent. During the arduous task of catheterizing her vein (very deep because of her obesity), I stuck myself with the large needle, already contaminated with her blood. Only after she was finally stabilized did I seek out medical attention for myself in the emergency department.

After a negative screening urinary pregnancy test, I was immediately put on prophylactic HIV medications. No HIV test on the patient had been previously recorded, and New York law prohibited ordering one without her consent. She was hepatitis C positive from her extensive intravenous drug use history. Hepatitis C is much more contagious than even HIV; yet there is no prophylaxis. I would require six months of monitoring to ensure that I had not contracted either virus from her. Because of the possible viral exposure and medication toxicity, I had to stop nursing ten-month-old Francesco immediately. He and I both suffered vastly from the abrupt loss of that beautiful contact between mother and child. The resuscitated patient was not very obliging about allowing an HIV test, even when made aware of the sacrifice that I had made. The colleague who had compromised both the patient's safety and my own was placed on brief probation. I hoped that the drug-addicted patient would see that I recognized, without condition, her worth as a human being. I hoped that my colleague would appreciate the impact of her actions (or nonaction) on others. While I have yet to know what ripple effect this intersection had on their lives, I know that my life changed infinitely.

I was very ill on the HIV medications: profound muscle aches, fatigue, nausea, vomiting. These intractable symptoms forced me to stop the medications before completing an adequate prophylactic course. Thankfully, by that time we had determined that the patient was HIV negative. Because my symptoms continued beyond my discontinuation of the prophylaxis, I was retested and confirmed to be negative for hepatitis. A serum pregnancy test was also run. It returned *positive* with inexplicably high levels of HCG (human chorionic gonadotropin) hormone. The levels were much greater than expected for a single fetus pregnancy, conceived in the period after the needle stick. I also had not had sex with my husband since the needle stick. I was both ill and fearful of exposing him to anything I may have contracted. It quickly became apparent that I had conceived just before the needle stick and that I was carrying *twins*. The initial urine pregnancy screen in the emergency department on the night of the needle stick had been a false negative. I was now about six weeks pregnant. Within twenty-four hours of the shock of recognizing that I was pregnant, I miscarried one of the twins. My obstetrician suspected that I would lose them both. I felt confident God was taking back the two lives that had been tainted by the awful medications I had taken. But I did not miscarry the second twin. She persisted. And while my husband strongly encouraged me to terminate the pregnancy, I turned to God in tearful prayer. This time it was not my mind, nor my heart, searching for an answer—it was my soul.

I allowed the pregnancy to continue, but at the end of my first trimester routine screening found that I had hepatitis C, with a high load of virus. I was in disbelief. The nature of my exposure should have conferred a less than 5 percent chance of becoming infected. How had the odds and God failed me? The lab director at Columbia was steadfast that this was a true positive. She referred me to the director of hepatology to discuss acute anti-hepatitis treatment. He knew me well from my training and advised me to terminate the pregnancy immediately. Finding an obstetrician willing to terminate in the second trimester would be challenging. I learned that my best chance at a cure would be a toxic yet potent protocol, to be started without hesitation. This news came to me on a Friday. I was asked to return to Columbia for genetic typing of the hepatitis C on Monday. I remember feeling shattered as I called the obstetrician covering that weekend. He compassionately listened to my predicament and agreed to a termination at the end of the following week.

That night I called in sick. I was due to work the same shift during which I had been exposed. As the universe would have it, the physician expected to cover for me was the same physician liable for my current state. She was back to work, off probation, and unhappy to be called in on a Friday night. I was beside myself with righteous fury. The probationary process had never required her to acknowledge her self-serving negligence toward me or the patient. Now, face to face with the rippling consequences of her actions, she was again shirking. That night my husband and I shared grief over the anticipated loss of our baby and fear over my own well-being. I sobbed all night, but it didn't serve as an outlet to the anguish that swelled into every part of my being. There was too little room in my head and heart to hold it all. I had the most dreadful headache and heartache of my life.

The following Saturday morning found me in the same state. My father-in-law, a devout man of the Greek Orthodox tradition, paid an unexpected visit to our home. Finding me in my tormented state, he asked in his broken and simple English what was wrong with me. My husband explained that I had just received news about having been infected with hepatitis months earlier and would now have to have an abortion to allow for treatment. George's father was enraged by our choice, a challenge to his faith. I quickly defended my position, stating that I had a greater responsibility to Taso and Francesco than to my unborn child. I was not about to risk chronic hepatitis and potential cirrhosis on moral grounds. While my reasoning was medically sound, I now recognize that my soul's commitment to Adreanna had wavered in the face of fear and exhaustion. While as a physician I might not have encouraged a patient to follow a similar path, I am now grateful that my father-in-law recognized an opportunity for a miracle. He invoked God and the energy of Saint Nicholas and offered me holy water to drink. Having nothing to lose, I drank the holy water. In doing so I was not actively exercising faith, but I *was* surrendering to God, not knowing what else I could do.

Days later I received notification that Monday's blood test could no longer detect hepatitis C. Doctors could not reconcile the incongruent results of tests done only a few days apart. They argued that there must have been a miscalibration of the machine that generated the prior positive test and viral load. The rational mind of science could not make sense of the sacred gift that I had been granted. Only the intuitive mind can assimilate this glimpse of divine consciousness and intercession. In spite of my traditional medical training, I was able to recognize that a miracle had occurred. I alerted my obstetrician that a termination was no longer called for.

Adreanna Nicola was born on October 30, 2006, nearly two weeks beyond her due date. Her middle name honored Saint Nicholas, whose energy, invoked by her *papouli* (grandfather), helped carry Adreanna forth into this world. Graciously recognizing that I was merely a vessel for her divine manifestation, I chose to experience her delivery fully, without medication. Adreanna was a natural birth at nine pounds, one ounce. While her first year of life was unremarkable, by her second year she was not babbling and would not do so for almost another full year. Adre is now nine years old and has very little verbal language. Notwithstanding the absence of words, she communicates her love so vibrantly and freely that she engages the soul of everyone she meets. Her love is so abundant and unconditional that I feel blessed to be part of her daily existence. Despite vast efforts to support a more "typical" development, Adreanna's life is unfolding beyond my will, desires, and expectations. Starting *in utero* she has taught me about faith, nonattachment, and the expression of Spirit on earth.

LOVE LESSONS FROM FRANCESCO

Francesco, my second son, was born after the apprehension-invoking words of the developmental pediatrician who diagnosed Taso with autism. Fear was similarly the favored tactic of the obstetrician who suggested that Francesco was not growing and required weekly/biweekly ultrasound and heart rate monitoring. He persuaded me to have an induction, convincing me my placenta would not sustain the forty weeks. (I had not yet learned to assert my confidence in God and nature, as I would in Adreanna's delivery.) Fear begot turmoil and a medical error ensued around the administration of Pitocin, the induction agent. This resulted in such intense, unrelenting uterine contractions that Francesco was compressed against my still closed cervix. His blood supply was compromised and his heart rate was transiently lost. Mercifully, my uterus relaxed and he was birthed naturally within a couple hours, larger than any of the estimates.

Francesco was so bonded to me that I suspect this was a recoiling response to the perception that he was being forcibly ejected from my uterus. I could not avoid holding him close to my heart in a Bjorn carrier I grew accustomed to wearing from morning until night. I learned to navigate the world with Francesco as a near-permanent appendage. I was home those days, engrossed in the mission of easing Taso out of his detached existence, encouraging him to tolerate the disorder of the natural world and its assault on his senses. Francesco just nestled close to me. After abruptly stopping nursing because of the needle stick exposure, I was further consumed by the emotional trauma of my early pregnancy with Adreanna. Francesco just watched and took it all in, "seeing" so much with his yet infantile eyes. We had not realized that Francesco's eyes had been adulterated even before he was born.

When Francesco was two years old, I noticed that those perceptive eyes I would peer into had moved out of alignment. His left eye did not seem to track with the right eye. My curiosity was piqued, as I am amblyopic (centrally blind) in my left eye. My brain, by the age of seven, had "turned off" the visual processing from a weak left eye because it could not reconcile the information presented by a stronger right eye—this is the medical understanding of amblyopia. But there had been an ancestral pattern of vision loss in my paternal family. My father had struggled with significant vision weakness. His sister had been involved in a motorcycle accident with a blunt physical trauma to her eye that permanently compromised its vision. Their mother, my paternal grandmother, had suffered a sharp, piercing trauma to her eye from a tailoring needle. Three generations of vision loss preceded Francesco.

Now, in the generation of my children, Francesco, most aligned by name and nature to my paternal lineage, was manifesting a weakness in his left eye. Concerned about a mild gaze discrepancy, I took Francesco to a highly recommended pediatric ophthalmologist. The physician promptly ascertained that Francesco was blind in his left eye. As he probed further into the depths of his eye, he identified a scar that had obliterated Francesco's macula. The scar was typical of that seen in congenital toxoplasmosis, an infection passed from mother to fetus after an exposure such as infested cat litter. Although we had no risk factors, testing confirmed that Francesco and I had indeed been exposed to toxoplasmosis.

How did this organism find its way into my energy system and access a line of communication with my unborn son such that he would manifest a weakness that he had been ancestrally predisposed to? Whether through trauma, neuromuscular weakness, or infection, eyesight was an Achilles' heel of sorts for me, my paternal family, and now Francesco. This sort of question would be part of the next (ongoing) phase of my development as a physician. I would never be able to appreciate the vastness that is healing, if I could not bow to the interplay (at times cross-generational) of physical, mental/emotional, and spiritual vulnerabilities. Clearly, there is no "physical" gene that could communicate a susceptibility to pluricausal blindness. Yet in our family that energetic imprint was transmitted in such a way that life events, even pathogens, aligned themselves to express a particular reality of sightlessness.

Several retina specialists prognosticated that the vision in Francesco's left eye was irrecoverable. Yet he was fortunate to have had just one eye affected. Both eyes are often blinded in congenital toxoplasmosis. Invoking the adaptive capacity of the body to heal, the primary ophthalmologist encouraged us to patch Francesco's right eye, "forcing" the left eye to see from areas that might have been spared. Slowly the left eye recovered some vision.

On February 17, 2010, when Francesco was nearly five years old, I noted an ominous sign in his right eye. It was Ash Wednesday, the first day of our Catholic Lent, and I was in church with the children for a late evening mass. It had been an emotionally challenging day for us as a family because our au pair had departed for her country of origin. Luisa had been with us for a year so that I could establish my medical practice. I had finally decided, in the wake of my occupational exposure and Francesco's illness, to leave critical care. There were much more intriguing avenues in medicine. I studied medical acupuncture through the Harvard School of Medicine and explored the energetic body and the energetic impact of food, herbs, thoughts, and emotions. In a leap of faith, I began my own practice, initially with no administrative support.

Francesco, now watching his mother return to her daily doctoring, actually grew very close to Luisa over the course of her year with us. Compounding the loss of Luisa, three days earlier, we had had one of those parental blunders whereby my husband and I each thought the other had Francesco. Instead he was briefly left unattended on the snow-covered playground hill on which we had been sledding. The brevity of the abandonment was unimportant, as Francesco's experience of desertion and helplessness over those few moments in the cold snow was enough to set his snowball of anxiety in motion.

The two experiences of loss breached Francesco's immunity, and pathology remanifested in his eyes. A follow-up visit to the ophthalmologist and a host of many other doctors, all with their own limited domain over my son's eye, nervous system, and immune system, generated varying theories on the etiology of the inflammation and nerve weakness now affecting his right eye. Somewhere in the ever more frustrating sequence of visits to doctors who proposed varying diagnoses I decided, with George's concurrence, that we need not look any further. We already had all the information within us about how to diagnose and treat our child.

Our friend, a holistic chiropractor, had assessed Francesco in the first days of Lent, just after the new symptoms emerged. He established through applied kinesiology—an interrogation of Francesco's energy system—that this was indeed reactivated toxoplasmosis in the right eye. Even though all of the ophthalmologists had asserted that there had been no toxoplasmosis in the right eye from which a reactivation could occur, we started Francesco on a homeopathic protocol. Months into our senseless investigations with the specialists, an examination under anesthesia and angiogram of the right eye diagnosed a peripheral toxoplasmosis scar in the right eye that had seeded the reactivation. The chiropractor had arrived at the correct diagnosis by querying Francesco's energy system. Relying on homeopathic remedies alone (Francesco poorly tolerated antibiotics), we were able to heal the psychoemotional, spiritual, and physical underpinnings of Francesco's worsened state. The parasite and inflammation became quiescent, and the vision in his right eye has been preserved,

What infinite and unforeseen possibilities for healing we could access if we doctors put aside our egos and our attachments and remain open to the answers revealed by the human energy system!

THE ULTIMATE LOVE LESSON

Francesco not infrequently complained of leg pains, almost always in his left leg. Later that same year, in early fall 2010, he awakened in the middle of the night, screaming horrifically: "Mommy, help me. It feels as if someone is cutting my leg off." I could not comprehend how he might have conjured up such a fear in his consciousness. He had never been exposed to such imagery. He had never met his amputated great-grandmother or any other amputee. Nor had he ever seen pictures of or heard anyone speak of what had befallen my grandmother. I was full of alarm and awe. I wondered if Francesco was somehow haunted by Ida's energy. The next day I found myself probing my mother and aunt about which leg Nonna had had amputated. They reminded me that it had been the right leg, not the left.

Weeks later the prophetic nature of Francesco's screams was made evident. On October 29, 2010, I was dragged, crushed, and run over by my own car. Much of the structure of my left lower leg and foot was amputated.

The day had been similar to others, except that in retrospect it seemed *fuller* from the start. Because it was Friday, two days before Halloween and one day before Adreanna's fourth birthday, there were a number of school celebrations to attend. I started the morning in Francesco's kindergarten Halloween celebration then went to my office to meet with a new patient for ninety minutes. Then I met with Sandy, a soul friend, whom I rarely had the opportunity to see in person. After our tea in Englewood, I headed over to my daughter's special needs program in Harrington Park, twenty minutes away. During my drive, I had an odd sense that something of large magnitude was imminent. I panicked and considered pulling off the road, but I did not want to be late for Adre's birthday/Halloween celebration. Following the celebration, I secured my fairy princess in our Honda Odyssey minivan and headed home. My boys were going to be displaying their costumes in their school parade, and I had hoped to make it in time. My head started throbbing with the all-too-familiar pain of an ensuing migraine headache. After arriving in our neighborhood just at the finish of their school parade, I pondered whether I would be up for following through with the plans I had made to meet childhood friends for dinner in Manhattan. Everything in my being wondered if I should go, but I was hesitant to cancel our plans, as we had been looking forward to this date for months. I asked Karol, the au pair who had replaced Luisa, to mind the children while I closed my eyes for a bit to try and ward off the migraine and regroup my energies. I lay down in my room and prayed quietly. When I roused myself, I told Karol that I would be leaving.

I believe I entered my car just before 6:00 P.M. with plans to pass by my mother's home and then head into the city. I never made it to either. I tried to navigate the minivan out of a tight space, blocked too closely by Karol's vehicle. Unsuccessful, I placed my car in park and planned to move the other car to facilitate my exit. As I stepped out of the car with my left foot leading, it started reversing down the incline of my drive. I desperately reached to engage the brake, but to no avail. I was ultimately dragged about forty feet, with my leg being crushed between the front tire and the

Belgium blocks bordering the driveway before the car ran over my leg and then stopped. I never lost consciousness while the accident crushed four of my five metatarsals and stripped the muscles and other structures off the top and side of my foot and midway up to my knee. My leg was lying at an odd angle as I reached down to bare bone and a bath of blood.

George had arrived home just as my car started on its reverse path. He was perplexed about what could be going on. Then he heard my screams and ran to the site of carnage. He detached himself enough to be of highest service to me in those moments, temporarily leaving my side to secure a belt to tourniquet my leg and to direct the au pair to call an ambulance. She was so overwrought and paralyzed by her emotions that she could not even make the phone call. Despite my certain immense pain (I can't recall that part of it), I was able to maintain enough clarity of mind to direct my husband through my cell phone contact list to my patient whose husband was the head of anesthesiology at Hackensack University Medical Center, the nearest trauma center. My readily available visual memories are the blue eyes of the police officer holding my hand as the paramedics were trying to safely get a board under me and my husband placing the IV through which I received morphine, which quickly brought on analgesia, amnesia, and sleep. I woke briefly in the emergency room, being made aware that they were taking me immediately to the operating room. The next time I awoke was in the surgical ICU to a team of doctors informing me that I would need an amputation below the knee. Too much of the bone, muscle, tendons, ligaments, skin, nerves, and blood vessels had been lost to deem the leg salvageable. I had spent months studying anatomy, but even as a doctor I had taken for granted so many things in my own physical anatomy. Beyond the wrappings that covered all of the severed areas, I saw my toes, somehow intact, connected via an intact sole of my foot, and it was challenging to imagine surgically removing parts that had been spared by the accident.

And then began the sacred intercessions that altered my path. First, a doctor who heard of my case asked my husband if he could meet me. When he entered my room, he appeared to be an angel. He embodied such tranquillity and invoked so much of my faith. As he pulled back my wound dressings, we spoke and realized that he and I were in fact neighbors and our boys had been in the same class: a beautiful synchronicity meant to show me that the universe was aligning for me. While doctors at Columbia Hospital for Special Surgery had concurred with the amputation, this divinely appointed doctor offered to assemble a "dream team" of surgeons for me. What the team proposed had only been done a handful of times: they would enter my chest wall and remove rib segments to graft into my foot as metatarsals and musculature to graft over the lacking areas of my foot and lower leg. Then they would graft skin from my thighs onto the newly placed musculature. The surgical team gave me a small window during which I could successfully undergo the surgery. If we waited too long and my blood became too viscous they would not be able to operate. Before that small window closed, they also needed to find an orthopedic surgeon who was willing to participate in this unprecedented surgery.

Most of the orthopedic surgeons worried that I might be disappointed with the outcome, if I should choose the reconstruction. They projected that after one to one and a half years of rehabilitation I might not be able to be functional in my life as a mother and physician. I would likely suffer chronic pain and be dissatisfied with the cosmetic outcome. I would never be able to wear a normal shoe on that foot. I feared all of these projections, but my husband encouraged me to make a decision based in hope and not fear. I will never forget the impact of his words. I started giving voice to the life I wanted to return to, which included hiking with my children and yoga. While I would be most certain to accomplish this with a prosthetic, I had a choice to make. In the forty-eight hours before the window would close on the surgery, I was assaulted with images of blurred words written on every surface, including the inside of my eyelids. I felt the urgency of a message that needed to be revealed to me. My soul friend Sandy encouraged me to quiet my mind so that I might receive the message. That night, because of an unusual decision to wean my epidural analgesic, my mind was so preoccupied with the intensity of physical pain that it could not quiet.

It was Sandy who was awakened with the message. She feverishly wrote in a half awake state, in a blackened room, ten pages of Spirit guidance. She apprehensively shared the content with me the following morning. I received the message as a gift. It shepherded me toward regeneration, suggesting that I would experience a "rebirth." So I decided to go along with the reconstructive surgery. The surgeon who had proposed it told me that he had sailed the Atlantic Ocean the summer before. That endeavor bespoke this willingness to choose faith over fear. He was my guy.

I underwent fourteen hours of deconstruction and reconstruction, and awoke on November 5, my birthday, now "rebirthday." On the same day as my initial incarnation, I was born again, like the phoenix. I awoke with a breathing tube down my airway, three tubes draining my chest wall, thighs covered in dressings over the removed skin, and a reconstructed left lower leg and foot held together by a cage of external pins driven into my bones. I had considerable pain, but my moments of *suffering* were few because I felt I was in the hands of the Divine in all its varied forms: the compassionate hands of the five nurses who rotated me in the bed and cleaned me, the nurse assistants, and even cleaning staff who wandered into the room with words of encouragement. Two young volunteer transporters, whose youth and inexperience had at first worried me, spoke to me from the Bible, reminding me that "the Lord [was] my shepherd and I [would] not want."

My blessings persisted throughout my nearly one month in the hospital and then nearly one month in in-patient rehabilitation. Whenever I was overwhelmed with fear or doubt, there was someone there, an old friend or a new one, to hold my hand. When I first tried to put my new limb vertical, off the edge of the bed, the rush of blood into the grafted bed of vasculature caused me such intense pain that I could not last more than five seconds. Nevertheless, my young yet wise nurse refreshed my confidence in my physical body's ability to revise itself to meet the new demands.

One particular embodiment of Spirit was in the form of my husband's cousin Rose. My husband and Rose had been estranged for twenty-five years because of a parental conflict. A few weeks before my accident we met for the first time when they asked me to treat George's uncle (Rose's father). We felt an instantaneous, timeless connection at the soul level. After my accident, Rose, a psychologist with a background in trauma, offered to commit herself to me during my healing, showing up for me in person every Monday and in spirit every day. She was the one greatest witness to the tremendous healing that unfolded for me. She would always say that she was "holding space" for me. Having never experienced that human offering, I did not recognize the generosity of it until much later. Rose allowed me to be exactly where I was in the healing process, without judgment, having full faith that Super-Intelligence (God) was at work in every moment. When I was back in my home but wheelchair bound and limited to the ground floor, Rose recognized my suffering in not being able to be upstairs with my family. Rose recognized when I needed to rejoin them. She patiently watched and graciously encouraged me to ascend the stairs on my rear with my externally fixed left leg outstretched. When I finally arrived at the top,

Rose snapped a picture of me, a testament to what she would call our "Make It Happen Mondays."

While I could not physically participate in the care of my children, my spirit was always with them and theirs with me. Adre signed "mama" incessantly in my absence. Francesco, after I was finally home, in his self-less attunement to me, said: "Mommy, it must have been really confusing for you to be in the hospital and then another hospital and then home only to return to the hospital again." What a healing gift from my child, who, at five and a half, was able to express empathically his understanding of my experience.

I returned to work well before I was fully healed. I was in a wheelchair, with external pins penetrating my bones to hold them in position. I was not any less able to be present for my patients because healing requires an extension of spirit on the part of the physician, no more and no less. I was walking in six months, much earlier than anyone's predictions. Speaking from experience, each day of my sacred work, I encourage my patients to open themselves up to that which can come to be when we exercise faith and fearlessness instead of fear and faithlessness.

Within my practice, I have been able to witness beautiful transformations even through the most tragic of circumstances. It is not a coincidence that a doctor's work is called his/her practice. Yogis call their coming to the mat their practice, a ritual and disciplined system for spiritual growth. The mat is the place where we face the challenges and tragedies in our lives. We also recognize the opportunity in those unanticipated, unwelcome events. If we grasp the opportunity, perhaps we can even transcend the condition. What I have become ever aware of is the physical body's capacity to take on disease and trauma to facilitate the expansion of its spirit or the spirit of another. Perhaps an ill state is an occasion for a grander experience of healing and grace.

If healing is seen as an act of grace, then the practice of medicine is nothing short of a ministry. In pledging the Hippocratic Oath, with all of my medical doctorate colleagues at Albert Einstein College of Medicine, I joined the ranks of many others who had preceded me in this ministry. My professional circle included medicine men and women, some designated by doctorates and some not, yet sacred healers nonetheless. More than 2,000 years after Hippocrates suggested the responsibility of a healer, we continue to honor the commitment. We all take the oath at our

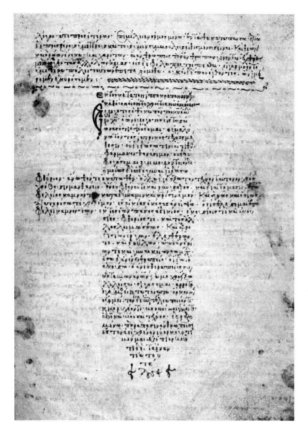

FIGURE 12.1 Twelfth-century Byzantine manuscript with
the Hippocratic oath written in the form of a cross, relating it visually to faith practices. Foto de la Biblioteca Vati-
cana (from Ira M. Rutkow, *Surgery: An Illustrated History*
[St. Louis, Mosby–Year Book, 1993], 27).

graduation, yet do we regard it as a covenant between doctor and patient?
In a twelfth-century Byzantine rendition of the Hippocratic Oath (shown in
the illustration) the ancestral doctor's words are embedded in a cross, suggesting that medicine is indeed a sacred endeavor. Seen as such, the practice
of sacred medicine is an evolution or rather a (r)evolution. It is a transformation that circles the healer back to our collective origins. The cross, seen
more broadly, beyond its Christian implications, is the intersection of God's
light, love, and wisdom as it descends and passes through the material plane

that is our physical existence. Healing happens at the point of intersection, which is the heart, manifest as love and compassion for self and other.

My most important teachings in healing came through my children, my greatest expressions of love, and ultimately through the loss in my own physical body, so I could intimately experience that love and grace.

As a holistic internist, I care for patients across the spectrum of their lives, through states of suffering and joy. I lovingly engage patients in leaps of faith regarding their potential to heal. This is in contrast to the fear that most often overrides them (and, too often, their other treating physicians). Fear has largely driven the extreme subspecialization in medicine, with most doctors practicing in a very small comfort zone and not venturing beyond that. I choose to practice broadly, welcoming any patient who seeks me out.

One of my most poignant journeys with a patient was with a woman who came to me in her late forties, after decades of loss and abuse, psychiatric illness, and drug addiction. She was "sober" but on six prescribed psychotropic medications. She was unable to fully participate in life, could not navigate her physical world, and could barely speak a coherent sentence. An exploration of her energetic system suggested hormone imbalances and neuro-immune manifestations related to a long-standing yet previously undiagnosed tick-borne illness. Laboratory testing corroborated these findings. Following cues, suggested through applied kinesiology, we were able to wean her off five medications and lowered the sixth significantly. I invited the prescribing neurologist to participate in this approach with me, but she replied that she had vehemently directed the patient at her last visit never to come off of any of the medications. Within weeks the patient was sharing with me some significant positive shifts in her life, thanking me for the opportunity to reexperience life as she had not done in quite some time. Her humble gratitude list included "writing and reading, smiling and laughing, appreciating music again, walking without falling, carrying things without dropping them, riding a bicycle." Together we expressed faith in the ability of her mind, body, and spirit to recover a state of balance.

For much of her course, I saw her once weekly *pro bono*, as she was unable to work and was uninsured. She reciprocated with tokens of gratitude: fresh fruit, animal figurines, seashells, whatever she happened upon in her reencounter with the world during the preceding week. One day she gave me a copy of the devotional book *God Calling*, which had been passed along to her by her mother, who had since departed. I was overwhelmed by the gesture, an affirmation of the transcendent nature of our physician-patient relationship. Whenever she expressed ambivalence about my seeing her without monetary reimbursement, I reminded her of her own message to me. It was simply "God calling" me to play this role in her life, and I was honored to be able to respond.

My healing evolution, or (r)evolution, like most paths that we walk in life, has been like an outward spiraling path. The point from which the spiral arises is that spark or "urge," which for me happened at age nine. There are nodes or points along the spiral that further define its path. Spiraling out beyond the plane of two dimensions, we never lose sight of the birthing point of the path, but encompass more, so that the perspective becomes more cosmic. God's calling me to be a medicine woman has been echoed into ever more sacred and universal ground. I continue to walk the path, physically challenged yet with increasing spiritual fortitude.

WORKS CITED

Bucky, Peter A., and Allen G. Weakland. 1992. *The Private Albert Einstein*. Kansas City: Andrews and McMeel.

Gibran, Kahlil. 1998 [1923]. *The Prophet*. New York: Alfred A Knopf.

Myss, Carolyn. 2003. *Sacred Contracts: Awakening Your Divine Potential*. New York: Three Rivers Press.

Thirteen

THE GROUND I STAND ON

LAUREN VITIELLO

THE LENTEN SPIRIT AND ASTRO BOY

It was while I was a child at St. Mary's grammar school that I developed a love/hate relationship with the Roman Catholic Church. Its glorious and mysterious ways were not easily grasped by the hands and minds of small children. My brother, sister, and I, however, attended St. Mary's "for the discipline," as my father ingloriously explained. My mother did not bother to offer an explanation for our enrollment in Catholic school because, unlike my father, she did not have to articulate why and what she did and felt. Such is the behavior of a believer. My father, however, was a doubter. At the very least, he was a questioner. He needed logical explanations for everything, and we, his family, were the sounding boards for his thoughts, many rational, others not.

My parents died a long time ago, and from them I inherited both a believing and a questioning mind. I grew up betwixt and between a crucifix and a question mark, yet somehow I was able to make sense of it all and create my professional, spiritual, and personal selves. I believe it was the constant straddling between belief and doubt that has helped me in the work I do today. In short, I am a gatekeeper. Professionally I allow or withhold, accept or reject. I have the legal responsibility to discern fact from fiction, to find who the innocents are among the disingenuous. By dispelling doubt through questioning, I am always on the cusp of believing. This constant cleaving and winnowing gives me what I hope is something very close to truth or at least a kernel of truth—a hard and tangible surety.

Privately I write memoir. Publicly my job is interviewing refugees and training other interviewers on the legal instruments for assessing factors that determine who meets the definition of "refugee" (*Handbook* 1992: 10–11).[1] It is with great respect and appreciation for the law, for the people who sit before me, and for the power dynamics that influence our words that I acknowledge my role as gatekeeper. I am a federal officer who exercises an authority to let in or keep out. This is just as much a fact as it is an honor. To say the least, gatekeeping is and should be an extraordinarily humbling experience. We in this profession are regularly confronted with our ignorance about the lives of those who sit before us, which we are called upon to judge.[2]

Engaging in complex conversations with refugee applicants also reinforces my sense of who *I* am. After years of face-to-face conversations with people who may never be able to return home,[3] inevitably I am led to ask myself the difficult questions that take me to territories beyond my comfort zone. What, literally and figuratively, is the ground I stand on? What constitutes "home" for me? Interviewers enter this field with a variety of identity markers, but to which do we give voice and authority? When do we privilege one aspect of who we are over another? It is critical to understand the filters that we use and how they inform our analytic process.

I don't consider myself Catholic, but Catholicism is as good a place as any to begin my small history (spelled with a lowercase "h"). If loved, a child who is empathetic and imaginative enough may learn to understand and articulate her own story. Taken together, these characteristics may also produce the kind of wisdom that helps a child mature to see with clarity the larger story, the one that places her in the flow of time from ancestors to the present. This is History with a capital "H." But clarity must necessarily begin with a small story.

I disliked much of my experience in Catholic school. I was constantly reminded that the letters of my cursive writing were irregularly sized, and deep inside I knew that only the quiet, obedient, and feminine girls would succeed and fully reach their potential under the guidance of Sisters Marie King, Helen Joseph, and Alice James, women of titular masculinity. What I did enjoy were the fantasies that grew in my mind from the Catholic teachings planted there. What child would not appreciate a good story about evildoers burning in hell, unbaptized babies suspended in limbo, and a perfect mother, the Mother of God in fact, standing on clouds in a white dress and blue robe, arms outstretched and palms upturned in a stance that is welcoming and giving—in short a happy child's idea of her mother.

Intertwined with doubting and believing in Catholicism, as I perceive it, is a constant oscillation between the opposite poles of loving and hating, hurting and helping, giving and taking. Whether I am storytelling or "storylistening,"[4] I am nostalgically pulled toward the seesawing of dichotomous thinking where a heaven must have a hell and vice versa. Such is the lopsided dualistic thinking that Westerners inherited from Socrates and René Descartes, two skeptical thinkers in our long history of thought who pushed the art of *not* believing to new heights (Elbow 2008–29: 3) or lows, as the case may be. Too easily this is the default: dogmatic frameworks, whether religious or secular, become a kind of brain furniture too big to move around and rearrange. But dogmatic thinking can serve as good a starting place as any as we grow into critical thinkers—so long as we remain aware of its limitations.

The season of Lent serves as the best example of how my love/hate relationship with Catholicism materialized. During the early months of spring I despised the nuns for forcing me to stay late after school on Fridays to participate in the Stations of the Cross, the virtual reenactment of Christ's walk up Mount Calvary. On those Friday afternoons I wanted to walk the mile home in the warm weather to play with my best friends, Roberta and Susan, the Presbyterians who lived next door and went to public school. To me, their lives were normal. Instead I remained at St. Mary's, where the Stations of the Cross were celebrated with an endless drone of prayers reverberating against the granite and concrete of the church walls and floor. Both priest and congregation muttered fifty Hail Marys while fondling the glass beads of the rosary, one rosary for each pair of hands, one bead for each prayer, five sets of ten beads for each Hail Mary, each set punctuated with a long Our Father on a fatter, more patriarchal bead, on and on through that endless loop. We held in our hands small pamphlets with a text and illustrations that depicted the end-of-life events of Jesus, from condemnation to entombment. Since my pamphlet was an older hand-me-down, the illustrations' colors and details were much more vibrant, so the humiliations that Christ suffered as the guards stripped him naked (pictured only to his hip bones!), flogged him, and pinned him to the cross by hammering nails through his palms and insteps were particularly vivid and therefore more indelibly fixed in my memory. It was always the hellish and freakish bits that attracted my greatest attention.[5] Ironically, years later I would be listening to stories even more gruesome than this.

The love part of my love/hate relationship was the fantasy life that I enjoyed during the Lenten season. The Roman Catholic Church wrapped all of its teachings in divine ritual. After the first ten minutes of the Stations of the Cross, when I was wishing I were somewhere else rather than seated in the hollow, shadowy cavern of St. Mary's church, fantasies took hold of my thoughts. The monotonous drone of prayer was hypnotic, and the residual odor of incense transported me to the otherworldly. Under the high ceilings, and in the coolness of cinder block walls, I imagined myself ascending above the rafters. Childhood megalomania? Perhaps. But what else could the priests and nuns expect of children who were subjected to the imagery that they presented as real? Holy beings were assumed into heaven (my first understanding of the word "assume"); patriarchs parted seas; the about-to-be-martyred fervently prayed in dens where hungry lions spared the faithful and would not maul and kill; an ark with mating pairs for all manner of fauna floated on a completely flooded world; poisonous snakes were turned to sticks; and cadavers rose from the dead. Why couldn't I, too, ascend to the heavens and be assumed? A small favor, really, for one little kid amid all this fantastical history. For years, I wanted to fly by my own propulsion. I wanted to be like Astro Boy, my cartoon hero with supernatural powers.[6] I wanted to be Astro Girl and save the world. In class I would daydream about robbers bursting into the classroom. I alone would disarm the villain and rescue sister and the other children. I, too, could perform miracles.

On occasion I attended a church service (not "mass") with my Presbyterian friends. Mysticism and fantasy were absent within their pastel-painted plaster walled church. There were no faint smells of frankincense and myrrh, no life-sized statues of saints with somber looks on their faces, their right arms bent upward at the elbow and two fingers raised as if to bestow a blessing. The congregants sang, the minister preached, the pews were the standard issue that I was accustomed to; but I had no longing to ascend or save anyone. I did not imagine shepherds keeping watch over sheep that were all woolly and covered in burrs stuck to the fuzzy off-white perimeter of their bodies. I imagined nothing special at all. I couldn't fly; and by the time Catholic grammar school was done with me, I truly believed that flying was the point. What were these Presbyterians trying to accomplish with their dull, dull words? This kind of normal, as it intruded into matters of faith, was not as appealing as I had supposed it might be. Which was more important to apply to my own life, the practical and real or the fantastical and imaginative?

The level of realism sculpted into the wood of all those saintly faces of all those Catholic statues was and is a constant reminder that it is possible to experience flight while walking on dirt. We are all surrounded by sky, the celestial, no matter what continent we live on, no matter how trivial or important we perceive our daily existence to be. It is sometimes possible to achieve greatness (or at least make a productive life), not necessarily by ascending, but by pushing forward. I had matured, expanded my understanding of geography, and added new dimension to my metaphorical vector: what I once understood as literally up and down I now comprehended transnationally and multidimensionally—in multiplanar display.

I grew up in Belleville, a town that sits on Newark's northern border in Essex County, New Jersey. The adults in my world, immigrants and the first- and second-generation Italian Catholics who predominantly populated Belleville at that time, were practical people. Their quotidian activities included doubling up on tea bags, reheating coffee, buying powdered milk, and knowing how to be clever with cans of salty anchovies and the feet of fresh-killed chickens.[7] At the beginning of the twentieth century my ancestors chose to leave their homes in Avellino and Teora, hamlets in the Apennine Mountains, east of Naples, Italy. There coffee and chickens were luxuries, and fantasy frequently animated the everyday. It is understandable, therefore, why my people made statues of other, more perfect people who resembled their own and who were better versions of themselves. They carved the torsos, arms, and hands of what they understood as beautiful and perfect beings, visually translating their role models and then assigning to each a miracle. All of these tangibles—the rosary beads, crosses, scapulae, religious medals, and amulets against the "evil eye" (*il malocchio*)—are transportable devices for making the fantastical intimate and tangible. In the words of Mary Apikos (1992: 63), it is "buying the doughnut to experience the hole."[8] "The more contact the individual has with ritual objects, the greater the probability of uncovering the value inherent in the belief or practice embodied by that object" (ibid.).

The stories I hear in my profession are of those who suffered unfathomable atrocities—ones that seem inconceivable in a modern world. The memoirs of three African writers, Ayaan Hirsi Ali, Ishmael Beah, and Grace Akallo, readily come to mind.[9] They survived the unspeakable. They physically, psychologically, and spiritually pushed through horrid past experiences, each becoming a kind of wounded healer (Sedgwick 2001: 34).[10] Having healed themselves, they have gained the respect, trust, and authority to take an active role in healing others. I have interviewed many with similar stories. Through these interviews I have learned that it is not only what is *given* to us through birth and inheritance; that which is missing or withheld also heroically guides us toward wholeness and any notion of normalcy. Yet not everyone is a hero, and not all are destined to become saints. Sometimes an untimely death arrives before the opportunity to succeed presents itself. Refugees who live to tell their stories often succeed by knowing which parts to hold onto and believe and which to discard or question. They make life and death decisions for themselves and others in extraordinary circumstances, and they do this while walking and pushing forward on the ground they stand on.

LAYING THE GROUNDWORK, BIT BY BIT

Cultural anthropologist Barbara Myerhoff defines the notion of "self" as "a creative and active process" (Metzger 1992: 247). What I find particularly appealing in Myerhoff's definition is how to recognize what makes the big, in fact, big. She asserts: it is the small and ordinary, the "debris," the "minute particulars," articulated in the process of becoming:

> A self is made, not given. It is a creative and active process of attending a life that must be heard, shaped, seen, said aloud into the world, finally enacted and woven into the lives of others. Then a life attended is not an act of narcissism or disregard for others; on the contrary, it is searching through the treasures and debris of ordinary existence for the clear points of intensity that do not erode, do not separate us, that are most intensely our own, yet

other people's too. The best lives and stories are made up of minute particulars that somehow are also universal and of use to others as well as oneself. (Metzger 1992: 247)

For me, it is the small, the humble, and the ordinary that perform most formidably because of the inherent nuance and irony in the details that increasingly lead to and ultimately construct greater meaning. This process of meaning-making is iterated by at least a couple of well-known Catholics, the current Pope Francis and Saint Thérèse of Lisieux, known for her "Little Way."[11] It is reasonable, for example, to think that all humans need to feel safe, especially children; but how do they get to that place of "feeling safe"?: through the compounding of daily experiences, small events that are mediated and framed by others.

These two verses, which I composed as poetry from the prose narrative of my journal entries, recall details of my early fishing experiences with my father:

My father and I, on rainless weekends,
would fish the surf late into the evenings
until time rolled out with the moon overhead
and just about midnight I'd make my bed
in the sand near his jacket and the old tackle box
and fall sound asleep with a day's worth of thoughts
of how clever I was, more clever than most
when I body surfed along the Atlantic coast
and swam farther out than my legs could stand
on the continental shelf, on the last bit of land.

It was just me, the stars, and the fisherman's tackle,
an inky-black sky, an old bucket once filled with spackle
where the air was clean and the gentle breezes warm,
when I was my happiest, when I wasn't forlorn,
with a sun-shined tan and my small muscles strong
before the hurting made me hurt, before the wearing made me worn
before the leaving left me out, and the tearing made me torn.
(Vitiello 2012)

I was my father's fishing buddy; in his company, as we prepared for and fished the Atlantic Ocean and its estuaries, I always felt safe. We made our own fishing weights by melting chunks of lead in an old pot on the kitchen stove and then pouring the brew into one-ounce, two-ounce, or heavier-gauge molds. The metallic smell hung heavy in the air above the pot. The hot liquid hardened instantly and took the shape of the pyramid-like molds. Released from the molds, the weights looked very much like silver charms, complete with an eyelet on top through which we threaded the fishing line. For me, the process of making lead weights from molds was magical, and my father explained the magic in a simple chemistry lesson.

When I share the "minute particulars" of this experience, either orally or in written form, listeners or readers can relate to my experience within a personal context that has most meaning for them. Indeed writers or storytellers hope that there might be universality to their words. Whatever the story, the teller of the story wants to be seen by others as a seamless and integrated self, a successful coalescence of a lifetime of many experiences, good and bad. Victor Turner uses the word "re-membering" to explain this process of becoming. In Turner's words:

> The focused unification provided by re-membering is requisite to sense and order. Through it, a life is given shape that extends back in the past and forward into the future, a simplified, edited tale where completeness may be sacrificed for moral and aesthetic purposes (Myerhoff 1980: 77).[12]

In my own memoir writing, I weave my fondest memories of fishing with my father together with the sadnesses that also colored my childhood.

I realize now that some of the most salient years of my development consisted, quite literally, of the feel of dried squid bits and the smell of methane gases that wafted off the back-bay sludge while I was fishing with my father. How, then, did the earth that I stood on as a child help me develop a coherent sense of what I wanted to do with my life? In large part, the answer lies in the fact that I was born into a family where there was compassion and empathy, where I was loved and expected to respect the amazing array of differences between my life and the lives of others. I had parents who were trusted by others notable for their inability to trust easily. I remember many instances in my childhood when people were treated indifferently, because they were poor, perceived as odd, or perhaps spoke no English—and in one case unable to speak at all. It is still a mystery to me how my father managed to befriend an elderly deaf man, the cook who worked in the kitchen behind closed doors in our neighborhood Chinese restaurant. The point is this: each time a refugee tells me his or her story, I realize that I am stepping into someone else's memoir. This is true intimacy—or at least has the potential to be. Because I write memoir to understand my own story, I have developed an honest interest in hearing and believing the stories of others.[13]

When refugees tell their stories of endurance and survival, I contextualize those stories within the larger social and political forces that have shaped their lives. I need this overarching History with a capital "H" to understand and appreciate with greater clarity how individual life histories and experience resonate within it. In writer/poet Deena Metzger's phrasing (1992: 59): "There is a story in the smallest moments and in the largest. There is a large story that each one of us is living into which all the other stories fit, like one Russian doll into another."

A SUBTLE SHIFT IN IMAGINATION: ESTELA'S STORY

What each and every one of us perceives as relevant, in any given situation, assuredly differs (sometimes widely) from the perceptions of those standing next to us and experiencing the very same event. Our experiences as individuals and members of any given social group yield a variant of "truth," which is reflected in our needs and wants. "First person oral historical narrative can frequently reveal alternative perspectives, particularly if collected from groups previously excluded from the historic record for reasons of political, geographic, class, gender, or ethnic affiliation" (Del Giudice 2009: 4).

The difficulty in reaching mutual understanding of what "it" is or how "it" was is as true for the would-be refugee as it is for the interviewer, with "it" being a whole constellation of events, physical memories, feelings, and social forces that shape the definitive moments that lead a refugee to seek refuge. It can be difficult, to say the least, for both the intending refugee and interviewer to find their way around the threads of context and meaning when each inhabits a world of experience wholly unrelated to the person seated before him or her, the other. "The asylum process can be seen as one in which the authorities try to make sense of the senseless" is one viable perspective (Bohmer and Shuman 2008: 170), especially when considering that "asylum officers and judges make a variety of assumptions about the narratives they hear to determine whether they are credible" (Bohmer and Shuman 2008: 154).[14] And what if the person seeking asylum or refugee status has been a victim of torture and suffers from post-traumatic stress disorder? What if the person on the other side of my desk is a child? In any given situation, the myriad communication networks that need to be connected and chasms that must be crossed are immense. How can we connect? How do we get to the other side of the chasm?

It is an understatement to say that we are dealing with matters of trust. These are not ordinary narratives. Sometimes it is inevitable that the dialog becomes therapeutic in nature, with the interviewer lending ego strength. Regular memories are recorded differently in the brain than memories about torture, which adds to the complexity and richness of the refugee narrative. Martha Stout (2006: 582) explains:

> In contrast, traumatic memories include chaotic fragments that are sealed off from modulation by subsequent experience. Such memory fragments are wordless, placeless, eternal, and long after the original trauma has receded into the past, the brain's record of it may consist only of isolated and thoroughly anonymous bits of emotion, image, and sensation that ring through the individual like a broken alarm.

To feel safe in telling these extraordinary narratives, the storyteller must believe that the listener possesses the rational control to handle the weight of the story and is standing on firm ground. The applicant must believe that the interviewer is willing to share the ground he or she stands on.

A while ago I interviewed a young girl from Central America who was repeatedly sexually assaulted by her father and male relatives. (Names and details have been withheld to protect the child's and mother's identity and to honor the code of confidentiality that is a part of the legal refugee process.) Sadly, this is not such an uncommon occurrence in my business. Feeling safe was certainly not part of Estela's narrative. At age seven, she was left behind in her village with her father and paternal grandparents when her mother,

María, left for the United States on "the Beast," the English translation of La Bestia, the Spanish nickname used by Central Americans for the train that originates in Chiapas, the southernmost Mexican state that borders Guatemala and terminates on the outskirts of Mexico City.[15] Like many migrants, María began her journey as "EWI" (Entered without Inspection) on the back of the Beast to seek employment and establish a new life in the United States. Her purpose was to support her family at home despite the absence of documentation or approval by the U.S. government. There are many like María and her daughter, mothers leaving children behind, planning either to return home one day to reunite with them or to help their children make their way to America. Estela was one of the "estimated 48,000 children who enter the United States from Central America and Mexico each year, illegally and without either of their parents" (Nazario 2007: 5).[16]

At age ten, when Estela first arrived in the United States through the paid assistance of a coyote (smuggler), it took many weeks for her to trust anyone, even her mother. She was reticent to speak. I told Estela that her name had a very special meaning, and that she must be an angel because her name "Estela" is very close to the Spanish word for "star"—*estrella*. "You must have come from heaven," I said. She seemed to like knowing this, and soon many details of her story trickled out—not so much because she believed I thought her an angel but because some children tend to be resilient and trusting of adults or perhaps because since her arrival in the United States she had been working with many specialists, including a school counselor and a child psychologist. Slowly, speaking to others about her experiences in Central America was getting easier. During the interview, Estela initially only went so far as to say that her father and some boy relatives "touched her." She didn't say where or how she was touched. I changed the subject and asked if she sought help from her grandmother (*abuela*). She did, but the old woman responded to Estela's request by admonishing her not to tell lies. Her grandmother shooed her away. In my world, a grandmother would explode off her overstuffed cut-velvet armchair, hustle over to the perpetrator, and whack him over the head with a frying pan—and that just for starters. But my world was not Estela's world. I had to enter into a world of "parallel universe thinking" and "identify alternatives to [my own] assumptions . . . rather than settling on a specific interpretation" (Peters 2007: 347).[17]

Storylistening is complex. Emotional responses are constant, one following another in quick split-second succession. They arise with each unfolding page of a story as it is told; each has its own evolution, depending on the imagination or biases of the listener. A statement is made, and an interviewer reacts: statement, reaction, statement, reaction. On it goes. And for the storyteller? He or she hears a question and in turn reacts: question, reaction, question, reaction. All of us suffer from "confirmatory bias" to some degree.[18] The emotional responses happen again and again throughout the storylistening and storytelling process, a continuous cycle beginning with the first reactive thought. During my interview with Estela I first thought to myself, "What kind of grandmother would not help this child?" I concluded that the grandmother may have had no other choice but to kowtow to her son and his vices. One reason might be that the grandmother felt no connection to or moral responsibility for Estela. My own biases led me to conclude that perhaps it was the grandmother's advanced age and her dependence on her vile son's virility and income that made it necessary for her not to believe or accept the girl's plea for help. I was able to "stumble upon the proper parallel universe (isomorphic attribution)" (Peters 2007: 347)—or at least one of the parallel universes that could exist for the grandmother and benefit Estela.

"Then what did you do?" I asked.

"I ran away to my aunt, but my father stole me back."

"Was he nice to you then?"

"No."

At the beginning of the interview, Estela's attorney handed me a psychologist's report printed on the stationery of a local police office. During a short period when Estela had run away from her father's home to live with her maternal aunt, the police investigated and issued an official report at the aunt's behest. It was clear that the police psychologist didn't believe Estela. One particular sentence in the report stood out: "The child has trouble relating to authority figures." I believed Estela and the story she told. I winced at the official's ignorant disregard for the safety of the child and what appeared to be a local government's attempt to prevent the levying of formal charges against the father. I wasn't surprised by such legal audacity in a country where "femicide" is a common occurrence,[19] but I needed Estela to be more forthcoming. I didn't need to hear her say the word "rape" or to even know that the word "rape" exists in Spanish or in English. Yet I needed Estela to provide details that were somewhat more explicit for the record I was making in order to support my legal finding. But this was a ten-year-old child sitting before me, who most probably did not understand the legal consequences of what she said.

During the interview Estela mentioned that her father frequently lay in her bed at night. Toward the end of our talk I asked my final question, which I prefaced with a brief apology: "Honey, I'm sorry, but I need you to answer something else. Was your father dressed when he came into your room?"

Estela responded: "It was always dark when he came into my bed after he drank alcohol. I couldn't see him, but I could feel him."

I granted Estela's application for asylum, and the third-party reviewer agreed with my decision.

Adults generally know the term "rape" and are not afraid to use it, at least for the most part. I did not need this child to describe the atrocities she endured, and I know I could not concern myself with thoughts about how *I* would have reacted to the situation if I had been the same age as Estela. Such thinking could lead to further misunderstandings (Peters 2007: 347–50). "The past can only be told as it truly *is*, not w*as*" (Schueb 1996: xix, quoting Immanuel Wallerstein).

"Lawyering for children in the twenty-first century is plainly a cross-cultural endeavor at almost every moment" (Peters 2007: 288). With Estela, I was swept into an experience alien to my frame of reference, but it was easy for me to believe her.

MOVING INTO, THROUGH, AND OUT OF A STORY

I always tell the officers that I train to formulate questions, not conclusions. It is easy to make erroneous assumptions, because as storylisteners we are constantly listening for those parts of a story with which *we* identify, substituting our own real experiences (or nostalgic ideals) for those of the other. We latch onto the words and images that we are familiar with because they remind us that we are all the same, our human hearts beating somewhere between sixty to one hundred beats per minute. It is the alikeness that most of us appreciate. It is at that moment of recognition that we enter the story and truly hear.[20]

Through our stories we begin the process of understanding one another, but the boundary between truth and fiction is hard to discern. The interviewer as storylistener must be able to distinguish between the two. Mark Twain understood the difference perfectly when he wrote:

> An autobiography is the truest of all books, for while it inevitably
> consists mainly of extinctions of the truth, shirkings of the truth,
> partial revealments of the truth, with hardly an instance of plain
> straight truth, the remorseless truth is there, between the lines.[21]

When I think of my own writing, I know that if it is *my* truth, it cannot be *the* truth, or *the only* truth. Storytellers and writers often conflate the larger social, political, and economic movements with their own personal history.

Interviewers must allow space for the push and pull of communication to subside so that a more intimate connection becomes possible and the truth is revealed. Refugee workers, the good listeners among them, will usually detect exaggerations and lies of both the "little white" and the "bald-faced" varieties, where desire for immigration and/or better economic status may be the real reason for filing a claim. Even in an authentic refugee narrative, exaggerations or white lies are inevitably expressed.[22] As the interlocutors alternate between speaking and listening, there are moments of mutual recognition of the other's experience that validate the purpose of communication and ignite the points of connection that each speaker/listener longs for. The good interviewer will recognize and mark common denominators with a pertinent comment or question and also call upon the refugee to give a better explanation of those areas where the story may have strayed too far into exaggeration. To do so is the utmost sign of respect that encourages the storyteller to continue speaking. After all, both parties are looking to stand on the common ground of truthfulness, or at least a close facsimile of truth with which both might agree.[23] This is isomorphic attribution as it is meant to be (Peters 2007: 347).

Often statements that I perceive as inconsistencies are not. The confusion that sometimes arises when two people examine the same topic from differing perspectives cannot be overly emphasized. What is important is that the lines of communication remain open and that the interviewer's role as gatekeeper is appropriately minimized. Therefore it is important for the interviewer to yield emotional space. This listening stance of openness and acceptance, a kind of emotional positioning, is the best point of departure for an interview—an interviewer's *stepping off* point, as I refer to it. Yielding is not a sign of weak interviewing skills. On the contrary, it shows that the storylistener comes into the conversation from a place of humility and deference. There is nothing wrong with being humble, respectful, or deferential, but there is everything wrong with not actually embracing those values, especially when considering the narratives of people afflicted by trauma or by the real fear of being harmed in the future.

The overall arc of the listening experience generally follows the model of what literacy learning scholar Judith Langer (1989: 3) describes when she writes about the experience of reading literature. It is worth appropriating Langer's "four recursive stances [that] readers take in relation to the text" and applying her theory to the listening act. Langer defines the stances as "[b]eing out and stepping in"; "being in and moving through"; "stepping back and rethinking what one knows"; and "stepping out and objectifying the experience" (ibid.). She goes on to say that "[r]eading is sense-making, an act of becoming—where new questions, insights, and understandings develop as the reading progresses, while understandings that were once held are subject to modification, reinterpretation, and even dismissal" (ibid.: 4). The same can be said about listening to the spoken narrative.

But jurisprudence—the law—is not literature: the protagonists are not fictitious; the narratives are judged; and life and death decisions are made for the applicants by others. "The law itself . . . can and sometimes does provide both the legal-rhetorical tropes and the venues for stories to be told and to unfold that are intimately tied to one's experience and identity" (Zagor 2014: 30). Matthew Zagor, social scientist and expert in judicial rhetoric, recognizes the "structural imbalances and societal influences that direct the narrative-generating process." In response to his own observation, Zagor asks a very important question: "Is our very obsession with self-narrating selves part of the problem?" In other words, does wanting to hear a good story interfere with the intentions of law? To support his inquiry, Zagor quotes another legal scholar, Richard Weisberg, who wrote that "to utter a popular trope like 'law is essentially narrative' . . . is simply to plead that law be treated as having a spiritual or emotional quality that might redeem the life of lawyers who 'crave enchantment'" (ibid.). Here Weisberg is making reference to Richard Sherwin's research (2000: 205) on the effect of popular culture on law: "We crave enchantment, but fear deceit":

> As the stories we hear and tell grow and weave their way into a larger mosaic, a discrete culture takes shape. There we find the archive of images, characters, plot lines and scenarios with which we make sense of ourselves and others and the world around us.

And there too lie the various tools of narrative, the techniques of meaning making, of persuasion and critical interpretation, which prompt (or perhaps alter) our opinions, produce knowledge, and cultivate judgment.

An interviewer is constantly moving in and out of the "images, characters, plot lines and scenarios" that constitute the details of a story. Interviewing officers are trained to question inconsistencies that may arise for a variety of reasons: the applicant may have contradicted factual statements that he or she had previously made in a written statement or made earlier during oral testimony; the applicant's version of the story seemingly contradicts known country conditions or other evidence; or the applicant's statement is implausible: for example, the applicant provided an eyewitness account of an event that he or she could not logically (plausibly) have observed (AOBTC 2002: 8). When such inconsistencies arise, an officer is obliged to tell the applicant what the inconsistency is and provide an opportunity to explain. It should be noted that asylum and refugee officers are required by regulation and trained to conduct *nonadversarial* interviews (AOBTC 2006: 6), the techniques for which are explicitly taught and tested in mock interview settings. After the applicant explains the inconsistency, the officer steps back and considers the reasonableness of the explanation and includes a credibility determination in a written assessment after the interview: "The applicant's explanation overcomes the inconsistency" or, in the alternative, "The explanation does not overcome the inconsistency," as the case may be.

Evaluation of credibility concerns also requires an interviewer to consider a variety of other factors that include (but by no means are limited to) the age of the applicant; his or her educational level, which may or may not affect the ability to communicate; whether or not the applicant was represented, which would contextualize his or her story within our legal framework; and the physical and mental health of the applicant. What should not be considered are U.S. policies toward the country of the applicant's origin and the applicant's personal, religious (or lack of religious), and political beliefs. In addition, officers and adjudicators must know and apply laws as established by international convention, statute, and precedent decisions. Do current country conditions support the applicant's claim, or have circumstances changed either for the applicant or within his or her home country that warrant special analysis? Are there indicators that an applicant may be barred from applying for asylum or refugee status because, for example, he or she was a persecutor (AOBT 2002: 6)? These concerns constitute a fraction of the many legal issues that an officer has to consider before, during, and after hearing oral testimony that is sometimes well rehearsed, sometimes divulged extemporaneously. All asylum and refugee officers receive several weeks of intensive, dedicated training before being assigned to one of eight asylum offices throughout the United States, to Washington, D.C., or to an overseas location.

"Rethinking what one knows" (compare Langer 1990: 229) is serious business in the adjudicator's world. The interview, subsequent analysis, and decision-writing processes require a variety of skill sets practiced at very sophisticated levels of accomplishment for an interviewing officer who must, perhaps, learn "a way to allocate more autonomy and discursive control to the refugee over a narration process that already allows, through the law, for the potential recognition of a meaningful refugee identity" (Zagor 2014: 31). I am always "stepping back and rethinking" and "stepping out and objectifying" to understand how an applicant's small story fits into the larger cultural context. It is during the writing process that I weave together the facts of the applicant's small story with the particular conditions in the applicant's home country. The intersection of the two is, I hope, the truth, but undeniably it will be the truth *as I understand it* (compare Langer 1990: 237–39).

A QUESTION, NOT A CONCLUSION

When I was a child, my older sister used to tease me because I had trouble using the expression "make believe." I consistently said, in the way a guileless child might, "make a belief." Perhaps this is what I have been struggling with for all these years—a way to make a belief. Earlier in this chapter I asked a couple of essential questions that I needed to answer for myself: Which is more important to apply to one's own life, the practical and real or the fantastical and imaginative? And what, literally and figuratively, is the ground I stand on? What constitutes "home" for me? When I was in Catholic school I believed, whether consciously or not, that the Bible stories I learned were improbable. But I loved the idea of them, and to love the idea of them was enough for me to suspend my beliefs in a parallel universe.

This ability to inhabit both worlds is at the heart of my believing mind. This ability is my "indelible beauty mark" (Apikos 2013).[24] Its imprint is not only the consequence of years of schooling within classroom walls that were infused with the dogma of organized Catholic religion; the scoldings and praise of Old World Italian parents; and the desire to be good and the feeling of guilt when I was not. Fantasy and imagination are not merely the consequential evidence of a dogmatically encrypted mind, of a child hallucinating in a church pew. Maybe they are the products of divine inheritance, and all humankind has a propensity toward sensing the divine in the world; or maybe all people merely possess both a need for the fantastical and imaginative and call this religion. As I experience it, fantasy prods my imagination: from such mental activities, humanitarian, moral, and ethical ideas are born. I like to think that my ideas are morally sound because they are embedded in the dialectics of good versus evil.

Recently I began calling myself an apatheticist:[25] I don't care about organized or disorganized religions; gods or goddesses; salvation or its loss; knowing or not knowing ultimate reality; or not knowing that there is not enough to ultimately know. It really doesn't matter. What matters is that we care and take care of ourselves and others, and, to sound a bit indelibly Christian, to be our brother's and sister's keeper (as well as their watchdog). It does not escape me that the gatekeeping work I do for a living, my work with refugees, smacks of the heavenly pearly gates metaphor with Saint Peter holding the key. But I do not believe that someone has to die to get to the other side, that there must be some kind of agent for salvation. As I have mentioned, I am an apatheticist with regard to such matters. In my role as adjudicator and trainer of federal officers who interview for a living, I understand the moral urgency to model acceptance and respect, to yield power and create the space where others can expand and create their own thoughts and ideas. In a word, it is important to *believe.*

A waiting room is the metaphorical limbo of refugee applicants, the interstitial space between what had been "home" and the unknown ground they will stand on. It is an awkward space for both storyteller and storylistener. From my perspective as a storylistener, I know that I am privileged. I am the writer of other people's stories *as I understand them.* And as a gatekeeper, I mediate the narratives of others. The storytellers have every right to declare that we "are not the victims of random and chaotic circumstances, that we, too, despite our grief or feelings of insignificance, are living meaningfully in a meaningful universe" (Metzger 1992: 55). And that, I conclude, is the entire point: no one is meaningless, and all lives are significant. It is true that all people access more or less privilege for one or another reason, but it is not for me to speculate why it is so. That is a job for mystics. My job is to remain aware of my privilege and not abuse it.

NOTES

The views and opinions expressed in this essay are those of the author and do not necessarily reflect the views and opinions of U.S. Citizenship and Immigration Services, specifically, the Asylum and Refugee Programs.

First and foremost, I dedicate this paper to my parents—"Nicky and Norma," as their contemporaries called them—and to Mary Apikos, my academic muse, whose spiritual, professional, and scholarly brilliance helped me better understand the ground I stand on. I also want to thank my other muses, all of whom are artists who have maintained their faith in my artistry: Karen Guancione, visual artist; Susan Narucki, voice artist; and Suzanne Reiman, performance artist. My ungirdled appreciation goes out to the women of my writing group, Jodie Goens and Shanna Koenig. I thank my fellow officers and the office support staff, colleagues who teach me on a daily basis, and the director of our office, Sue Raufer, who makes professional space for good teaching and learning. I can say with confidence that we all appreciate her leadership. And finally, I dedicate this chapter to my sister and brother, Michelle and Nick, Jr., whose sibling rivalry and love I cannot do without.

1. "According to Article 1 A (2) of the 1951 Convention [Relating to the Status of Refugees], the term 'refugee' shall apply to any person who: 'As a result of the events occurring before 1 January 1951 and owing to well-founded fear for being persecuted for reasons of race, religion, nationality, membership in a particular social group or political opinion, is outside the country of his nationality and is unable or, owing to such fear, is unwilling to avail himself of the protection of that country; or who, not having a nationality and being outside the country of his former habitual residence as a result of such events, is unable or, owing to such fear, is unwilling to return to it'" (*Handbook* 1992: 10–11).

2. "Parallel universes also confront a lawyer with the vastness of his or her ignorance about the client's life and circumstances" (Peters 2007: 347).

3. Generally speaking, applicants who are granted refugee status cannot return to their home countries except for brief visits under extraordinary, unavoidable circumstances, such as the death of a close relative. A return to the country from which the refugee sought protection presumes that he or she no longer fears persecution.

4. Building on the work of Fran Stallings (1988) and Charles Tart (1972), Brian Sturm (1999: 2, see also 2000: 287-90): analyzes how people who listen to stories "may enter an altered state of consciousness" in what Stallings refers to as the "storylistening trance."

5. Sturm (1999: 7) observes: "Internally, mental visualizations are stimulated as the listener creates images to match the descriptions of the storyteller; the emotions are activated in response to character emotions, the teller's tones of voice, or plot elements; and there are kinesthetic responses to the story in the form of shivers, moans, and sighs."

6. Per *Wikipedia*: "*Astro Boy,* known in Japan by its original name *Mighty Atom* (. . . *Tetsuan Atomu* [literally, Iron Arm Atom]) is a Japanese manga [*anime*] series written and illustrated by Osamu Tezuka from 1952 to 1968. The story follows the adventures of an android named Astro Boy and a selection of other characters" (https://en.wikipedia. org/wiki/Astro_Boy).

7. When talking about the Italian peasantry, ethnomusicologist Catalano and musician Fina define the word "simple" as meaning not easy. "The word *simple* constitutes a basic concept in understanding peasant life and worldview. It is intended here not as the usual paternalistic expression of the dominant culture's view of the peasantry but as *creative ingenuity*. What is simple, as applied to any type of tool, clothing, choice of food, or manifestation of oral culture at large, is readily understood in an efficient, direct, and practical way. . . . The art of improvising, developed through centuries of living at severe subsistence levels, makes the peasant a rather sophisticated human being" (Del Giudice 2009: 121).

8. Per Apikos (1992: 75), "While objects may be the harbingers of meaning, and they may serve as mnemonics for facilitating an altered state of consciousness, we should not forget that objects are merely the messengers. The real message is encoded in the unseen, hidden recesses of an object's attributes. Symbolic objects either refer the participant to a primary experience or memory involving a specific time or place, or they refer to a secondary experience involving the physical senses or perception." In referencing theologian Rudolf Otto, Apikos (ibid., 75) comments that he "recognized the importance of objects to negotiate belief." In Otto's own words (1950 [1923]: 27), "this feeling or consciousness of the 'wholly other' will attach itself to, or sometimes be indirectly aroused by means of, objects." "Wholly Other cannot, strictly speaking, be taught, it can only be evoked, awakened in the mind; and everything that comes 'of the spirit' must be awakened" (ibid.: 7).

9. There are many autobiographies well worth reading by those forced to leave their homeland as refugees. The works of these three authors are a random sampling of authors whose works I found inspiring. They are the stories by former residents/ citizens of African countries (perhaps the population I have worked with more than any other refugee population): Somalia, Sierra Leone, and Uganda, respectively.

10. Central to the work of psychologist Carl Jung is the idea that the physician or clinician derives great therapeutic skill from his (or her in an updated context) own agony. Jung based this archetype on the Greek myth of Chiron, the wounded centaur who was a legendary healer. Jung wrote: "We could say, without too much exaggeration, that a good half of every treatment that probes at all deeply consists in the doctor's examining himself, for only what he can put right in himself can he hope to put right in the patient. This, and nothing else, is the meaning of the Greek myth of the wounded physician" (Sedgwick 2001: 2).

11. Saint Thérèse of Lisieux (1873–97) was known as "the Little Flower" for her humility and simplicity. It is also worth noting that the current pope, Pope Francis, is the first

Jesuit pope (Jesuits are known for their work in education and social justice), and the first from the Southern Hemisphere, born in Buenos Aires, Argentina.

12. Myerhoff (1980: 77) beautifully enlarges Victor Turner's theory of "Re-membering" in her article for *Parabola*: "Victor Turner has used the term 'Re-membering,' bracketing it by the hyphen to distinguish from ordinary recollection. Re-membering, he offers, is the reaggregation of one's members, the figures who properly belong to one's life story, one's own prior selves, the significant others without which the story cannot be completed. Re-membering, then, is a purposive, significant unification, different from the passive, continuous, fragmentary flickering of images and feelings that accompany other activities in the normal flow of consciousness. The focused unification provided by re-membering is requisite to sense and order. Through it, a life is given shape that extends back in the past and forward into the future, a simplified, edited tale where completeness may be sacrificed for moral and aesthetic purposes."

13. In this essay I am not concerned with refugee narratives that are wholly fabricated, a common occurrence because of the great legal and economic benefits that refugee status bestows upon the beneficiary.

14. Shuman and Bohmer (2008: 154) list assumptions of adjudicators as "(1) assumptions about the motivations of the applicants, (2) assumptions about the behavior and beliefs of the applicants (including the legitimacy of their fears), (3) assumptions about the motivations and behaviors of the persecutors, (4) assumptions about appropriate knowledge of the applicants, (5) assumptions about the likelihood and meaning of the help many asylum seekers have received, especially to help them escape."

15. *Which Way Home* features the stories of several Central American children as they journeyed to the United States aboard La Bestia (Cammisa 2009).

16. In *Enrique's Journey* author Sonia Nazario (2007: 26) explains how Enrique's mother, Lourdes, supports her son while working in the United States: "Money from Lourdes helps Enrique, too, and he realizes it. If she were here [in Honduras, not in the United States], he knows where he might well be: scavenging in the trash dump across town. Lourdes knows it too; as a girl, she herself worked the dump. Enrique knows children as young as six or seven whose single mothers have stayed at home and who have had to root through the waste in order to eat." In the text of this chapter I quote Nazario's research, which estimates the number of children who enter the United States from Central America and Mexico for the period closest to the time of her research. More headlines on the recent influx of undocumented or unauthorized immigrants from a variety of news sources range from the sensationalism of *Fox News* ("Agencies Buying Hotel Rooms for Surge of Mexican Illegal Immigrants, Others Released," August 12, 2013) to centrism in the *New York Times* (Todd Miller, "War on the Border," August 17, 2013) and advocacy in *Human Rights Watch* (Grace Meng, "Dispatches: Jail Won't Deter Migrants from US," August 6, 2013).

17. Jean Koh Peters, a legal expert in child, family, and refugee law, advises lawyers working with children "to identify alternatives to assumptions he or she may make about the client's behavior. . . . When faced with a client's behavior, a lawyer should force himself or herself to brainstorm multiple explanations for the client's behavior rather than settling on a specific interpretation" (Peters 2007: 347). The concept of

"parallel universe thinking" also appears in other disciplines such as child psychology, educational theory, and other social sciences. Peters applies the concept of parallel universe thinking specifically to lawyer-client relationships, citing Raymonde Carroll (1987: 20): "Very plainly, I see cultural analysis as a means of perceiving as 'normal' things which initially seem 'bizarre' or 'strange' among people of a culture different from one's own. To manage this, I must imagine a universe in which the 'shocking' act can take place and seem normal, can take on meaning without even being noticed. In other words, I must try to enter, for an instant, the cultural imagination of the other."

18. "In psychology and cognitive science, confirmation bias (or confirmatory bias) is a tendency to search for or interpret information in a way that confirms one's preconceptions" (*Science Daily*: http://www.sciencedaily.com/articles/c/confirmation_bias .htm). For example, it is not unusual for applicants—refugee or otherwise—to have the preconceived notion that gatekeepers may look upon them unfavorably. Likewise, it would not be unusual for gatekeepers to have the preconceived notion that the person before them is misrepresenting the truth in order to gain an immigration and/or economic benefit. Both parties, interviewer and applicant, may gravitate toward one or the other side of the doubting-believing spectrum. As a trainer of interviewers, I fully understand why officers possess one prejudice or another. No one is pure and guileless. What is important, however, is that the gatekeeping interviewer be able to recognize his or her own biases and practice parallel universe thinking in the preparation, analysis, and adjudication of each case. For an extraordinary historical essay on how one gatekeeper was actually killed in the line of gatekeeping duty, I highly recommend *Killing the Poormaster* by Holly Metz (2012). The story of an unemployed Italian mason, Joe Scutellaro, who was charged with murder during the years of the Great Depression aptly illustrates how the role of confirmation bias is played out in the extreme.

19. From the World Health Organization (2012): "Femicide is generally understood to involve intentional murder of women because they are women, but broader definitions include any killings of women or girls. . . . Femicide is usually perpetrated by men, but sometimes female family members may be involved. Femicide differs from male homicide in specific ways. For example, most cases of femicide are committed by partners or ex-partners, and involve ongoing abuse in the home, threats or intimidation, sexual violence or situations where women have less power or fewer resources than their partner."

20. In "The Enchanted Imagination" Sturm (1999) builds upon the literary criticism/ philosophy of Louise Rosenblatt (1978), wherein she applies transactional theory analysis to the reader and written text: the author creates a simple "text," while the reader creates a "poem." Sturm extends Rosenblatt's theory by making the storylistener analogous with the "reader." As Sturm (1999: 2) (and I) see it, the listener, too, creates his or her own little "poem" vis-à-vis Rosenblatt's theory: "The storyteller recounts the 'text,' while the listeners create the true 'story' based on the verbal text and overlaid with personal images and memories. While there is a continual feedback loop present in any storytelling event—as the teller changes the story to accommodate the audience—the unit of study, following Rosenblatt's thesis, is not the storyteller's performance but the listener's experience."

21. From Twain's letter to William D. Howells, March 14, 1904 (www.twainquotes.com).
22. In this chapter I am not concerned with refugee narratives that are wholly fabricated, a common occurrence because of the great legal and economic benefits that refugee status bestows upon the beneficiary. An authentic refugee narrative, in this context, is one that is overall truthful: the applicant's story is internally consistent and corroborated by country conditions and other evidence.
23. It is my contention that refugee and asylum adjudicators must remain open to novel ways of understanding the applicant's narrative. Even in those situations where the claims may be justifiably denied (for example, when the applicant's unwillingness to return to his or her home country is not based on objective fear but rather on the inability to find work), the adjudicator should always listen without the prejudice and weight of precedential legal history, because opinions and analyses do evolve over time. Yesterday's laws and policies are frequently reanalyzed, overturned, or at least given fresh perspective. Change may not happen quickly or perhaps not at all; but it is worth considering that legal evolution *may* begin when a refugee or asylum officer relates to the narrative in a novel way and then applies an equally novel analysis in the adjudication. Consider this unusual analogy: there is more than a casual similarity in how the concept of "risk" is understood when comparing the narratives of those who were or may have been exposed to the HIV virus and the narratives of those who have been seriously harmed or have a well-founded fear of persecution. The parallel is found in how the experts, whether medical or legal, filter the narratives they hear, which are the stories of the nonexperts, the very people that the professionals treat and judge. Folklorist Diane Goldstein (2004: xiii) postulates in her introduction ("Philosophizing in a War Zone") that "[s]tory and science are interrelated, interactive, and ultimately constitute each other." She further explains that "[t]he greatest asset of lay experience is in precisely those areas of thinking and relating to information most criticized by medical authorities. . . . Through narration, health information comes to life, exploring, affirming, rejecting, and sometimes replacing information that is offered by powerful outsiders without true cultural contextualization" (2004: 171–72). To reiterate, in much the way that scientific knowledge progresses and gains insight by listening to the patient, so, too, does asylum and refugee law evolve with the stories of the applicants that are *truly listened to and heard.*
24. Mary Apikos is not only to be thanked for the "doughnut and hole" metaphor, but for the beautiful metaphor of "the indelible beauty mark" as well (Apikos 2013).
25. I thank Deborah Klahr for this perfectly descriptive label.

WORKS CITED

Apikos, Mary. 2013. Personal communication. August 23.
———. 1992. "Buying the Doughnut to Experience the Hole." In *Meaning, Measure, and Morality of Materialism*, ed. Floyd W. Rudman and Marsha Titchins, 63–76. Provo, UT: Association for Consumer Research.

Asylum Officer Basic Training Course (AOBTC). 2006. *Interviewing Part I: Overview of Nonadversarial Interview*. Washington, DC: U.S. Citizenship and Immigration Services, RAIO Asylum Division.

———. 2002. *Making an Asylum Decision*. Washington, DC: U.S. Citizenship and Immigration Services, RAIO Asylum Division (https://www.uscis.gov/sites/default /files/USCIS/Humanitarian/Refugees%20%26%20Asylum/Asylum/AOBTC %20Lesson%20Plans/AOBT-Making-an-Asylum-Decision-3aug10.pdf).

Bohmer, Carol, and Amy Shuman. 2008. *Rejecting Refugees: Political Asylum in the 21st Century*. New York: Routledge.

Cammisa, Rebecca, director. 2009. *Which Way Home*. DVD. HBO Films (1 hour, 30 minutes).

Carroll, Raymonde. 1987. *Cultural Misunderstandings: The French-American Experience*. Trans. Carol Volk. Chicago: University of Chicago Press.

Catalano, Roberto, and Enzo Fina. 2009. "Simple Does Not Mean Easy: Oral Traditional Values, Music, and the Musicàntica Experience." In *Oral History, Oral Culture, and Italian Americans*, ed. Luisa Del Giudice, 119–34. New York: Palgrave Macmillan.

Del Giudice, Luisa, ed. 2009. *Oral History, Oral Culture, and Italian Americans*. New York: Palgrave Macmillan.

Elbow, Peter. 2008–9. "The Believing Game or Methodological Believing." *Journal for the Assembly of Expanded Perspectives on Learning* 14, no. 1 (Winter): 1–11.

Goldstein, Diane E. 2004. *Once upon a Virus: AIDS Legends and Vernacular Risk Perception*. Logan: Utah State University Press.

Handbook on Procedures and Criteria for Determining Refugee Status. 1992. 2nd ed. Geneva, Switzerland: Office of the United Nations High Commissioner for Refugees

Langer, Judith. 1989. "The Process of Understanding Literature." National Research Center on Literature Teaching and Learning University at Albany, State University of New York. Report Series 2.1 (http://www.albany.edu/cela/reports/langer /langerprocess.pdf).

Metz, Holly. 2012. *Killing the Poormaster: A Saga of Poverty, Corruption, and Murder in the Great Depression*. Chicago: Lawrence Hill Books.

Metzger, Deena. 1992. *Writing for Your Life*. San Francisco: HarperCollins.

Miller, Todd. 203. "War on the Border." August 17, 2013.

Myerhoff, Barbara. 1980. "Re-membered Lives." *Parabola* 5, no. 1: 74–77.

Nazario, Sonia. 2007. *Enrique's Journey: The Story of a Boy's Odyssey to Reunite with His Mother*. New York: Random House.

Otto, Rudolf. 1950 [1923]. *The Idea of the Holy*. New York: Oxford University Press.

Peters, Jean Koh. 2007. "Representing the Child-in Context: Five Habits of Cross Cultural Lawyering." In *Representing Children in Child Protective Proceedings: Ethical and Practical Dimensions*, 285–364. 3rd ed. N.p.: LexisNexis.

Rosenblatt, Louise M. 1978. *The Reader, the Text, the Poem: Transactional Theory of the Literary Work*. Carbondale and Edwardsville: Southern Illinois University Press.

Schueb, Harold. 1996. "Introduction." In *The Tongue Is Fire: South African Storytellers and Apartheid*, xv–xxvi. Madison: University of Wisconsin Press.

Sedgwick, David. 2001. "Introduction." In *Jungian Psychotherapy: The Therapeutic Relationship*, 1–17. New York: Taylor and Francis.

Sherwin, Richard K. 2000. *When Law Goes Pop: The Vanishing Line between Law and Popular Culture*. Chicago: University of Chicago Press.

Shuman, Amy, and Carol Bohmer. 2004. "Representing Trauma: Political Asylum Narrative." *Journal of American Folklore* 117: 394–414.

Stallings, Fran. 1988. "The Web of Silence: Storytelling's Power to Hypnotize." *National Storytelling Journal* (Spring/Summer): 6–19.

Stout, Martha. 2006. "When I Woke Up Tuesday Morning, It was Friday." *The New Humanities Reader*, ed. Richard E. Miller and Kurt Spellmeyer, 578–99. 2nd ed. Boston, MA: Houghton Mifflin Company.

Sturm, Brian W. 2000. "The 'Storylistening' Trance Experience." *Journal of American Folklore* 113 (449): 287–304.

———. 1999. "The Enchanted Imagination: Storytelling's Power to Entrance Listeners." *Research Journal of the American Association of School Librarians* 2: 1–20.

Tart, Charles T. 1972. "Scientific Foundations for the Study of Altered States of Consciousness." *Journal of Transpersonal Psychology* 18: 93–124.

Vitiello, Lauren. 2012. *Barberone the Poem*. Public reading at Club at La Mama Theatre, April 23.

World Health Organization. 2012. "Understanding and Addressing Violence against Women: Femicide." http://www.who.int/iris/bitstream/10665/77421/1/WHO_RHR _12.38_eng.pdf.

Zagor, Matthew. 2014. "Recognition and Narrative Identities: The Legal Creation, Alienation and Liberation of the Refugee." ANU College of Law Research Paper No. 11-22. Available at SSRN: http://papers.ssrn.com/sol3/papers.cfm?abstract_id= 1906507.

CONTRIBUTORS

CHARLENE VILLASEÑOR BLACK, whose research and teaching focuses on the art of the Hispanic world, is professor of art history and Chicana/o Studies at UCLA. Her widely reviewed book *Creating the Cult of St. Joseph: Art and Gender in the Spanish Empire* was awarded the College Art Association Millard Meiss prize. She is currently finishing *Transforming Saints: Women, Art, and Conversion in Mexico and Spain, 1521–1800*, which considers the translation and transformation of images of the Madonna, St. Anne, St. Librada, and Mary Magdalene from Old World to New. She has held grants from the American Council of Learned Societies (ACLS), Fulbright, Mellon, Woodrow Wilson, and Getty Foundations, and the National Endowment for the Humanities. She has published extensively on the politics of religious art and transatlantic exchange. Villaseñor Black is also actively engaged in the Chicana/o art scene. She recently edited *Tradition and Transformation: Chicana/o Art from the 1970s through the 1990s*, Shifra M. Goldman's final book. She is the editor of *Aztlán: A Journal of Chicano Studies*, the leading journal in the field. Her upbringing as a working-class Catholic Chicana/o from Arizona forged her identity as a border-crossing early modernist and inspirational teacher.

MARY ELLEN BROWN is professor emerita, Indiana University Bloomington, where she has taught in the folklore, English, and Women's Studies departments and also, in the course of her career, directed Women's Studies and the Institute for Advanced Study as well as editing the *Journal of Folklore Research*. Her research has almost always focused on the ballad, a vernacular form with ties to both oral and literary worlds, and on Scotland and things Scottish. She has sought to explore the intellectual history of this persistent literary genre and those who have collected, edited, and even written ballads, frequently employing the methodology "historical ethnography." This work has been aided by the Guggenheim and Mellon

Foundations, a Fulbright Research fellowship, the ACLS, her university, and others. She is a fellow of the American Folklore Society. A child and grandchild of the manse, she has almost unconsciously chosen her subjects because of Scots Presbyterian inflections, recognizing, however latterly, the enormous influence of her natal heritage.

LUISA DEL GIUDICE is an independent scholar, former university academic (University of California—Los Angeles, Addis Ababa University, Ethiopia), public sector educator (founder-director of the Italian Oral History Institute), and community activist. She has published and lectured widely on Italian and Italian American and Canadian folklife, ethnology, and oral history and has produced many innovative public programs on Italian, Mediterranean, regional, and folk culture and local history in Los Angeles. In 2008 she was named an honorary fellow of the American Folklore Society and knighted by the Italian Republic. She is the coordinator of the Watts Towers Common Ground Initiative and editor of *Sabato Rodia's Towers in Watts: Art, Migrations, Development* (New York: Fordham University Press, 2014).

EDVIGE GIUNTA is a professor of English at New Jersey City University. She teaches memoir, women writers, immigrant literature, and other literature and writing courses. Her books include *Writing with an Accent: Contemporary Italian American Women Authors* and the co-edited anthologies *The Milk of Almonds: Italian American Women Writers on Food and Culture*; *Italian American Writers on New Jersey*; *Teaching Italian American Literature, Film, and Popular Culture*; *Embroidered Stories: Interpreting Women's Domestic Needlework from the Italian Diaspora*; and *Personal Effects: Essays on Memoir, Teaching, and Culture in the Work of Louise DeSalvo*. In 2011 she became a certified yoga instructor.

KAREN GUANCIONE has been awarded a Mid Atlantic Arts Foundation Artists and Communities Grant, four New Jersey State Council on the Arts Fellowships, a Ford Foundation Grant, a Puffin Foundation Grant, and an Arts and Culture Exhibition Grant from the Nathan Cummings Foundation. Her work has been exhibited worldwide and is in numerous public and private collections. Her interdisciplinary art includes large-scale installations, performance, sculpture, printmaking, papermaking, book arts, and video. She has curated many exhibitions, is an adjunct professor of art at the State University of New York (SUNY Purchase), Montclair State University, and Middlesex County College and has been a visiting artist and lecturer at Pratt Institute, Rutgers University, and numerous schools and institutions in the United States and abroad. For over a decade she has served as artistic director/guest curator of the annual New Jersey Book Arts Symposium and Exhibition. She is the first-time recipient of the Erena Rae Award for Art and Social Justice. She recently collaborated on the production of *Cuatro Corridos*, a multidisciplinary chamber opera about human trafficking that is now touring in the United States and Mexico.

JENNIFER GUGLIELMO is an associate professor of history at Smith College and specializes in histories of labor, race, women, migration, transnational cultures and activisms, and revolutionary social movements in the modern United States. She is the author of *Living the Revolution: Italian Women's Resistance and Radicalism in New York City, 1880–1945* (2010), which received the Theodore Saloutos Memorial Award for best book in U.S. immigration history from the Immigration and Ethnic History Society, the Helen and Howard R. Marraro Book Prize from the American Historical Association and Society for Italian Historical Studies, and honorable mention from the Berkshire Conference of Women Historians' Book Prize. She also received the Organization of American Historians Lerner-Scott Prize in 2003 for the best doctoral dissertation in U.S. women's history. Her work has been funded by the Social Science Research Council and the American Association of University Women. Her publications also include *Are Italians White?: How Race Is Made In America* (co-edited with Salvatore Salerno, 2003), which was published in Italy as *Gli Italiani sono bianchi?: Come l'America ha costruito la razza* (2006), as well as several essays.

JOANNE LESLIE is the archdeacon of the Episcopal Diocese of Los Angeles. She taught as an adjunct faculty member in the Community Health Sciences Department of the UCLA Fielding School of Public Health for fifteen years and was a co-founder of the Pacific Institute for Women's Health. Dr. Leslie has both a master's degree and doctorate in International Health from the Johns Hopkins Bloomberg School of Public Health in Baltimore. She received a Certificate of Theological Studies in 2001 from the Church Divinity School of the Pacific in Berkeley, California. She has published extensively in the areas of maternal and child health, food and nutrition policy, and ethnic disparities in health. She is a sought-after preacher throughout the Diocese of Los Angeles. Dr. Leslie lives with her husband, Walter, in Santa Monica, California. They each have three adult children and, between them, thirteen grandchildren.

SABINA MAGLIOCCO is a professor of anthropology at California State University, Northridge. A recipient of Guggenheim, National Endowment for the Humanities, Fulbright, and Hewlett fellowships and an honorary fellow of the American Folklore Society, she has published on religion, folklore, foodways, festival, and witchcraft in Europe and the United States and is a leading authority on the modern Pagan movement. She is the author of numerous books and articles, including *The Two Madonnas: The Politics of Festival in a Sardinian Community* (1993, 2005), *Witching Culture: Folklore and Neo-Paganism in America* (2004), *Neopagan Sacred Art and Altars: Making Things Whole* (2001), and with filmmaker John M. Bishop produced the documentary film series *Oss Tales*, on a May Day custom in Cornwall and its reclamation by American Pagans. Her current research is on animals in the spiritual imagination.

ANNALISA PASTORE was born to an immigrant Italian family and raised in Brooklyn, New York. She was the first in her family to pursue graduate and postgraduate training. She attended Yale University and then taught young people before entering medical school. She completed her training at Columbia University Medical Center then expanded upon that training at Harvard University. She has layered onto her Christian faith studies of metaphysics, Kabbalah, and Buddhist philosophy. She recently certified as a yoga teacher. She brings to her patients her understanding of functional medicine, wellness as viewed by both Eastern and Western traditions, and an ever-expanding awareness of psychoemotional and spiritual fortitude. She founded and directs the Center for Holistic and Integrative Medicine, in Englewood, New Jersey, bringing together like-minded holistic and integrative practitioners under one roof. She also co-founded Sacred Healing Coalition, a nonprofit organization to further the transformation of patients and communities.

GRACE SCHIRESON is a Zen abbess, president of Shogaku Zen Institute (a Zen teachers' training seminary), and a clinical psychologist. She received her doctorate in clinical psychology at the Wright Institute in Berkeley, California. She leads two practice centers and a retreat center under the Central Valley Zen Foundation. She is the author of *Zen Women: Beyond Tea Ladies, Iron Maidens, and Macho Masters* (Boston: Wisdom, 2009) and has published articles in *Shambhala Sun, Buddhadharma*, and *Tricycle* magazines. She has also been anthologized in the Zen books *The Book of Mu, Receiving the Marrow*, and *The Hidden Lamp* as well as in a book on spiritual training: *The Arts of Contemplative Care*. She received Dharma transmission from Sojun Mel Weitsman Roshi of the Suzuki Roshi Zen lineage. The late Fukushima Keido Roshi of Tofukuji Monastery, Kyoto, asked her to teach the kōan that she studied with him during her practice there. She has been married for forty-five years and lives with her husband part time on Stanford campus and at her Zen retreat center, Empty Nest Zendo in North Fork, California. She has two grown sons and four grandchildren.

LAUREN VITIELLO is a Training Officer with the Newark Asylum Office (U.S. Citizenship and Immigration Services). She trains and provides mentorship to new officers who interview and adjudicate applications for people fleeing oppression, persecution, and torture. She has an M.A. in teaching from Columbia University and taught for many years, most notably at SUNY Buffalo. Vitiello has read from her novel in verse, *Barberone the Poem,* at La Mama's Ellen Stewart Theatre in New York City. She writes about the emotional complexity of her own family, the children of Italian American immigrants in the second half of the twentieth century. In her writing she explores the intersection of politics, economics, and culture and the weight of history and memory on immigrants as individuals, families, and communities. She grew up and lives in Belleville, New Jersey, but spends much of her writing time in Northampton, Massachusetts.

WILLOW YOUNG is an International Association for Analytical Psychology–certified Jungian analyst with the C. G. Jung Study Center of Southern California in private practice in Santa Barbara and Ventura, California. Her research is focused on the study of C. G. Jung's psychology and the reality of the psyche. Young presented the following seminars as part of Pacifica Graduate Institute's Legacy Tour at Eranos in Zurich and Ascona, Switzerland: "Jung and Nature: The Nourishing Life of the Soul" and "The Psyche Soma Dynamism in the Asklepion Healing Tradition." She is a core professor at Pacifica Graduate Institute, where she serves as chair of the Counseling Psychology Program. Her training in the cultural archetypes of the collective unconscious includes graduate studies at Saybrook University, Pacifica Graduate Institute, and undergraduate studies in world arts and cultures at UCLA, with grant-supported fieldwork in Guatemala.

CHRISTINE ZINNI was awarded a Ph.D. in American Studies from the State University of New York at Buffalo in 2007. She teaches courses in Indigenous Studies, Food and Culture, and Museum Studies at the State University of New York at Brockport and directs a Food and Culture of the Aegean Study abroad program. She also works as a videographer for and with Native American groups. She recently completed a video documentary on indigenous women's activism. Published book chapters focused on the oral histories, collective memories, and migration stories of Italian American needleworkers, stoneworkers, and musicians in western New York include "Stitches in Air: Needlework, Spirituality and Service among Italian American women of Batavia, New York," in *Embroidered Stories: Italian Women of the Diaspora*, ed. Edvige Giunta and Joseph Sciorra (Jackson: University of Mississippi Press, 2014); "Play Me a Tarantella, Polka or Jazz: The Currency of the Piano Accordion in Italian American Culture," in *The Accordion in the Americas*, ed. Helena Simonett (Champaign-Urbana: University of Illinois Press, 2012); and "Cantastorie: Ethnography as Storysinging," in *Oral History, Oral Culture and Italian Americans*, ed. Luisa Del Giudice (New York: Palgrave Macmillan Press, 2009).

INDEX